DATE DUE

			PRINTED IN U.S.A.

The Blackwell Encyclopedic Dictionary of Management Information Systems

About the Editors

Cary L. Cooper is Professor of Organizational Psychology at the Manchester School of Management (UMIST), UK. He has also been appointed Pro-Vice-Chancellor at the University of Manchester Institute of Science and Technology (UMIST). He is the author of over 80 books, has written over 250 scholarly articles and is editor of *The Journal of Organizational Behavior*. He is also the Founding President of the British Academy of Management.

Chris Argyris is the James B. Conant Professor of Education and Organizational Behavior at the Graduate School of Business, Harvard University. He has written many books and received numerous awards, including the Irwin Award by the Academy of Management for lifetime contributions to the disciplines of management. Recently, the Chris Argyris Chair in Social Psychology of Organizations has been established at Yale University.

About the Volume Editor

Gordon B. Davis is the Honeywell Professor of Management Information Systems at the Carlson School of Management, University of Minnesota. He is recognized internationally as one of the principal founders and intellectual architects of the academic field of Management Information Systems. He has authored 21 books and over 150 scholarly articles. He has been involved in establishing academic journals, scholarly conferences, and model curricula for the field of information systems.

The Blackwell Encyclopedic Dictionary of Management Information Systems

Edited by Gordon B. Davis

Carlson School of Management

First published 1997

First published in USA 1997

2 4 6 8 10 9 7 5 3 1

Blackwell Publishers Ltd
108 Cowley Road
Oxford OX4 1JF
UK

Blackwell Publishers Inc.
238 Main Street
Cambridge, Massachusetts 02142, USA

Library of Congress Cataloging-in-Publication Data

The Blackwell encyclopedic dictionary of management information systems/
   edited by Gordon Davis.
      p. cm. — (Blackwell encyclopedia of management)
    Includes bibliographical references and index.
    ISBN 1-55786-948-0 (alk. paper)
    1. Business–Data processing–Dictionaries.   2. Management
    information systems–Dictionaries.   3. System analysis-
    -Dictionaries.   4. Office management–Dictionaries.   I. Davis,
    Gordon Bitter.   II. Series.
    HF5548.2.B524   1997   96–30373
    658.4′038′011—dc20   CIP

British Library Cataloguing in Publication Data
CIP catalogue record for this book is available from the British Library.

ISBN 1557869-480

Typeset in 9½ on 11pt Ehrhardt by Page Brothers, Norwich
Printed in Great Britain by T. J. Press (Padstow) Ltd

This book is printed on acid-free paper

—— Preface ——

Computer-based information and communications systems are critical resources for competing successfully in the information age. These systems are vital to products, services, and management processes. A new organization function has been established to plan, implement, and manage the information technology infrastructures and systems required by an organization. An academic discipline has emerged to teach and research the use of information technologies in organizations and the management of information resources. The size of investment in information resources and its importance to the effectiveness and efficiency of organizations justify the business function and corresponding academic discipline.

A variety of names are applied to the new organization function and academic discipline. The term, Management Information Systems or MIS, is widely used. Other often-used terms are information systems and information management. Management information systems is used for this encyclopedic dictionary of the field both because it is the most widely used and also because it clearly identifies the management and organization context for the systems.

A useful starting point for a user of *The Blackwell Encyclopedic Dictionary of Management Information Systems* is the article, MANAGEMENT INFORMATION SYSTEMS. It defines and describes the scope of the organization function and academic discipline. Historical background is contained in the article, HISTORY OF ORGANIZATIONAL USE OF INFORMATION TECHNOLOGY. Underlying concepts are found in articles on INFORMATION CONCEPTS and SYSTEM CONCEPTS APPLIED TO INFORMATION SYSTEMS.

The focus of this encyclopedic dictionary is on information systems in organizations and the management of information resources. There are articles describing the concepts, processes, and tools employed in planning, building, and managing information systems. The coverage does not include technical details of information and communications technologies,. However, since management information systems employ these technologies, there are management-level explanations of technical terms that are relevant to organization dialogue about requirements and applications.

The articles and definitions in the dictionary have been written by academic and professional colleagues working in the field of management information systems. They have responded well to instructions to make the descriptions technically correct but understandable to a reader who is not a specialist in the field.

Gordon B. Davis

—— Contributors ——

Dennis Adams
University of Houston

Soon Ang
Nanyang Technological University

David Bahn
University of Minnesota

Colleen Bauder
Georgia State University

Robert J. Benson
Washington University and the Beta Group

Robert W. Blanning
Vanderbilt University

Paul L. Bowen
University of Queensland

Eric S. Boyles
University of Minnesota

Susan A. Brown
Indiana University

Heather E. Carlson
University of Minnesota

Chris Carr
University of Minnesota

Norman L. Chervany
University of Minnesota

Roger H. L. Chiang
Nanyang Technological University

Rosann Collins
University of South Florida

Amit Das
Nanyang Technological University

Michael Davern
University of Minnesota

Gordon B. Davis
University of Minnesota

Gerardine DeSanctis
Duke University

Gary W. Dickson
North Carolina State University

Robert Evaristo
University of Denver

Gordon C. Everest
University of Minnesota

Mark A. Fuller
Baylor University

David Gefen
Georgia State University

Tim Goles
University of Houston

Stefano Grazioli
University of Texas

J. Scott Hamilton
Manufacturing Guild

Nancy K. Herther
University of Minnesota

Loke Soo Hsu
National University of Singapore

Blake Ives
Southern Methodist University

Brian D. Janz
University of Memphis

Sirkka L. Jarvenpaa
University of Texas at Austin

Jesper M. Johansson
University of Minnesota

Julie E. Kendall
Rutgers University

Kenneth E. Kendall
Rutgers University

Kyung Kyu Kim
Inha University

William R. King
University of Pittsburgh

Barbara Klein
University of Michigan, Dearborn

Frank Land
London School of Economics and Political Science

Donald J. McCubbrey
University of Denver

D. Harrison McKnight
University of Minnesota

Ephraim R. McLean
Georgia State University

Salvatore T. March
University of Minnesota

Richard O. Mason
Southern Methodist University

Enid Mumford
Manchester Business School

William D. Nance
San Jose State University

J. David Naumann
University of Minnesota

R. Ryan Nelson
University of Virginia

Boon-Siong Neo
Nanyang Technological University

Kathryn Ritgerod Nickles
Wake Forest University

Fred Niederman
University of Baltimore

T. William Olle
T. William Olle Associates

Barry Peiper
Delux Corporation

Reagan M. Ramsower
Baylor University

Sangkyu Rho
Seoul National University

Djenan Ridjanovic
Université Laval

Mark A. Serva
Baylor University

Sandra Slaughter
Carnegie Mellon University

H. Jeff Smith
Georgetown University

Randy Snyder
Carnegie Technology Group Inc.

Christina Soh
Nanyang Technological University

Kevin Stolarick
Country Companies Insurance Group

Detmar W. Straub
Georgia State University

Jonathan K. Trower
Baylor University

Narayan S. Umanath
University of Tulsa

Lester A. Wanninger Jr
University of Minnesota

Hugh Watson
University of Georgia

Ron Weber
University of Queensland

James C. Wetherbe
University of Minnesota

Chee Sing Yap
National University of Singapore

A

accounting use of information technology The use of information technology in accounting is reflected in an *accounting information system* (AIS). It is an information system that collects, stores, processes, and reports information regarding the financial transactions of an organization. A major objective of an accounting information system is to provide the necessary controls over the processing of transactions to ensure that the organization's financial activities are recorded and reported accurately, fairly, and on a timely basis.

Accounting information systems are the most common information systems utilized in business. Every firm uses at least one. They are a combination of manual (i.e. people-oriented) and automated (i.e. computer-based) components that work together to accomplish the accounting system objectives. Due to the critical and often enterprise-wide role of accounting applications, an organization's set of integrated accounting applications may be its largest information system. The accounting information system can be described in terms of its processing activities and its use in business accounting cycles.

Accounting Information Processing Activities

Accounting information systems are a subset of the broader category of organizational information systems. As such, they perform the basic data processing functions.

In the input stage, the system collects and records data such as sales orders, shipping data, and vendor payments into the system. Forms such as invoices or bank deposit slips that contain the input data are called source documents. If necessary, data from non-machine-readable source documents (such as a hand-written price tag) are entered into machine-readable form for use in subsequent computerized processing. Common AIS input devices include keyboards for manual data entry, scanners to read universal product codes (UPCs, or bar codes), and magnetic ink character readers (MICR) in banking.

In the processing stage, accounting applications perform primary accounting operations, utilizing the data that was collected in the input stage. The most common data processing operation is the updating of organizational files and databases to reflect the completion of a transaction. Transaction processing typically uses one of two modes: batch or online. In batch processing, individual transactions are accumulated over a specified period of time (hourly, daily, weekly, etc.) and are then processed as a group to update the relevant files on a periodic basis. A payroll system is an example of an application that is typically processed in batch mode. In online processing, relevant files are updated immediately, one transaction at a time, as the transaction occurs. Online systems are more complex and expensive than batch systems, but they provide greater database integrity since they reflect a more accurate state of the world. A sales order entry system that updates the inventory file immediately upon completion of a purchase is an example of an application that utilizes online processing.

In the output stage, an accounting system produces documents that describe financial transactions that have been processed. At the single transaction level, a customer's sales receipt or a bank's deposit receipt are examples of outputs. Examples of outputs that depict aggregated transactions include monthly bank statements and packing slips for a product shipment. At an even more aggregate level, and perhaps most commonly identified as an example of an output from an accounting information system, corporate financial statements summarize the entire set of financial transactions in which an organization has engaged during a specified period of time.

An accounting information system involves a significant amount of data storage. Two major types of data are typically stored in an AIS: master data and transaction data. A master file can be thought of as a record of the *people and things* with which the organization interacts and stores data. Examples include customers (name, address, phone number, etc.), vendors, and products (item number, price, quantity on hand). Transaction data describes *events* that occur about which the organization needs to retain an accurate record. Examples include sales, purchases, and payments.

Business Accounting Cycles

Accounting information systems are used to support the activities that take place in many functional areas of an organization. In general, they support five fundamental business cycles: (a) revenues; (b) purchases; (c) operations; (d) human resources; and (e) financial management/reporting.

The *revenues cycle* is comprised of all transaction activities that bring operating revenue directly into the organization. Focusing on the company's sales and receivables activities, systems that support the revenues cycle include order entry, sales automation, billing, accounts receivable, and cash receipts systems. Since the public interacts most frequently with revenue cycle applications, these components are typically the most visible external accounting applications in an organization.

Purchase, or procurement, cycle transactions bring raw materials and supplies into the organization. Rather than bringing in revenue, the procurement function focuses on obtaining the physical inputs (and incurring the accompanying costs) that are required to produce the organization's goods and services. Applications that support the purchasing cycle include purchase order, accounts payable, and cash disbursement systems. One change in automating the procurement cycle is the use of ELECTRONIC DATA INTERCHANGE (EDI), whereby two trading partners exchange docu-

ments such as purchase orders, invoices, and payments electronically (and instantaneously) rather than relying on mailed paper transaction documents.

Operations cycle transactions transform the procurement cycle inputs into the goods and services that are sold through the revenue cycle. A critical component within the operations cycle is inventory management, which links purchasing activities to sales activities. Essentially, all organizations have some form of operational inventory management requirement. In a manufacturing firm, inventory transactions involve purchasing raw materials inventory from suppliers, transforming those raw materials into manufacturing work-in-progress inventory, and eventually producing finished goods inventory that is ready for sale. In a wholesaling or retailing organization, inventory management operations involve acquiring products from suppliers, storing them as necessary, and distributing them to customers.

The *human resources cycle* accounting systems focus primarily on the processing of payroll and related expenses (taxes, benefits, sick leave, etc.). Payroll systems are often processed in batch mode, due to their relatively stable and repetitive nature. Due to processing repetitiveness and simplicity, payroll systems are a common accounting function that many organizations outsource to firms that specialize in such data-processing activities.

Financial management and reporting applications involve the general ledger system and reporting business results through the financial reporting system. It requires recording all transactions (business events) accurately and promptly, maintaining a complete and accurate set of account balances, and compiling and reporting all financial results to appropriate parties on a timely basis. The financial management and reporting system is an integrating application for the accounting system. It combines the financial activities of all the other business cycles into an integrated set of statements that provide a broad and comprehensive view of the organization. These outputs can be used by management and stockholders to evaluate the company's performance and to make decisions regarding corrective actions that may be needed.

WILLIAM D. NANCE

ACM The Association for Computing Machinery is the largest, broad-based international computer and information system society (*see* ASSOCIATIONS AND SOCIETIES FOR INFORMATION SYSTEMS PROFESSIONALS).

ADA A general purpose programming language sponsored by the United States Department of Defense. It is especially suited for the programming of large, long-lived systems with a need for ongoing maintenance. It supports modern programming structured techniques and concurrent processing.

agency theory applied to information systems Agency theory examines the contracts between a party (the principal) who delegates work to another (the agent). Agency relations become problematic when the principal and agent have conflicting goals and when it is difficult or costly for the principal to monitor the performance of the agent. When goals are incongruent, the agent is assumed to have a different set of incentive structures from the principal; the agent will consume perquisites out of the principal's resources and make suboptimal decisions. These activities produce efficiency losses to the principal. To counter these losses, the principal designs contracts to align the goals at the lowest possible costs. Costs can arise from providing incentives and from monitoring to ensure that the agent is acting for the principal's interests.

Agency theory can offer insights for information systems. First, principals can design information systems to monitor the actions of agents. Electronic communication systems, electronic feedback systems, and electronic monitoring systems are examples of monitoring devices that can be implemented to ensure that agents' behaviour is aligned with principals' interests.

Secondly, information systems professionals themselves often enter into agency relationships with other stakeholders in organizations and agency problems can arise. Important examples of such agency relationships include systems development, outsourcing, and end-user computing.

Systems Development

As principals, users often engage information system (IS) professionals as agents to develop information systems on their behalf. Due to a lack of understanding and knowledge of each other's domain, goal conflict may arise between the two parties. To reduce agency costs, one or both parties must try to narrow goal differences. IS professionals can invite users to participate more actively throughout the development lifecycle. This gives the users more opportunities to verify requirements and ensure that the final system is aligned with user needs. Further, users may request that the information system produce information-rich documentation so that monitoring is made easier and more readily available to users.

Outsourcing

In any outsourcing arrangement, the client company (principal) is usually motivated to shift its IS operations to external vendors who can carry out the work at the lowest possible cost. The vendor, on the other hand, may be looking for high profit in the arrangement. There is thus an economic goal conflict. To protect its interests, the client will increase its monitoring of the vendor. This can be achieved by requesting regular operational performance measures from the vendor, frequent meetings with the vendor to review progress of outstanding projects, and independent auditors to review benchmarks and internal controls of the vendor.

End-user Computing

Agency theory can help explain the dynamics of end-user computing. End users develop information systems themselves with little IS involvement. End-user computing, interpreted in agency theoretic terms, is a mechanism for reducing agency problems by eliminating the agency relationship between the user and IS professional.

SOON ANG

AIS The Association for Information Systems is an international society for information system academies (*see* ASSOCIATIONS AND SOCIETIES FOR INFORMATION SYSTEMS PROFESSIONALS).

artificial intelligence The attempt to program computers to perform tasks that require intelligence when performed by humans is known as *artificial intelligence*. Examples of such tasks are visual perception, understanding natural language, game-playing, theorem-proving, medical diagnosis, and engineering design.

Beginning in the late 1950s, AI researchers have modeled a variety of problems (such as playing checkers or proving theorems in mathematics) in terms of state space search. A *state* denotes a particular configuration of the components of a problem. The position of pieces on a chess board and the structure of terms in a mathematical expression are examples of states (for the problems of chess-playing and theorem-proving, respectively). The application of a permissible operator (such as a legal move in the game of chess or an expansion of terms in a mathematical expression) alters the state of a problem. The set of all possible states, together with the operators that enable transitions among them, constitutes the *state space* representation of a problem.

The solution of an AI problem consists of a search through the state space, i.e. the successive application of operators until the final state of the problem matches the desired goal state (a checkmate in chess or the simplest expression of a theorem). Unless the problem is very limited in scope (e.g. playing tic-tac-toe), the state space is hopelessly large for an exhaustive search (the game of chess has more than 10^{120} states). Additional knowledge (beyond the rules of the game) is required to guide the state space search in promising directions. This search control knowledge is commonly called *heuristic knowledge*. The process of problem-solving in AI described above is called *heuristic search* (Newell & Simon, 1976).

Chess-playing and theorem-proving are examples of tasks where the careful application of logic has to be supplemented by heuristic knowledge to produce an efficient solution. As AI research progressed, it was discovered that specialized tasks, such as diagnosis, design, and planning, require even more knowledge to formulate (in state space terms) and solve (through heuristic search). In order for knowledge to facilitate the solution of an otherwise intractable problem, the knowledge must be represented in a suitable form for use by a computer program. Methods of reasoning about the knowledge to apply it to a particular situation must also be specified. The representation of domain knowledge and efficient methods of reasoning with it have become central concerns of AI since the 1970s (Feigenbaum & McCorduck, 1983). Certain formalisms, including if–then rules, semantic networks, frames, and predicate logic, have been developed to represent and utilize knowledge efficiently in problem-solving.

AI methods have been successfully applied to problems in computer vision, robotics, knowledge-based systems (*see* EXPERT SYSTEMS; KNOWLEDGE BASE), understanding natural language and machine learning (the extraction of patterns from large volumes of data). AI-based computer systems have been successfully deployed in manufacturing to support the design and diagnosis of products and processes. In services, AI has been applied to a variety of tasks, including medical diagnosis, financial statement analysis, and logistics management. In addition to dedicated AI systems, AI techniques have also been used to improve the user interfaces of conventional information systems.

See also **Cognitive science and information systems**

Bibliography

Newell, A. & Simon, H. A. (1976). Computer science as empirical inquiry: symbols and search. *Communications of the ACM*, **19** (3), 113–26.

Feigenbaum, E. A. & McCorduck, P. (1983). *The Fifth Generation: Artificial Intelligence and Japan's*

Computer Challenge to the World. Reading, MA: Addison-Wesley.

AMIT DAS

ASCII A commonly used code for alphabetic, numeric, and special characters is the American Standard Code for Information Interchange (ASCII). The original ASCII standard code used seven bits. An extended ASCII code employs eight bits (*see* CODING OF DATA FOR INFORMATION PROCESSING.

assessment of management information system In order to evaluate the resources being spent on information management and whether or not it is meeting organizational needs, assessment of the MANAGEMENT INFORMATION SYSTEM function can be performed periodically. The evaluation should be carried out within the context of the organization and its strategies and plans.

There are two persistent questions relative to the information systems of an organization:

1 How much should be spent on information systems? (allocation of organizational resources to information systems).
2 How good are the information systems and the function that supports them? (evaluation of organization, management, and services of the information systems function).

Within industries, spending levels on information systems differ substantially among successful companies. Within the constraints of resource availability, how much should be spent depends on two factors: (1) what the organization wants to achieve with information technology; and (2) how much it must spend to be competitive. Companies differ in culture, capabilities, and the way they use information technology, so what organizations wish to achieve will differ; industries differ in their use of information technology, so what organizations must spend to be competitive will differ by industry. This suggests that information systems can only be evaluated within their organizational and environmental context.

An in-context approach to information system assessment provides the framework for investigating these key management questions. The in-context assessment framework is presented as a complete assessment approach. A company may wish to perform a complete, comprehensive assessment, but it is more likely that the assessment will be targeted at a high-level evaluation or at a specific problem area. The value of the in-context assessment framework is in identifying factors to be included in assessment and in defining the overall context for targeted assessments.

The Context for Information Systems

The information architecture of a company serves an organization which: (1) exists in an industry with a competitive environment; (2) has a specific organizational structure, management style, and culture; and (3) has specific information requirements. These define the overall context for assessment of the information management function and the portfolio of information system applications.

The existing *industry context and competitive environment* define what is expected of information systems at the current time. This can change as new applications and new information products (and other innovations) are used to change the industry structure and basis of competitive advantage. The relevant assessment questions should do more than merely determine whether information systems meet industry and environmental norms. Since information technology can help achieve competitive advantage by changing the way the organization or the industry operates, the MIS function and information systems should also be assessed on participation in competitive innovation and change.

Organizations differ in the way they approach problems and the way they respond to competitive pressures. These differences are reflected in the *organizational structure, culture, and management style* of the organization. This context is important in an assessment of how well the information systems fit the organization as it currently exists. The assessment can also identify changes in information systems that are necessary to support strategic changes in culture and organization.

Overview of the Process

A complete, comprehensive assessment of information systems can be divided into four stages, each of which is subdivided into a series of assessment activities that focus on the major areas of interest. The four stages represent a logical order of assessment in that there is a sequential dependency between the various stages. This suggests that assessment should proceed in a systematic fashion, since the activities within each stage build upon knowledge gained in prior stages. However, within each stage there is only a limited dependency between the individual activities, so the sequence of these may be determined by specific priorities or by convenience factors.

In general, it may be possible to postpone or even omit a particular activity within a given stage, although it is probably inadvisable to omit a stage altogether. When an assessment is targeted or limited in scope, the stages provide a framework for doing enough investigation to establish an appropriate context for the area of assessment interest. For example, a targeted assessment of END-USER COMPUTING should first establish some context consisting of relevant organizational context and infrastructure context. For a limited assessment with a wide scope, the framework identifies the range of things to be considered, even though the depth of analysis may be limited. The framework of four stages and the areas of assessment are as follows:

Stage I: Analysis of the organizational context for information systems
 1 Analysis of the industry and competitive environment of the organization
 2 Analysis of the historical development, culture, structure, and activities of the organization
 3 Analysis of the organization's requirements for information and technology support

Stage II: Assessment of the information system infrastructure
 4 Assessment of information systems architecture of applications and databases
 5 Assessment of the technical architecture for information systems
 6 Assessment of organization and management structure for information systems

 7 Assessment of the investment in information systems

Stage III: Assessment of the organizational interface for information systems
 8 Assessment of information system planning and control
 9 Assessment of information system use
10 Assessment of end-user computing

Stage IV: Assessment of information system activities
11 Assessment of application development and maintenance
12 Assessment of information system operations
13 Assessment of capacity planning and technology acquisition
14 Assessment of information system support functions
15 Assessment of information system safeguards
16 Assessment of information system personnel management

The steps in the assessment framework are organized in a top-down fashion. They proceed from the most general topic of competitive environment and company structure to the overall structure of information systems and the service level being provided to the management interface between information system and organization and then to the specific activities within the information system function. The evaluation of the information management function is an organizational evaluation; it deals with processes more than outcomes.

 1 *Stage I: Analysis of the organizational context for information systems.* At the conclusion of this stage of analysis, there should be a clear definition of competitive forces, major competitors, and key success factors in the market. There should be an understanding of the way the organization has responded to the competitive environment through its organization, policies, culture, etc. There should be an appreciation at a general level of the organization's requirements for information and support services and how these relate to the context of the organization and its environment.

2 *Stage II: Assessment of the information system infrastructure.* After establishing the organizational context in stage I, stage II of the assessment analyzes the various components of the information system's infrastructure, i.e. the institutional structures and established processes that define the organization's information system's capability. The infrastructure is viewed in four dimensions: an *information dimension* (the application systems and databases that provide information support); a *technical dimension* (the architecture of computer equipment, system or non-application software, and telecommunications facilities); an *organizational dimension* (the organization and management structure of the information systems function); and an *economic dimension* (the organization's investment in information systems).

3 *Stage III: Assessment of the organizational interface for information systems.* Having assessed the institutional structures that represent the established information system's capability, the next stage is to evaluate the management processes that act as the essential interface between these structures and the rest of the organization. There is an assessment of information system planning and control to evaluate the existence of these processes and their quality. Assessment of information system use examines how effectively the organization uses its information system and meets the real needs of its users.

4 *Stage IV: Assessment of information system activities.* The last stage covers assessment of activities and management within the information system function. There are six activities that encompass the assessment of individual functions contained within the information system. Assessment of *application development and maintenance* is an evaluation of the methods and procedures for systems developed by professional programmers. The use of standard methods, methodologies, and development tools are included. Assessment of *information system operations* looks at the organization and management of operations. It includes an evaluation of facilities, use of operations software, and scheduling of work. Assess-

ment of *capacity planning and technology acquisition* examines the processes by which the information management function tracks utilization, forecasts needs, employs performance measurement tools, and evaluates alternatives. The step also evaluates the processes by which new technologies are identified and considered for use. Assessment of *information system support functions* is an evaluation of the way that the function deals with its customers, the users of applications, and end users who need support. Assessment of *information system safeguards* is a study of the security measures and backup and recovery provisions. It may focus on how well the organization has done in studying security issues and in providing for backup and recovery. Assessment of *information system personnel management* considers the current personnel policies and procedures and evaluates how they are working in terms of recruitment, upgrading, and retention.

The assessment framework guides the assessment team in organizing its work, collecting data, and structuring its analysis and reporting. All activities performed by the MIS function are assessed within the organizational context of what is expected of MIS. These expectations are calibrated by the context of competitive environment and organizational strategy. Targeted evaluations, such as an assessment of MIS personnel management, are performed within the overall context.

GORDON B. DAVIS

associations and societies for information systems professionals Several associations and societies have been founded, or have evolved from other groups, since the invention of the electronic digital computer. Some of them are quite technical in nature, while others are strongly managerial in character. The latter group of associations will be our focus here.

There is no one international body that captures the attention and loyalty of all those involved in information system activity, both professional and academic. Each country has one or more groups which cater for the specialized interests of its members. For example, in Australia, there is the Australian Computer Society (ACS); and in the United Kingdom, the British Computer Society (BCS). In the case of the United States, there are several competing professional associations vying for members' attention.

The best known broad international society is the International Federation for Information Processing (IFIP), founded under the auspices of UNESCO in 1960 and currently head-quartered in Laxenburg, Austria. It is governed by a General Assembly, consisting of member representatives from 45 national computer societies. IFIP's mission is to be the leading, truly international, apolitical organization which encourages and assists in the development, exploitation, and application of information technology for the benefit of all people.

IFIP sponsors a general World Congress every two years and has a regular newsletter. Most of its technical activities are conducted through special-interest technical committees (TC) and working groups (WG). Of special interest is IFIP Technical Committee 8 (TC8) on Information Systems. TC8 was founded in 1975 (growing out of WG2.6 on Databases) and at present contains seven Working Groups: WG8.1 on the Design and Evaluation of Information Systems (founded in 1976); WG8.2 on the Interaction of Information Systems and the Organization (1977); WG8.3 on Decision Support Systems (1981); WG8.4 on Office Information Systems (1986); WG8.5 on Information Systems in Public Administration (1988); WG8.6 on the Diffusion, Transfer, and Implementation of Information Technology (1992); and WG8.7 on Informatics in International Business Enterprises. The titles of these working groups give a good indication of the scope of the interests of the members of TC8. Each of the working groups has an annual or biannual working conference, sometimes singly and sometimes in combination, with each conference having published proceedings. While TC8's scope of interest and international coverage is broad, it has a relatively small membership of a few hundred individuals, mostly academics.

The oldest computing society is the Association for Computing Machinery (ACM) founded in the United States in 1947. Headquartered in New York City and covering all aspects of computing, computer engineering, and computer science, ACM now has 85,000 members worldwide. Its flagship journal is the monthly *Communications of the ACM*, first published in 1958. In addition, ACM publishes 14 other journals and numerous newsletters from its 34 special interest groups (SIGs). More than 60 technical conferences a year are sponsored by ACM and its SIGs, chapters, and regions, attracting over 75,000 attendees.

Among ACM's special interest groups, that on Management Information Systems (SIG-MIS), formerly known as the Special Interest Group on Business Data Processing (SIGBDP), is the second oldest of all the SIGs, having been founded in Los Angeles, California, in 1961. Aimed at the organizational and managerial uses of information technology, this SIG has published *The DATA BASE for Advances in Information Systems* (or *DATA BASE* for short) since 1969. With an international readership of nearly 3,000, *DATA BASE* is the oldest scholarly publication devoted to the business aspects of computing.

Another SIG of interest to information systems professionals is the Special Interest Group on Computer Personnel Research (SIGCPR). Founded in 1962 as an independent group and subsequently affiliated with ACM, SIGCPR has held annual conferences, with published proceedings, nearly every year since its founding. It publishes *Computer Personnel* on a quarterly basis; and, like SIGMIS, has a membership comprised mainly of faculty members and other research-oriented individuals.

While the primary focus of ACM is on the computer, The Institute for Management Sciences (TIMS), headquartered in Providence, Rhode Island, is concerned with management processes and techniques, especially those using quantitative approaches. Recently, TIMS merged with the Operations Research Society of America (ORSA) to form the Institute for Operations Research and the Management Sciences (INFORMS). The combined membership of INFORMS is approximately 13,000 worldwide. The main journal of INFORMS is *Management Science*, which began publication in 1953 and has been an important outlet for the publication of information systems research. In 1990, TIMS, along with its College on

Information Systems, began publishing *Information Systems Research* which has now emerged as INFORMS' primary publishing outlet for information systems research. INFORMS also holds annual research conferences, both within the United States and at international venues. The College of Information Systems (INFORM-CIS) meets in conjunction with these conferences, as well as publishing a regular newsletter. INFORM-CIS currently has approximately 550 members.

The newest of the large academic information societies is the Association for Information Systems (AIS), founded in 1995 and headquartered in Pittsburgh, Pennsylvania. With over 1,400 members, AIS is organized around three regions: Asia/Pacific, Europe/Africa/Mid East, and the Americas. Annual or biannual meetings are planned for each of the regions with the International Conference on Information Systems being the one research-oriented conference for the entire association. At present, AIS publishes no journals of its own, but provides discounted subscriptions to other journals, such as the *MIS Quarterly* (published at the University of Minnesota since 1977).

In addition to academically oriented associations, there are a number of professionally oriented groups. The oldest and largest of these is the Data Processing Management Association (DPMA), founded in 1951 and originally known as the National Machine Accountants Association (the name was changed in 1962). There are currently 12,000 regular members and 5,000 student members organized into 240 chapters throughout North America. DPMA has long had a strong emphasis on education for its members.

Another group is the Association for Systems Management (ASM), founded in 1947 as the Systems and Procedures Association and renamed ASM in 1968. It currently has over 3,500 members and publishes the *Journal of Systems Management*.

A noteworthy international professional society is the Society for Information Management (SIM). Founded in 1969 as the Society for Management Information Systems, SIM membership consists of 3,000 senior executives worldwide who are committed to advancing the management and use of information technology to achieve business objectives. SIM members are typically corporate and divisional head of information systems (IS) organizations, their IS management staff, leading academics, consultants, and other leaders who shape or influence the management and use of information technology. SIM, along with the University of Minnesota, publishes the *MIS Quarterly*.

The leading international conference for information system researchers is the International Conference on Information Systems. Founded in 1980, the annual conference averages over 1,000 in attendance. Proceedings are published by ICIS and are available after the conference through ACM.

EPHRAIM R. McLEAN and COLLEEN BAUDER

asynchronous transmission mode   ATM is a high-speed switching protocol. It is an important data transmission method because it provides efficient use of band width in transmitting messages. An ATM cell or packet is a fixed length of 53 bytes. It accommodates well to transmissions requiring a constant bit rate, such as video and audio. It can operate at different speeds.

auditing of information systems   An audit of an information system (IS) is an examination, by qualified persons, of documentation, procedures, operations, programs, and data for the purposes of identifying and correcting weaknesses in an organization's information systems. Objectives of the IS audit function are to safeguard IS assets, maintain data integrity, and ensure that IS functions are performed efficiently and effectively.

IS audits are undertaken by two types of auditors. *External auditors* are concerned primarily with financial information systems. They focus on evaluating IS controls that affect the reliability of financial data. *Internal auditors* recommend and design appropriate IS controls. They often serve on IS project teams or review the specifications produced by IS project teams.

Risks Associated with Information Systems

Information systems can significantly affect the success of many organizations. The development, implementation, operation, and maintenance of information systems, however, are subject to substantial risks.

1 *Information systems required for organizational continuity.* Many organizations cannot function without their information systems, e.g., airlines cannot schedule flights or book seats and banks cannot process checks. These organizations would cease to exist if their information systems remained inoperative for only short periods.

2 *High cost of information systems.* Many organizations have made substantial investments to develop and implement information systems. These investments sometimes account for more than 50 percent of their total capital investment. Moreover, information systems often are costly to operate and maintain. Significant losses can be incurred if they do not deliver expected benefits.

3 *Information systems affect employee behavior.* Information systems can be used to control and reward employee performance. Incorrect or inadequate information can result in dysfunctional behavior, e.g. employee morale may drop because employees believe that they have not been evaluated correctly.

4 *Intra- and interorganizational information sharing.* Information systems enable information to be exchanged among individuals inside and outside organizations. An organization's ability to respond to change may depend on how well employees can exchange information among themselves. Its desirability as a trading partner may depend on how well it can exchange information with other organizations.

5 *High risk of failure.* Despite their high cost, many information systems fail, i.e. they are never placed in use, abandoned after a short service life, or not used for decision-making purposes. Even organizations known for their IS expertise sometimes have dramatic failures.

6 *High cost of software failures.* Software failures can cause both direct and indirect losses. Direct losses can occur from malfunctions that arise in physical processes or financial processes, e.g. environmental pollution by an out-of-control nuclear reactor or overpayments to creditors by a faulty

electronic funds transfer system. Indirect losses arise through damage to reputation, e.g. loss of customer goodwill through errors in customer invoices.

7 *Data security violations.* Computer systems sometimes contain confidential information such as military secrets, financial data, and personal details. If IS controls fail to maintain the privacy of this information, national security can be jeopardized, competitive advantages can be lost, and individual lives can be ruined.

Performing an IS Audit

Auditors perform several phases of work during an IS audit.

Background investigation

Audits are concerned with assessing and reducing risks. To assess the general risks associated with an organization and its information systems, auditors investigate and evaluate environmental factors, such as:

1 *Industry.* The reliance of organizations on information systems depends in part on the nature of the industry in which they compete. For example, information systems are likely to be more critical to financial services organizations than to mining companies.

2 *Organizational structure.* As control becomes more decentralized, the likelihood of variations in the quality of controls and personnel increases. Decentralized organizations also increase the demands on information systems to provide more diverse information about the performance of their subunits.

3 *Personnel.* The integrity and competence of senior management, internal auditors, and IS personnel affect how external auditors approach the audit. If senior management lacks integrity, external auditors may decline the entire engagement. If internal auditors lack competence, they may be unable to design appropriate controls or to properly evaluate IS functions and applications. If IS personnel lack competence, they may make inappropriate choices from hardware and software alternatives, develop error-prone systems, or fail to take advantage of strategic IS opportunities.

4 *Hardware*. When external auditors accept an engagement, they represent themselves as having the competence and knowledge required to conduct the engagement properly. For an IS audit, this includes having adequate knowledge of the hardware used by the client organization.

5 *Database management system (DBMS)*. Many controls are implemented in an information system via the capabilities provided by a DATABASE MANAGEMENT SYSTEM. For example, IS personnel often use DBMSs to implement input, processing, and output controls. Auditors must have a thorough understanding of any DBMS used by an organization to be able to evaluate the quality of controls.

6 *Languages*. To evaluate application functions, auditors must understand the computer languages used by an organization. For example, at times auditors must read program source code to evaluate whether control weaknesses exist in a program.

Planning

Once background information has been obtained, an audit must be planned. The following tasks must be undertaken:

1 *Setting priorities*. Auditors often cannot examine all an organization's information systems. Some systems (e.g. financial reporting systems) must be examined each year, others on a rotating schedule, and others not at all. Auditors select systems to evaluate based on the purpose of the audit and the importance of the system to the organization.

2 *Determining required procedures and evidence*. Auditors consider the sensitivity, criticality, pervasiveness, and implementation characteristics of each system when determining procedures to perform and evidence to collect. Evidence is obtained from documentation, physical inspection, questionnaires, interviews, and test data.

Evidence collection

To evaluate the reliability of controls in an information system, auditors use various means of evidence collection including:

1 *Documentation*. Auditors usually begin their procedures by inspecting documentation. Documentation provides evidence about how the system was developed, what controls are supposed to exist, and what functions the system is supposed to perform.

2 *Questionnaires and interviews*. Auditors use questionnaires and interviews to gather information from IS personnel about how the system operates, known weaknesses with the system, and future plans. They may also use questionnaires and interviews to gather information from users about the effectiveness of the IS function and to identify problems with specific information systems.

3 *Testing*. Auditors perform compliance testing to verify that the system contains the controls and performs the functions described in the documentation. They then use test data to verify that the system responds correctly to typical input, to unusual but acceptable input, and to illegal input.

4 *Generalized audit software (GAS) and query languages*. GAS and query languages allow auditors to examine existing data. They use these tools to identify potential problems or inconsistent relationships among data, generate control totals that they can check against other evidence, and produce samples for further investigation, e.g. a list of customers to contact to confirm the unpaid balances of their accounts.

5 *Concurrent auditing techniques*. Concurrent auditing techniques collect evidence about the information system while it operates. These techniques include software routines embedded in a system that record random or unusual transactions as they are being processed.

Evidence evaluation
Experienced IS auditors evaluate and interpret the evidence gathered. They use the piecemeal evidence collected during an audit to arrive at overall decisions about the quality of the information systems they have examined.

Report

The audit report should indicate both strong and weak points in the systems examined by the auditors. For each weak point, the report should indicate its seriousness, suggest the priority for remedying the weakness, and where possible indicate a way of correcting the weakness. Auditors address their report to the audit committee of the board of directors or, if no audit committee exists, to the chief executive officer.

Follow-up

Auditors follow-up at appropriate intervals to determine that IS strengths are being maintained and that IS weaknesses are being corrected.

Information System Controls

Information system controls consist of generalized IS procedures, generalized programmed controls, application-specific programmed controls, and miscellaneous controls. Internal auditors help design and implement information system controls. External auditors evaluate whether the controls are working effectively and make suggestions for improvements.

Generalized information system procedures

IS procedures control the overall IS management environment in which information systems are developed, implemented, operated, and maintained. They include IS planning, personnel, disaster recovery, systems development, configuration control, and data administration procedures.

1 In *IS planning*, management develops plans to ensure that information systems meet the organization's strategic, managerial, operational, and regulatory information requirements. Management also establishes general procedures and guidelines to control the development, implementation, operation, and maintenance of information systems.

2 *Personnel procedures* include hiring, compensation, training, job assignments, and supervision. They are important because IS personnel, especially highly skilled programmers, can often circumvent controls. Organizations attract and retain high-quality IS personnel by providing adequate compensation, on-going training programs, and interesting job assignments.

3 *Disaster recovery procedures* protect data and ensure that IS operations can be resumed in a timely manner if hardware, software, or facilities are lost, damaged, or destroyed. Disaster recovery techniques include making program and data backups, using fault-tolerant hardware and software, and establishing alternative processing sites.

4 *Systems development procedures* prescribe the steps to be used to build new systems. By following a defined methodology, systems can be developed that are more likely to meet cost and time constraints, to have high reliability, to integrate easily with other systems, and to be resilient to change.

5 *Configuration control procedures* define the approach to be used to modify existing systems. They ensure that modifications are acceptable to all users, that these modifications do not introduce errors or inconsistencies, and that the system retains its resiliency.

6 *Data administration procedures* maintain and enhance the value of data stored in information systems. They embody the organization's strategy to ensure data is authorized, accurate, complete, and timely.

Generalized programmed controls

Generalized programmed controls are software and hardware controls that apply to the operation of all information systems. They include boundary controls; communication controls; operating system controls; and database controls.

1 *Boundary controls* govern access to computer hardware, software, and data. They include physical access controls and passwords.

2 *Communication controls* maintain the integrity and privacy of data transmitted between the user and the system or between information systems. They include data transmission protocols, which determine that messages sent are the same as messages received, and encryption, which scrambles messages so that they cannot be understood by unauthorized persons.

3 *Operating system controls* govern access to files and programs, regulate computer resource use (e.g. disk space and processor

time), and manage and protect processes currently being executed.

4 *Database controls* provide more extensive access controls over data than operating system controls. Data in databases is often encrypted to ensure that database controls are enforced, i.e. that users must access data through the database management system rather than accessing data directly. Database controls include concurrency controls to ensure that changes made by one user are not corrupted by changes made simultaneously by another user and view controls to limit access to a subset of data in the database.

Application-specific programmed controls

Application-specific controls are software controls that apply to the operation of individual information systems, e.g. an inventory information system. They include input controls; processing controls; and output controls.

1 *Input controls* seek to minimize data errors entering the information system. They include menus, data entry screens, and interactive help to facilitate data entry; range and format checks to ensure the accuracy of individual values; completeness and reasonableness checks to ensure the accuracy of records; and batch checks (e.g. dollar amount totals) to ensure the accuracy of groups of records.

2 *Processing controls* ensure that correct files are accessed and that software executes correctly. Processing controls include file labels to ensure that the correct data is accessed, file existence checks to ensure that all the data needed for a process is accessible, and commit and rollback functions to ensure that update processes produce consistent results.

3 *Output controls* determine the data that users can receive. They include physical restrictions that limit access to secure terminals, printers, and other output devices; and system backups to recover if the current data or programs are lost or damaged. Because of the interactive nature of the exchange between the system and the users in online systems, the boundary and com-

munication controls discussed above also function as output controls.

Miscellaneous controls

Miscellaneous controls are other measures organizations can take to maximize system availability and to protect against improper use of their information systems. They include fault tolerance; access logs; system logs; and security notices.

1 *Fault tolerance* involves using duplicate processing units, storage devices, and/or software to provide an immediate backup system. Fault tolerance becomes more desirable as hardware costs decline and the criticality of computerized information systems increases.

2 *Access logs* record who accessed or attempted to access an information system, when the access or attempted access occurred, and what applications or data were accessed. Proper control procedures include regular review and analysis of logs to detect security threats.

3 *System logs* record extraordinary events detected by the operating system. Internal events recorded on system logs include write failures, disk-capacity warnings, and device-access problems. External events recorded on system logs include repeated attempts by unauthorized users to access the system. Management must regularly review and analyze these logs.

4 *Security notices/patches*. When weaknesses in operating systems, database management systems, or similar software are discovered, known users are notified and provided with modifications (patches) to remedy the problem. Proper control procedures for organizations that use the software include reading the notices and applying the modifications correctly on a timely basis.

Impact of Changing Technology

The incentives for organizations to implement successful information systems are increasing because of competitive pressures, gains in the expected net benefits from IS projects, and expanding access to information technology. Threats to information systems are increasing as access to and knowledge of computers increase. Public awareness of IS capabilities are increasing users' expectations and engendering less tolerance of weaknesses in organizations' information systems.

As the importance of IS increases, so does the significance of the IS audit function. Changes in information technology, integration of information technology with organizational functions, and threats to information systems are increasing the demands on IS auditors for technical knowledge, understanding of organizational functions, and integration of both areas with internal controls. The importance of the IS audit function and demands for greater exper-

tise are causing many auditors to specialize in particular areas of technology.

PAUL L. BOWEN and RON WEBER

automated teller machine   ATMs are used in consumer (retail) banking. Customers may withdraw cash or enter deposits from remote locations. ATMs are typically connected to a network that allows customers from different banks or holding different credit cards to use them (*see* ELECTRONIC FUNDS TRANSFER).

———— B ————

bar code A method of coding data using vertical bars of differing widths, bar codes are used to identify products and inventory items. They are widely used in commerce to mark items being sold in retail stores. A universal product code (UPC) is assigned to a product and placed on a small rectangular space on the product package. The UPC or bar code can be read by a hand scanner or by a check-out counter scanner connected to a cash register. In the case of a retail store, the data scanned from the bar code is input to a computer that looks up the price and provides it to the cash register. The computer also collects data for inventory updating and sales analysis.

GORDON B. DAVIS

batch processing A term applied to periodic processing of transactions that are assembled into batches (*see* PROCESSING METHODS FOR INFORMATION SYSTEMS).

bulletin boards Computer bulletin boards can be a valuable source of information for organizations. Three different types of information-sharing groups have evolved: (a) bulletin board systems; (b) commercial discussion groups, and (c) personal discussion groups. Bulletin board systems are independent systems created and operated by entrepreneurs or organizations. The largest bulletin board system is the Usenet. These news groups number in the tens of thousands and are globally distributed over the INTERNET. The Usenet evolved with no central organizational structure. It has been the source of controversy and even legislation because of the lack of control over its contents.

A second class of discussion groups and information services is provided by the major commercial online vendors. The services are marketed for a relatively low monthly fee and hourly charge. They are one of the primary sources of technical information provided by information industry vendors. Vendors assign staff to follow their bulletin boards, post replies, announce problem solutions, and post upgrades. A third source of bulletin board/discussion group information is a personal discussion group. Discussion groups may have a large number of users, but there are also specialized groups with small numbers of dedicated participants.

Search tools are available for discussion groups and bulletin boards. Many newsgroup discussions are archived. A user looking for information that might have been discussed in a particular newsgroup can search its archive and retrieve relevant comments. In some newsgroups, volunteers accumulate important information and periodically post it as FAQs (frequently asked questions).

Bulletin boards are commonly supported within organizations. Most electronic mail systems support bulletin boards. These may be used to access and disseminate useful information within the organization.

GORDON B. DAVIS and J. DAVID NAUMANN

byte A byte consists of 8 bits plus a parity bit. It is a basic unit for coding information for computer processing and for addressing units of computer storage. In processing, bytes may be combined for addressing or processing purposes.

C

C and C++ C is a high-level programming language that takes into account machine-level considerations. There are a number of high level instructions to simplify programming. It has been used in writing UNIX operating systems and for applications to be run on microcomputers and workstations. Programs in C for one computer tend to be easily transported to another computer.

C++ is a variation of the C language that incorporates principles of object-oriented programming. It has the advantage of being similar to the C language but the disadvantage of not meeting all of the conditions of an object-oriented programming language. *See also* PROGRAMMING LANGUAGES.

careers in information systems Information systems (IS) professionals are people who acquire, develop, manage, and maintain hardware, software, and telecommunication networks, and offer computing and information services to users. There is a wide spectrum of information systems professionals who play various roles in the management and development of information systems. The major categories of IS careers are:

1 *Chief information officers* (CIOs). CHIEF INFORMATION OFFICERS are top corporate officers responsible for the overall IS functions in organizations. CIOs offer leadership in managing the information resources of the firm, and in directing the power of information technology toward the strategic objectives of the firm.
2 *Data center IS professionals.* These include computer operations managers; database administrators; network specialists; systems programmers; and computer operators who are involved in computer capacity planning and management; disaster recovery; hardware and systems software maintenance; and production or job scheduling.
3 *Software development and maintenance teams.* These comprise application programmers who develop software using programming languages and software tools; systems analysts who determine user requirements and design the systems specifications; and project managers who oversee and coordinate teams of programmers and systems analysts in developing specific application systems.
4 *End-user IS professionals.* These are responsible for the acquisition, maintenance, and help-desk support of personal computer use in the organization.

Career Orientations of IS Professionals

Igbaria et al. (1991) found that IS professionals are diverse in their career orientations, i.e. in their interests, self-perceived talents, values, and motives that shape their career decisions (see also Ginzberg & Baroudi, 1988). Technical and managerial orientations are two dominant themes among IS professionals. People in technical jobs such as systems programmers, application programmers, and systems engineers are more technically oriented, while those in managerial jobs such as systems analysts, project leaders, and managers are more managerially oriented. The study by Igbaria et al. (1991) found that the match between job type and career orientation of IS professionals is important because such a match leads to higher job satisfaction, stronger organizational commitment and lower intentions to leave the organization. The implication of this study is that management should take into account differences in employee interests and orientations and provide job opportunities that match employee needs.

Future Directions for IS Professionals

Two important factors influence the evolution of IS work: the expansion of end-user computing and the outsourcing of IS services. With the advent of client-server technologies, powerful personal computers, and software languages that are easy to use, end-users have been increasingly developing and managing their own computing applications, rather than relying on the organization's IS employees. This trend has contributed to the downsizing of the IS group within organizations. It will also affect the nature of IS work. Rather than providing complete information system services to the organization, IS professionals may provide support for end-user developed systems or may concentrate on developing and managing only major, company-wide applications.

The organization of IS work is also changing. Traditionally, firms that require a specific skills set will employ a worker under a long-term employment contract where the worker works all year round at the employer's place of business, except for vacations and holidays. Unless they resign or have their services terminated, employees are assumed to remain with the employer until death or retirement. From the legal perspective, both parties have rights and responsibilities accorded to them by both common law and employment statutes governing the employer–employee relationship. Accordingly, it is not uncommon for IS workers to remain attached to single employers during their entire careers.

Careers built upon long-term employment relationships with single organizations work well in situations where the skills sets required by the firm are relatively stable over time. However, in information systems, firms are finding that alternative employment arrangements, such as contract work, are becoming more important and attractive because of the increasingly rapid evolution of technology (see Slaughter & Ang, 1995). Cutting-edge technologies typically enjoy lifespans of only two years. Skills of IS personnel therefore erode very rapidly. Operating in short windows of stable technological environments, IS organizations with a stable and static workforce anchored in traditional employment relationships continually face the problem of needing to upgrade the skills of the workforce. In many cases, organizations may feel that commitment to training the internal workforce is self-defeating. Because technologies move so rapidly, by the time an organization invests in and trains its IS staff in a certain technology, that technology may already have become obsolete.

Accordingly, the number of organizations using contract workers for IS work is growing dramatically, particularly with the rapid diffusion of IS outsourcing where organizations are contracting out the services of the entire IS department to independent contractors or service-providers. Consequently, IS careers no longer take place in single organizations. Rather, as contract workers, IS professionals are not attached to any single organization for a long period of time. Instead, they are independent and self-employed, hired on a fixed-term basis for a specific skill through an agreed-upon contract. The contract may provide a fixed duration of service or may operate on a job-by-job basis. From the worker's point of view, contract work provides an opportunity to establish a special expertise or professional status within an industry. In fact, it is often regarded as a way for workers to focus on the aspects of their profession they most enjoy (e.g. programming instead of managing software projects) without having to deal with corporate politics or pressures to move up the expected career ladder.

The trends toward outsourcing and careers based on contract work arrangements imply an increasing interorganizational division of IS labor in the future, as work formerly conducted within organizational boundaries and under the administrative control of a single enterprise is parceled out to more specialized individuals or organizational entities. The implication for IS professionals is that they can no longer solely rely on building careers by moving upwards in single organizations. Rather, IS professionals must consciously plan to upgrade and reskill themselves in light of competence-destroying technologies. They must also be cognizant of new career opportunities offered by outsourcing arrangements. For example, ideal IS professionals in outsourcing must possess not only a combination of technical and practical knowledge, skills, and abilities, but also negotiation and bargaining skills to sustain a flexible partnership that demands intense relationship-building and continual recommitment from top to bottom of both client organizations and service-providers.

Bibliography

Ginzberg, M. H. & Baroudi, J. J. (1988). MIS careers – a theoretical perspective. *Communications of the ACM*, **31** (5), 586–94.

Igbaria, M., Greenhaus, J. H. & Parasuraman, S. (1991). Career orientations of MIS employees: an empirical analysis. *MIS Quarterly*, **15** (2), 151–70.

Slaughter, S. A. & Ang, S. (1995). Information systems employment structures in the USA and Singapore: a cross-cultural comparison. *Information Technology and People*, **8** (2), 17–36.

SOON ANG and SANDRA SLAUGHTER

CASE: computer-aided software/system engineering   The term "computer-aided software or system engineering" (CASE) applies to tools that assist developers to analyze, design, and construct software applications or information systems. A software system is developed to provide a solution to a problem. This requires the problem domain to be analyzed before a solution is proposed and a solution to be designed before a software system is constructed. Once constructed, the system is maintained. After use, it may evolve and change. This software system life-cycle is not necessarily sequential, nor are all phases in the cycle exercised every time. There are different approaches to the development (analysis, design, and construction) of software systems, as well as different formalisms and notations to represent requirements and design during software life-cycle phase.

There are two broad categories of CASE tools – upper and lower. Upper CASE tools are used in the analysis and design, while lower CASE tools are used in the construction of information systems. A repository is used to pass analysis and design representations, often called models, to a lower CASE tool. A lower CASE tool is also called an application or code generator. It has a language to add more implementation details to

a design and provides a facility to generate program instruction. All artifacts in the development process are stored in a repository. In this way, they can be used to maintain and evolve a software system from the analysis and design perspective, providing higher-quality software. In addition, they can be reused in other projects to increase software development productivity.

A CASE tool is, itself, a data-intensive software system. It consists of a repository of analysis, design, and construction data about another software system, and a graphical interface that looks at the repository data through the eyes of a specific notation (formalism or language). The primary concept that distinguishes a CASE tool from a DATABASE MANAGEMENT SYSTEM is its meta-model. A meta-model is a repository schema, which determines what kind of data is going to be kept in the repository about systems which are built with the help of the CASE tool.

One of the important features of CASE tools is support for modeling of a problem domain and modeling information system components. One of the most-used notations to analyze a problem domain is a data flow diagram (DFD). DFD has four concepts with graphical representations: external entities, business processes, data flows, and data stores. External entities provide specific entry and exit points to or from an organization unit being analyzed. Business processes transform, move, or store organizational data represented as data flows or data stores. A process relies on organizational resources to accomplish its tasks. If a process at hand is complex, it can be decomposed into lower-level processes that are graphically represented in another diagram. This top-down graphical decomposition of processes is a significant feature of the DFD formalism.

In an information system application, there are four major components: business data, user applications (interfaces), business policies (rules), and business tasks (services). In general, each component is represented and designed using a different formalism. A CASE tool may support only one of them, or an integrated combination of them. In object-oriented analysis and design tools, the components are integrated through a common model of classes (entities) and their relationships.

Business data, once analyzed in the context of business processes, is described with the CASE tool using a variation of an entity-relationship formalism. An entity (or a class) is used to describe similar objects. A relationship is used to relate objects to each other. An attribute is used to describe either an object or a relationship. User applications are designed based on user data views using presentation layouts and use scenarios. A data view is derived from business data and is structured in such a way to support user needs. View data may be presented to a user in different forms. The interaction between a user and various forms is documented by one or more use scenarios. Business policies are often described in state transition diagrams. An entity or its view passes through different states in its life. A state transition is caused by an event. This may be a business task and is often subject to a condition. Business policies may be described through a sequence of state transitions, events, and conditions. Business tasks are specified by their names, parameters, and results, together with pre- and post-conditions. They usually describe a behavior of an entity, a data view or an application form.

DJENAN RIDJANOVIC

CD-ROM A CD-ROM or compact disk is a form of information storage, in which information is stored digitally and read by readers/drives using low-intensity lasers. Each aluminum and plastic 12 millimeter (4.72 inches) disk holds 500–650 megabytes of information; however, given new compression techniques, much more information – text, audio, video, etc. – can be stored. Audio CDs were first released in 1982 (replacing vinyl long-playing records); CD-ROM (compact disk read-only memory) was introduced in 1985. Other versions of the CD, such as CD-recordable, CD-interactive, and erasable CDs, have since been introduced. All products must be licensed from inventors Sony (Japan) and Philips (The Netherlands), guaranteeing a high level of standardization. ISO standards for the file format (ISO 9660) also ensure standardization. Advantages of compact disks for storage include easily available and low-cost media and drive devices, standardiza-

tion, large capacity, portability, huge and growing installed base of drives, durability and stability of the medium and the ability to store and retrieve multiple data types on a single disk. Disadvantages include the 10–15-year life of an average CD-ROM disk, relatively slow access times (compared to hard drive systems) and the increasing availability of other high-density storage options. CD products are ideal for data sets that are relatively static or for which many copies of the same data are required. Widespread commercial acceptance guarantees a useful life of 10–20 years for traditional data storage applications.

NANCY K. HERTHER

cellular technology in information systems Cellular communication systems are used not only for telephone communications but also for information processing. A portable computer can download information from a central computer and upload customer or other information. Using this technology allows a salesperson or other customer representative to interact with a customer while communicating with applications and databases at a central location. For example, a sales representative at a customer's office can transmit an order via cellular technology and receive immediately a confirmed delivery date for the order from the organization's main computer.

GORDON B. DAVIS

chargeback in information systems Pricing information system (IS) services and charging organization units for services rendered is practiced by many organizations. Chargeback systems range from simple to complex.

Many organizations treat centralized IS services as an unallocated cost. In this view, IS is a cost center, since it incurs expenses, but does not directly contribute to enhancing revenue. As an "unallocated cost center," IS services are essentially free to the users in the organization. This strategy is useful in the initiation and adoption/adaptation stages of IT assimilation in an organization, because it creates a climate conducive to user experimentation with IT. However, lack of accountability inherent in this approach can lead to misuse and abuse of IS resources. In addition, the IS unit is insulated from competitive pressures and operational efficiencies.

When IS is well integrated in an organization, controlling for efficient and effective use of IT resources by the organizational units becomes a critical issue. An allocated cost center for IT resources promotes responsible use of IS services by the organizational units because the users are held accountable for the IT resources consumed; that is, they are charged.

How an organization uses chargeback information for control purposes is the key determinant of chargeback system effectiveness. Characteristics of a chargeback system, such as understandability, controllability, cost–benefit incidence and accountability, have a moderating effect. IT management control structure is defined as the set of control mechanisms that integrate IT activities with the rest of the organization operations. The maturity of assimilation of IT in an organization is also found to interact with IT management control structure in determining chargeback system effectiveness.

Research on chargeback systems has focused on the perceptions of the users and the providers of IS services (e.g. perception of fairness, satisfaction, perceived effectiveness). Other key questions are:

1 How should the IS services function be organized (allocated or unallocated cost centers, profit centers, or even investment centers)?
2 Which of these strategies will be conducive to what operating environment?
3 If costs are allocated, how should the transfer price be determined: market-based, cost-based, or dual pricing scheme?

Outsourcing IS services has emerged as a feasible alternative for controlling costs. The majority of the research to date has assessed chargeback schemes for a centralized IS services scenario. Distributed computing based on CLIENT/SERVER ARCHITECTURE has shifted management of several key IS functions to user and IS personnel, who assume internal consulting roles in addition to managing core technologies such as telecommunications net-

works. These changes require different methods of chargeback.

KYU KIM and NARAYAN S. UMANATH

chief information officer The chief information officer (CIO) is the highest-ranking manager responsible for the management of information resources and information technology within an organization. Although the position of CIO varies from organization to organization, the CIO often reports to the president and chief executive officer. The position usually has two broad responsibilities: (a) the management of information technology (e.g. hardware, software, and networks); and (b) the management of the information resources (applications, databases, and personnel) used by the organization.

As the most senior information technology officer, it is the CIO's responsibility to understand the organization's mission and objectives and the potential benefits of using information technology. The CIO's challenge is to seek out opportunities where information technology can be deployed to achieve organization objectives as well as to find ways in which information technology can be used to gain competitive advantage.

The aggressive use of information technology and the growth in the creation, need, and use of information has focused the CIO on corporate information as a manageable resource. In this role, the CIO must understand how information is used by the organization in accomplishing its objectives and how to best manage this information as a critical and valuable corporate asset.

BRIAN D. JANZ

client/server architecture The term "client/ server" refers to a logical architecture that describes a way of subdividing tasks among processors in a network. Client/server applications and systems are distinguished from other logical architectures (such as hierarchical and peer-to-peer) by dividing tasks into two components: a client with which the user is generally in direct contact and a server which performs relatively standardized tasks for a set of clients. Multiple clients can be programmed to use the results of server activities; a single client can access one or more servers to perform a variety of tasks. Frequently, a personal computer or workstation is used for the client, while a workstation, minicomputer, mainframe, or supercomputer is used for the server. However, the logical client/server design can be implemented with other hardware patterns and may also be implemented on a single machine. One computer within a network can host both client and server programs.

The client/server architecture can be extended to computer resources in an enterprise network. In such a design, each client system has potential access to a variety of servers in the enterprise. The users have access to the entire range of enterprise computing (within their specified security-oriented limits). An objective is efficiency across the enterprise by shifting some computing from centralized locations to the client location, making greater use of the organization's total combined computing capacity.

The client portion of the application typically provides a user interface, screens for data input or specification of a data retrieval, text-editing capabilities, and error processing. Resources needed by the client, such as printers, database access, image processing, and security, are likely to be managed by a particular server. Client/server systems are inherently more complex than centralized mainframe applications because they require management of and coordination among client, server, and communications components.

Designers of client/server systems must decide where to conduct processing. The developer has the dual objectives of doing processing at client locations (which are presumably dedicated to a particular user), while not overloading network traffic by moving large volumes of raw data. In general, processing is more cost-effective at the client site and input–output tasks more cost-effective at the server site (Renaud, 1993).

The concept of client/server architecture is often linked to distribution of computing. Organizational computing is moved from the mainframe to smaller hardware. Using processing capabilities of both the client and server

worksites, and replacing relatively expensive larger equipment with relatively less-expensive smaller equipment, cost savings and more responsive computing are potentially attainable. By linking client/server architecture with RE-ENGINEERING or application redesign, additional streamlining can occur. In this scenario, redundant or unnecessary activities are eliminated and sequential processes can be replaced by concurrent or parallel processes.

Some issues and difficulties with implementation of client/server designs include:

1 Developing the architecture in an environment of existing hardware and software configurations that may not be compatible throughout an organization.
2 Distributing of processing across different sites such that availability (reliability) and performance (both throughput and response time) are maintained.
3 Training and orienting technical and user personnel to new development methods and uses.
4 Ensuring security for all elements of a decentralized system.
5 Transitioning from centralized mainframe-oriented systems while continuing to operate the enterprise effectively.
6 Planning for smooth operations as the number of users (clients) increases.

Bibliography

Renaud, P. E. (1993). *Introduction to Client/Server Systems.* New York: John Wiley.

FRED NIEDERMAN

COBOL   A procedural programming language designed to address problems in business data processing. The acronym COBOL stands for COmmon Business Oriented Language. COBOL has been the most widely used programming language in business. Billions of lines of COBOL are in use throughout the world.

The effort to develop COBOL was started in the late 1950s by a group of private individuals from academia and industry. This group obtained assistance from the United States Department of Defense to set up the Committee on Data Systems Languages (CODASYL).

CODASYL was responsible for the first standard of COBOL, called COBOL 60. The United States Department of Defense soon adopted COBOL 60 and propagated it as a standard. Other standards of the language have been defined by the American National Standards Institute (ANSI), beginning in 1974 with ANSI-74 COBOL.

The development of COBOL was motivated by business needs that were not well supported by other languages at that time. These needs included efficient retrieval and storage of large data files, manipulation of business financial data, formatting of business data onto reports, and English-like syntax that could be understood by non-programmers.

COBOL successfully addressed the need for retrieving and storing data files by supporting sequential, random, and indexed file access, as well as the ability to define hierarchical records of data. These features allowed COBOL programs to access data in any order from a file, process it, and store it in a new order. COBOL addressed the need to manipulate business data by supporting fixed-point arithmetic which prevented inaccurate computation of business data. COBOL addressed the need to format business data by providing data types tailored to the display of financial information. COBOL was unsuccessful in providing a syntax that could be understood by non-programmers. The language uses many English words in its syntax, but the meaning of a COBOL program cannot easily be understood by someone untrained in the language.

A COBOL program is composed of four divisions.

1 The *identification division* gives the name of the program, its author, the date the program was written and other information that other users may find helpful in understanding or maintaining the program.

2 The *environment division* comprises two separate sections: the *configuration section* which holds information about the way in which a specific machine implements COBOL; and the *input–output section*, which describes external devices that will be accessed during execution of the program.

3 The *data division* defines all of the program variables, data structures, and data types

that the program uses. The data division contains the *file section* and the *working storage section*, among others. The file section describes data that comes from external files and the working storage section describes data computed from program input. The data division defines three data types: numeric, alphanumeric, and alphabetic. Numeric data is represented by the number 9, alphanumeric data is represented by the letter X, and alphabetic data (which includes the space character) is represented by the letter A (or the letter B for representing spaces). These types are combined to define the size of a program variable. For example, a numeric variable that is three digits long would be represented as 999.

4 The *procedure division* contains program logic to compute, manipulate data, and to iterate and branch through program execution. Most COBOL statements in the procedure division begin with a verb. Common data manipulation statements use the verbs *add*, *subtract*, *multiply*, *divide*, *compute*, and *move*. The *perform* verb is commonly used to iterate through program execution. The word *if* is used to begin statements that cause program branching.

The following COBOL program provides a simple example of the four COBOL divisions and shows some common COBOL statements. The program takes an input file containing the hours worked (IN-HOURS) and the rate of pay (IN-RATE) for a group of employees. Sample program input is shown immediately following the sample program. In the procedure division the program computes the pay due each employee (PAY-DETAIL) and computes the total pay (PAY-TOTAL) for all employees. This computation appears in the paragraph called 3000-PROCESS-INPUT and is accomplished using the verbs COMPUTE and ADD. Each employee's hours worked, rate of pay, and pay due is printed out as shown in the sample program output. Report headings that appear on the output are defined in the data division and used in the procedure division. For example HDR1 is defined in line 000760, moved into an

A small COBOL program example

```
000010 PROCESS NOCMPR2 08/18/95
000020 IDENTIFICATION DIVISION.MN75COBL
000030 PROGRAM-ID. COBOLPGM. LV002
000040 AUTHOR. YOUR NAME.
000050 DATE-COMPILED.
000060
000070***********************************************
000080* SYSTEM: INSERT YOUR SYSTEM NAME
000090* PROGRAM: PRINT A PAY AMOUNT
000100*
000110* PROPERTY OF: YOUR COMPANY NAME
000120***********************************************
000130* CHANGES:
000140* 08/15/95 - INITIAL CONCEPTION
000150*
000160*
000170***ENDREMARKS*************************************************
000180
000190 ENVIRONMENT DIVISION.
000200 CONFIGURATION SECTION.
000210 SOURCE-COMPUTER. IBM-370.
000220 OBJECT-COMPUTER. IBM-370.
000230 SPECIAL-NAMES.
000240 C01 IS TOP-OF-PAGE
000250 C12 IS BOTTOM-OF-PAGE.
000260
000270 INPUT-OUTPUT SECTION.
000280 FILE-CONTROL.
000290
000300 SELECT IN-FILE ASSIGN TO INFILE.
000310
000320 SELECT REPORT-FILE ASSIGN TO RPTFILE.
000330
000340
000350 DATA DIVISION.
000360
000370 FILE SECTION.
000380* --------------- INPUT FILES --------------------
000390
000400 FD IN-FILE
000410 LABEL RECORDS ARE STANDARD
000420 RECORDING MODE IS F
000430 BLOCK CONTAINS 0 RECORDS
000440 RECORD CONTAINS 80 CHARACTERS
000450 DATA RECORD IS IN-REC.
000460
000470 01 IN-REC.
       05 IN-REC-TYPE PIC   X(3).
       05 IN-HOURS PIC S9(5).
       05 IN-RATE PIC
        S9(3)V99.
       05 FILLER PIC X(67).
000530
000540* ------------------- OUTPUT FILES ----------------
000550
000560 FD REPORT-FILE
000570 LABEL RECORDS ARE STANDARD
000580 BLOCK CONTAINS 0 RECORDS
000590 DATA RECORD IS RPT-RECORD.
000600 01 RPT-RECORD PIC X(133).
000610
000620
000630 WORKING-STORAGE SECTION.
000640 01 FLAGS.
000650 05 EOF-FLAG PIC X VALUE 'N'.
000660 88 EOF-INPUT VALUE 'Y'.
000670
000680 01 HOLDERS.
000690 05 PAY-DETAIL PIC S9(5)V99 VALUE ZEROS.
000700 05 PAY-TOTAL PIC S9(7)V99 VALUE ZEROS.
000701
000710
000720***********************************************
000730** REPORT HEADINGS **
```

```
000740***********************************************
000750
000760 01 HDR1.
000770 05 FILLER PIC X VALUE SPACES.
000780 05 FILLER PIC X(29)
000790 VALUE 'A COBOL PROGRAM COMPUTING PAY'.
000800 05 FILLER PIC X(103) VALUE SPACES.
000810
000820 01 HDR2.
000830 05 FILLER PIC X(5) VALUE SPACES.
000840 05 FILLER PIC X(5)
000850 VALUE 'HOURS'.
000860 05 FILLER PIC X(5) VALUE SPACES.
000870 05 FILLER PIC X(5)
000880 VALUE ' RATE'.
000890 05 FILLER PIC X(5) VALUE SPACES.
000900 05 FILLER PIC X(5)
000910 VALUE ' PAY '.
000920 05 FILLER PIC X(103) VALUE SPACES.
000930
000940***********************************************
000950** REPORT DETAILS **
000960***********************************************
000970
000980 01 DETAIL-LINE.
000990 05 FILLER PIC X(5) VALUE SPACES.
001000 05 PRT-HOURS PIC X(5).
001010 05 FILLER PIC X(3) VALUE SPACES.
001020 05 PRT-RATE PIC $$$9.99.
001030 05 FILLER PIC X(1) VALUE SPACES.
001040 05 PRT-PAY-DETAIL PIC $$$$9.99.
001050 05 FILLER PIC X(103) VALUE SPACES.
001060
001070 01 TOTAL-LINE.
001080 05 FILLER PIC X(5) VALUE SPACES.
001090 05 FILLER PIC X(5) VALUE
001100 'TOTAL'.
001110 05 FILLER PIC X(10) VALUE SPACES.
001120 05 PRT-PAY-TOTAL PIC $$$$$9.99.
001130 05 FILLER PIC X(103) VALUE SPACES.
001140
001150 01 SEPARATOR.
001160 05 FILLER PIC X(19) VALUE SPACES.
001170 05 FILLER PIC X(11) VALUE
001180 '==========='.
001190 05 FILLER PIC X(103) VALUE SPACES.
001200
001210 01 BLANK-LINE.
001220 05 FILLER PIC X(133) VALUE SPACES.
001230
001240 PROCEDURE DIVISION.
001250
001260 0000-MAIN-LINE.
001270
001280 OPEN INPUT IN-FILE,
001290 OUTPUT REPORT-FILE.
001300
001310 PERFORM 1000-INITIALIZE.
001320 PERFORM 2000-READ-INPUT.
001330 PERFORM 9000-PRINT-HEADER.
001340 PERFORM UNTIL EOF-INPUT
001350 PERFORM 3000-PROCESS-INPUT
001360 PERFORM 9100-PRINT-DETAIL
001370 PERFORM 2000-READ-INPUT
001380 END-PERFORM.
001390
001400 PERFORM 9200-PRINT-TOTAL.
001410
001420 CLOSE IN-FILE,
001430 REPORT-FILE.
001440
001450 STOP RUN.
001460
001470 1000-INITIALIZE.
001480
```

```
001490 MOVE ZEROS TO IN-
              HOURS
              IN-RATE
PAY-DETAIL
001500 PAY-TOTAL.
001510
001520 2000-READ-INPUT.
001530 READ IN-FILE
001540 AT END MOVE 'Y' TO EOF-FLAG.
001550
001560
001570
001580
001590 3000-PROCESS-INPUT.
001600
001610 IF IN-REC-TYPE = '$$$'
001620 COMPUTE PAY-DETAIL = IN-HOURS * IN-RATE
001630 ADD PAY-DETAIL TO PAY-TOTAL
001640 END-IF.
001650
001660
001670 9000-PRINT-HEADER.
001680
001690 MOVE HDR1 TO RPT-RECORD.
001700 WRITE RPT-RECORD AFTER ADVANCING TOP-OF-PAGE.
001710 MOVE HDR2 TO RPT-RECORD.
001720 WRITE RPT-RECORD FROM HDR2 AFTER ADVANCING 3 LINES.
001730 MOVE BLANK-LINE TO RPT-RECORD.
001740 WRITE RPT-RECORD AFTER ADVANCING 2 LINES.
001750
001760 9100-PRINT-DETAIL.
001770
001780 MOVE IN-HOURS TO PRT-HOURS.
001790 MOVE IN-RATE TO PRT-RATE.
001800 MOVE PAY-DETAIL TO PRT-PAY-DETAIL.
001810 MOVE DETAIL-LINE TO RPT-RECORD.
001820 WRITE RPT-RECORD.
001830 MOVE ZEROS TO PAY-DETAIL.
001840
001850
001860 9200-PRINT-TOTAL.
001870
001880 MOVE SEPARATOR TO RPT-RECORD.
001890 WRITE RPT-RECORD AFTER ADVANCING 2 LINES.
001900 MOVE PAY-TOTAL TO PRT-PAY-TOTAL.
001910 MOVE TOTAL-LINE TO RPT-RECORD.
001920 WRITE RPT-RECORD.
```

Sample program input

```
$$$0002501000
$$$0003001100
$$$0003500500
$$$0000505000
$$$0004002000
```

Sample program output

```
A COBOL PROGRAM COMPUTING PAY

HOURS   RATE   PAY

00025   $10.00    $250.00
00030   $11.00    $330.00
00035    $5.00    $175.00
00005  $250.00   $1250.00
00040   $20.00    $800.00

===========
TOTAL          $2805.00
```

output variable in line 001690, and written to the report in line 001700.

RANDY SNYDER

coding of data for information processing
Coding is required for information processing because data in natural form (as data on documents, the documents themselves, voice, pictures, diagrams, etc.) is not suitable for computer storage or processing. The data in its various forms must be encoded in a representation using binary digits. For output, the process is reversed: digital codes are converted to representations such as printed characters, diagrams, pictures, voice, etc. Even though inputs and outputs take many forms, the concepts underlying coding data digitally are similar. Closely related to digital coding is data compression. Coding may be efficient for input but not efficient for storage or transmission. Most data coding methods result in significant redundancy. Compression methods reduce redundancy and thereby reduce the storage and transmission requirements.

Analog versus Digital Representation

Information can be represented in either analog or digital form, corresponding to continuous or discrete representations. Although human processing of voice, sound, image, and motion is analog, computer information processing is based entirely on digital equivalents. This means that anything a computer is to process must be converted from analog inputs to digital coding. For output, it must be converted from internal digital coding back to analog for presentation to humans.

Analog methods are still in use in voice communication, entertainment media, and some telephone technology. In human speech communication, sounds are continuous waveforms that are produced by the speaker's vocal chords, sent through the air, and reconstructed by the ears of the recipient. When microphones and speakers are used, they also employ analog electromagnetic waveforms. Until fairly recently, methods for storing sound were based on storing analog waveforms on the magnetic surface of a disk or tape. Similarly,

video programs are broadcast in analog signal form, flow over cable as analog signals, and are stored on VCR tape as analog signals.

In contrast, a digital signal is a voltage or current that represents two states. The digital codes represented by digital signals provide information for reconstructing an analog signal if there is need for an analog output. Newer data transport facilities, recordings, telephone communications, and other systems employ digital devices and digital coding. There are basically two reasons for the dominance of digital devices and digital coding. The first is the simplicity and low cost of electronic components based on the two states that represent binary digits; the second is the increase in quality by using digital coding error detection and error correction methods.

Coding of Alphanumeric Characters

If computers only processed numeric digits, the coding scheme could be quite simple. To encode the 10 numeric digits from 0 to 9 requires a code with a set of four binary digits (bits) with values of 0 or 1.

Numeric value	Digital code
0	0000
1	0001
2	0010
3	0011
4	0100
5	0101
6	0110
7	0111
8	1000
9	1001

Computers need to represent not only numeric characters but also alphabetic and special characters. The size of the code needs to increase. The basic coding and storage unit for personal computers consists of a set of 8 bits called a *byte*. An 8-bit code can encode 256 different input characters. A byte is sufficient for upper and lower case letters (that need different codes) as well as a large number of special characters. It is not sufficient when different non-Roman language characters such as Hebrew and Greek are included. The coding method must expand to use two bytes (that can encode 65,536 symbols). The fundamental principle is that the code size must increase as more characters are included. A commonly used code for alphabetic, numeric and special characters is the American Standard Code for Information Interchange (ASCII). The original ASCII standard code used 7 bits. An extended ASCII code employs 8 bits.

Various coding schemes have implications for data processing and communication. The coding will affect the way data items are ordered. For example, if the capital letters are given a smaller numeric value than lower case letters, the three words, Alpha, Beta, Gamma will be sorted by the computer in that order; however, if the words are Alpha, beta, Gamma, they will be ordered as Alpha, Gamma, beta. There are ways to deal with this problem but the underlying concept is that coding has implications for processing.

Coding of Pictures and Graphics

The screen used for computer output displays alphanumeric data, graphics, pictures, and video. If the screen needed to display only alphanumeric characters and simple line drawings, the display device could encode these as combinations of lines. However, in a full GRAPHICAL USER INTERFACE, the screen consists of thousands of tiny dots, each of which can have a picture value of white, black, gray, or color. These individual picture elements are called pixels (or pels). A digitized picture is composed of a large number of pixels. The number of pixels represented can vary with different implementations of the technology. For example, a widely used display standard for personal computers is 640 pixels across by 480 pixels high. The number of dots to be encoded per unit of area determines the size of each pixel and also the texture of the result. A fairly small number of pixels gives a rough picture in which the individual dots are clearly visible. A large number of picture elements makes the picture smooth and sharp, so that individual pixels cannot be identified by the viewer.

The size of the code for a pixel depends on the variations that must be encoded. If a pixel is either black or white, then the code for a pixel can be a single bit with 0 representing white and 1 representing black. If a pixel can be only a few basic colors, a half-byte of four bits can encode 16 different colors. If a pixel can represent 256 different colors, one byte is used for each pixel. This is currently sufficient for many high-resolution personal computer displays. If a pixel needs to represent more colors and shades of colors, a 3 byte (24 bit) coding is used to represent 256 levels for each of the primary colors. With 24 bits, over 16 million variations of color can be coded to represent the full range distinguishable by the human eye.

Coding of Voice and Sound

A sound is captured by a microphone or reproduced by a speaker as a continuous waveform. The analog method for coding voice and sound is to capture and store the waveform. With digital technology, however, analog waveforms are encoded with digital codes in such a way that they can eventually be reconverted to analog.

Analog to digital conversion is performed by measuring the analog signal at frequent intervals and encoding the measurement as a digital value. In telephony, for example, sampling is done at 8,000 times per second. Each measurement is encoded as one of 256 voltage levels using 8 bits. This means a voice or sound message requires 64,000 bits per second, or 480,000 bytes per minute. To produce the sound for humans, digital to analog conversion recreates the analog signal for a stereo speaker by generating the appropriate voltages from the digital codes. This same principle is used for other sound encoding such as music compact disk, but a much higher sampling rate is used to capture all of the music signal.

Coding of Video with Motion

Motion video consists of separate pictures that change rapidly. Each new image is displayed often enough that the human vision system blends it into continuous motion. This occurs when a picture is completely redrawn about 15 times per second. For comparison, the USA standard for broadcast TV, NTSC (National Television Systems Committee) video, has about 480 rows of 725 pixels repeated 30 times per second. If it were digitally encoded at 1 byte per pixel, it would require 10 million bytes per second of video (plus audio).

Compression

The need for compression is based on costs of storage and communication, limits of storage technology, and convenience. Compression reduces the cost of storage by reducing the storage needed. For example, most software packages use compression to reduce the number of diskettes that must be distributed. The algorithm to decompress the data is included in the installation program. Information communication is often a significant cost. Compression reduces redundant information and speeds transmission. The costs of storage devices continue to decrease, but the architecture of most systems places limits on available storage capacity. When copying data files, compression makes the operation more convenient because it reduces the volume of media required.

There are many different procedures or algorithms for data compression. The simplest example of data compression is called "space suppression." Space suppression takes advantage of the presence of frequently occurring strings of the space character, something that was once very significant in computer generated reports sent to remote printers. In space suppression, each string of spaces is replaced at the transmitter by a flag code and a count of the number of spaces. The receiver then replaces the flag code and count with the specified number of spaces. A similar scheme is used by facsimile transmission.

For data compression, variations on an algorithm by Lempel and Ziv are very common. Data files are compressed for storage and transmission, often to less than half of their original length. The LZ approach is related to space suppression, but is able to substitute short codes for virtually every string that repeats once or more in a file. Lempel–Ziv type algorithms are built into high-speed modems. They are also the basis for many software products that effectively double the capacity of disk storage.

These approaches to compression are called "loss-less" since the exact bit-pattern of the original is always completely restored. Loss-less compression is often not necessary in communicating sound, graphics, and motion images. By carefully developing compression algorithms that leave out just the content of an image that is not noticeable (or least noticeable) to humans, high compression ratios have been defined. For example, the JPEG (Joint Photographic Experts Group) standard for images provide loss-less compression of about $3:1$, but can approach ratios of $50:1$ with some loss of the original signal.

Motion video compression can rely on all of the above techniques, and some additional characteristics of both the human vision system and motion pictures. Most of the time, only a small part of the video image changes from one frame to the next. By encoding only the changes over time, very high-quality compressed video can have compression ratios of more than $200:1$. For example, the MPEG-2 (Moving Picture Experts Group) standard for high-definition TV will compress from an original picture of 1.2 billion bits per second to less than 6 million.

GORDON B. DAVIS and J. DAVID NAUMANN

cognitive science and information systems   Cognitive science is the interdisciplinary study of intelligent behavior. The disciplines contributing to cognitive science include ARTIFICIAL INTELLIGENCE, psychology, linguistics, anthropology, philosophy, and neuroscience (Gardner, 1985). The range of intelligent behaviors investigated by cognitive scientists extends from commonplace tasks such as vision and locomotion to skilled problem-solving in specialized domains like medicine, engineering, and law.

A key area of focus within cognitive science has been the development of computational models of intelligent behavior. Computational models identify the knowledge and reasoning processes underlying an aspect of intelligent behavior and encode these representations and processes in computer programs to reproduce the behavior. Such computer programs have been developed to model game-playing, theorem-proving, natural language understanding, diagnosis of physical systems, and design of various artifacts. The adequacy of a computational model is assessed by examining the performance of a computer program embodying the model.

The relevance of cognitive science to information systems is twofold. Frameworks drawn from cognitive science improve our understanding of work tasks that information systems are designed to support. Understanding of work tasks enables us to design more effective and usable information systems. Cognitive science also contributes directly to the design of a class of information systems called EXPERT SYSTEMS. These systems (which are designed to mimic the problem-solving behavior of human experts) are developed using principles and methods of cognitive science.

Bibliography

Gardner, H. (1985). *The Mind's New Science: A History of the Cognitive Revolution*. New York: Basic Books.

AMIT DAS

compression   Methods to reduce the storage requirements for program and data files (*see* CODING OF DATA FOR INFORMATION PROCESSING).

computer hardware architecture   Computer hardware is one of the elements in an operational computer system for information processing. The components of the hardware system form a computer hardware architecture. The basic building block for all computer hardware is the chip. Computer hardware systems differ in size, complexity, and power. However, every computer system for information processing includes hardware and software to perform processing functions and store data; many have communications capabilities.

Computer Hardware Chips

A chip is a rectangular piece of silicon on which an integrated circuit has been etched. The process of producing computer chips starts with a crystal of silicon that is sliced into thin circular wafers. Circuits are etched on the wafer by a process of masking and diffusion. The process forms and connects transistors, resisters, diodes, etc. that make up circuits. The wafer is sliced into several chips. Each chip is mounted in a package with pins for plugging the chip into a board.

The circuits can be designed to be microprocessor chips, memory chips, or input–output interface chips. A microprocessor is a chip which contains the traditional functions of the central processing unit of a computer. It contains an arithmetic/logic unit, a control unit (to direct and synchronize operations), and registers to use during operations. The microprocessor is essentially a computer on a chip. It can be programmed to perform arithmetic functions, execute logic, select among alternatives, and direct functions. High-performance chips have extended features such as floating point arithmetic.

Memory chips are of two major types: read-only memory (ROM) and random access memory (RAM). The ROM chips are used for permanent programs written as part of the manufacturing process, and a user cannot alter them. The instructions are read from ROM as part of processing, but there is no writing to ROM chips. PROMs (programmable read-only memories are like ROM memory but can be programmed after manufacture).

RAM chips are used for primary storage (main memory) containing user data and application programs being processed. Data may be read from this storage and data stored in it. It is volatile in the sense that data stored there is lost if power is interrupted. The storage capacity is expressed in thousands (using the symbol K for thousands of bytes of storage) or millions using the symbol MB (for megabytes). A byte is the basic unit of storage. One byte can store, for example, one alphanumeric character. Sets of bytes are used for more complex elements.

The microprocessor uses an internal bus architecture. A bus is a common path for all signals. All functional units are connected to the bus. An electrical signal is sent down the bus and selects the connecting path that will take it to its destination. Different signals are kept from interfering by synchronizing signals and controls. Several internal buses may be used to increase speed. An important characteristic of chips and buses is the size of the internal data path on the chip and on the buses, i.e. how many signals are sent and used simultaneously. By analogy, it is the number of lanes on which traffic can move in parallel. At the PC level, high performance computers have 32-bit or 64-

bit architecture. Very large computers also use integrated circuits. However, the circuits are very dense and require special cooling and other design features.

Because of the basic power of the microprocessor, one approach to computer design has been to create microprocessors with a large number of complex instructions. This design is termed CISC (complex instruction set computer). The advantage is the ability to create complex instructions that handle complex situations. The disadvantages are the decoding delays and the need for more than one instruction cycle. An alternative approach is RISC (reduced instruction set computer) in which instructions are limited to simple ones that can be executed in one cycle. As a result, for some applications, an RISC processor may require more instructions but may take less time to execute. For other applications, a CISC processor may be faster.

In the design of computers, both microprocessor code and software can be used to present the user with a machine that appears to have characteristics that are not in the physical hardware. The machine the programmer or user deals with is a conceptual or logical machine, often termed a virtual machine.

Basic Hardware in a Computer System

Basic hardware equipment in a computer system for information processing supports the following functions:

1 Entry or input of data and instructions to the computer.
2 Computation, control, and primary storage (central processing unit or CPU).
3 Secondary storage.
4 Output from the computer.
5 Data communications (not always present).

Equipment connected directly to the computer (through cables or communications lines) during use is termed "online;" equipment used separately and not connected is "offline." In some cases, the same device may be used online for some applications and offline for others.

Input of data for information processing comes from four hardware sources: direct online entry from a keyboard of a terminal, microcomputer or other input device; offline data preparation using terminals or microcomputers; reading of data from machine-readable documents or package coding; and data stored in files. "Entry" and "input" are often used interchangeably, although recording data at a keyboard is usually termed "entry," while reading of stored data is usually termed "input" (*see* INPUT DEVICES).

The central processing unit (CPU) of a computer system contains the arithmetic logic unit, the control unit, registers, and primary storage or "memory." A clock establishes the timing for operations.

● The arithmetic logic unit contains circuitry that performs arithmetic operations (add, subtract, multiply, etc.) and logic operations.

● The control unit retrieves and interprets instructions, provides instructions to the other units, and sends timing signals.

● Registers are used to hold data during execution of arithmetic and logic operations. A computer will have a number of registers because of the need to hold several items at the same time.

● Primary storage is used for data and instructions to be processed. Access to primary or main storage is very fast compared to secondary storage access but still relatively slow compared to processing speeds. There are design methods to improve access; one of these is to use an additional, very fast access memory termed a *cache* memory to hold instructions and data that are actively being used.

The clock for the CPU provides signals that are used in synchronizing operations. A crystal delivers these signals at a predetermined rate. This rate, stated in terms of megahertz (MHz), is the clock speed for a computer.

Most computers use a sequential flow of instruction processing. Alternative processing architectures, found primarily in supercomputers, are pipelining or vector processing. In pipelining, operations are divided into a number of independent steps to be performed in parallel by different parts of the computer. In vector processing, the same operation is performed simultaneously on all the elements of a vector or pair of vectors.

Secondary storage is supplementary to the primary storage contained in the CPU. It has larger capacity and is less expensive but slower relative to primary storage. It is therefore used to hold data files plus programs not currently in use. Also, unlike most primary storage, it is not volatile; stored data is not affected by shutting off power (or a power outage). The most common secondary storage media are magnetic disk, magnetic diskettes, and magnetic tape (reel and cassette). Storage technology is changing rapidly with the storage capacity of each storage medium increasing and the cost per character stored decreasing (*see* COMPUTER STORAGE).

Output employs devices such as the computer display screen, printer, or voice output unit (*see* OUTPUT DEVICES). One of the developments in hardware for output is multimedia output. A person using a computer may receive output from the display screen as text, graphics, or pictures. The picture can be still or moving. There can be sound in the form of music, tones, spoken words, and so forth (*see* MULTIMEDIA).

Classes of Computer Systems

There is a wide variety of computer systems in terms of size and power. Four classes are often identified: supercomputers, mainframe (large-scale) computers, minicomputers, and microcomputers. Supercomputers are designed for applications requiring very high-speed computation and large primary storage. Large-scale or medium computers have very large secondary storage capacities, very powerful CPUs, and highly sophisticated operating systems. They can support multiple jobs executing concurrently and online processing from many remote locations at once. Minicomputers are smaller than the large mainframes and relatively less expensive. Each minicomputer may support online processing from multiple remote locations. In many organizations, multiple minicomputers with communications capabilities are used instead of a single large-scale computer. MICROCOMPUTERS are small and typically have a simple operating system, one keyboard input unit, one monitor (visual display unit), and one printer. Large capacity microcomputers are often termed workstations.

Computers in an organization system are usually interconnected by networks (*see* TELE-COMMUNICATION). The processing work is distributed among the computers. The traditional architecture for interconnected computer systems was a hierarchy with the mainframe computer in control. An alternative architecture is for several computers, called clients, to make use of the facilities of a shared computer, called a server (*see* CLIENT/SERVER ARCHITECTURE). The clients are in control; the server makes available resources on demand such as programs and data.

Other Computer Hardware Devices

Process control applications of information technology focus on managing the equipment in a production process. A computer, called a programmable logic controller, can be used to automatically control production equipment performing tasks, such as measuring and disbursing raw materials, executing the treatment steps, and feeding product (and labels) to packaging.

GORDON B. DAVIS

computer operating system   The operating system (OS) provides the interface between the application programs and/or the user and the computer hardware. The operating system manages the resources provided by the computer hardware and allocates their services to the application programs and the user. There are several common features of an operating system: hardware input/output management; memory subsystem management; file system management; device management; user management; and user interfaces.

Hardware Input/Output Management

This feature of the operating system manages the execution and flow of data between the central processing unit (CPU) and the various subsystems such as memory, COMPUTER STORAGE, INPUT DEVICES, and OUTPUT DEVICES. The simplest form of an operating system in this regard is a single-tasking OS. A single-tasking OS only works on one task at a time. However, most operating systems today involve some form of multi-tasking, where several tasks can be executed at, what to the user seems like, the same time. This means that the operating system needs to somehow allocate the processing resources fairly to the different tasks. These tasks can belong to a single user, as in a single-user operating system such as the MacOS and Windows95; or they can belong to several users, as in multi-user operating systems such as UNIX and VMS.

Memory Subsystem Management

Tasks processed by the CPU need data. This data is held in the memory subsystem, consisting of several types of memory, such as random access memory (RAM), read-only memory (ROM), cache, and so on. The operating system is responsible for managing access to the memory in order to ensure the integrity of the data stored there. The applications and the user thus do not need to specify where in memory something is to be stored. The OS assigns data to a storage location and maintains a record of it. Without this feature, a process might overwrite vital data used by another process.

File System Management

Data in the memory subsystem may need to be stored in secondary storage. This can be a hard disk, a floppy disk, a tape, or several other types of device. Regardless of the storage device, the OS manages the transfer and keeps track of storage so that data can later be retrieved.

Device Management

Communication with users is accomplished through monitors, keyboards, mice, printers, hard drives, and so on. The management of these subsystems is also left to the operating system. In some operating systems (e.g. UNIX), this area coincides to a great extent with the file system management. The reason is that devices can be conceptually viewed as files; for example, to print something, copy it to the file associated with the printer. Whatever the paradigm, devices need to be handled so that they can communicate with the rest of the computer, and this is also done by the operating system.

User Management

In multi-user operating systems, it is very important to manage access to computing resources. This function is often delegated to the operating system. The operating system keeps track of the users, the directories, and files

they are allowed to access, and what actions are permitted.

User Interface

This function of the operating system enables users to interface directly with the operating system. This is normally done through some sort of shell. The shell may provide a graphical user interface. The shell may be separate but appear to be part of the operating system or be integrated in it.

Many of the features of operating systems can be handed over to other utilities. For example, user management can be handled by a utility, and another shell can be substituted for the one that comes with the operating system. In some cases, the operating system has become "kernel-ized," meaning that it only provides the most basic services, and relies on other utilities to provide the higher-level services.

JESPER M. JOHANSSON

computer program   A computer program is a set of instructions that performs processing for a task. Examples of programs used in business processing are programs to update the payroll file, do depreciation analysis, apply customer payments to accounts receivable, and so forth. The instructions in a program perform input, output, and processing functions. A program written for an application does not contain all functions needed. Many standard functions are provided by the operating system of the computer. For example, a program may specify data to be printed and the format; the management of the printing operation is handled by the COMPUTER OPERATING SYSTEM.

A computer program is typically subdivided into routines and modules. A program routine is a set of instructions within a program. It is a way of subdividing the program into parts for purposes of development and maintenance. A program module is a building block for a program or program routine. A subroutine is a reusable routine that is written to be used (called) by a program. A program object is a reusable routine that encapsulates both data and methods.

The instructions in a program are organized into program control structures to control execution within a module. The three basic control structures are sequence, alternation, and repetition. Sequence control means that instructions are executed in sequence, one after another. Alternation and repetition incorporate decisions. The program evaluates a condition described in a program statement as being true or false. Program execution follows different paths depending on the result. In alternation, a program selects from alternative program paths. The statement takes the general form of *if* (condition) *then* perform one set of instructions *else* perform another set of instructions. The repetition or looping control structure specifies repetition of a sequence of instructions. During each repetition, there may be changes in the data or execution. At each repetition, a condition is evaluated; when the condition is satisfied, the repetition ceases and the program continues with other instructions.

Two central concepts in program design are reusability and modular design. Reusability refers to the design of modules and program objects, so that they can be used over again in any program requiring the processing performed by the modules. Reusable code modules support standardization. Since they are carefully checked for errors, they reduce potential program errors. They are stored in a code module or program object library accessible by programmers.

Modular design (often called structured design) is based on decomposition of programs into modular structures. The concept is that a program should be divided into different functions and subfunctions. By subdividing in this way, modules can be designed to be relatively independent. Independence of a module means that there should be no instruction in some other module that affects it in unknown ways. In structured design, the modules are organized as a hierarchy. A high-level function is subdivided into several subfunctions, and so forth.

A program to be run by a computer is in the executable machine language of the computer. This is termed an "object program." Programs are written in a computer programming language or using a program development system. The program in this language or notation is termed the "source program." The conversion from a source program to an object program is performed by a translation program termed an "assembler" or "compiler."

Computer programs of any size are complex artificial systems. Since there are many possible paths through a program, it is difficult and sometimes impossible to test a program for all possible conditions. To achieve correctness and other quality attributes, computer programs are developed by a process often referred to as SOFTWARE ENGINEERING. The process emphasizes a disciplined approach to requirement, decomposition into modules, coding and testing of modules, testing of the complete program, and documentation. The process of program repair and enhancement is termed MAINTENANCE.

Traditional program design has emphasized a modular structure with reuse through subroutines. Data and processing using the data were separated, so that changes to processing statements or data would not require changing the programming statements or data definitions. An emerging program design paradigm is an OBJECT-ORIENTED PROGRAM in which reusable program objects are designed with processing methods and data encapsulated within the objects. An objective is to increase the reuse of program routines by providing tested program objects for common operations.

Macros are program routines that can be run (played) by other programs. They are often written in connection with microcomputer software to automate sequences of operations or add functionality to a spreadsheet or report program. Macro recorders are provided by application packages to assist users in developing macros. Macros can be developed by using a macro recorder. The user turns on the macro recorder, executes the instructions to be automated, and stores the result. This is programming by doing. It is effective for routines involving only sequences. To add alternation or repetition structures to a macro requires programming in the macro language. Macro programs can be employed to create applications that rely on the facilities of the package. A macro program written to be used with a spreadsheet processor will be a spreadsheet-based application. There are libraries of macros provided by software package vendors and independent suppliers.

GORDON B. DAVIS

computer storage   This is generally classified as primary and secondary. Primary storage is associated with the central processing unit (CPU); it holds programs in use and data being processed. Secondary storage is larger capacity storage than primary storage; it holds programs not in use and data not in active processing. Storage devices employ chip technology, magnetic storage technology, and optical storage technology. Secondary storage is often classed as direct access and serial access. Because of the price/performance characteristics of storage devices, systems employ a range of devices, including chips for primary storage, disk storage for fast access secondary storage, magnetic tape for slower access offline storage, and optical disk for large data storage.

Primary Storage

The most common primary storage devices are memory chips. Memory chips are of two major types: read-only memory (ROM) and random access memory (RAM). The ROM chips are used for permanent programs. RAM chips are used for primary storage (main memory) containing user data and application programs being processed. Data may be read from this storage and data stored in it. It is volatile in the sense that data stored there is lost if power is interrupted.

Secondary Storage

Secondary storage uses magnetic or optical technologies. Most secondary storage utilizes magnetic media. A medium such as metal disk, plastic diskette, or plastic tape is coated with a metallic oxide. The coating can be magnetized. Tiny areas on the coating are treated as small magnets. Polarity at an area is set in one of two ways in order to store one of two values. Data can be read without altering the polarity. Secondary storage is read or written by passing the magnetic media under a read-write head that either reads the polarity that is present in each tiny segment or changes the polarity to record new data. In microcomputers, disk storage consists of the "hard disk" that is part of the hardware and removable diskettes.

Optical storage uses a metal disk with a coating. Data is recorded using very small dots. The recorded data is read by a laser beam. The use of the laser means that there is little danger of head crashes and the density of storage is much higher than with magnetic disks. The most common optical storage in use is write-once-read-many (often referred to as WORM) and CD-ROM (compact disk read-only memory). The high capacity and low cost per unit of storage makes optical storage very attractive for applications such as databases of text data, an encyclopedia, reference volumes, research literature, and so forth. The disadvantages are fairly slow access time plus the write-once characteristic. However, read and write optical storage devices can also be used.

Performance Characteristics of Direct and Serial Access Storage

The two types of secondary storage most widely used are magnetic disks and magnetic tapes. Disk and tape technologies represent two different types of physical access mechanisms: direct access and serial access. Direct access devices, such as disks, support a variety of physical storage and access structures. Magnetic tape will efficiently support only sequential access. Although both disks and tapes are widely used, the trend is toward disk for storage of active files and magnetic tape for backup and archival storage. This reflects a general tradeoff between the low cost and high capacity of tape and the faster direct access of disks. Optical disk storage is generally used for large read-only files.

A direct access storage device (DASD) can access any storage location without first accessing the location preceding it. The dominant DASD is disk. The storage medium is a round disk with a substratum of metal or plastic covered by a coating that can be polarized in two directions to store binary coded data. The recording areas are concentric circles called tracks on the surface of the disk. Depending on the design of the disk storage device, the tracks may be further divided into sectors. Each disk surface has an address; each track on a disk surface has an address; and each sector (if used) has an address. The address of a particular record in storage would thus be the surface, track, and sector addresses combined; these serve to locate the particular sector in which the record is stored.

DASDs have been called "random access devices," implying that the time to access any record at random is the same regardless of its location. This term is not completely accurate because the time required to access a storage location is somewhat dependent upon the current location of the read-write head. If the record immediately preceding (physically) the one desired has just been read, the read-write head is already positioned over the record to be read. But if the last record was on a different track, arm movement may be required to obtain the next record. This is in contrast to primary storage where there is no difference in read time among different storage locations. The time to read any location on a disk is composed of two major elements: the seek time to position the read-write arm and the time for the disk to revolve so that the location to be read moves under the read-write head (rotational delay).

Magnetic tape is termed a serial access device because a given stored record cannot be read until the records preceding it on the storage medium have been read. With a magnetic tape, the average time required to access a particular record at random is approximately one-half the time required to read the entire file, because on average half the records need to be read. Accessing of records in random order is therefore very inefficient, and because of this, files stored on magnetic tape are normally organized and processed in sequential order. Thus, magnetic tape is acceptable for applications for which sequential ordering of records for processing is natural, such as archival storage of transaction history.

The speed of access or data transfer rate for magnetic tape is based on three characteristics of the tape and the tape drive: tape density (characters per inch), tape speed (inches per second), and the size of interblock gap (for tapes using a tape record block scheme). There are other tape unit designs. For example, tape units called streaming tape are designed for backup units that record continuously without blocking of records.

Future of Storage Devices

Size of storage on devices has increased steadily and price has dropped continuously. The result has been a rapid increase in price performance for computer storage. This trend is expected to continue for a number of years. There is room for significant improvement in primary storage

devices, magnetic storage devices, and optical storage. There are also alternative storage devices that may prove to be competitive.

GORDON B. DAVIS

computer-supported cooperative work Advances in technologies, such as networks, TELECOMMUNICATION, file-sharing systems, and MULTIMEDIA devices, have led to the development of computer-supported cooperative work or collaborative computing systems. Computer-supported cooperative work (CSCW) is the use of computer-based technology to facilitate work tasks involving multiple parties. CSCW refers to software applications and their use, and not to the more rudimentary technologies (such as networks, databases, videoconferencing, etc.) that make CSCW possible. In this sense, CSCW is not a type of technology, but a technology application. CSCW designers take component technologies, integrate them, and develop functionality that will service the needs of a work group. Common examples of CSCW include electronic messaging, joint authoring, discussion databases, workflow management, and electronic meetings.

CSCW can be described in terms of collaboration concepts, computer systems design, application types, and impact on work groups.

Collaboration Concepts

Because most, if not all, work involves some degree of interface between two or more parties, many organizational tasks can be conceived in terms of a cooperative work process. The unique focus of CSCW is on the interface between co-working parties, that is, on their collaboration. Those aspects of work which are done independently are of less concern in CSCW, except in so far as the inputs or outputs of one work process affect those of another work process. Tasks which are done entirely in a joint manner are of particular concern to CSCW designers. Business meetings and classroom learning represent extreme examples of CSCW, because all parties are present and actively working together in those contexts. Other collaborative work settings include systems development, business planning, project design, report development, forms passing, and joint decision-making. CSCW is concerned with the design of systems to support these kinds of collaborative work activities.

The parties involved in a cooperative work process are not restricted to people. They can be documents, machines, or transactions. Shared work among computer processors, for example, can fall within the domain of CSCW, as can the flow of paperwork through an office environment. Central to cooperative work processes is the concept of *coordination*. Coordination is the synchronous aspect of a cooperative work process, the juncture of dependency between two otherwise independent work tasks. Once the coordination required for a cooperative work task has been fully specified, a system can be designed to support coordination. Typically, a cooperative work task has many coordination processes within it, some of which are performed by people and some of which are computerized. CSCW is concerned with augmenting the computer-based coordination within cooperative work tasks.

Computer Systems Design

Whereas the development of user-friendly software for individual work has been driven by the principle of WYSIWYG, or "what you see is what you get," the development of collaborative systems has been driven by the principle of WYSIWIS, or "what you see is what I see." Collaborative design involves the creation of *shared workspaces* in which multiple parties access common computer files. Computer bulletin boards exemplify this principle, as many people can post articles and share the bulletin board space. Similarly, collaborative word-processing applications allow multiple authors to develop a common document.

Major issues in CSCW design include data management, media selection, and multi-user interfaces. Data management involves specification of private versus shared information, determining which information will be exchanged and in what format, and specifying information security and ownership procedures, such as which party involved in the collaboration is able to change common information and under what conditions. Issues of file updating and concurrency control are critical in CSCW design, since more than one party may have the capability to update a common data file at the same time. Maintaining accurate, current, and nonredundant data can be a complicated process in a CSCW system that is simultaneously utilized by many parties. Designers are increasingly interested in creating *group memories*, or a shared KNOWLEDGE BASE, whereby uses of CSCW applications result in historical repositories that can serve as resources for future coordination needs. Advances in group memory management may lead to further automation of coordination activities and the embedding of intelligence into CSCW applications.

Media for CSCW include text, sound, graphics, and/or video. Since so much of cooperative work involves interpersonal conversation, many CSCW designs include either a voice component or the ability to exchange text-based messages in real time (instantaneously). CSCW systems are increasingly multimedia, as in computer conferencing and electronic meeting systems. The CSCW designer must understand human communication processes and the relative impact of various communication media on the ability of people to work together effectively.

CSCW systems require multi-user interfaces, that is, simultaneous access to system components by more than one party. The CSCW interface must accommodate different people, different input and display preferences, and different learning styles. As an example, consider a large electronic whiteboard used in a conference room setting. Some meeting participants may wish to draw freehand on the board, while others prefer to display documents typed within a word processor. More than one participant may want to use the board during the meeting; and everyone may want to leave the meeting with copies of material placed on the board so that they can work on it privately at a later time. The CSCW designer must assure flexibility for multiple forms of input, manipulation, and output of system data. Further, any one user may require the ability to track information as it stops or flows between various parties involved in the cooperative activity. The use of *threading* in electronic bulletin boards illustrates this latter capability; bulletin board postings are arranged to indicate the content, timing, and party involved in the posting:

The corporate plan is being developed
(M. Jones), 6/9/95
Suggested item for the corporate plan
(K. Finch), 6/9/95
Comment on Finch's suggestion
(M. Blar), 6/10/95
Comment on Finch's suggestion
(E. Wharch), 6/12/95
Comment on Wharch's comment
(M. Jones), 6/16/95
Another suggested item for the corporate plan
(G. Parch), 6/23/95

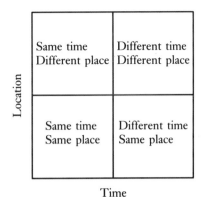

Time

Figure 1   Four major settings for CSCW applications

Application Types

CSCW applications are often referred to as *groupware*. The term "groupware" usually refers to a software system, whereas the broader CSCW term refers to the application of that software in a collaborative work task. Nevertheless, groupware and CSCW are sometimes used interchangeably.

CSCW applications can be distinguished along a number of dimensions, the most important being the *time* and *place* of the coordination involved. Four general types of CSCW settings are possible (*see* figure 1):

1 *Same time, same place.* All parties are co-located when the coordination takes place, such as in a group meeting.
2 *Same time, different place.* Parties coordinate at the same time but work in different physical locations, such as in a teleconference.
3 *Different time, same place.* Parties move through the same location but at different points in time, such as in shared office spaces or meeting rooms.
4 *Different time, different place.* Coordination is entirely asynchronous and physically dispersed, as in electronic bulletin board discussions. Coordination becomes more difficult, and the opportunities for computer support therefore greater, as coordination moves beyond the same time, same place setting to more dispersed, asynchronous work settings.

Some CSCW applications are commercially available as "off-the-shelf" software, whereas others are custom built to suit specialized coordination needs. Most commercial software vendors today offer some types of CSCW applications. In addition to the coordination settings which they support, CSCW applications can also be differentiated in terms of their various features, the numbers of parties they accommodate, and the type of work or task which they support. Some of the more widely available CSCW applications today are as follows:

● electronic mail

● calendaring

● computer conferencing

● conversation management

● electronic bulletin boards

● electronic discussion groups

● electronic meeting systems

● group decision support

● project management systems

● group writing and editing

● document sharing

● joint authoring/editing

● workflow management

Electronic meeting systems (EMS) are a special type of CSCW system designed specifically for group meetings. To the extent that an EMS contains facilities to support decision-making, it is a GROUP DECISION SUPPORT SYSTEM

(GDSS). An EMS provides such facilities as electronic agendas, electronic whiteboards, shared notepads, and group writing programs. A GDSS may include these facilities as well but also includes group decision models, such as risk analysis, forecasting, and choice algorithms.

Impact on Work Groups

CSCW systems aim to smooth the linkages among the activities in a coordination task, resulting in tighter integration among otherwise independent or loosely coupled tasks. CSCW systems also aim to enhance the overall quality of the coordination endeavor.

Efficiency gains can be realized as CSCW systems automate systems that previously were done through manual means. For example, phone calls or typed memos can be replaced with electronic mail. Documents can be exchanged electronically instead of through traditional mail systems, and manual whiteboards in meeting rooms can be replaced with computerized boards. Automation can reduce costs, decrease the time required to complete a work task, and/or make the coordination process easier and less stressful for those involved.

CSCW systems also can create new possibilities for coordination, linking work processes that otherwise were not connected. For example, a CSCW system may allow participants in a project, who would otherwise work independently, to access each others' materials, even if project participants are not in the same location. Similarly, CSCW systems can enable strangers to discuss common problems and solutions via bulletin boards; popular Usenets on the INTERNET illustrate this CSCW application. CSCW systems which pool the knowledge of multiple parties to solve complex problems bring a level of sophistication to the work setting that inevitably will have a significant impact on the business or organizational setting in which that work is conducted.

CSCW systems are having a major impact on business process re-engineering, on the support of mobile, dispersed workers, and on the creation of the "virtual organization." Business process re-engineering requires that work be redesigned to yield a "leaner" organization, with a minimal number of business processes and rapid workflow. CSCW contributes to re-engineering as it supports specific, multi-party coordination tasks. Electronic communication systems, workflow systems, and project management software have been particularly helpful in re-engineering efforts. Similarly, CSCW is facilitating the trend toward a more mobile, dispersed workforce. Work-at-home, the ability to communicate with co-workers while traveling, and the use of contract workers who electronically link to work facilities, are all made possible due to CSCW developments such as electronic mail, scheduling software, computer conferencing, and electronic meeting systems.

The effectiveness of a CSCW system depends on the design of the technology, the task(s) for which it is used, and how it is used. Users may compare one CSCW system to another to see which is the most effective for a given work task. But equally significant in determining CSCW effectiveness is the way in which the CSCW system is managed. For example, researchers have found that the same electronic conferencing system brought many benefits to one group or organization but brought no advantages at all in other groups or settings. Solid understanding of how work is to change with a new system, adequate training of all parties involved, and a commitment to an efficient, participative management style are among the factors thought to be critical to successful CSCW adoption.

At the extreme, a geographically dispersed workforce makes possible an organization without physical facilities, that is, a virtual organization. Collaboration occurs across time and space, with workers located in homes or office sites of their choice. Work occurs in shared computerized spaces connected via electronic networks; and there is little formal management structure, as workers operate with a high amount of professional independence. Research societies, consulting agencies, and brokerage firms illustrate the kinds of work suited to virtual forms of organizing. Many forecasters anticipate proliferation of virtual organizations in the future, with CSCW systems facilitating this trend.

The development of CSCW systems blends perspectives from the disciplines of economics, computer science, communication, social psychology, and management. Since CSCW is a rather new area of management information systems, techniques for systems design and methods for assessing CSCW impacts are still in their early stages.

Bibliography

Galegher, J., Kraut, R. E. & Egido, C. (eds) (1990). *Intellectual Teamwork: The Social and Technological Bases of Cooperative Work*. Hillsdale, NJ: Lawrence Erlbaum.

Greenberg, S. (Ed.) (1991). *Computer Supported Cooperative Work and Groupware*. New York: Academic Press.

Malone, T. W. & Crowston, K. (1994). Toward an interdisciplinary theory of coordination. *Computing Surveys*, 261.

GERARDINE DESANCTIS

critical success factors   CSF is a method of eliciting information system requirements by asking informants to define factors critical to the success of their activity or system. Requirements are derived from these factors (*see* REQUIREMENTS DETERMINATION FOR INFORMATION SYSTEMS).

—— D ——

data The stored, symbolic, or encoded representation of information; lexically recorded individual pieces of information or facts. Historically, data was the plural of "datum," but is now also generally used in the singular as a collective noun.

See also **Data structures(s); Information concepts**

GORDON C. EVEREST

data administration Data management refers to the function of managing the data resources of an enterprise. This includes collecting, storing, and maintaining (updating) data, making it available for use, and protecting the integrity of those data resources. Data management involves both a human component and a machine component. Human responsibility and accountability rest in the position of a data(base) administrator (DBA). Data management is enabled through the use of a DATABASE MANAGEMENT SYSTEM (DBMS) and related tools.

Data administration is the human and organizational locus of responsibility for data(base) management. It is responsible for creating and maintaining the information asset resources of an organization, particularly as embodied in computerized databases. Data administration includes the functions of:

- the design and formal definition of databases

- evaluating, selecting, and installing database management tools (DBMS)

- training and helping people use those tools to access the databases

- assisting in application systems development to ensure that data requirements are satisfied

- monitoring the operation of database systems to ensure adequate levels of performance

- protecting the existence, quality, integrity, security, and privacy of data

Database administrators work with users, system developers, and managers. A data administration staff requires a complement of technical and administrative skills to carry out these functions. They may have a variety of computerized support tools to assist in their tasks.

GORDON C. EVEREST

data dictionary The data dictionary is a reference work of data about data, i.e. metadata. It defines each data element contained in an information system, specifies both its logical and physical characteristics, and provides information concerning how it is used.

Historically, the data dictionary was created to extend the information about data provided by the database schema. The database schema written using the database definition language (DDL) of a DATABASE MANAGEMENT SYSTEM (DBMS) contains sufficient information for computer access and processing. However, the database schema usually contained insufficient information for those who used, managed, and maintained the database.

The concept of a data dictionary has been extended to system development. When system analysts develop data flow diagrams during the analysis and design of an information system, they usually create a data dictionary. It is a catalog that defines the contents of data flows and data stores of data flow diagrams.

Many database management systems and CASE: COMPUTER-AIDED SOFTWARE/SYSTEM ENGINEERING tools have an automated data dictionary utility. This utility stores not only information about database schemas and data flow diagrams, but also other information such as design decisions, usage standard, and user information. This information is available for query and manipulation by users and software packages. The terms system catalog, data repository, and data dictionary are often used as synonyms.

ROGER H. L. CHIANG

data modeling, logical   Logical data modeling is a process by which the data requirements of an organization or an application area are represented. A data modeling formalism defines a set of constructs used in the representation. A logical data model represents the "things" that are of interest (e.g. customers, employees, inventory items, orders); their characteristics (e.g. customers are identified by customer number and are described by: customer name, credit limit, etc.); and their interrelationships (e.g. each order must be associated with a single customer). It can be validated by end users to ensure accuracy of the data requirements.

Numerous formalisms have been proposed, such as the entity relationship (ER) model and the object relationship model. Such formalisms are termed *semantic* data models to differentiate them from *traditional* data models (hierarchic, network, and relational) used by commercial DATABASE MANAGEMENT SYSTEMS (DBMSs) to represent a database schema. Object-oriented data models extend the semantic data modeling by explicitly representing processes (behavior) as well as data structure.

Four basic constructs are common among data models: entity, attribute, relationship, and identifier. An *entity* is a category or grouping of objects (people, things, events) or roles (e.g. employee, customer) each sharing a common set of attributes and relationships. The objects are termed: *entity-instances* (e.g. the employee with

employee number 12314, the customer with customer number 5958). Some formalisms refer to the category as an *entity-type* and the instances as *entities*.

An *attribute* is a characteristic of an entity-instance. Attributes may be single- or multi-valued, mandatory or optional. Each employee, for example, may be required to have exactly one value for the attribute social security number (single-valued and mandatory), and may be allowed to have zero or more values for the attribute dependent first name (multi-valued and optional).

A *relationship* is an association among entities. Any number of entities may participate in a relationship and a relationship can associate zero or more instances of one entity with zero or more instances of other participating entities. The number of entities participating in a relationship is termed the *degree* of the relationship. A relationship between two entities is termed a *binary* relationship. A relationship among *n* entities is termed an *n-ary* relationship. Each entity in a relationship has a minimum and maximum *cardinality*, i.e. the minimum and maximum number of relationship instances in which one entity-instance must/may participate. Furthermore, a relationship itself may have attributes.

If the minimum cardinality of an entity in a relationship is one or greater, then that entity is said to be *dependent* upon the other entity or entities in the relationship. This type of dependency is termed a *referential integrity constraint*.

Data modeling formalisms vary in their definitions of attributes and relationships. The most restrictive formalisms:

- limit attributes to a single value

- require all instances of an entity to have a value for each attribute

- allow only binary relationships

- disallow many-to-many relationships

- only allow entities to have attributes

Proponents of such formalisms claim simplicity of formalism and consistency of definition. However, data models expressed in such formalisms must include additional entities to

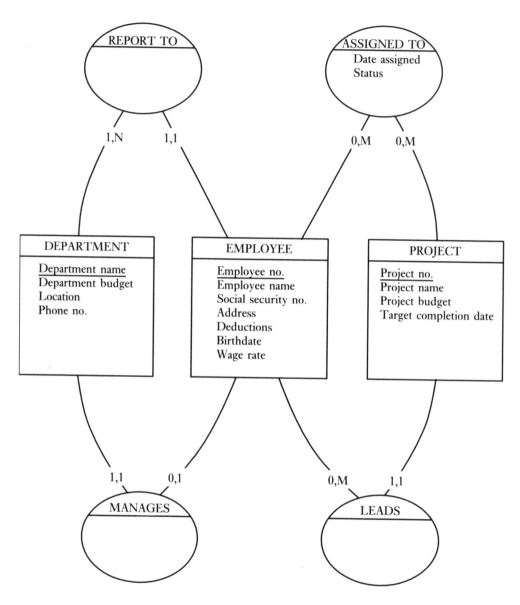

Figure 1   Basic data model

represent multi-valued attributes, *n*-ary relationships, and many-to-many relationships.

Each entity has at least one set of attributes and relationships, termed an *identifier*, whose values uniquely distinguish its instances. Given the value of an identifier, there is at most one corresponding instance of that entity. Employee number 12314, for example, identifies one

employee; customer number 5958 identifies one customer.

Figure 1 is a graphic representation of a data model in a variation of the entity relationship (ER) formalism. There are three entities: *Department*, *Employee*, and *Project*. Each is represented by a rectangle with the name of the entity at the top. Attributes are listed inside the rectangle. Relationships are represented by ovals with arcs connecting the related entities. The relationship name is in the upper portion of the oval. Attributes, if any, are listed in the lower portion. Minimum and maximum cardinality are specified on the arc nearest the entity. Identifiers are underlined.

Employee and *Project* are related through the relationship *Assigned to*. This is a many-to-many relationship (maximum cardinality for each entity is greater than one) with no dependencies (minimum cardinality for each entity is zero). One employee can be *Assigned to* many projects and one project can have many employees *Assigned to* it. However, an employee can exist without being *Assigned to* a project, and a project can exist without having any employees *Assigned to* it. The relationship has attributes, Date Assigned and Status. In a more restrictive data modeling formalism this relationship would need to be represented as an entity (say *Assignment*) with *Employee* and *Project* each having a one-to-many relationship with it.

There are two relationships between *Employee* and *Department*: *Report to* and *Manages*. The first associates employees with the departments to which they administratively report. It specifies that each employee must *Report to* exactly one department and a department must have one or more employees *Report to* it (maximum cardinality is one for *Employee* and many for *Department*; minimum cardinality is one for both *Employee* and *Department*). Thus, *Employee* and *Department* are mutually dependent along the *Report to* relationship.

The second relationship associates each department with the one employee who *Manages* it. All departments must have a manager; however, not all employees manage a department. The fact that some employees participate in the *Manages* relationship suggests that the category *Employee* is heterogeneous. It contains at least two subsets of employees: those who manage departments and those who do not. The relationship *Leads* between *Employee* and *Project* is similarly defined, except that an employee can lead many projects. Thus there are possibly four subsets of *Employee*: department managers, project leaders, both, and neither.

Generalization was introduced to increase the fidelity of data models for such situations. Generalization allows the modeler to identify subsets of entities, termed *subtypes*, and to define how these subsets interrelate. This concept, central to the object-oriented paradigm, includes the notion of *inheritance*. A subtype inherits all attributes and relationships from the entity (its *supertype*). This type of relationship is also termed an *ISA* (is a) relationship – each instance of the subtype *is a(n)* instance of the supertype.

An entity may have many subtypes and it may be a subtype of many other entities. If all entities have at most one supertype, then the structure is termed a *generalization hierarchy*. If an entity is a subtype of more than one entity, then the structure is termed a *generalization lattice*. Two types of constraints characterize generalization structures: *exclusion* and *cover*. An exclusion constraint on a set of subtypes specifies that an instance of the supertype can be in at most one of the subtypes. A cover constraint specifies that each instance of the supertype is in at least one of the subtypes. Their combination, termed *partition*, specifies that each instance of the supertype is in one and only one subtype.

A more accurate representation of employees, department managers, and project leaders and their association with departments and projects uses generalization as shown in figure 2. *Manager* and *Leader* are subtypes of *Employee*. This is indicated by an arrow from the subtype to the supertype. Using generalization it is clear that the *Manages* and *Leads* relationships apply only to subsets of employees. An exclusion constraint specifies that employees who are department managers cannot also be project leaders (the circled x on a line connecting the two subtypes of *Employee*).

Since each manager is an employee, *Manager* inherits all attributes and relationships from *Employee*. In addition, *Manager* has the attributes Parking Space Number and Credit Card Number that do not apply to employees who are not managers. Similarly, *Leader* has attributes Date Certified and Responsibility Level. If generalization were not used, these would need to be included as optional attributes of *Employee*.

Whenever a relationship has an entity whose minimum cardinality is zero or there are optional attributes of an entity, generalization can be used to decompose that entity into one or

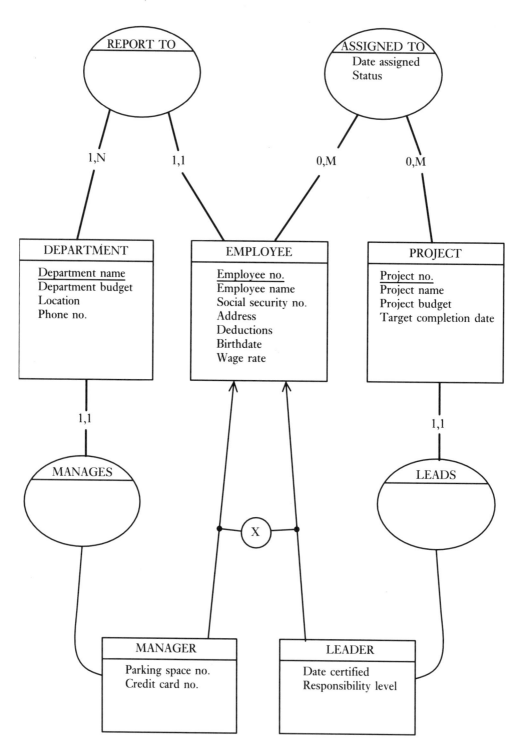

Figure 2 Data model with generation hierarchy

```
Sample Company, Inc.                          INVOICE
111 Any Street                                No.      Date
Anytown, USA                                  157289   10/02/90


Bill to:
     Customer no. 0361

     Local Grocery Store          Customer PO:      3291
     132 Local Street             Terms:            Net 30
     Localtown, USA               FOB point:        Anytown
```

Line no.	Pro- duct no.	Product description	Unit of sale	Quantity			Unit price	Discount	Extension
				Order	Ship	Backord.			
1	2157	Cheerios	Carton	40	40	0	50.00	5%	1900.00
2	2283	Oat Rings	Each	300	200	100	2.00	0%	400.00
3	0579	Corn Flakes	Carton	30	30	0	40.00	10%	1080.00

```
                                   Order gross          3380.00
                                   Tax at 6%             202.80
                                                        _____
                                   Order net            3177.20
```

Figure 3   Sample invoice document

more subtypes. By using generalization in this way, the data model increases its fidelity to the domain; however, it also becomes more complex and may be more difficult to validate.

Data modeling is a part of an overall process of developing a system representation. Numerous techniques have been proposed; however, the process remains highly subjective. The key tasks are:

- identify the entities

- establish relationships

- determine and assign attributes to entities

- represent constraints

The developed data model must be cross-validated with other representations of the information system such as process and behavior representations.

Key approaches to data modeling are document analysis (transactions and reports) and analysis of sentences describing the operation of the organization. It is extremely common for an organization to create artificial identifiers for important entities. These identifiers invariably appear on reports or transaction documents as <entity> Number (or No. or num) or as some other obvious designator of an identifier. To analyze a document, examine each heading on the document and classify it as representing: (a) an entity (its identifier); (b) an attribute; or (c) calculated data. This determination is done by an analyst in conjunction with the end users.

Consider the invoice document illustrated in figure 3. A scan of that document reveals 21 headings: Invoice no.; Invoice date; Customer no.; Bill to address; Customer PO; Terms; FOB point; Line no.; Product no.; Product description; Unit of sale; Quantity ordered; Quantity shipped; Quantity backordered; Unit price;

Discount; Extension; Order gross; Tax; Freight; and Order net. Recalling the definition of an entity as any "thing" about which information is maintained, we classify Invoice no., Customer no., and Product no. as entity identifiers. Tax, Order gross, and Order net are classified as calculated values. All others are classified as attributes. For each entity identifier, the entity is named: Invoice no. identifies *Invoice*, Customer no. identifies *Customer*, and Product no. identifies *Product*.

Secondly, we establish relationships. The following sentence describes the business operation. "Invoices are sent to customers." The nouns "invoices" and "customers" correspond to entities; the verb phrase "are sent" corresponds to a relationship. We choose to call the relationship *Responsible for* rather than *Are sent* to better reflect the nature of the business concept. The relevant questions are: "How many customers are responsible for a single invoice?" (one); "Can an invoice exist without a customer who is responsible for it?" (no); "Can a single customer be responsible for more than one invoice?" (yes); and "Can a customer exist without having any invoices?" (yes). This specifies a one-to-many relationship between *Customer* and *Invoice* with minimum cardinality zero for *Customer* and one for *Invoice*.

Thirdly, we assign attributes. Attributes can be assigned using *functional dependencies* (or *multi-valued dependencies* for multi-valued attributes). A functional dependency is a mathematical specification indicating that the value of an attribute is determined by the value of an identifier ($x \rightarrow y$, where x is an identifier and y is an attribute). Each attribute must be fully functionally dependent upon the identifier and on no other attributes or relationships. This process of assigning attributes is termed *normalizing* the data model.

Invoice is identified by Invoice no. and has attributes, Invoice date, Customer PO, Terms, FOB point, Tax, and Freight. *Customer* is identified by Customer no. and has attributes, Bill to address, and Terms. The attribute, Terms, has been assigned to both *Invoice* and *Customer*. That is, two functional dependencies were identified, Invoice no. $\rightarrow$ Terms and Customer no. $\rightarrow$ Terms. Terms is fully functionally dependent upon more than one identifier. There are three possibilities. First, there

may be two different attributes referenced by the name, Terms, the Invoice terms (for a specific invoice) and the normal Customer terms (which may be changed for a specific invoice). In this case, they should be given different names. Otherwise, Terms must describe *either Customer* or *Invoice*. If Terms describes *Invoice* then a customer could have invoices with different terms and the identified functional dependency Customer no. $\rightarrow$ Terms is in error. Terms should be removed from *Customer*. If Terms describes *Customer*, then all invoices for a customer must have the same terms and the functional dependency Invoice no. $\rightarrow$ Terms is a *transitive*. That is, Invoice no. $\rightarrow$ Customer no. $\rightarrow$ Terms. In this case, Terms should be removed from *Invoice*. Figure 3 illustrates the first case.

Continuing the analysis, the sentence, "Invoices specify products shipped," results in the many-to-many relationship *Specifies shipment* between *Invoice* and *Product* with minimum cardinality zero for *Product* and one for *Invoice*. Attributes of this relationship are, Line no., Quantity ordered, Quantity shipped, Quantity backordered, and Order price (Unit price is an attribute of *Product* which may be different from the Order price for the product; this differentiation is particularly important if the price of a product can change between the time a product is ordered and the time it is invoiced). Its identifier is the combination of Line no. and the relationship with *Invoice*. In formalisms that disallow many-to-many relationships, it would be transformed into an entity called *Lineitem*.

How can *one product* be on more than one invoice? This assumes that what is meant by *one product* is not one instance of the product, but one *type* of product. In contrast to Customer no., which identifies one instance of *Customer*, and Invoice no., which identifies one instance of an invoice, Product no. identifies one type of product, the instances of which are completely interchangeable. The customer is being invoiced for some quantity of this product. In figure 3, for example, "Cheerios" is Product no. 2157, sold in units of cartons. Local Grocery Store is being invoiced for 40 cartons of this product. Presumably 40 more cartons of this product could be shipped (and invoiced) to a different customer.

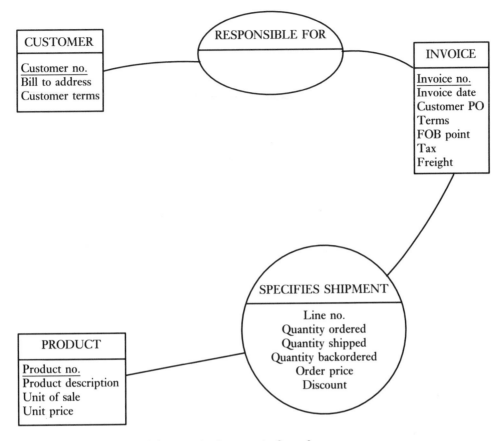

Figure 4 Data model derived from invoice document in figure 3

Finally, we review the model to ensure that all attributes are assigned to an entity, that algorithms and base attributes are specified for all calculated attributes and that all important generalizations are identified. The value of explicitly recognizing subtypes depends on the degree of heterogeneity within an entity. The purpose of the data model is to communicate the meaning of the data. If the introduction of subtypes confuses rather than clarifies, they should not be introduced.

Referring to figure 4, some customers may not have any outstanding invoices (*Customer* is not dependent upon *Invoice*). Thus there are two subtypes of customer: those with invoices and those without. If this is the only distinction, it is probably not worthwhile to explicitly recognize the subtypes. If, on the other hand, customers with invoices have additional attri-

butes or are viewed differently from customers without invoices, then subtypes should be created.

SALVATORE T. MARCH

data modeling, physical Given a description of the logical data content and activities for an application, physical data modeling is concerned with designing efficient structures and algorithms for the storage and retrieval of that data. A physical data model describes the details of how data is stored and accessed. The efficiency of a physical data model is determined by such factors as: the volume and intrinsic structure of the data, the frequency and content of retrievals and updates, and the accessing characteristics of the data-storage media.

There are two major aspects of a physical data model: *record structures* and *access paths*. Record structures define the representation, grouping, and interconnection of elementary data units (attributes and instances). Access paths define the algorithms and system data used to store and retrieve the data. Given the characteristics of common data storage media, a general rule for physical data modeling is to store data together that is used together.

A DATABASE MANAGEMENT SYSTEM can be characterized by the record structures that it supports. Relational database management systems typically restrict record structures to flat tables interconnected via data values (foreign keys). Object-oriented database management systems typically support complex record structures in which objects of different classes can be nested and interconnected via system pointers (object identifiers).

Record structures are defined from an application's logical data model. All information in the logical data model (i.e. attributes and relationships) must be represented in the record structures. Record structures may, however, *nest* or *fragment* logical entities, *replicate* attributes, and define *aggregate* data items in order to increase efficiency. Nesting entities implies storing attributes of related entities in the same file. Fragmenting an entity implies storing subsets of an entity's attributes or instances in separate files. Replicating attributes means copying specific attributes in related files. Aggregate data items hold values calculated from other attributes.

There are two types of access paths: primary and secondary. Both supply mechanisms for accessing records by their *key* attribute(s). Primary access paths use the *primary key* to determine the physical positioning of records within the file. Secondary access paths are used strictly for retrieval by the *secondary key*.

There are three major types of primary access paths: sequential, indexed sequential, and algorithmic. Sequential access paths position records in physical sequence. Often they use chronological sequence as the key due to the high cost of record insertion using an attribute-based key (to insert a record anywhere but at the end of a sequential file requires all records in the file after the insertion point to be moved to make room for the inserted record).

Indexed sequential access paths also organize records in physical sequence, but only within disk *blocks*. Typically, a disk block can store a number of data records. An additional *index* file maintains the logical sequence of blocks. There is one record in the index for each block. It contains the primary key of the first record in the block and a pointer to the block (i.e. the block address). Records in the index are also stored in blocks and sequenced by primary key. An index may be indexed, forming a *tree-structured* or *hierarchical* index.

To insert a record into an indexed sequential file, the index is searched to find the appropriate block and all records in the block after the insertion point are moved to make room for the new record. If there is not sufficient room in the block, an *overflow* mechanism is invoked. A common overflow mechanism, termed block *splitting*, adds a new block to the file, moving half of the records (those with the larger primary keys) to the new block. A new record is added to the index. If there is insufficient room in the appropriate index block to accommodate a new record, the index block must be split.

Algorithmic or *hashed* access paths allocate a number of disk blocks for file storage and calculate the block in which to store records. For example, if 100 blocks were allocated for the storage of employee records, a possible hashing algorithm would be to take the last two digits of the employee number (primary key) as the block number for that employee (this results in a number between 00 and 99). If more records hash to the same block than fit on the block, an overflow mechanism is employed. *Dynamic hashing* and *extensible hashing* use index structures to enable file growth.

Consider the following simple record structure for an order processing application:

Salesperson [s-no, s-name, s-address, s-commission]

Customer [c-no, c-name, c-address, c-credit, c-terms, s-no]

Order [o-no, o-date, o-shipped, o-terms, c-no, s-no]

Lineitem [o-no, l-no, p-no, li-quantity, li-discount]

Product [p-no, p-description, p-price, p-quantity-on-hand]

Consistent with relational database management systems, it has a file (table) for each entity having a field (data item) for each attribute and a field (foreign key) for each (many-to-one) relationship. Consider producing a report of orders, including customer, salesperson, lineitem, and product information. All five files would need to be combined (joined). A number of different methods can be used to accomplish this, depending on the access paths implemented (e.g. merge join, index join).

Efficiency can be improved for this report in several ways. Joins with *Customer*, *Salesperson*, and *Product* can be eliminated if the needed *Salesperson* and *Customer* attributes (s-name, c-name, c-address) are *replicated* (copied) in the *Order* file and the needed *Product* attributes (p-description, p-price) are replicated in the *Lineitem* file. However, this increases the size of the *Order* file and of the *Lineitem* file and incurs additional update, storage, and transfer costs. When an order is added, the replicated customer and salesperson data must be copied to it; when a lineitem is added, the replicated product information must be copied to it. Furthermore, it violates *third normal form* – if updates to salesperson or customer data must be reflected in the *Order* file, then additional update costs must also be incurred. Similarly for updates to the *Product* file. Efficiencies are gained if the reduction in retrieval costs exceed the increase in storage and maintenance costs.

Alternatively, the *Lineitem* file could be nested within the *Order* file. That is, lineitems could be stored as a repeating group within the *Order* file. In this way, order and related lineitem data are stored in the same block and accessed at the same time. While this has retrieval advantages for printing orders, it violates *first normal form* and may not be supported by the target database management system. Furthermore, it makes access to lineitems, e.g. for product sales analysis, more complicated.

For the record structure given above, producing a report of the gross sales for each order requires access to all lineitems for each order in the report. If an aggregate data item, say *order-gross*, holding the order's gross sale was added to the *Order file*, then only this file would need to be accessed and the cost to produce the report would be reduced. This data item would, of course, need to be maintained when lineitems for an order were added, deleted, or modified.

To select appropriate record structures and access paths for an application, tradeoffs among retrieval and update activities sharing the database must be considered. Replicated and aggregate data can improve the efficiency of retrieval activities that use this data, but actually worsen it for retrieval activities that do not use it. Furthermore, it increases maintenance and storage costs. Similarly, secondary indexes can improve retrieval efficiency, but increase maintenance and storage costs.

SALVATORE T. MARCH

data processing *see* PROCESSING METHODS FOR INFORMATION SYSTEMS

data structure(s) Data structure refers to the method of organizing the DATA in a DATABASE, which may be as simple as a single FILE. Under a record-based organization scheme, a database is a collection of one or more files or tables. Multiple files/tables are generally explicitly interrelated, though formally defined interfile relationships are not necessary to constitute a database.

A database schema (or data model) is the *definition* of a data structure or a database, whereas the database contains the actual data. For example,

Employee: NAME(char), UNIT(num,4),
JOBCODE(num,4), TITLE(char),
BIRTH(date), SALARY(money)

could be the schema definition for information about an entity type called *Employee*. The *Employee* entity is described by a set of defined *attributes* or data items, along with a definition of the type of values for each attribute. Data for an example *instance* of the *Employee* type entity could be:

Callagan, R. F. 2100 5210 Secretary
1955/06/06 $28,000

This data could be stored in a *record* in the database. A collection of several such records constitutes a file or table in the database. In the relational model, a file is called a table with each record being a *row* and each attribute or data item being a *column* in the table.

A data structure can relate to three or four distinct levels, depending upon its perspective and purpose. The ANSI/SPARC Committee (1978) defined three levels of database schema: external, conceptual, and internal. The *external schema* defines how a particular user, group of users, or an application (program) views a portion of the database of interest to them. This view (also called a subschema) can relate to a screen display, a report, or a query.

The *conceptual schema* defines the entire database from the global perspective of the database administrator (*see* DATA ADMINISTRATION,) who takes an enterprise-wide view (which is still a chosen scope of interest). The conceptual schema is generally a high-level logical view, expressed without the constraints of implementation in a particular DATABASE MANAGEMENT SYSTEM. This has led some to speak of the global schema on two levels: the conceptual schema and the *logical schema* definition for implementation. The *internal schema* defines the physical stored representation of a database.

A data structure contains information about entities, their attributes, and relationships in the domain of interest. Data structures are classed into those that form records and those that do not. In a record-based data-structuring scheme, the attributes are represented by data items or columns in a table. The attribute values are stored together in records. Similar records (describing the same type of entity) are collected together in files or rows in tables. All the data in a database may be collected into a single file structure or multiple file structures. Each file may be "flat," that is, where there is at most one value for each attribute, or *hierarchical*, where data items may be multivalued; a record may contain nested repeating groups of data items. For example, an *Employee* record may contain multiple *Skills* for each employee or may contain multiple addresses (consisting of the group of items: street number and name, city, state, zip/mail code).

Network and *relational* data structures are both multifile structures. The main difference is that, in a relational data structure, each table must have a flat file structure, that is, all

attribute domains are single valued or "atomic." More general network data structures may permit many-to-many relationships, as well as ternary (and higher) relationships. Non-record-based data structures can be thought of as "no file" structures (*see* OBJECT-ROLE-MODELING).

Data structures can also be distinguished on the basis of their physical structure and accessing mechanisms. The main access alternatives are indexing and key transformation ("hashing").

Traditionally, databases contained formatted fields of numbers and symbolic strings of characters. More recently, databases are intended to store heterogeneous information to support more complex applications such as MULTIMEDIA, graphics, computer-aided design, and geographical information systems. Extended forms of information include text, graphics (bit-mapped and vector graphics), audio, and moving video. Some database management systems allow the definition of a general purpose data item, called a BLOB (binary large object). A BLOB can be used to represent a graphic image, a spreadsheet, a complex text document, an audio clip, or a moving video clip. Usually some other application must be designated which stores, retrieves, displays, prints, and edits a particular type of BLOB.

A *multidimensional* database is intended to support complex queries and reporting for executive information systems and management decision-making. They are the basis for DATA WAREHOUSING applications. A multidimensional database is characterized by extensive classification and cross-referencing of the data, and a retrieval facility which allows much richer manipulation and analysis of the data, now called online analytic processing (OLAP).

Bibliography

ANSI/SPARC Committee (1978). *Information Systems*, 3(3).

GORDON C. EVEREST

data warehousing   W. H. Inmon, a pioneer in the field of data warehousing, offers the following definition: "A data warehouse is a subject-oriented, integrated, time-variant, nonvolatile collection of data in support of management's decision-making process" (Inmon, 1992, p. 29). A subject-oriented view allows users to easily locate and access the data they need. Because the warehouse is nonvolatile and time-variant, users can perform historical or trend analysis. Because the data in the warehouse is integrated, users can examine and join together data generated from many different applications.

In an operational view, a data warehouse is a collection of data from multiple applications, files, databases, found throughout the organization in operational systems and stored in a consistent, structured format. The data stored in the warehouse is a copy and a summary of data from these multiple sources reorganized for easy and efficient retrieval. This combination of content, structure, and access provides the availability benefits to data-warehouse users.

The data warehouse provides a foundation for analytical processing by separating operational and decisional data processing. There are fundamental differences between these kinds of processing. Operational processing involves the detailed, day-to-day procedures in which data is accessed and updated with short response times. Decisional processing refers to the analytical activities involved in looking across the organization for information to use in management analysis and decision-making. Because data in the data warehouse is integrated, has historical perspective and is stored at both summary and detail levels, a company can perform more substantive, accurate, and consistent analyses using the data warehouse as a foundation for DECISION SUPPORT SYSTEMS, EXECUTIVE INFORMATION SYSTEMS, and access tools. In theory, there is no reason why both operational and decision support systems cannot be based on the same data. In practice, there are many organizational advantages in having two parallel systems. One major advantage is eliminating the immediate need to migrate legacy information systems to an integrated architecture.

Most large organizations are constrained by existing system designs. Typically, information systems are large, old, written in COBOL, and file based. They are essential to the organization's business and must be operational at all times. Today, they pose one of the most serious problems for large organizations. Problems of failures, maintenance, inappropriate functional-ity, lack of design documentation, and poor performance can be very costly.

Many organizations are working to re-engineer legacy information systems. It requires a major change in almost every aspect of information system design, development, and management. Building a data warehouse architecture, without major changes to existing systems, may be the first step an organization should take to respond to the problems of legacy systems. By reducing the volume of data in the legacy systems environment, the data warehouse architecture streamlines systems so that both operational and decision processing can be done more efficiently. In addition, it reduces the amount of maintenance typically done in legacy systems.

Operational systems are separated from decision support systems by introducing redundant but better quality data to support business needs. As with any redundant data, it has to be properly managed to be up to date. Redundant data stored in a data warehouse is derived from data sources found in legacy systems. With respect to legacy data, warehouse data is the derivation target. However, with respect to user views of data, warehouse data is the derivation source. This derivation link between legacy data, warehouse data, and user views represents the essence of data warehousing.

The link between legacy systems and a data warehouse is supported by extraction and transformation tools. Besides extracting data, they map the source data to the target database. They also automatically generate the program instructions for data transformations. Next, the tools integrate and transform the data before moving it to the warehouse. This step can include converting fields and values and summarizing, condensing, and converting data from one platform or database to another.

The second category of tools consists of DATABASE MANAGEMENT SYSTEMS (DBMS). A DBMS is used to house a data warehouse. This category is dominated by well-known DBMSs, although there are specialized systems designed and developed specifically for data warehousing. Making up the third category are the data access and view tools for the end user. The primary objective of a data warehouse is to provide data for user summary or other data views. Users are interested more in analytical than operational data, since different types of business analyses are only possible from summary data. For example, different statistics on sales (total, average, minimal, maximal, number of sales, variance, standard deviation) are basic indicators of how a company is doing. They are often done within a specific time frame (time dimension), in a specific geographical area (space dimension), for a specific product or a type of products (form dimension). Hence, indicators and dimensions are two major characteristics of user data requirements supported by this category of data warehousing tool.

In summary, a data warehouse is a permanent, integral part of an organization's portfolio of information systems. In a global and highly competitive environment, a data warehouse is like a critical system designed, managed, and exploited for management decision-making.

Bibliography

Inmon, W. H. (1992). *Building the Data Warehouse*. New York: Wiley–QED.

DJENAN RIDJANOVIC

database   An organized collection of DATA, the term is generally used for collections of data stored within a computer system and used within an organizational context. Thus, a database is a mechanized, shared, formally defined, and centrally controlled collection of data used in an organization (Everest. 1986, p. 11). The simplest form of a database consists of a single FILE, although some prefer to reserve the term database for data collections consisting of multiple, interrelated files. In a computer, a DATABASE MANAGEMENT SYSTEM (DBMS) is used to manage databases.

DATA MODELING is the process of designing the content and structure of a database (*see* DATA STRUCTURE(S)). A data model is a representation of some portion of the real world domain of interest to some organization or set of users. Data modelers or database designers develop a data model based upon the collective perceptions of specialists in the user domain. Some data modeling scheme (formalism, technique) or methodology guides the preparation and presentation of a data model.

The data model specifies the constructs, combination rules, and constraints used in designing and building a database.

Bibliography

Everest, G. C. (1986). *Database Management*. New York: McGraw-Hill.

GORDON C. EVEREST

database management system   A computerized system for creating and maintaining databases. A minimal database management system (DBMS) performs the following functions:

- defines a database

- stores and accesses data

- retrieves and displays or prints data in response to a request

- maintains data in the database (insert, modify, delete)

- maintains the integrity of the stored data according to its defined structure and constraint rules

The request for data may come directly and interactively from human users, or from programs or stored procedures through some application programming interface (API). A DBMS may be designed to operate in a variety of environments: multi-user, client/server, host-based, etc. in which case additional functionality and interfaces are required.

DBMSs can be classified on various bases. Perhaps the most common is on the underlying data structure: hierarchical, network, and relational (which is not a complete taxonomy since it leaves out the single flat file, and the object-role data model; *see* OBJECT ROLE MODELING). Another basis for classifying DBMSs is on their purpose or role within the platform of an information system. Client DBMSs are primarily intended for the *ad hoc*, interactive end user. They usually have simplified data structuring capabilities and rich, easy-to-use, data access, query, reporting, and manipulation capabilities. They may or may not offer the ability for a user-written program to access the database, either from a standard programming language, such as

COBOL or C, or using a built-in programming language.

Development DBMSs provide capabilities for the system developer to build application systems. They provide an interface to one or more programming languages (which may include their own built-in language). They generally provide facilities to define menus, screens, queries, reports, and user views, which can all be combined to build an application information system. DBMSs primarily intended for system developers may also include facilities for the interactive end user.

Many DBMSs run mainly on a personal computer platform. The next tier of DBMS primarily runs on mini- or mainframe computers or in a network environment (though most also run on PCs) and generally offer higher levels of functionality. Most include facilities for both the interactive end user and the system developer. They are generally distinguished by offering a richer programming language interface, triggers and stored procedures, enhanced backup and recovery, greater access and quality control, concurrent update control, synchronization and replication management, etc. Another class of DBMS is the database server, intended primarily to run in a network and provide services to a set of clients. A database server does not normally interface directly with human users (although such facilities could be provided by the same vendor).

In the evolution of DBMSs and data languages, there are different generations. The third generation of programming languages, such as COBOL and PASCAL, gave rise to the first generation of DBMSs. They read and write records one at a time from a single file. Fourth-generation languages (4GL) are specifically designed to process and retrieve sets of records, even from multiple files or tables, in a single statement. The dominant 4GL is SQL (pronounced 'sequel') for which there is now an ANSI and ISO standard. A second-generation DBMS incorporates a fourth-generation language. Most DBMSs today provide some flavor of SQL, whether directly to the end user, to the application programmer (perhaps as extensions to a conventional programming language), underneath an easy-to-use prompting interface, or at the interface between the client DBMS and the database server.

The next or third generation of DBMS is an object-oriented DBMS or simply an object management system (*see* OBJECT-ORIENTED DATABASE MANAGEMENT SYSTEM). An OODBMS incorporates the principles of object-orientation in its programming language and its user interface(s), while still providing all the functionality of a second-generation DBMS. The third generation of DBMS is marked by some of the following:

- higher level of semantics in the definition of the database (or object base)

- handling heterogeneous, multimedia forms of information

- explicitly representing the temporal and spatial dimensions of information

- offering a natural language user interface

- employing rules of inference (as in EXPERT SYSTEMS)

- operating in a distributed or client/server environment.

GORDON C. EVEREST

debugging of computer programs   Debugging is a programming technique or process used to find and correct computer program errors or mistakes, known as bugs. Debugging is performed to create robust programs, programs that compute reliable results for a broad range of input values, and reject illegal input. Different types of errors (bugs) in computers are identified and corrected using different debugging techniques. Bugs are commonly divided into three types: syntactic errors, logical errors, and algorithmic errors.

Syntactic errors occur when one or more program statements violate the construction rules (syntax) of the language being used. For example, the syntax of many languages requires that a period be placed at the end of a program statement. If a period is not present where required, a syntactic error will occur. Syntactic errors can exist in an otherwise logically correct program. The errors may occur because of statement entry mistakes or careless programming, or because the programmer had an incomplete or flawed understanding of language syntax. Syntactic errors are usually the easiest type of error to debug. The program compiler or interpreter who detects a syntactic error can produce diagnostic messages that identify the part of the program that contains the error and may also identify the kind of syntax error as well.

To debug syntactic errors, a programmer locates and displays the portion of the source code identified in the error message. The programmer determines how to modify the source code by comparing it to a correct definition of the programming language being used. This can be accomplished by examining a description of the language syntax or by looking at examples of correct code that uses similar syntactical constructs. The programmer then modifies the source code and attempts to compile or interpret it again to see if the error has been corrected. All syntax errors must be corrected before a program can be executed.

Logical errors occur when a program instructs a computer to execute valid instructions that produce an unwanted behavior in the computer. Logical errors are sometimes called *semantic errors* because the meaning of the program instruction is inconsistent with desired behavior. Typical logical errors include causing programmed loops to run erratically, misassigning memory, or improperly formatting output data.

One debugging technique used by programmers to locate a logical error is to strategically embed temporary print or display statements in the program flow, allowing them to limit error search to small portions of the program. Programmers also limit their search for logical errors by using their knowledge of a program to focus on the parts responsible for program behaviors in error. After narrowing the search area, programmers examine the suspect logic and mentally rehearse the program's behavior to determine exactly how the logic is in error. To correct the bug, the programmer rewrites program statements, resolves any new syntactic errors that are introduced, and re-executes the program to verify that its behavior is correct.

Algorithmic errors occur when a program works correctly for most, but not all, combinations of program input. Algorithmic errors can be difficult to detect and correct because it is often infeasible or impossible to test every possible combination of program input. A common approach for detecting algorithmic errors is to test the program with widely varying input values and with large samples of data the program is written to process. Incorrect results identified for only a specific combination of input data alert a programmer to the existence of algorithmic errors. The peculiarities of the input data used in the test are used to locate and rewrite parts of the program.

RANDY SNYDER

decision support systems Decision support systems (DSS) process, store, and present information to support managerial decision-making. The task of decision-making can vary greatly between functions within an organization, between individual decision-makers who have different styles of taking action, between different tasks or types of decisions, and between organizations. Therefore, decision support systems take different forms. The DSS supports decision-makers in understanding the nature of the environment and in assessing probable consequences of various alternative actions, but does not "make the decision."

DSSs consist of applications built from tools with a user interface appropriate to decision-makers. The applications access data and employ models to support managerial decision-making. Data may be gathered from a single process from within an organization (such as customer transactions), from multiple processes (these often provide links between separate processes for receiving revenue and for disbursing funds), and/or from outside data sources such as online databases or customer help (or complaint) lines. Data-oriented DSS can be used, for example, to search a sales transaction database looking for subsets of clients that share particular characteristics and define a segment. Models are frequently financial or statistical in nature but may also include optimization or other mathematical tools. They are used to refine, shape, and organize the data. Financial models can be used for "what if" analysis in projecting the effect of changing policies or macroeconomic conditions on the probable effectiveness of various actions.

The DSS user interface allows the user to directly manipulate data and/or models and to format the output as desired. For example, a typical DSS will allow the user to examine timeline data as either tables or graphs. DSS with Windows-style features may allow shifting from one format to another with a keystroke or mouse action. Similarly, a DSS can draw data from organizational transaction processing systems and deposit it within a spreadsheet or database package on the user's desk for their further manipulation. As an example, a DSS application for a hospital might be constructed to support bidding on a contract with a health maintenance organization. Such an application would be built from data for clinical costs, patient revenue, and physician preferences gathered from various departments based on historical data derived from operational processes. Where such bidding on contracts might be a recurring task, the application would be built to be updated with current data.

The DSS may be designed to support one or more of Herbert Simon's phases of decision-making: intelligence, design, and choice. Intelligence is the gathering of information about the nature of the problem; design is formulating alternative action plans or solutions to the problem; and choice is selecting among the alternatives. In the hospital scenario, the DSS may support the intelligence activity by periodically drawing information from clinical and financial transactions, by integrating internal data with information drawn from external sources that provide baselines of activity or a basis for forecasting. The DSS can support alternative designs by comparing proposed contracts for profitability, given varying demand and cost scenarios. It can support choice by comparing alternative scenarios on various criteria selected by senior managers. It will present ranking of alternatives and the relative sensitivity to changes for particular criteria.

A DSS may be designed for top, middle, and lower management levels. In the hospital scenario, for example, a comprehensive DSS can provide information for high-level executives formulating major contracts; for middle managers ensuring that medical resources are available for implementing the contract; and for operational managers selecting the most cost-effective techniques for providing direct care.

The purpose of a DSS is to provide relevant data as a mechanism for managers to make decisions based on an understanding of the environment and an examination of relevant alternatives. As a by-product, managers tend to have more confidence in their decision, knowing that their investigation has been thorough. They have more effective means to communicate their decision to peers and to persuade others to implement the decision. A successful DSS will provide some combination of better decisions (where the link between decisions and outcomes can be demonstrated), more efficient use of time in decision-making and more satisfaction or confidence with the decision-making process.

DSSs can be built in a number of ways. For a particular decision or problem, the DSS may be built using a prototype model. PROTOTYPING emphasizes quick development of an approximation of the final system. The user observes the prototype and provides feedback on how to improve it. Development and feedback proceed in an iterative fashion until the user is satisfied. Where the DSS aims to provide a wide array of corporate data for repetitive use over many decisions, a repository for data is built with interfaces to draw or receive data from other corporate systems. Such a system is likely to have both structured reports that are regularly updated and a more complex interface that specialists can use to generate detailed *ad hoc* reports. The term DSS has generally been applied to corporate or department-wide decision-making systems; however, personal computing tools, such as spreadsheets and database packages, allow knowledge workers to develop DSS procedures to support individual decision-making.

Expanding on the original concept of DSS are EXECUTIVE INFORMATION SYSTEMS (EIS) and GROUP DECISION SUPPORT SYSTEMS (GDSS). The EIS supports senior managers in terms of specific decision-making and in monitoring key indicators of progress for their organization. The GDSS supports decision-making by groups or teams rather than by single individuals. In addition to tools for supporting data and modeling, the GDSS generally will have meeting support tools that automate brainstorming and voting functions.

Bibliography

Alter, S. L. (1980). *Decision Support Systems: Current Practice and Continuing Challenges*. Reading, MA: Addison-Wesley.

DeSanctis, G. & Gallupe, B. (1987). Group decision support systems: a new frontier. *Management Science*, 33 (5), 43–59.

Gorry, G. M. & Scott-Morton, M. S. (1971). A framework for management information systems. *Sloan Management Review*, 13 (1), 55–70.

Houdeshel, G. & Watson, H. J. (1987). The management information and decision support (MIDS) system at Lockheed-Georgia. *MIS Quarterly*, 11 (2), 127–40.

Silver, M. S. (1991). Decisional guidance for computer-based decision support. *MIS Quarterly*, 15 (1) 105–22.

Simon, H. (1977). *The New Science of Management Decision*. Englewood Cliffs, NJ: Prentice-Hall.

Sprague, R. H. Jr (1980). A framework for the development of decision support systems. *MIS Quarterly*, 4 (4), 1–26.

Sprague, R. H. Jr & Carlson, E. D. (1982). *Building Effective Decision Support Systems*. Englewood Cliffs, NJ: Prentice-Hall.

Watson, H. J. et al. (eds) (1992). *Executive Support Systems*. New York: Wiley.

FRED NIEDERMAN

desktop publishing   The use of a microcomputer-based hardware and software system to design and produce high-quality documents. The features of desktop publishing systems enable combinations and enhancement of text and graphic elements (photographs, line drawings, borders) in a design that is appropriate for a document's audience and purpose. Desktop publishing is commonly used to prepare short documents such as brochures, newsletters, announcements, and programs, as well as lengthy documents such as books, catalogs, and technical manuals.

Before desktop publishing became available, document design and production involved many manual processes, such as cutting and pasting text and graphics on a layout board and the services of specialists (graphic designers, typesetters). The process was slow, required much coordination between activities, and was expensive. At various stages in document preparation, decisions about text, graphics, and format were final. Changes made after those decision points were very expensive and time consuming.

With desktop publishing, the entire document preparation process is done by one person at a workstation, and changes to any aspect of the document can be quickly and easily done at any time. The typical desktop publishing workstation includes a microcomputer with a large, high-resolution graphics screen; a scanner; a mouse or digitizer board; a desktop publishing program; word and graphics processing programs; and a laser printer. The text and graphics for a publication are entered and edited by using the keyboard, mouse, scanner, and the word and graphics processing programs. Layout, editing, and enhancement of the text and graphics is done in the desktop publishing program.

Basic word processing program functions (column formats, text alignment, multiple type fonts and styles, graphics insertion, style sheets) offer limited document design capabilities. For example, text can be put into columns with a word processing program, but if graphics or more than one font size or type is used, it is difficult to align text at the top and bottom of columns. Desktop publishing programs enable fine control of text through features such as *kerning* (minute adjustments in placement of letters on a line), *leading* (spacing additions between lines of text in very small increments), *ligatures* (letter combinations such as "fi" that typesetters usually place close together) and text wrap (specification of the space between text and graphics for each line of text). Photographs, drawings, and text can be cropped, sized, rotated, and stretched for design effect and for exact placement on the page. Many programs include extensive font and graphics libraries, as well as functions that manage multiple projects and associated files. Printing of proofs and camera-ready copy of documents is typically done on a laser printer at the workstation, although some programs will also produce color separations and files that directly drive very high-resolution, commercial typesetters.

Low-end desktop publishing programs are available for occasional, personal use. These programs are easy to use, have a reduced set of features, and include templates for common publications, such as newsletters and fliers. Full-featured, professional-level programs are used by desktop publishing specialists, who may work out of their homes as freelancers, in advertising and publications departments of large organizations, or in small businesses that specialize in professional document creation and production.

ROSANN COLLINS

distributed systems Organizational information requirements have traditionally been met either by a large mainframe computer (i.e. a centralized system) or by a collection of small independent computers (i.e. a decentralized system). However, neither system can completely satisfy the rapidly changing needs of the users. In a centralized system, users can share information, but typically rely on an information systems department to provide access to it. In a decentralized system, users can typically access information themselves, but cannot easily share it across the organization. By connecting decentralized computer systems, users can not only access information themselves but also share it across the organization. A distributed system is a collection of computer systems that are interconnected by a communication network; it provides users and applications transparent access to data, computational power, and other computing resources.

What is a Distributed System?

The term *distributed system* has been applied to systems with widely different structures and characteristics (e.g. computer network, multiprocessor system). Rather than trying to precisely define it, a distributed system can be described by answering the following questions: (a) what is being distributed?; (b) what are the characteristics of a distributed system?; and (c) what is and is not an example of a distributed system?

What is being distributed? The definition of a distributed system assumes that multiple computers or *processing units* are connected via some communication network. A processing unit is an autonomous computer system including CPU, storage, and operating system. In addition to processing units, both process and data could be distributed. Processes of applications may be

divided into subsets and distributed to a number of processing units. Data used by applications may be distributed to a number of processing units.

Characteristics of a distributed system. A distributed system in general has the following characteristics:

- multiple, possibly heterogeneous, processing units

- electronic connections via a communication network

- single system image providing transparent access to at least some of its resources (e.g. file, application)

- significant interaction among processing units

As processes and data are distributed to multiple processing units, coordination is required to provide adequate services. If the services can be provided to users without much interaction between processing units (i.e. communication and coordination between units), it would be difficult to call such a system "distributed."

Such coordination should be transparent to users. Transparency is the key to a distributed system. Ideally, users should not see a distributed system at all. They should see a single system which provides a number of services and resources. They should not have to know where the resources are in order to accomplish their tasks. In reality, this ideal situation is not typically achieved and users are aware that they are using a distributed system.

Examples of distributed systems. Consider the system shown in figure 1. It represents a geographically distributed organization where each region has its own computer (i.e. processing unit). All computers are interconnected via dedicated or dial-up telephone lines. Most of a region's work is done on its own computer. Users, however, can submit jobs to a remote computer via communication lines. Is this a distributed system? It has multiple processing units interconnected by a communication network. It may or may not provide some form of single system image, depending on the methods by which remote jobs can be submitted. Most likely, however, the user would need to be aware

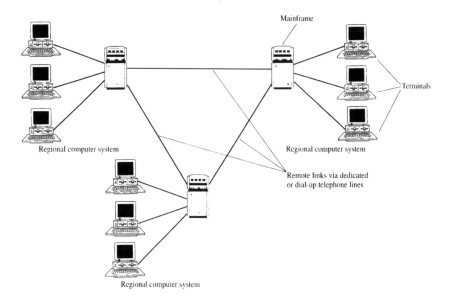

Figure 1   Regional computers connected via remote links

that he/she is submitting a remote job. Furthermore, there is minimal interaction among processing units in providing services. Therefore, this would not be considered to be a distributed system.

Figure 2 shows a system where intelligent terminals (e.g. workstations) are connected to a general purpose computer (e.g. database server). Is this a distributed system? This system also has multiple processing units interconnected via a network. It has a single system view. There are interactions between the server and work-stations. However, this cannot be considered to be a distributed system. This is because intelligent terminals are not autonomous pro-cessing units. The interaction between the server and the terminal is a master/slave relationship and there are no interactions between terminals. This system is rather a centralized system.

Figure 3 shows a distributed database system where the database is stored at several compu-ters (i.e. database servers). In this system, users can write a query against the database as if it were stored at a single computer. In order to

satisfy a user request, the system performs the following steps:

1 Determining where the needed data is located.
2 Determining an access strategy that specifies which copy of the data to access (and when), where the data will be processed, and how it will be routed.
3 Sending request messages to the appropriate servers.
4 Accessing and processing data at each of these servers.
5 Routing the response to the requesting server for final processing.

If (a copy of) all the data required by a retrieval request is located at the requesting node, then only local accessing and processing are needed (step 4). However, if some needed data is not located at the requesting server, then data must be accessed from, and possibly processed at, other servers. Is this a distributed system? There are multiple processing units and they are interconnected via a communication network. Users see only one database. If the user's query requires data that is stored at more

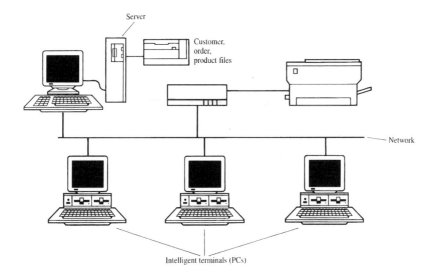

Figure 2   LAN-based database system

than one server, the servers must cooperate to answer the query. This is clearly a distributed system.

Components of a Distributed System

A distributed system consists of several components. The essential components to provide transparency are: network, directory service, and file system.

Network

A network provides the mechanism for processing units to communicate with each other. A computer network consists of a set of computer systems, termed *nodes*, interconnected via communication *links*. It allows multiple computers to exchange data and share resources (e.g. printer).

Given a set of nodes, the network topology defines how these nodes are connected. Examples of network topologies are meshed, star, bus, and ring topologies. The links in a network can utilize different technologies and have varying speeds and channel capacities.

Distributed directory service

In addition to being connected, a distributed system must know where resources are located. Finding resources (e.g. data and application) in a distributed system is the task of the directory service. It must map a large number of system objects (e.g. files, functions, printers, etc.) to user-oriented names. A distributed directory service makes distribution transparent to users. Users do not have to know the location of a remote file, application, or printer.

Distributed file system

A distributed file system provides transparent access to any files on the network. It utilizes a directory service to locate files. To enhance retrieval efficiency, files can be redundantly stored at multiple nodes. Such redundancy increases the complexity of a file system. If there are multiple copies of the same file, the file system first locates its copies using the directory service and must determine how and where read-only access will be performed. Furthermore, consistency among multiple copies of data must be maintained by the file system as the files are updated. Concurrency control/

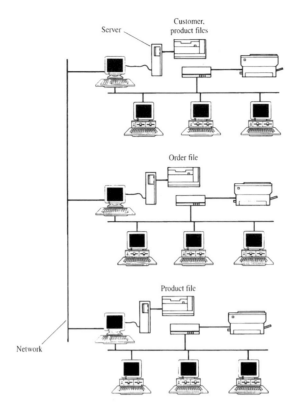

Figure 3   Distributed database system

recovery mechanisms are responsible for maintaining consistency among multiple copies of the same file.

Why Distribute?

Distributed systems can yield significant cost and performance advantages over centralized systems for organizations. These advantages include improved system performance (i.e. response time), reduced system costs, improved reliability/availability, and scalability.

System performance (i.e. response time) can be improved if regularly used applications and data are close to their users. If requests can be processed locally, communication delays due to remote access can be avoided. Furthermore, since each node handles only a portion of the requests, contention for CPU and disk input/output services is reduced. System performance can be further improved by exploiting the parallelism inherent in distributed systems.

System costs can be reduced. A system of smaller computers is less expensive than a single central computer with equivalent computing power. Further, communication costs can be reduced if the regularly used applications and data are local to their users. Reliability/availability is improved since system crashes or link failures do not cause a total system failure. Even though some of the resources may be inaccessible, distributed systems can still provide limited service. If the same resources are provided by more than one node, reliability/availability is further improved, since only one of the nodes providing the resources needs to be available. Scalability is also improved. In a distributed environment, it is much easier to accommodate increases in system capacity. Major system overhauls are seldom necessary. Expansion can usually be handled by adding processing and storage power to the network.

However, there are several disadvantages. Distributed systems are much more complex than a centralized system. First of all, there are many more components in distributed systems (software as well as hardware). Therefore, distributed systems can be quite difficult to implement and manage. Maintaining adequate security can be a serious problem. Since users as well as resources are distributed, maintaining security over the network is much more difficult than in a centralized environment.

Bibliography

Ozsu, M. & Valduriez, P. (1991). *Principles of Distributed Database Systems*. Englewood Cliffs, NJ: Prentice-Hall.

Stallings, W. & Van Slyke, R. (1994). *Business Data Communications*, 2nd edn. London: Macmillan.

SANGKYU RHO

DPMA   The Data Processing Management Association is an international organization of information system professionals (*see* ASSOCIATIONS AND SOCIETIES FOR INFORMATION SYSTEMS PROFESSIONALS).

E

education and training in use of informa-tion technology Effective use of IT is one of the prime determinants of success for organizations as well as individuals. The rapid advances in IT have created a gap between what most individuals know about the technology and what is required for its effective exploitation. Research suggests that most information system failures stem from a lack of user acceptance rather than poor technical quality. Education and training in IT may therefore have priority in human resource development.

Learning Knowledge and Skills

Learning is a relatively permanent change in behavior occurring as a result of experience. The distinction between learning via *education* and learning via *training* is important. In general, education teaches problem-solving approaches, while focusing on the ability to reason abstractly. Training, on the other hand, provides the tools (i.e. skills) for implementing problem-solving approaches, while focusing on the ability to work concretely. Education helps the student choose his or her activity; training helps the participant improve his or her performance in it.

Six general areas of knowledge/skills are required by employees using IT.

1 *Organizational overview:* includes objectives, purpose, opportunities, constraints, and internal and external functioning.
2 *Organizational skills:* includes interpersonal behavior, group dynamics, and project management.
3 *Target organizational unit:* includes objectives, purpose, functions, resources, links with other internal and external units, and problems.

4 *General IT knowledge:* includes hardware and software concepts, IT potential, organizational IT policies and plans, and existing IT applications.
5 *Technical skills:* includes methods and techniques required to perform IT-related tasks.
6 *IT product:* includes purpose, design, required procedures, and documentation of a specific information system.

The Learning Process

The learning process consists of three main phases: pre-education/training, formal education/training, and post-education/training. Additionally, trainee, software, task/job, and organizational characteristics influence key decisions made at each phase of the process.

1 *Pre-education/training phase.* This phase concerns a broad range of factors, from needs assessment to the development of instructional materials.
2 *Formal education/training phase.* A key question in this phase relates to the method of training delivery (face-to-face, video, computer-based, or some combination). Methods that incorporate hands-on use, behavior-modeling, good conceptual models, manuals that encourage exploratory learning, and training previews have been shown to be effective. A second question is who will facilitate the training: outside consultants, in-house trainers, or the learners themselves through some form of self-study?
3 *Post-education/training phase.* The primary focus of this phase tends to be on the evaluation of the education/training process (e.g. was the instructor effective?). However,

Table 1 The content–level framework for education/training needs assessment

Level	Content		
	Person	Task	Organizational
Individual	*Cell 1.1* What knowledge and skills do specific individuals need to learn for effective performance?	*Cell 1.2* What are the knowledge and skill requirements necessary for the accomplishment of specific tasks by an individual?	*Cell 1.3* How do the goals of an individual affect or constrain performance, motivation to learn, or training effectiveness?
Subunit	*Cell 2.1* What skill mix is needed for successful job performance within a given work group, e.g. interpersonal skills, teamwork skills?	*Cell 2.2* What activities, technologies, and behaviors should be trained for effective task performance within a given subunit?	*Cell 2.3* How do work group goals and culture affect or constrain performance or training effectiveness?
Organizational	*Cell 3.1* How does the organization tie human resource planning (i.e. HR analysis, skills inventories, forecasting of workforce demand and supply and forecasting of skill mix) to strategic planning?	*Cell 3.2* What are the core work processes and technologies of the organization?	*Cell 3.3* How do organizational goals, objectives, and resources affect whether and where training is needed?

managers are interested in the longer-term effect of education/training.

Ability, Acceptance, and Productivity

Essentially, through its impact on end-user ability, education and training serve to enhance acceptance by impacting the perceived ease of use and usefulness of information technology. Ability refers to the quality of having sufficient IT-related knowledge/skill to accomplish an objective. An organization's desire to improve white-collar productivity through more effective IT utilization is the primary motivation for the measurement of end-user abilities. Productivity benefits from IT result from both efficiently supplied and effectively utilized IT products and services. In addition, the decentralization of computer usage via end-user computing has prompted arguments that utilization is directly related to user knowledge and skills.

Careful needs assessment (see table 1) and systematic evaluation are needed to guide improvements in user education and training. Where needs assessment identifies the objectives of education/training, evaluation measures the accomplishment of objectives.

R. RYAN NELSON

electronic commerce Electronic commerce is the application of computer and communications technology so as to enhance or redefine business transactions between firms and their customers, suppliers, or other business partners. Prior to the era of information technology, the customer–supplier relationship usually involved a person-to-person exchange of cash or its equivalent for a product or service. Today's business transactions have usually been enhanced by a variety of electronic and communication devices. Some have made transactions more efficient, such as the use of scanning equipment at the point of purchase, or terminals to authorize credit. Automated teller machines (ATM) provide cost efficiencies to the bank while giving customers 24 hour access to banking services. Enhanced service and lower costs are also shared characteristics of self-service fueling stations, automated highway toll systems, debit cards, and so on. Time, as in the ATM example, can be stretched via innovative use of technology; but while time expands, distances can be collapsed. For instance, online reservation systems give customers and travel agents access to a worldwide assortment of travel products. Similarly, order entry systems, coupled with televised home shopping networks, provide customers in their home with the ability to order a product and ensure its availability.

Although the above examples are all targeted at transactions involving consumers, similar systems have evolved to make the business relationship between corporate buyers and suppliers more efficient and effective. By adopting standardized formats for common transactions, commerce between organizations can be largely automated. Such ELECTRONIC DATA INTERCHANGE (EDI) systems, for instance, permit a large retailer to electronically place orders with its major suppliers. Some retailers now routinely provide their suppliers with online access to the detailed store sales information generated by their check-out scanners. With this data the supplier can help decrease inventory carrying costs while better serving customers. Similar electronic linkages let retailers instantly interact with freight carriers, warehouses, distributors, banks, government agencies, and other business partners.

The Future of Electronic Commerce

The next generation of electronic commerce appears likely to transform rather than just enhance the relationship between customer and supplier. It will lead to new products, new formats for old products, and new marketing and distribution channels. Emerging global data highways such as the INTERNET give individual customers the opportunity to electronically shop for products or services throughout the world. Suppliers, big or small, now have inexpensive access to a worldwide marketplace. Start-up

airlines use reservation systems to reach a worldwide market relatively inexpensively; similarly, a small producer of golf clubs in California or of cowboy hats in Arizona can, without benefit of distributors or retail stores, sell merchandise in England or Australia by use of the Internet's WORLD WIDE WEB. Services and information-based products, such as music recordings or commercial art, are even more likely to benefit from these highways. The spouse of a professor in Montana can establish an Internet-based business providing copy-editing or translation service to journals throughout the world and employ TELECOM-MUTING copy-editors and translators from Ireland, India, or Peru. A fashion advertiser in New York can employ a design team consisting of independent contractors, perhaps including a photographer and model in Paris, a graphic artist in Hawaii, a fashion reporter in Milan, and layout specialists in New York and Melbourne. In such examples of COMPUTER-SUPPORTED COOPERATIVE WORK, as the work day ends in one part of the world, a time-constrained project can be handed off to others many time zones away.

Enhancing Customer Service

Although many people think that electronic ordering and payment are essential elements of electronic commerce, they are among the riskier transactions and are usually not necessary for significant improvement in customer service. The emerging examples of electronic commerce enhance the purchasing process in a wide variety of ways, often by providing the customer with better access to information about the product and its uses. For instance, a number of firms in high-technology industries are providing interested prospective customers with solicited announcements of new products via electronic mail notification. Additional marketing and technical information can then be retrieved by the customer from an online data repository accessible via the Internet or a proprietary network. Such customer-driven information systems can, sometimes in only a matter of minutes, let the customer determine if a particular product is potentially useful.

Similar marketing repositories can identify retail outlets where the product can be purchased, prospective customers can listen to segments of recorded music, or test out software prior to purchase. In some instances, such as in the semiconductor industry, customers can design or help to design the products. Customers with access to the World Wide Web are being given the ability to design simple made-to-order products such as T-shirts, business cards, flower arrangements, and so on, thus providing us with a small taste of the opportunities in electronic commerce that should soon follow.

After the sale, there are continued opportunities to enhance the customer's use of the product. For instance, Federal Express uses the World Wide Web to let customers track the process of package deliveries. Similarly, Millipore, a manufacturer of filtration equipment and chemicals, gives its customers access to a database showing how their various chemical products react with other chemicals. Software developers are providing updates online, and computer manufacturers provide access to their internal help desk support DATABASES. In a similar manner, car companies might provide customers with maintenance histories of particular cars or mortgage companies details on escrow accounts and the like.

Products Appropriate for Electronic Distribution

Eventually, however, many products will be ordered, paid for, and even delivered electronically. It is still not obvious what products will be the best candidates to move to an electronic distribution system, but among the likely attributes are those that are information-based, are time sensitive in their value, and are expensive to distribute by current means. Prospective customers who are already connected to electronic networks would also seem to be necessary and, fortunately, this pool is rapidly expanding. Software, information databases, and CD-music are examples of likely candidates, and electronic marketing and distribution channels have recently emerged for many products within these product classes. As the price of computers and communication decreases, the quality of the customer interface will increase. Computers will also become more and more portable as they are increasingly connected to cellular communication networks. With these improvements, more and more aspects of electronic commerce will become

possible (including realistic face-to-face video-conferencing) and more products will be sold and distributed electronically.

New Business Rules

Although inevitable and rapidly approaching, the future of electronic commerce is difficult to predict based on today's business rules. The new technologies will create new business rules. One new rule has been mentioned already: that firms will inexpensively, although perhaps unintentionally, market to an audience throughout the world. A second emerging rule is that customers will increasingly have to be motivated to pull marketing information from the network rather than having it pushed at them as in traditional advertising. Firms will need to find creative ways to ensure that customers find their product descriptions. A variety of new mechanisms will have to be pursued. For instance, in the past a professor requiring a new textbook for a course might have looked at the publisher's catalogs, the list of free examination copies distributed by the publishers, or spoken to a publisher's representative (all marketing channels designed and controlled by publishers). In the future that instructor might be more likely to go and look on the network to see what book an admired professor had listed in his course syllabus, seek guidance from a discussion list of peers teaching the same course, or query a professional association's edited information repository of resource information for the particular course. None of these marketing channels is directly controlled by the publisher and each provides a worldwide channel for an independent producer, say a textbook-writing professor, to take advantage of.

The example of the professor assumes that there will be a future requirement for textbooks. A third business rule likely to change is the form of products, particularly information-based products (e.g. books, magazines, music, theater, movies, education), which potentially can be electronically distributed. A heritage of paper-driven commerce has left us with product packages such as books, journals, music recordings, catalogs, yellow page directories, and so on. These packages are often tied to the economics of paper-based production. In the distant future, for instance, the publisher of a scholarly journal should be less likely to wait three months and then publish a largely unrelated set of articles (a heritage traceable to the economics of the printing process). A more likely model is for individual scholarly works to be published electronically as they are accepted by their peers. So, too, perhaps for the works of performing artists, which might be released one title at a time and carefully targeted, perhaps by using the World Wide Web to reach members of a performer's fan club located throughout the world.

The ability to target a relatively small group for high margin returns is likely to be a fourth rule of the new electronic commerce. Textbooks are likely to fall victim to such personalization. They may be replaced by loose modules of knowledge woven together by an individual faculty. Already we are seeing versions of this with tailored textbooks now being offered by some publishers. These permit an individual faculty member to select from among a set of candidate chapters, cases, articles, and perhaps his or her own publications.

Market targeting and personalization can be as narrow as a single customer. For instance, an electronic newspaper might be individually tailored to the interests of a particular subscriber. Similarly, yellow page-like searches of electronic *databases* can generate not only indexes but advertisements based on the search criteria.

Barriers to Innovations in Electronic Commerce

Electronic commerce still faces many barriers. As electronic commerce moves away from proprietary networks and toward the open and largely unregulated Internet, there will be increased opportunities for fraud. SECURITY OF INFORMATION SYSTEM procedures are being devised to authenticate the identity of both the buyer and seller and to permit the transfer of payments in a secure manner. The issue of fraud and security is not unique to the Internet, however, and some level of loss will probably be acceptable. Nevertheless, the current publicity surrounding the weaknesses of the Internet have delayed the involvement of many firms. Technological problems beyond security must be overcome. At present the Internet is a relatively slow and unreliable delivery mechanism that can make even the most professional market presence appear

poorly conceived. For instance, using electronic networks to display graphic images or transfer sound gives a prospective customer a richer view of the product, but they take a long time to transfer, particularly for users from countries remote from the computer providing the data.

There are also operational problems to overcome. The availability of a worldwide distribution system, though convenient, can often extend a firm's marketing reach beyond its ability to distribute or support. Further, products and brands that are tailored to particular cultures or countries may be difficult to differentiate or even inappropriate on a global marketing platform. Dealing with multiple languages is another operational concern as is providing 24 hours a day manned support systems.

A variety of public policy issues must also be addressed, and from an international context. One is the issue of PRIVACY IN INFORMATION SYSTEMS; customers worry that their purchase behavior will be available without their permission or that they will be the targets of unsolicited mailings. The technical solutions related to the security of financial transactions, particularly data encryption, raise other public policy issues such as whether a government will let its citizens use a security scheme that cannot be broken by government security specialists. To condone the use of these programs may leave society open to threats from criminals and other governments, as well as from tax avoiders. The protection of intellectual property issues is another concern. The CLIENT/SERVER ARCHITECTURE of the Internet makes it very easy to appropriate and modify images, sounds, text, and the general look and feel of the productions of others. Variations in the protection of intellectual property from one country to another further complicate the problem. Some areas of electronic commerce also are perceived as socially unacceptable in a particular culture. Pornography, gambling, or information on the making of nuclear weapons are uses of the Internet that could lead to attempts to create and enforce regulations. Such regulations, though probably difficult to enforce for illegitimate businesses, could nevertheless have negative consequences for legitimate businesses. But, because of the ability to quickly relocate electronic businesses anywhere in the world, the regulatory issues are complicated and not readily solved by regulation within any one country.

The magnitude of change that electronic commerce will mean for many industries suggests that there will be institutional resistance to protect the status quo and past investments. Such resistance, coupled with the relatively low costs of entry for early participants, will produce many new start-up firms, some of which are likely to be very successful. Industry boundaries are likely to shift and new forms of business evolve. On the other hand, these same factors will lead to an increase in the amount of economic disruption experienced by many currently successful firms and industries. Such disruptions are likely to be widespread and painful for many sectors of societies and their economies.

BLAKE IVES

electronic data interchange   EDI is the computer-to-computer exchange of standard business documents in a standard data format. Each of the three elements in the definition is important. "Computer-to-computer" means that paper business documents are not sent. The phrase "standard business documents" means that EDI is restricted to standard business documents such as purchase orders, order acknowledgments, shipping notices, invoices and the like. "Standard data format" means that the trading partners have agreed that each standard business document (e.g. a purchase order) will always be transmitted using an agreed-upon standard data format, so that the computer systems on each end will be able to properly interpret the meaning of streams of data sent as EDI transactions. Using EDI in place of paper-based transactions and the mail, results in greater speed, increased accuracy and lower costs. EDI is an essential feature of just-in-time (JIT) systems in the manufacturing sector and quick-response (QR) systems in the retailing sector.

Electronic data interchange (EDI) was a precursor to an emerging business paradigm called ELECTRONIC COMMERCE. EDI and electronic commerce have been used to gain strategic advantage. EDI is also a special case of the larger business paradigm of INTERORGANI-

ZATIONAL SYSTEMS (IOS). One of the ways that EDI in electronic commerce is used to gain competitive advantage is for two trading partners to use the techniques of EDI to re-engineer the processes they share along the manufacturing, distribution, and retailing supply chain.

EDI has been in use for over 25 years. The dominant pattern of diffusion has been called "hub and spoke." In a hub-and-spoke pattern, a large customer (the hub) pressures its suppliers (spokes) to do business using EDI. From the perspective of a "spoke" company, they must use EDI when requested to do so by one of their important customers or they will not receive any more orders from them. In early systems, suppliers had to accept EDI transactions from their customers in a data format that was proprietary to the customer and not standard.

The Development of Standards

Industry groups developed industry-wide standards for EDI transactions. In the US automobile industry, for example, it soon became apparent that if suppliers had to process incoming orders in a unique proprietary standard adopted by each of its major customers, the burden would be severe. Accordingly, the industry group MEMA (Motor and Equipment Manufacturers Association) facilitated the development of a standard that would be used by all of its members. Similar proprietary standards arose in other industries. When it became apparent that cross-industry standards would be beneficial, inasmuch as industry members did business with trading partners outside their own industry, or with government, the cross-industry standards ANSI X12 and, later, EDIFACT were developed and put into widespread use. ANSI X12 is most popular with EDI users in the US, Canada, and Australia, while EDIFACT is more widely used in Europe and in international trade generally.

The Role of Value-added Networks

Value-added networks (VANs) have made it easier for trading partners to overcome the obstacles of connectivity and standards incompatibility, particularly when a company is dealing with hundreds of trading partners. Rather than establish an individual telecommunications link with each of its EDI trading partners, a supplier connects its computer with the VAN a few times each day and transmits all of its EDI transactions to any of its customers. The VAN receives them and places them in the electronic mailbox of each customer. When the customers' computers dial in to the VAN, they collect all EDI transactions waiting in their electronic mailbox. Before signing off, the supplier's computer will collect all EDI transactions in its electronic mailbox, placed there earlier by the VAN when it received them from the supplier's EDI trading partners.

In addition to the switching and store-and-forward messaging services offered by the VANs, they also offer translation services. For example, General Motors could transmit a purchase order to one of its suppliers in a format dictated by the design of GM's internal purchase order computer system. The VAN (for a fee) will translate the purchase orders into a predetermined standard format, such as ANSI X12. When the supplier picks up its orders from GM (and from other customers) they are all in the same standard ANSI X12 format. The supplier then has the VAN translate its customers' orders from ANSI X12 to the format required by its internal order entry computer system application. Should either trading party decide it would be cheaper to translate on their own premises, they would simply acquire one of the many commercially available software packages designed for that purpose. Some of the reasons for using a private network instead of a VAN are high performance, fixed costs, and greater security.

The VANs have played an important part in facilitating EDI. They will often offer to help hub companies engage their trading partners in an EDI relationship and offer consultation and training services, translation software, model trading partner agreements, and the like.

Organizational Placement of the EDI Function

Until very recently, EDI did not have high visibility with top executives or with information systems (IS) executives. Sales professionals realized that EDI was an important business issue. The result has been that many EDI managers found themselves with a small EDI staff attached to the sales and marketing organization. As the strategic uses of EDI have

become more generally known, many CEOs and CIOs have placed EDI much higher on their priority lists and the EDI function has assumed a more prominent role in many companies.

DONALD J. MCCUBBREY

electronic funds transfer   Systems for electronic funds transfer (EFT) are used in both consumer banking and commercial banking. In consumer or retail banking, the most common application is the use of automatic teller machines (ATMs). ATMs are connected via networks so that a customer may access funds from remote locations. ATMs support both credit cards and debit cards. Credit cards result in charges to a credit card account. Debit cards provide immediate withdrawal of funds from a checking or savings account. In commercial banking, electronic funds transfer is used to transfer funds between banks or large corporations. These fund transfers are handled over specialized funds-transfer networks, both national and international.

GORDON B. DAVIS

electronic mail   E-mail permits two people to communicate via a computer by allowing a sender to compose and send a message to another person. Depending on the system configuration, the recipient of the message may be within the same company or in another country. In its simplest form, electronic mail involves the transmission of a text message, although more advanced capabilities are often available. E-mail is typically used when interactive dialog – that is, face-to-face or telephone conversation – is not necessary.

For an e-mail message to be sent, the sender must know the recipient's e-mail address. The Internet form for an e-mail address is usually *person@domain*, where *domain* is an electronic mail provider at a company, college or university, government agency, or organization. *Person* is the recipient's unique e-mail address for that particular electronic mail provider. The "@" symbol is not optional and must separate the two parts of the e-mail address.

Public versus Private E-mail Providers

To be able to send a message, a person needs to have access to a personal computer or computer terminal and must have a registered account with a public or private e-mail provider. Public providers are third-party vendors who supply computer space and accounts for a fee for people desiring to send and receive e-mail messages. Subscribers to public electronic mail providers can access their accounts typically by using a connected computer terminal or by dialing into the system via a modem. Some examples of public e-mail providers and their e-mail systems include AT&T Information Services (AT&T Mail), MCI International (MCI-Mail), and The Source Computing (The Source). Information services companies are also popular e-mail providers. These companies provide benefits in addition to electronic mail, such as usenet groups, online reference books, and Internet access. Examples of information services companies include CompuServe, America On-line, and Prodigy.

Private e-mail providers include companies which own and operate their own electronic mail network and software. By being a private provider, the company can tailor its e-mail system to its own individual needs. Security can also be more easily maintained, since all electronic mail communication remains within the company. Maintaining the system remains the biggest disadvantage for private e-mail providers. Companies must purchase, modify, and maintain the hardware and the electronic mail software, which requires a staff of analysts and programmers. An additional disadvantage is reduced connectivity: for employees to send messages to people outside the private network (e.g. in another company), the company's private e-mail system must be connected to a public e-mail provider.

Advantages of Electronic Mail

Electronic mail has many of the same advantages as a traditional letter sent through the postal service. Written communication is often the best medium to communicate lengthy messages or complex ideas, and the recipient does not need to be present for the message to be successfully received. Similarly, the recipient of the message can decide when to read the message, take time to consider an appropriate response, and answer whenever he or she desires.

Although electronic mail is similar to traditional mail, electronic mail has other unique advantages. Electronic mail is fast. Delivery of a traditional letter can take one or more days; over e-mail, the recipient will usually receive the message within a few minutes to an hour. In addition, a letter can be easily sent to multiple recipients simply by adding the recipients' e-mail addresses to the message header. Received letters can be forwarded quickly to other recipients without additional modification. To save time, users are usually able to access the names and e-mail addresses of others within the organization. On some systems, the sender can even monitor a posted letter's status to determine if the recipient has seen or read the e-mail message.

Additional considerations have made e-mail increasingly popular in recent years. From a cost perspective, electronic mail can reduce costly long-distance telephone calls and the need for intraorganizational postal services. Electronic mail also can increase communication among different organizational levels of a company. Upper management becomes more accessible through e-mail contact; they – in turn – can directly address the concerns of lower-level employees. Moreover, because of dial-in capabilities, employees can check their e-mail even when they are out of town or out of the country.

While the most basic features of an electronic mail system are inserting, deleting, and moving text, most systems now offer more advanced capabilities. Proofing tools, such as an integrated spellchecker and thesaurus, are becoming more common. In addition to standard text, more recent electronic mail packages allow users to attach formatted documents, spreadsheets, software applications, and even sound and video to enhance the communicability of the message. While all of these capabilities are not offered by every electronic mail package, most offer an assortment to enhance written communication within the organization.

In summary, electronic mail provides many of the services required in today's competitive business environment. Managers can use e-mail to schedule meetings and even to monitor employee morale. Electronic mail can also increase organizational communication. Because of the quick turnaround time, e-mail can be an effective medium to encourage the exchange of ideas among employees, and even between workers and management. The functionality and increased communication provided by electronic mail assures that it will be a central tool in achieving an automated workplace.

MARK A. SERVA

electronic meeting systems   *see* GROUP DECISION SUPPORT SYSTEMS

encryption   The coding of a data transmission or data in storage so that it cannot be understood without decoding. The original data is processed using an encoding algorithm to create a complex data coding that is not meaningful without decoding. Encryption can be done using software or using processes built into encryption chips. Encryption systems typically employ a key used by the encoder to produce a ciphered output. The recipient of the message employs the same key in decoding. An alternative approach is a public enciphering key that is different from a private deciphering key. This allows the enciphering key to be distributed to multiple users without compromising the deciphering key.

GORDON B. DAVIS

end-user computing   Prior to the 1980s, the information systems (IS) function maintained a virtual monopoly over the acquisition, deployment, and operation of information technology resources. Many of these responsibilities have been transferred to those who use the information. These are termed "end users." Three major forces explain the transformation process:

1 *Hardware and software improvements* have increased the availability, affordability, and usability of information technologies. Microcomputers, personal productivity software (e.g. spreadsheets, database management systems, and word processing), fourth-generation languages, personal peripheral devices (e.g. mice, pen-based interfaces, and laser printers), tele-communications and networks support widespread individual use of information technology.
2 Enhanced *computer-related knowledge and skills* within the end-use community have motivated and enabled end users to use IS products and technologies.
3 An *organizational environment* conducive toward end-user computing (EUC) has fostered the employment of EUC products and technologies as productivity enhancement tools.

Types of End Users

End-user computing is a diverse phenomenon. End users can be categorized based on variables such as computer skill, method of use, application focus, education and training requirements, and need for ongoing support. Four categories represent end users:

1 *Non-programming end users.* These users access computerized data through a limited menu or graphical user interface (GUI)-based environment. They follow a well-defined set of procedures. Software is provided by others.
2 *Command-level users.* Users perform inquiries and simple calculations such as summation and generate unique reports for their own purposes. They understand the availability database(s) and are able to specify, access, and manipulate information.
3 *End-user programmers.* These users utilize both command and procedural languages directly for their individual information needs. They develop their own applications, some of which are used by others. Use by others is a by-product of what is essentially analytic programming performed on a "personal basis" by quantitatively oriented managers and professionals.
4 *Functional support personnel.* They support other end users within their particular functional area. By virtue of their skill with information technology, they have become informal centers of systems design and development expertise. In spite of the time spent supporting other end users, these individuals do not view themselves as programmers or IS professionals. Rather

they are market researchers, financial analysts, and so forth, whose primary task within their function is to provide tools and processes to access and analyze data.

Benefits and Risks

There are a number of significant advantages to end-user development applications. First, EUC provides some relief from the shortage of development personnel. A common complaint by users is that they cannot get the IS solutions they need when they need them. There are not enough analysts and programmers to keep up with the demand.

Secondly, EUC eliminates the problem of REQUIREMENTS DETERMINATION FOR INFORMATION SYSTEMS by IS personnel. One of the major problems in information systems is the eliciting of a complete and correct set of requirements. Various techniques and methodologies have been proposed, but it still remains a difficult process. The problem is made more difficult because the analyst is an outsider who must be able to communicate with a user in eliciting the requirements that the user may not fully understand him or herself. While having users develop their own system may not eliminate the problem of obtaining requirements, it does place an "insider" in the role of requirements problem-solver.

Thirdly, EUC transfers the IS implementation process to end users. This transfer effectively eliminates the potential conflict from technical system experts and non-technical users, one of the major reasons why systems are not utilized. Users may develop less sophisticated systems when they do the design and development themselves, but they will use them.

EUC also poses a number of serious risks to the organization. First, elimination of the role of systems analyst also results in the elimination of an external reviewer throughout the development process. The systems analyst provides an organizational mechanism for enforcing standards, supplying technical expertise, and providing an independent review of requirements.

Secondly, there are limits to a user's ability to identify correct and complete requirements for an application. For example, human cognitive limits stem from behavior based on anchoring and adjustment, concreteness, recency, intuitive

statistical analysis, and the structure of the problem space. In addition, errors in decision-making relative to requirements result from over-analysis and inefficient search, solving the wrong problem and applying a wrong analysis or model. Thirdly, there is often a lack of user knowledge and acceptance of application quality assurance procedures for development and operation. This risk is evidenced in testing, documentation, validation procedures, audit trails, and operating controls.

Management of EUC

The challenge for organizations is to find ways to manage EUC to maximize the benefits of EUC while minimizing the risks. Though management may be perceived as encompassing many different attributes, the three most critical attributes relating to EUC are the following:

1 *Policy setting and planning*. Policy setting identifies appropriate EUC practices and clarifies the acceptable form of outcomes concerning EUC activities. Planning efforts are aimed at identifying goals/objectives and establishing the framework for coordination and allocation of resources to EUC activities.
2 *Support*. EUC support refers to activities such as provision of tools and training opportunities that enhance the development and growth of EUC in organizations.
3 *Control*. Control processes ensure that planned activities are performed effectively/efficiently and in compliance with policies and plans.

End-user computing is expected to be a permanent phenomenon. It requires resources that must be managed carefully to ensure proper diffusion and use within the organization. Technical and managerial infrastructures need to be created to support EUC at all levels of the organization (i.e. individual, departmental/work group, and organizational).

R. RYAN NELSON

enterprise architecture This describes the structure of a company in terms of means of production, customer service, strategy and objectives, and use of information and information technology. It provides models to portray component parts of a company and how they work together to achieve its business mission and goals. It connects the company's business structure, use of information and information technology, and the technology architectures needed.

Enterprise architecture is a family of related architecture components. These include information architecture, organization and business process architecture, and information technology architecture. Each consists of architectural representations, definitions of architecture entities, their relationships, and specifications of function and purpose. Enterprise architecture guides the construction and development of business organizations and business processes, and the construction and development of supporting information systems.

Diagrams and schematics are commonly used to represent enterprise architecture. For example, an entity-relationship diagram may portray enterprise information architecture, and an organization chart may portray the enterprise management structure. Such diagrams and schematics come from other disciplines such as organizational design. They have been adapted to describe enterprise architecture.

Enterprise architecture is a holistic representation of all the components of the enterprise, and the use of graphics and schematics are used to emphasize all the parts of the enterprise, and

how they are interrelated. Data and process models originally designed for computer application development are used in describing information architecture. For example, entity-relationship diagrams that describe information as a set of business entities (e.g. customer and products) and how they relate (e.g. customers order products) can also be used to represent an enterprise information architecture. Similarly, IDEF (Integration DEFinition) is a systems function and information modeling tool, but it can be used to portray an enterprise business process architecture.

Enterprise architectures are used to deal with intraorganizational processes, interorganizational cooperation and coordination, and their shared use of information and information technologies. Business developments, such as outsourcing, partnerships, alliances, and ELECTRONIC DATA INTERCHANGE, extend the need for architecture across company boundaries.

New technologies add to the need for enterprise architecture. Client-server approaches (*see* CLIENT/SERVER ARCHITECTURE) and related communications networks enable distribution of information and computer applications throughout the enterprise. The need for architecture includes rapid information technology proliferation, incompatible and non-communicating application systems, multiple networks, inaccessible data in parts of the enterprise, piecemeal technical solutions to business problems, uncoordinated developments in common areas of the

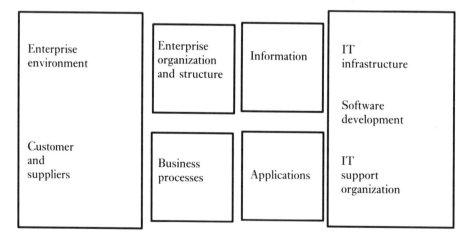

Figure 1   Components of enterprise architecture

enterprise, unintegrated data, and inadequate integrity and security of results.

Components of Enterprise Architecture

An enterprise architecture consists of several related architectures. The set of related architectures describes different · elements of the enterprise. Figure 1 shows six common architecture components: the enterprise environment, the enterprise organization and structure, business processes, information, application systems, and IT support infrastructures.

The *enterprise environment* architecture describes the business and technical connections between the enterprise and its customers, suppliers, and competitors. EDI (electronic data interchange) is one common element of such connections, and the Internet is a recent addition to the enterprise environment.

Enterprise organization and structure architectures are often represented as hierarchies or networks reflecting the organization of an enterprise. The models describe its components, its division or departments, the functions to be carried out by each part, and key business performance measures. Elements of the organization model include organizational roles, responsibilities, and relationships with other organizational units including customers, suppliers, and government.

Business process architectures describe the business processes used in the enterprise to provide goods and services. *Information* architectures describe the information required to support the enterprise business activities. *Application systems* architectures specify the software portfolios that deliver business functionality to the departments and business processes.

IT infrastructure architectures describe the organization's computers, ranging from mainframe through personal computers. It also specifies the network architectures that define the communications and messaging technologies that connect the enterprise. Software development architectures define the environment in which the enterprise acquires or develops applications. This includes case tools, database and data management environments, and automated development tools. IT support architectures specify the configuration of IT organizations, whether centralized or decentralized throughout the enterprise. Such support architectures include help-desk and support services, as well as development and operational organization support.

The importance of enterprise architecture lies in the interrelationship of the various models. For example, connecting the information architecture to the supporting information technology architecture is critical to delivering information. Connecting the information architecture to the business process architecture is critical to assure that every process functions optimally.

ROBERT J. BENSON

ER diagrams   An entity-relationship (ER) diagram is a conceptual data schema that depicts various categories of data and their associations within an organization or information system. It does not specify how the data is organized, implemented, used, or maintained physically within the organization or information system. An ER diagram is constructed according to the ER model. It is used in the conceptual design of information systems, especially databases. The ER model was introduced by Peter Chen in 1976. It is only one of many possible diagramming conventions, but it has wide acceptance. In 1988, the American National Standards Institute (ANSI) chose the ER model as the standard for information resource dictionary systems. The basic modeling concepts provided by the ER model are entities, relationships, and attributes.

Entities and Entity Types

Entities represent instances of real-world objects. Any object about which someone chooses to collect data is an entity. Entities of the same class are collected into entity types, e.g. *employee* and *project*. The concept of entity is the most fundamental modeling concept in the ER model. Each entity type is described by a name and a set of attributes. Entities from the same entity type have common attributes. Usually, the name of an entity type is a noun. In an ER diagram, entity types are depicted as rectangular boxes.

Relationships and Relationship Types

Relationships represent associations among entities. *Employees work-on projects*, for example, represent associations between the entities *employees* and *projects*. There must be at least two entity occurrences participating in each occurrence of a relationship. Entities that take part in a relationship are called the participating entities of the relationship.

Similar to entity types, relationships of the same kind are grouped into a relationship type, e.g. *work-on* In an ER diagram, relationship types are depicted as diamond-shaped boxes, which are connected by straight lines to the rectangular boxes representing the participating entity types. Usually, the name of a relationship type is a verb which is displayed in the diamond-shaped box. Properties are usually specified for the relationship types: degree, cardinalities, and attributes.

Degree. The degree of a relationship type is the number of participating entity types. Although relationships can be of any degree, the ones that occur most commonly are binary. A binary relationship type has two participating entity types. For example, the relationship type *work-on* between *employee* and *project* is a binary relationship type.

Cardinalities. The cardinality specifies the number of relationship instances in which an entity can participate. The cardinality can be represented by its lower and upper bounds, called *Min* and *Max*, respectively. Consider a binary relationship *work-on*. The *Min/Max* values of the cardinality indicate the minimum and maximum occurrences of the entity type employee that can occur for each occurrence of the entity type *project*, and vice versa. If each occurrence of *employee* can have exactly one corresponding occurrence of *project*, then the *Min/Max* cardinalities for *employee* are (1,1). On the other hand, if each occurrence of *project* can have many occurrences of *employee*, then the *Min/Max* cardinalities for *project* are $(1, n)$, where n denotes "many." There are three basic cardinality ratios for binary relationship types: $1:1$ (one-to-one), $1:n$ (one-to-many), and $n:n$ (many-to-many).

Attributes. Entities and relationships have properties, represented as attributes. Some attributes may be identifiers (keys). The identifiers form the set of candidate keys for an entity type from which one is designated as the primary key. Similar to entity types, relationship types can have attributes. Consider the binary relationship type *work-on*. The start date that an employee works at a particular project can be relationship attribute of *work-on*. It is neither an attribute of *employee* nor an attribute of *project*, because its existence depends on the combination of participating entities in a relationship instance.

ROGER H. L. CHIANG

ergonomics As applied to information systems, ergonomics is the design of equipment and user interfaces that fit the capabilities of human users (*see* HUMAN–COMPUTER INTERACTION). In the design of the keyboard, for example, ergonomic principles will result in a keyboard that does not overstress the hands of the human operator. In the design of a GRAPHICAL USER INTERFACE, ergonomic and human–computer interaction principles result in a screen that fits human cognitive capabilities.

GORDON B. DAVIS

errors in information systems As organizations incorporate more decision-making in information systems, the consequences of information system errors may increase. Even small errors may be magnified through the repeated application of an automated process. Information system error is a failure of a system to achieve the outcome intended by its user or designer. Such errors can be generated by either faults at the user interface or faults in system processing.

Interface errors occur in input and output. Input interface errors are due to user failure (e.g. data entry errors) or poor quality of the input information (e.g. the use of obsolete data). Output interface errors are due to user failure (e.g. misreading a display of information) or poor quality of the output information (e.g. an incomplete report).

Processing errors occur during the execution of computer programs that operate on acquired data. Processing errors can be categorized as knowledge errors, software errors, and execution errors. Knowledge errors occur when the system achieves its intended function but does not satisfy the requirements of the problem (e.g. the system uses the straight-line method of depreciation instead of the required double-digit method). Software errors occur when the system fails to achieve its intended function because of bugs in a computer program (e.g. the program creates a new record for a customer who has moved instead of updating the existing record). Execution errors occur when the system fails to achieve the function specified by the software because of a hardware or operator failure (e.g. a computer operator executes an obsolete version of a program).

Both prevention and detection are employed to reduce system errors. Prevention of information system errors is based on increasing the reliability and accuracy of the input and output interface and processing. Interface errors can be prevented by guiding or constraining user actions. This can be achieved through user-centered design or through user training. Processing errors can be prevented through software engineering practices such as systematic testing and reviews of requirements, designs, and code.

Complete prevention of errors is generally impractical and expensive, so error detection is also needed. Redundancy checks and consistency checks are the main mechanisms for detecting errors. Redundancy checks are based on duplication of information. Examples at the interface level include redundant data entry and check digits. At the processing level, examples are various control totals used to verify completeness of processing. Redundancy checks are particularly effective in the presence of random disturbances. However, they do not detect systematic errors.

Consistency checks identify conflicts between information and a standard. Examples of consistency checks at the interface level include programmed integrity constraints and spell checkers. Consistency checks at the processing level ensure that the relationships among processed data values are valid. Consistency

checks can detect both random and systematic errors.

STEFANO GRAZIOLI and BARBARA KLEIN

ethics of computer use   Ethics is the study and evaluation of human conduct in the light of moral principles. In an information society, human conduct is greatly influenced by the use of computers, communication devices, and other forms of information technology. Using information technology inevitably creates ethical issues: situations in which an agent's acts, which were undertaken in order to achieve his or her own goals, materially affect one or more stakeholders' ability to achieve their goals. The affected parties may either be helped or harmed (ethics work for the good as well as for bad or evil).

A moral agent can be an individual, a profession, an organization, or an entire society. Agents must address several central questions when facing an ethical issue: "What action should I take?," "How should I live my life?," or "What kind of person or organization do I want to be?" These questions are eternal; they deal with the good, the right or the just. The context in which they must be answered, however, changes with every major change in technology and social organization. The transition from ancient Egyptian and Greek societies to the *polis* of fifth-century BC Athens, required the reflections of a Socrates, a Plato and an Aristotle to redefine the meaning of "the good" and of virtue in the newly emerged social system. Similarly, in the modern day, there has been a transition from an industrial society, rooted in machines that augment physical energy and the organizational values of Taylor and Ford, to a knowledge- or information-based society. The new society is founded on computers and communication technologies and tends toward flatter, more highly networked, organizational units with intensive external relationships. All of this change requires a fundamental re-examination of ethics and morality (*see*, for example, INTERORGANIZATIONAL SYSTEMS).

Ethics requires the examination of an issue from several crucial points of view. What is the agent's duty (deontology)? What are the results of the act (consequentialism)? What does it say about the agent's character (virtue)? And is the outcome fair (justice)? The questions are universal, but their application is shaped fundamentally by the nature of an information society. In the contemporary information society, at least seven crucial issues face moral agents at the individual, professional, organizational, and societal levels.

(1) *Technologically induced social change*   Technology is generally implemented in order to secure economic and social gains. In the process, however, the flow and the balance of benefits and burdens to the stakeholders in the social system are changed. Some people win; others lose, physically, psychologically, economically, or socially. Resulting from this redistribution of social status is a set of ethical issues that managers and MIS professionals must resolve, such as worker displacement, under-employment or "dumbing down" of jobs, depersonalization, new health hazards, over-reliance on technology, spatial reallocation (e.g. TELECOMMUTING), technological illiteracy, and the need for education and training.

(2) *Privacy*   Modern information technology makes the acquisition and integration of information about people and their behavior and its storage, processing, dissemination, and use feasible and economical. On the one hand, some of this information is wanted and needed by decision-makers in business, government, and other organizations; on the other hand, some of it is gathered at the ethical cost of invading individual privacy. Sensitive, sometimes quite intimate, information about people is revealed to those who do not have a legitimate need to know it or who are not authorized by the subject party to know it. Managers must balance their temptation to acquire this data against their obligation to respect the privacy and autonomy of others. This ethical issue has led to the adoption of principles of fair information practices based on the concept of informed consent: no personal information should be acquired on a secret basis; an individual should be able to discover personal information that is being kept about him or her; the individual should be able to correct the record; the individual

who gives consent for the collection of information for one purpose should be able to prohibit its collection for use for any other purpose; and any party collecting and handling personal information must assure its accuracy and reliability (see also below) and take reasonable precautions to prevent its misuse. Relevant US legislation includes the Freedom of Information Act of 1966, the Fair Credit Reporting Act of 1970, the Privacy Act of 1974, and the Privacy Protection Act of 1980 (*see* PRIVACY IN INFORMATION SYSTEMS).

(3) *Property*   Property is something that can be possessed, controlled, or owned while excluding others from these privileges. As John Locke argued in the seventeenth century, people earn the right to make something their property by virtue of their physical and intellectual labor. Because information is intangible and mental, however, and it is symbolic, readily reproducible, facility transmittable, easily shared, and highly "leakable," it is difficult to exercise this right effectively with intellectual property. One's intellectual property is a source of wealth and value; consequently, other people are motivated, tempted and, frequently, able to take it without compensating its owner. Managers must steward and safeguard their organization's intellectual property and ensure that their organizations and employees respect the property of others. This leads to issues such as software piracy, fraud, and theft in electronic funds transfers and accounts, and copyright infringements of all types. A related class of issues is program damage such as is caused by software viruses, worms, logic bombs and Trojan horses. Relevant US legislation includes the Copyright Act of 1976, the Electronic Funds Transfer Act of 1980, the Semiconductor Chip Protection Act of 1984, the Computer Fraud and Abuse Act of 1986, and proposed computer virus legislation (*see* SECURITY OF INFORMATION SYSTEMS).

One's intellectual capability and know-how is also property. Initiatives in the name of ARTIFICIAL INTELLIGENCE and EXPERT SYSTEMS to delve into a worker's mind, to capture the principles of his or her reasoning, and to program them into computer systems, may also violate or compromise the property rights of that individual (*see* KNOWLEDGE BASE).

(4) *Accuracy and reliability* In an information society most people rely on information to make decisions that materially affect their lives and the lives of others. They depend on computers, communication devices, and other technologies to provide this information. Errors in information can result in bad decisions, personal trauma, and significant harm to other, often innocent, parties. Users are entitled to receive information that is accurate, reliable, valid, and of high quality (at least, adequate for the purposes to which they intend to put it). But this also entails a significant opportunity cost. Error-free, high-quality information can be approximated only if substantial resources are allocated to the processes by which it is produced. Consequently, managers must make an ethical tradeoff between conserving the resources and competencies under their control and allocating them to produce higher-quality information. In any case, a certain minimal, socially acceptable, level of accuracy is required of all information and information systems.

(5) *Burden* The cost of providing information at any level of accuracy or quality is borne, usually, by a limited class of people. For managers, this raises a question of fairness: are the providers unduly burdened and adequately compensated for their contributions? At the governmental level, the Federal Paperwork Reduction Act of 1980 represents an attempt to relieve US citizens of some of the burdens involved in filling out forms.

(6) *Access* Information is the primary currency in an information society and in information-intensive organizations. Managers are responsible for its just and equitable allocation. In order to participate effectively in a democratic society, people must have access to information concerning things that affect their work and their lives; and, therefore, they must have access to a minimal level of technology for handling information and they must receive an adequate level of general and technological education.

(7) *Power* Power is the ability to influence or control other individuals or organizations. Its acquisition and use engenders responsibility. Information, including the capability to produce and handle it, is a fundamental source of power and a generator of responsibility. The principal intent of the strategic and marketing use of information technology, for example, is to enhance this power base. Wielding this power, however, must result in considerable help or harm to others. In industry, for example, capturing vital information sources can result in monopolistic power, which, in a free market economy, raises serious questions for managers and for government as to how this power is to be channeled, allocated, and used responsibly (*see* STRATEGIC USE OF INFORMATION TECHNOLOGY).

The combined forces of technological "push" and demand "pull" will only serve to exacerbate these ethical issues for managers in the future as the increased use of information technology results in more information being made generally available. The availability of information creates its own demand due to its perceived benefits; and, consequently, more parties hasten to use the information in order to secure its benefits for themselves.

Bibliography

Johnson, D. G. (1985). *Computer Ethics*. Englewood Cliffs, NJ: Prentice-Hall.
Johnson, D. G. & Snapper, J. W. (1985). *Ethical Issues in the Use of Computers*. Belmont, CA: Wadsworth.
Mason, R. O., Mason, F. M. & Culnan, M. J. (1995). *Ethics of Information Management*. Thousand Oaks, CA: Sage Publications Inc.
Oz, E. (1994). *Ethics for the Information Age*. Dubuque, IA: Wm. C. Brown Communications Inc.

RICHARD O. MASON

executive information systems An executive information system (EIS) is a computerized system that provides executives with internal and external information relevant to their strategic management. Characteristics typical of an EIS include:

- custom-tailored to individual executives
- extracts, filters, compresses, and tracks critical data
- provides current status information, trend analysis, exception reports, and drill down
- accesses and integrates a broad range of internal and external data
- user friendly and requires minimal training
- used directly by executives without intermediaries
- presents graphical, tabular, and textual information
- provides support for electronic communications
- provides data analysis capabilities
- provides organizing tools

Development of an EIS

Organizations develop an EIS for a variety of reasons. Some are to achieve more timely, relevant, concise, complete, or better information. Other reasons are to be more responsive to changing market conditions, to support a total quality management program, or to facilitate downsizing of the organization. Critical to the success of an EIS is a strong high-level executive sponsor (such as the CEO). The sponsor initiates the project, allocates the needed resources, participates in the system's design, uses the system, and handles political resistance. Usually an EIS is developed by executive mandate rather than a comprehensive cost–benefit analysis. Executive sponsors also appoint operating sponsors to oversee the day-to-day development of the system. The operating sponsor may be selected from information systems or a functional area. This sponsor selects the EIS staff, draws up plans for the system's development, and helps resolve routine issues and problems.

The EIS staff is responsible for building, operating, and enhancing the system. The group must combine solid technical, business, and interpersonal skills. This staff performs tasks such as determining information requirements, evaluating hardware and software, designing screens, installing local area networks, and accessing needed data. An EIS includes a variety of internal and external and hard and soft information. Organizational databases and analyst spreadsheets are major sources of internal data. External data may come from marketing intelligence and electronic news and stock price databases. Soft information in the form of explanations, assessments, and predictions are sometimes included as annotations to screens in order to enhance the user understanding of the harder information displayed.

Evolution of EISs

Most systems are developed using special-purpose EIS software. A strong current trend is the use of client/server rather than mainframe-oriented software. EISs are developed using a prototype/evolutionary development methodology. There is seldom a final product; they evolve in response to new or changing information requirements, the need to add new applications and capabilities (e.g. decision support systems), and to satisfy the needs of additional users.

While a firm's executives are the primary audience for an EIS, successful systems frequently spread to additional users. Powerful push/pull forces are at work. The executives want to "push" the systems down to lower-level organizational personnel so that they can benefit from the system, while this same personnel want to "pull" the system down in order to see the information that higher-level executives are using. This process tends to extend the EIS to a broader audience than the top executives.

HUGH WATSON

expert systems   Computer programs designed to mimic the problem-solving activity of human experts in specialized domains are known as expert systems. Human expertise is characterized by extensive knowledge of the problem domain (Chi et al., 1988). For a computer program to attain a comparable level of performance, the domain knowledge of human experts must be captured and represented in the program. Because of the centrality of domain knowledge in problem-solving, expert systems are also known as knowledge-based systems (*see* KNOWLEDGE BASE).

The Structure of Expert Systems

The development of an expert system begins with the acquisition of knowledge from a human expert. A systems professional (known as a knowledge engineer) works closely with a domain expert to accumulate and organize a body of explicit knowledge relevant to the problem being solved. Since expert knowledge is often tacit (difficult to articulate), a variety of methods is used in the knowledge acquisition process. These methods include interviewing, analysis of past records of expert decisions, and observation of experts engaged in their natural activity.

Once a body of domain knowledge has been acquired, the knowledge must be represented in a form suitable for use in a computer program. A number of knowledge representation formalisms have been developed over the years. The most common of these are if–then rules (also called condition–action rules or production rules), though other formalisms such as frames and predicate logic have also been implemented in some commercial systems.

If–then rules, as their name suggests, have two parts: a set of conditions necessary for the rule to "fire" (the *if* part), and a set of actions or consequences resulting from the application of the rule (the *then* part). Two hypothetical rules from the field of automobile repair may be:

Rule 1: if (CAR DOES NOT START) then (CHECK BATTERY), and

Rule 2: if (BATTERY OK) then (CHECK FUEL SUBSYSTEM)

A rule-based expert system contains a large number of such if–then rules. The set of rules in an expert system is collectively called the *knowledge base* of the expert system.

Problems are solved by the expert system by composing the individual stored rules into sequences that connect the initial state to the goal state. The composition of individual rules into sequences is called *chaining*; both backward and forward chaining systems are possible. In *backward chaining*, reasoning proceeds from the goal state to identify the prior states leading to the observed outcome. Diagnostic expert systems often employ backward chaining to identify fault hypotheses which would account for the observed malfunction. In *forward chaining*, reasoning starts at the initial state and progresses through successive states until an acceptable goal state is found. A design expert system may use forward chaining to generate a configuration of components that satisfies certain constraints. Certain problems are better suited to backward chaining, while others are better solved by forward chaining. It is also possible to combine the use of both forms of reasoning in a single expert system. The part of the expert system program that performs reasoning on the knowledge base is called the INFERENCE ENGINE.

While each if–then rule has a simple structure, the programming of rule-based expert systems becomes complex as the number of rules in the system increases (commercial systems may have thousands of rules). Clever pattern-matching algorithms have been devised to identify all the rules whose *if* conditions are satisfied in each state of problem-solving. Selecting one of the applicable rules as the most promising one to fire (called *conflict resolution*) is also a non-trivial programming task.

The knowledge in an expert system may not be completely deterministic, i.e. there may be uncertainty in the relation between the *if* and the *then* parts of a rule. For instance, finding a chemical pattern in a sample from a drilling site does not guarantee the presence of oil, it only provides probabilistic evidence. To represent such uncertainty in rules and propagate it through the reasoning process, a variety of methods (certainty factors, Bayesian networks, Dempster–Shafer theory, and fuzzy sets) have been developed. Because of their capacity to process uncertain information, expert systems are not restricted to choosing single alternatives; instead, they can rank a set of alternatives in order of their likelihood, given the information available.

Though the reasoning processes of expert systems are based on formal logic, human reasoning does not always closely follow the tenets of formal logic. One such characteristic of human reasoning is non-monotonicity – the possibility that conclusions, once accepted, may be revised in view of new information. Implementing non-monotonic reasoning enables an expert system to mimic the human expert's reasoning more closely, but implementing such a capability is a formidable programming task.

In addition to a knowledge base and an inference engine, some expert systems also have rudimentary capabilities for explaining the reasoning behind the system's conclusions or requests for information. In most cases, the explanation facility is little more than a trace of the rules fired to produce the conclusion, but even such a minimalist explanation is better than having none at all, and provides some insight into the operation of the system.

Some expert systems also attempt to automate the knowledge acquisition process by conducting a dialog with the user. An analysis of the knowledge base identifies the items of knowledge that can be used to generate hypotheses or choose among them. The user is then requested for these items of information through a structured question-and-answer dialog, and his/her responses are incorporated into the knowledge base. Automated knowledge acquisition opens up the possibility of improving system performance with usage.

Commercial Applications of Expert Systems

Significant commercial interest in expert systems was generated by the pioneering systems of the early 1980s: MYCIN (Buchanan & Shortliffe, 1984) in medical diagnosis; R1 (McDermott, 1982) in computer system configuration; and PROSPECTOR in mineral exploration. These programs amply demonstrated the power of knowledge-intensive approaches in solving otherwise intractable problems. The early programs were all hand-crafted in the LISP programming language, took multiple man-years of effort (from domain experts as well as software designers), and ran on special-purpose hardware. Though some high-technology companies invested in similar hand-crafted expert systems for their own applications, the popularity of expert systems technology in the business world spread mainly after inexpensive expert system "shells" became available.

An *expert system shell* is a commercially available programming environment that allows the entry of domain knowledge in the form of rules. An inference engine (usually capable of forward as well as backward chaining) is included in the shell, and a graphic user interface facilitates the entry of rules and the observation of system performance. Many commercial shells also include interfaces to other software such as databases and programming languages. The availability of inexpensive shells running on desktop computers enabled individuals and organizations to create their own expert systems with minimal effort, and a large number of such systems appeared in organizations. With domain experts increasingly able to enter rules by themselves, the difficulties of knowledge acquisition were significantly reduced. In some ways, expert system shells became vehicles for END-USER COMPUTING, by which means skilled professionals, such as engineers and scientists, could institutionalize their personal expertise.

Today, expert systems are widely used in businesses to perform tasks ranging from diagnosis of manufacturing processes to credit approval by credit card companies. By encapsulating human expertise in computer programs, expert systems make such expertise durable, portable, and affordable. Numerous organizational scholars have also written about the organizational impacts of formalizing knowledge into expert systems.

Current Directions in Expert Systems Research

The first generation of expert systems, though commercially successful, had several shortcomings. They did not differentiate clearly between the knowledge used to construct the state space formulation of a problem and the knowledge used to guide heuristic search. This gave the knowledge acquisition process a somewhat haphazard character, making it prone to cost and time overruns. First-generation expert systems were made up entirely of an undifferentiated set of if–then associations. While this simplified the control structure of the programs, maintenance of the expert system in the face of rule additions became a problem (since the newly added rule could conflict with any of the existing rules). First-generation systems were also remarkably brittle, in the sense that any question even slightly outside the precisely defined scope of the system would evoke a "don't know" response.

Research into the second generation of expert systems (mid-1980s to the present) has sought to reframe the expert system development process as a modeling activity. Attempts are now made to create and use explicit models of the domain to which the expert system will be applied. The use of explicit models in expert systems overcomes many of the difficulties of the earlier-generation systems. Models provide a hierarchical organization for the knowledge in a system: the structure of the underlying model is clearly differentiated from associational if–then rules about the behavior of the model. The focus on a model also provides guidance to the knowledge acquisition process through the separation of domain knowledge from search control knowledge. Hopes have been expressed about the potential reusability of models across tasks and systems, thus simplifying maintenance. Finally, a model-based approach also has the potential to deal with novelty, hence it may produce less brittle expert systems.

Traditionally, knowledge acquisition has been a frequent bottleneck in the development of expert systems. An active area of current research is the attempt to bypass the knowledge acquisition bottleneck through machine learning. Machine learning programs take as input a set of past cases (containing observed symptoms as well as expert judgments) and attempt to detect regularities in the relation between the symptoms of a case and the judgment of the expert in that case. Given sufficient data, it is possible to approximate the heuristics used by the expert in making his/her judgments, alleviating the need for the first-hand acquisition of this knowledge. The machine-generated heuristic knowledge can be programmed easily into an expert system.

See also **Artificial intelligence; Cognitive science and information systems**

Bibliography

Chi, M. T. H., Glaser, R. & Farr, M. (eds) (1988). *The Nature of Expertise*. Hillsdale, NJ: Lawrence Erlbaum.

Buchanan, B. G. & Shortliffe, E. H. (1984). *Rule-based Expert Programs: the MYCIN Experiments of the Stanford Heuristic Programming Project*. Reading, MA: Addison-Wesley.

McDermott, J. (1982). R1: a rule-based configurer of computer systems. *Artificial Intelligence*, **19** (1), 39–88.

AMIT DAS

explanation systems   Explanation systems are incorporated into EXPERT SYSTEMS in order to explain to users the logic applied by the expert system in arriving at the recommended solution.

F

failure of information system applications
Failed information system applications result in high costs for organizations and potentially serious consequences for individuals whose lives or property depend on them. For these reasons, understanding why applications fail is useful for both organizational management and information systems professionals who design, develop, implement, and manage applications.

Failed information system applications refer to results at one end of a continuum that ranges from complete and obvious failure to high success. Applications found at the failure end of the spectrum are judged as failures because they do not meet or exceed some threshold of performance on one or more key dimensions. For example, an application may fail to meet users' expectations for streamlining work or the implementation of an application may be plagued by delays. In either case, the application may be redesigned, under-utilized, or even abandoned. Although there are many reasons for abandoning an application, the clearest measure of failure occurs when the application is discarded with the *perception* that it was a failure.

Perceptions of system stakeholders (users and others who are interested in the success or failure of the application) are key to understanding or diagnosing information system failure. Stakeholders' views vary, affecting their opinions and diagnoses of the system. An application that may be considered successful according to one view may be considered a failure by another. For example, someone who holds a *technological imperative view* considers only the hardware, software, and data components of a system and, thus, sees information system failure as a hardware failure, software failure, data failure, or any combination of these.

Remedial measures according to this view involve redoing (correctly) system analysis and design, accompanied by the willing participation of everyone involved in the development cycle procedures. Any failure according to this view is regarded as a failure of the developers or users and not a failure of the technology.

To those who hold an *organizational culture view*, the technology is seen as an artifact that must adapt to the needs of the people and the organization. A failed information system is one that does not serve well the individuals within the organization or fit the organization's activities or rituals. According to this view, redesigning an application to conform better to the organization may prevent system failure.

To the stakeholder who holds a *political view*, the development, implementation, and use of the information system application all provide a context within which power may be exercised by a person, group, or other organizational unit. The purposes of the information system are secondary to the exercise of power. Preventing application failure thus requires strong support from individuals or units within the organization whose primary interest is a political agenda.

Another view, the *sociotechnical view*, sees an information system as a social system that uses information technology. Because of the interaction between technology and the social system, an application is likely to fail when the social and technical considerations are not well integrated. For example, if technical considerations dominate the development and implementation process and future users are ignored, user resistance may cause the application to fail. To prevent failure in this case, the sociotechnical view suggests that users become effective participants in the design process.

Bibliography

Davis, G. B., Lee, A., Nickles, K. R., Chatterjee, S., Hartung, R. & Wu, Y. (1992). Diagnosis of an information system failure. *Information and Management*, **23**, 293–318.

Lyytinen, K. & Hirschheim, R. (1987). Information systems failures: a survey and classification of the empirical literature. *Oxford Surveys in IT*, **4**, 257–309.

Lucas, H. C. (1975). *Why Information Systems Fail.* New York: Columbia University Press.

KATHRYN RITGEROD NICKLES

file A particular form of data organization in which all the stored data is organized according to a single connotation, represented by the primary key or identifier. A collection of data about a set of entities possessing some common characteristics (that is, entities of the same type). From a mechanistic perspective, a file is a collection of entries or records, each record containing values for a set of data items. Each entry relates to and describes an entity in the application domain of the user (the universe of discourse for the file). A file is the simplest case of a DATABASE.

GORDON C. EVEREST

file transfer protocol A provider of information may make it available in the form of a file to be copied by anyone who has access privileges and access software.

The most common protocol for file transfer is the File Transfer Protocol (FTP). Developed as part of the ARPANET project to aid transfer of research among universities and other research sites, it is now a standard Internet protocol. The FTP protocol is built in to many communication software tools. The user specifies file transfer using FTP by selecting an option.

FTP is employed to transfer data files, program files, software corrections, manuals, and a variety of other data. The transfer can be in either direction. For example, many software providers establish files that users can FTP in order to get software modifications. The software modifications obtained in this way are used in the same way as modifications on diskettes. In general, a user needs to know whether the data in the files is text data or is binary coded. This affects the options for file transfer.

The most frequent use of FTP for information retrieval is known as anonymous FTP. In this convention, the FTP server (the source of the information) establishes an account named "anonymous." Users (clients) connect to the account using "anonymous" as a user name with their e-mail names as passwords. Many current versions of FTP client software hide technical and procedure details from their users and make anonymous FTP connections automatically. The user may use a graphical interface to specify transfer to or from a remote computer directory.

GORDON B. DAVIS and J. DAVID NAUMANN

flowchart Flowcharts describe the flow of work in a system or the flow of processing and logic in a program. Both system flowcharts and program flowcharts employ the same set of symbols. Program flowcharts are typically used in informal design but are not usually included in formal documentation because of the difficulty of updating them when programs are altered.

FORTRAN An algebraic programming language (FORmula TRANslator) (*see* PROGRAMMING LANGUAGES). Figure 1 illustrates the format:

```
PRINT *, 'Volume of a Square Pyramid'
PRINT *
PRINT *, 'What is the length of one side of the base in'
PRINT *, 'feet or meters?'
READ *, SIDE
PRINT *, 'How high is the pyramid in feet or meters?'
READ *, HEIGHT
VOLUME = (HEIGHT*SIDE**2)/3
PRINT *, 'The pyramid volume is', VOLUME, ' cubic feet or meters.'
STOP
END
```

Figure 1   Statement illustrating the format of FORTRAN

where:

PRINT* means to print a line using the standard printer

READ* means to accept data from standard input device such as a keyboard

* means multiply

/ means divide

** means exponentiate

G

genetic algorithms A class of robust and efficient search methods based on the concept of adaptation in natural organisms, genetic algorithms (GA) have been successfully applied to complex problems in diverse fields, including optimization (e.g. traveling salesperson problem) and machine learning (e.g. rule induction).

The basic ideas of GA are:

1 A representation of solutions, typically in the form of bit strings, likened to genes in a living organism.

2 A pool of solutions likened to a population or generation of living organisms, each having a genetic make-up.

3 A Darwinian notion of "fitness," which governs the selection of parents who will produce offspring in the next generation.

4 Genetic operators, which derive the genetic make-up of an offspring from that of its parents (and possible random "mutation").

5 Survival of the fittest where the less fit solutions are more likely to be removed from the solution pool at each generation (do not survive into the next generation).

To illustrate these components, consider a simple optimization problem. Suppose we want to maximize the function $f(x) = -x^2 + 22x + 279$ on the integer interval [0,31]. A solution, x, can be represented by five bits as a binary number. For example, 01001 represents 9. A genetic algorithm begins by randomly generating an initial pool of solutions (i.e. the *population*). The pool should be large enough to ensure a reasonable sample of the actual solution space, but not so large as to make the algorithm approach exhaustive enumeration. Table 1 shows an initial population of size 4 for the sample problem. During each iteration, called a *generation*, the solutions in the pool are evaluated using some measure of fitness or performance. In the example problem, solutions can be evaluated in terms of the value of the function.

Table 1 Initial population

Individual	x	$f(x)$ (Fitness)
11101	29	76
00101	5	364
01110	14	391
10100	20	319

After evaluating the fitness of each solution in the pool, some of the solutions are selected to be parents. Parents can be selected randomly or probabilistically with the selection probability for any solution being proportional to its fitness. Parents are paired and genetic operators applied to produce new solutions, called *offspring*. A new generation is formed by selecting solutions (parents and offspring) so as to keep the pool size constant. Solutions can be selected randomly or based on their performance.

The genetic operators commonly used to produce offspring are crossover and mutation. *Crossover* is the primary genetic operator. It operates on two solutions (parents) at a time and generates offspring by combining segments from both parents. A simple way to achieve crossover, as illustrated in table 2, is to select a cut point at random and produce offspring by concatenating the segment of one parent to the left of the cut point with that of the other parent to the right of the cut point. A second offspring can be produced by combining the opposite segments. Selecting solutions based on performance yields the population in table 3 for the second generation. *Mutation* generates a new solution by independently modifying one or second generation. *Mutation* generates a new solution by independently modifying one or more gene values of an existing solution, selected at random. It serves to guarantee that the probability of searching a particular subspace of the solution space is never zero. Finally, a genetic algorithm terminates when a prespecified stopping condition is satisfied, typically some number of generations.

Table 2   Crossover operation

Parent 1	00101
Parent 2	01110
	↑
	cut point
Offspring 1	00110
Offspring 2	01101

Although greatly simplified, the above example provides insight into why genetic algorithms are effective. As crossover combines solutions, a number of partial solutions, termed *schemas* (e.g. 0****, *1**1, 01***), having good performance, begin to emerge in multiple solutions. Parents with above-average performance are expected to contain some number of good schemas (e.g. 01***). With a probabilistic selection process, such parents are likely to produce more offspring than those with below-average performance (which are expected not to contain as many good schemas). Over successive iterations (generations), the number of good schemas represented in the pool tends to increase, and the number of bad schemas tends to decrease. Therefore, the average performance of the pool tends to improve.

Table 3   Second-generation population

Individual	x	$f(x)$ (Fitness)
00101	5	364
01110	14	391
00110	6	375
01101	13	396

Bibliography

Goldberg, D. E. (1989). *Genetic Algorithms in Search, Optimization, and Machine Learning.* New York: Addison-Wesley.

Holland, J. H. (1992). *Adaptation in Natural and Artificial Systems.* Cambridge, MA: MIT Press.

SANGKYU RHO

graphical user interface   A graphical user interface (GUI) is used in almost all personal computer and workstation applications. The screen presents the user with an accurate representation of an input form, a document, a report, etc. Menus, icons, and buttons are represented graphically. This has been termed "what you see is what you get" (WYSIWYG). The graphical user interface extends to direct manipulation of objects of interest such as schematic diagrams, process control flows, simulations, and games. Graphical user interfaces are also used for menu selection, form fill-in, and icon selection to invoke operations.

GORDON B. DAVIS

graphics in information systems   Graphics are used for analyzing, presenting, and communicating data. Their increased use has occurred due to a heightened need for better and more relevant information and the availability of low-cost computer graphics tools. Graphics can help identify key variables and trends, highlight important relationships among variables, and demonstrate subtle but important deviations or exceptions. However, confusing and misleading graphs can also be produced.

Graphics are abstract pictures conveying information about numbers and relationships among numbers using points, lines, a coordinate system, numbers, symbols, words, shading and color. Statistical graphics, such as scatter plots, time-series charts, and multivariate displays, were invented during the period 1750–1800. Graphics capabilities became available to managers in the early 1980s with spreadsheet, database, and statistics software. The software allowed nearly automatic conversion of data already stored in computer readable files to two-dimensional or three-dimensional graphics such as pie charts, bar or line graphs, scatter plots, and contour charts.

A common belief among professionals and managers is that graphs provide more appealing as well as more effective presentations of data. Graphical representations are inherently more

Graphics are, however, not necessarily more effective than text or tables. Different graphical formats are not equivalent to each other nor to tables; each graphical format has its own particular uses and limitations. For example, horizontal bar graphs suffer from different human perceptual biases and limitations than vertical bar charts. The effectiveness of a particular graph is dependent upon other factors besides the particular graph format used; namely, the purpose of the task and the experience of the user (Jarvenpaa & Dickson, 1988).

In general, tasks where graphs perform well are those that require display of relational information. For example, in a bar graph, the heights of the adjacent bars emphasize the relational perspective of the data, not the specific heights of each bar. By contrast, when the task involves presentation of specific data values, a tabular form is superior. The relational aspect of information typically becomes more emphasized with larger data sets. With small data sets, individual numbers are often as important as the relative dimensions of the data. Tufte (1983) recommends the use of tables for data sets of 20 numbers or less.

The leading theory explaining the effectiveness of presentation formats is "encoding specificity" that deals with how perceptual mechanisms and memory interact in human information processing. The theory argues that the recall of information is highest if the circumstances surrounding the acquisition of that information are recreated at the time of recall of the information. In the information systems literature, the theory has been extended to decision-making processes as "cognitive fit" (Vessey, 1991). Simply stated, this means that information should be presented in the form that creates a problem representation that best supports the decision and recall strategies (methods and processes) required to perform a particular task. In decision support, a graphic display form should directly support the structure of the problem. Besides the issue of task, there is a significant education and training component to the efficacy of presentation formats. Business people often prefer tables to graphics unless a large amount of data is summarized because they have more exposure to tables.

The two fundamental rules for the construction of graphics are that (a) physical measures on the surface of the graph should be proportional to the numerical values being portrayed; and that (b) graphs are well labeled in terms of their scales, grids, and titles. These principles are violated, for example, when the starting baseline of a line graph is at a number other than zero or the time frame or scale varies from one graph to another without any notification. Used properly, graphs have an important role in analyzing, presenting, and communicating information for decision-making, but the use of graphics requires a manager to understand the relative advantages and disadvantages of graphs, as well as the ability to correctly perceive and interpret graphs.

Bibliography

Jarvenpaa, S. L. & Dickson, G. W. (1988). Graphics and managerial decision making: research based guidelines. *Communications of the ACM*, **31** (6), 764–74.

Tufte, E. R. (1983). *The Visual Display of Quantitative Information*. Cheshire, CT: Graphics Press.

Vessey, I. (1991). Cognitive fit: a theory-based analysis of the graphs versus tables literature. *Decision Sciences*, **22**, 219–40.

SIRKKA L. JARVENPAA

group decision support systems A class of COMPUTER-SUPPORTED COOPERATIVE WORK system intended for use in group problem-solving, planning, choice, and other decision tasks. A GDSS specifically targets group decision-making, whereas CSCW systems support a broader range of multiparty work activities. A GDSS may be created simply by applying a single-user DECISION SUPPORT SYSTEM (DSS) to a problem confronting a group. For example, a board of directors may use a forecasting model to project sales and expenses for a new business; a project team may apply risk analysis to compare possible courses of action; or an engineering group may use computerized optimization techniques to evaluate approaches to producing chemical compounds. These are very rudimentary forms of GDSS. More sophisticated GDSSs bring facilities that are specially designed for use by groups. In this sense, a GDSS means more than simply applying a DSS to a group context.

Particular implementations vary, but most GDSSs include two types of facilities to support group decision-making: (a) discussion management; and (b) decision modeling. These are two general approaches to group problem-solving that have been used in organizations for many years, and a GDSS adds computerization to each of these longstanding approaches.

The *discussion* approach to group problem-solving involves bringing various experts and/or stakeholders together to identify issues and provide an environment for resolution. The strength of the discussion approach is that talking about a problem in a group setting can lead to divergent perspectives on the problem's causes and creative thinking about how to solve it. Group discussion provides broad input on a problem, which can facilitate rapid idea generation and commitment to implementation of solutions. Decision *modeling* involves formulation of a mathematical representation of the problem and solution tradeoffs. Once modeled, the problem is "solved" by using one or more algorithms deemed appropriate for the model. In some cases the models are spatial as well as mathematical, using graphical techniques to display variables and relationships to the group. The strengths of the group modeling approach are that it allows consideration of many variables and relationships simultaneously, and multiple parties can provide inputs to the model specification and analysis. Mathematical models facilitate rational analysis of complex problems and help to overcome the cognitive limitations of a decision-making group. Inputs to the model can be objective or opinion-based. A GDSS contains facilities to support group discussion and modeling.

GDSS Functionality

Discussion support.

To support group discussion, GDSSs include facilities for group note-taking, idea organization (clustering), voting and opinion polling, candid commenting, and storage and retrieval of meeting minutes. Additional facilities might include anonymous recording of individual inputs and step-by-step procedures for using the features within the system. Groups might

create their own step-by-step procedures, piecing together features according to the particular needs of their meeting. Alternatively, they might use pre-established discussion procedures, such as Robert Rules of Order or a meeting protocol, to guide their discussion.

Decision modeling

To support decision analysis, GDSSs take decision models developed for individual use, such as multi-criteria modeling, forecasting, and risk analysis, and explode their components to accommodate input from multiple parties. For example, a multi-attribute utility model might be exploded to allow several $(2-n)$ people to (a) generate criteria; (b) weight criteria; (c) identify alternatives; (d) rate alternatives against criteria; and (e) calculate a relative score for each alternative. The model may generate various types of outputs for the group, such as lists of criteria, the average weight given by group members to each criterion, lists of alternatives, and average ratings given to each alternative on each criterion. More sophisticated GDSSs may provide extensive statistics on the model outputs, graphical display of group opinions, and the opportunity to change the parameters of the model and perform dynamic "what-if" analyses. Expansion of individual decision models to accommodate multi-party input, processing, and output requires extensive computer programming and numerous design decisions regarding how data should be entered, processed, and displayed.

GDSS Operation

Typically, groups do not rely upon a GDSS for their entire problem-solving process but rather use a subset of available features at various points during their deliberations. Verbal discussion in a meeting, or electronic messaging in the case of dispersed groups, supplements use of the GDSS. The typical setting for GDSS use today is the face-to-face meeting (rather than dispersed conferences) (see figure 1). In a GDSS-supported meeting, each participant has a workstation through which ideas, votes, comments, and so on can be entered. Usually, such information is entered anonymously. Simultaneous and anonymous entry of information speeds up the data-gathering process and encourages group members to be creative and

PUBLIC SCREEN

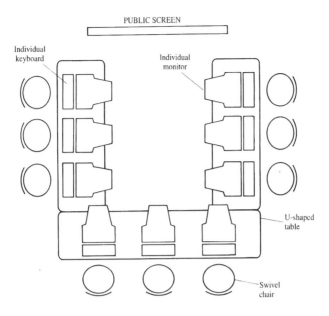

Individual keyboard

Individual monitor

U-shaped table

Swivel chair

Figure 1   Typical GDSS configuration for a face-to-face meeting

Simultaneous and anonymous entry of information speeds up the data-gathering process and encourages group members to be creative and uninhibited in self-expression. Once entered, information then can be publicly shared on a common viewing screen or software window, which provides a focal point for the group discussion. In a face-to-face meeting the common screen is physically located in the front of the room. If group members are dispersed across a network, public information is viewed in a designated window or screen at the individual's private workstation. A network is needed to connect all of the workstations together into a common workstation, or server, where the heart of the GDSS software resides.

Design Rationale

GDSS design is based on a systems view of group decision-making in which the group's size, styles of interacting and other characteristics are *inputs* along with the task at hand to the group decision *process*. The group's decision process occurs as members exchange information with one another and work to solve the problem that they confront. Depending on the nature of the group's decision and related processes, certain *outcomes* will result. Group decision outcomes can be described in terms of their quality, the time required for the group to reach the solution, the total number of ideas generated, the degree of consensus among members about the final solution, and members' willingness to implement the solution. *Feedback* in the system occurs as decision outcomes serve as inputs to future interactions that group members undertake. The entire group decision process takes place within a broader social context, such as a particular organization, institution, or society, which has a dynamic relationship with the group's decision system, affecting how inputs to interaction are defined and how the group decision process is conducted.

GDSS designers treat the inputs to the decision process as givens and proceed to consider how the group interaction process might be improved. That is, given a particular

Table 1   Examples of GDSS functionality to support group processes

Group process	Possible GDSS functionality
Discussion	
Participation	Anonymous, simultaneous entry of ideas followed by display of idea lists on a common viewing screen
Influence	Weighting ideas (weights of all ideas sum to 1000 points); ranking, or ordering, ideas; rating, or scaling ideas (such as on a 1–7 scale); voting yes/no on each idea
Leadership	Combining weights either equally or according to a scheme that favors influence by certain members, such as the leader or experts
	Providing the leader with functions that are not accessible to other users
Emotional expression	Candid commenting, opinion polling
Conflict management	Issue identification and analysis, stakeholder analysis; statement of positions and graphics to illustrate shifts in positions over time
Memory	Group note-taking, storage and retrieval of meeting minutes, clustering ideas into common categories or themes
Decision analysis	
Problem structuring	Agenda management, outlining, problem formulation techniques, cognitive mapping
Idea generation	Electronic brainstorming, nominal group technique, creativity techniques
Alternatives evaluation	Multi-criteria decision models, risk analysis, stakeholder analysis, contingency analysis
Impact assessment	Forecasting models, scenario analysis
Implementation planning	Planning techniques, budget models

problem, a set of people responsible for resolving it, and a specific social context, then how might technology be designed to facilitate analysis and resolution of the problem? GDSS designers have relied heavily on a large body of research which documents the difficulties that groups experience during decision-making and methods for overcoming these difficulties. The literature indicates that groups are more creative, engage in more thorough analysis, reach higher-quality decisions, and gain higher commitment to solution implementation when there is full and even participation in the decision process, rather than low participation or dominance by a few members. Unfortunately, groups often have difficulty achieving full and even participation in their deliberations due to the *process losses* associated with interpersonal communication. In other words, when one person faces a decision, energy focuses solely on problem analysis and solution, but in a group

setting, tremendous energy is expended in regulating interpersonal communication and dealing with socioemotional issues, such as conflict, influence, and the like.

Group researchers argue that process losses can be overcome and decision-making improved if groups are supplied with process interventions that promote more even participation, appreciation of multiple viewpoints, and systematic reasoning. Group discussion techniques and decision models provide these kinds of interventions, and GDSS designers often begin by automating techniques that originally were designed to be implemented manually or with minimal computer support. For example, computer files and view screens can be used instead of flipcharts or electronic blackboards; keyboards can be used instead of index cards or round-robin voice voting; and inputs to decision models can be made via electronic files or by members themselves, rather than by a special facilitator or modeling expert. A key aspect of the GDSS design is separate, but linked, facilities for managing individual (private) versus group (public) work.

GDSS Design Alternatives

GDSS design is centered around providing discussion and modeling support to a group's decision process. Table 1 shows how GDSS designers map system functionality to group process needs. Systems vary, of course, in their specific features and implementation, and there are several useful dimensions for distinguishing among GDSS designs.

Comprehensiveness

The degree to which the GDSS offers a full range of functionality. The more extensive the system's functionality, the more comprehensive it is. More comprehensive GDSSs can be applied to a variety of decisions, whereas less comprehensive systems target particular aspects of the group problem-solving process (e.g. idea generation, impact assessment) or particular types of decisions (e.g. transportation, agriculture). More comprehensive systems also may be more complex and may require training or other forms of guidance to facilitate their operation.

Restrictiveness

The degree to which the GDSS limits the decision-making process to a particular sequence of operation or problem-solving procedure. Whereas comprehensiveness concerns *what* functions are available, restrictiveness governs *how* the functional options are used. More restrictive GDSSs attempt to guide the group through a structured method of applying the available options. Less restrictive GDSSs offer no prespecified decision path, so the group is free to choose among the options and use them in any order.

Decisional guidance

The degree to which the GDSS enlightens or persuades users as they choose among the system options. Decisional guidance may be *informative* (providing pertinent information that enlightens the selection or use of options but without suggesting how to proceed) or *suggestive* (providing judgmental recommendations on what procedures or data to apply and

how to apply them). The guidance may be *predefined*, with a fixed set of guidelines that are available to all groups that use the system) or *dynamic*, applying intelligence so that the system can "learn" in response to the progress of the particular user group.

Interface

The GDSS software interface might be described along a number of dimensions, but a key dimension is the *representation* that members work with as they interact with the software. Representations may be *process-oriented*, emphasizing actions that the group can undertake, such as defining the problem, evaluating alternative solutions, or formulating future strategies. The process-oriented interface presents the group with procedures for formulating or solving the problem, and data (usually in the form of member opinions or comments) is created as the procedures are applied. Alternatively, *data-oriented* representations emphasize information associated with the particular problem, such as health information, soil data, or public opinion surveys. The interface then allows the group to apply processes (such as decision models) to the available data. To date, most GDSSs favor the use of process representations as the dominant interface, with data representations being secondary.

Information exchange

Some GDSSs support creation and sharing of only *task-related* information (such as problems, alternatives, criteria, or strategies), whereas others support exchange of *socioemotional* information as well (such as expressions of frustration or praise, joking, or the overall mood of the group). The *pattern* of information exchange supported by the GDSS also can vary across system implementations. Information exchange patterns in GDSSs may include:

1 *One-to-all communication*: all information entered into the system becomes public, or available to all members of the group.
2 *One-to-one communication*: individual members can selectively communicate with other members as part of the group decision process.

3 *Subgroup communication*: group members are divided into subgroups, and models or messages operate based on these subgroups.

Finally, the *storage* of information in the GDSS can affect information exchange in the group. Alternative storage designs include:

1 *Complete histories*: comments, votes, model outputs, or other information created during the problem-solving process are stored as a continuing history with new information added as the group process unfolds.
2 *Dynamic replacement*: only the most recently generated data is presented to the group; historical information is either deleted or stored outside of the group's active workspace.
3 *Keyed storage*: Data is organized according to some meaningful scheme, such as by date, by topic, or by group member.

The content, pattern, and storage of information exchange supported by the GDSS are critical design decisions that potentially can affect the decision process the group experiences as it attempts to understand and resolve the problem at hand.

Control over functionality

Who determines what functions are made available to the group, the sequencing of those functions, and when or how they are applied? Alternative designs include:

1 *User controlled*: each group member has access to all system functions, and the members select and apply the functions as they see fit.
2 *Leader controlled*: a group leader or facilitator, who has access to full system functionality, determines the subset of functionality that is presented to members.
3 *Shared control*: system operation is divided among various parties, such as between the leader and members. The shared control mode can be implemented in a variety of ways. For example, to support negotiations,

operations may be divided between members representing different sides of an issue. An alternative design is to share control among a leader, group members, and a technician, with the technician performing functions that are too complex for group members, such as file retrieval or complex data manipulations.

Private versus public work.

To support *private work*, the GDSS facilitates individual recording of ideas, comments, votes, and the like, and responds to whatever commands the individual enters at his or her workstation. *Public work* represents an aggregation of individual work and is located in the shared workspace. In some implementations, only a group leader or representative can control operation of the shared workspace. In other systems, each group member has direct access to the shared workspace and is free to control its operation. Usually, at least some of the public GDSS functions operate automatically. Determining the content and configuration of private and public workspaces is an important issue in GDSS design.

Bibliography

Bostrom, R. P., Watson, R. T. & Kinney, S. T. (1992). *Computer Augmented Teamwork: A Guided Tour*. New York: Van Nostrand Reinhold.

Jessup, L. M. & Valacich, J. (eds) (1993). *Group Support Systems: New Perspectives*. New York: Macmillan.

Nunamaker Jr, J. F., Dennis, A. R., Valacich, J. S., Vogel, D. R. & George, J. F. (1991). Electronic meeting systems to support group work: theory and practice at Arizona. *Communications of the ACM*, **34** (7), 30–39.

GERARDINE DESANCTIS and
GARY W. DICKSON

groupware   *see* COMPUTER-SUPPORTED COOPERATIVE WORK

H

history of organizational use of information technology Individuals and organizations have come to depend on calculating and computing machinery for increasing amounts of accurate and timely information. Mathematicians and philosophers, among the first to use calculating devices, developed sophisticated techniques for representing, manipulating, and analyzing information. Entrepreneurs and inventors gradually adapted these tools and techniques to the problems faced by merchants, factory owners, and government agencies. By the twentieth century, engineers and scientists contributed fundamental insights into the design of calculating machinery, components, materials, and programming. At each stage in the development of computing machines, a constellation of economic, social, and technological factors combined to reduce cost while improving speed and reliability of computation.

Early Aids to Calculation

Efforts to mechanize calculation began in the early seventeenth century as mathematicians and philosophers like William Schickard (1591–1635), Blaise Pascal (1623–62), and Gottfried Wilhelm von Leibnitz (1646–1716) devised some of the first mechanical aids to calculation (Aspray, 1990). These devices represented numerical digits on gear wheels and performed calculations as these components moved. By 1820 the first commercial adding machine, the "Arithmometer," was invented by Charles Xavier Thomas for the French insurance industry. Similar devices were developed by Frank S. Baldwin (1838–1925), Dorr E. Felt (1862–1930), and William S. Burroughs (1857–98), and improved the accuracy of accountants and office managers. Business professionals of the nineteenth century developed accounting techniques that relied heavily on mechanical calculating machinery and office equipment.

The English mathematician Charles Babbage (1792–1871) designed some of the most sophisticated mechanical calculating machines of the nineteenth century (Swade, 1991). Babbage's difference and analytical engines were never constructed during his lifetime, but they incorporated several of the key concepts found in later computer architectures and were designed to function automatically by following a sequence of instructions stored on punched cards.

Punched-card Tabulating Systems

The growth of government bureaucracies and more complex business organizations heightened interest in the collecting, processing, and storing of information toward the end of the nineteenth century. Beginning in the 1890s, organizations like the US Bureau of the Census and the New York Central Railroad began to use punched-card based tabulating systems developed by Herman Hollerith (1860–1929) to collate and analyze information (Norberg, 1990). Tabulating equipment used electrical sensors to read information encoded onto paper cards, and in turn perform a set of basic calculations. Hollerith incorporated the Tabulating Machine Company (TMC) in 1896 and produced a complete system of tabulating equipment. Hollerith's main competitor, James Powers, founded the Powers Accounting Machine Company in 1911. Between 1914 and 1930, these two firms introduced machines with increasingly faster sorting speeds, greater density of card data, and modest improvements in calculating ability. Eventually TMC was sold to the Computer Tabulating Recording Company (CTR) headed by Thomas J. Watson in 1911. In

1924 CTR changed its name to International Business Machines (IBM) and continued to manufacture and lease tabulating equipment until the emergence of electronic computers in the late 1950s. In general, tabulating systems prepared businesses and government agencies for many of the applications that would later be performed with digital computers.

Mechanical to Electromechanical Machines

While business organizations made heavy use of punched-card tabulating equipment, several mechanical and electromechanical calculating machines were developed during the 1930s and 1940s that foreshadowed the development of electronic digital computers. These machines used electromechanical devices to perform calculations, and functioned as special purpose machines for use by scientists and engineers (Ceruzzi, 1983). Konrad Zuse, an engineering student in Berlin, designed and constructed a series of electromechanical calculators beginning in 1938 with his Z1 machine. At Bell Telephone Laboratories, George Stibitz and Samuel Williams also developed special purpose, electromechanical computers beginning in 1939 that assisted engineers in the analysis of complex electrical networks. Howard Aiken, a Harvard University physics professor, joined with IBM to build an electromechanical machine, the Harvard Mark I or IBM ASCC, for scientific work in 1939. While Aiken's relationship with IBM was unstable, a series of machines was developed by Harvard that included the Harvard Mark II (1947), Harvard Mark III (1949), and the Harvard Mark IV (1952). A series of mechanically based, analog computers, called differential analyzers, was developed under the direction of Vannever Bush at MIT from the 1920s to the 1940s that demonstrated the potential and limitations of analog computing devices. John Atanasoff at the University of Iowa, from 1938 to 1942, developed a computing device to solve systems of linear equations.

Early Electronic Digital Computers

During the Second World War the US military sponsored a number of R&D projects that resulted in some of the core technologies used in early computer designs. In June 1943 John W. Mauchley (1907–80) and J. Presper Eckert received a grant from the US Army to design and construct the ENIAC (Electronic Numerical Integrator and Computer) at the University of Pennsylvania (Stern, 1981. This machine was completed in December 1945. Weighing several tons and containing over 18,000 vacuum tubes, the ENIAC was programmed through plugboards and manual switches. Soon after the completion of the ENIAC, John von Neumann (1903–57) articulated the concept of the internally stored, automatically executed, programmable computer in his "First Draft Report on the EDVAC" of June 1945. This led to the construction of several stored program computers, like the IAS machine. Started in 1946, this machine was constructed at Princeton under the guidance of von Neumann, and the design specifications for this machine quickly diffused to other projects, including the development of the IBM 701. British engineers, working at the University of Cambridge, Manchester University, and the National Physical Laboratory, made fundamental advances in computing technology during the 1950s. A significant accomplishment was the development of William's tube memory technology by F. C. Williams at Manchester University. Maurice V. Wilkes contributed to the development of true, stored program computers during this period.

MIT's Whirlwind computer project represents one of the last large machines constructed as a result of the war. It was designed to perform real-time simulation of aircraft performance (Redmond & Smith, 1980). Completed in 1951 under the direction of Jay W. Forrester, the Whirlwind computer made substantial advances in the design of high-speed circuits and pioneered the use of ferrite core memory. Many of these advances were later implemented in the SAGE computer system to monitor aircraft that operated between 1963 and 1980.

Emergence of the Computer Industry

By the mid-1950s, electronic digital computers had migrated from scientific laboratories and military projects into the business sector (Cortada, 1993). While less than a dozen computers existed at this time, their numbers rapidly increased as firms started to view computers as a potentially profitable product. After purchasing the Eckert–Mauchley Computer Corporation in 1950, Remmington Rand developed the UNIVAC I with the first installation in 1951 at the Bureau of the Census. This machine's central processor contained some 5,000 vacuum tubes and used a mercury delay-line for main memory. The installation of one of these machines at General Electric, for use in payroll and general accounting applications, in 1954 marked the beginning of the commercial computer industry in America. Similar early business use of computers was begun in Great Britain. UNIVAC's customers used their machines for general accounting and transaction processing applications. Remmington Rand, renamed Sperry Rand in 1955, grew to be a major force in the early computer market and competed against IBM with its UNIVAC 80 and 90, UNIVAC II (1957), and UNIVAC 1108, 1110 computers.

In the 1940s IBM held a leadership position in the punched-card tabulator and office machine markets. Digital computers represented a potentially disruptive product to IBM's established line of punched-card tabulating equipment and IBM's senior management approached this technology with caution (Bashe et al., 1986). One of IBM's first efforts in digital computing involved the development of its Defense Calculator, later called the IBM 701, in 1952. IBM also developed a companion system, the IBM 702, for business customers.

By 1954 IBM had also developed a smaller system, initially intended to extend the capabilities of punched-card equipment, called the IBM 650. This machine used magnetic-drum technology for its main memory and was one of the most successful general purpose commercial computers. Organizations like Caterpillar Tractor and the Chrysler Corporation used the 650 for inventory control and manufacturing processing applications. Many universities also acquired their first digital computer through a discount leasing program for the IBM 650, and the availability of these machines encouraged the establishment of computer science departments in many American universities. While IBM came to dominate the computer industry by 1960, other computer manufacturers also developed so called "first-generation computers." Some of the most prominent firms included the Datamatic Corporation, Burroughs, RCA, and the Philco Corporation

which introduced the first transistorized computer, the Philco Transac S-2000.

Growing Acceptance

The computers developed in the late 1950s demonstrated the feasibility of manufacturing fast digital computers for a limited, largely scientific market; however, most of the calculations required in business activities continued to be done on punched-card equipment. In the first half of the 1960s, however, several new systems made their way into the market and increased the acceptance of digital computers. In general, these machines used individual transistors as logic circuit components and ferrite-core devices for memory. The lower cost and higher reliability of these systems convinced many business leaders to invest in computing technology. The development of higher-level languages like COBOL and FORTRAN also made these machines easier to program. As machines of greater power and flexibility emerged throughout the 1960s, business organizations began to explore the computer as a tool for management control and planning applications.

By the late 1950s, IBM's management had refocused its energies on the digital computing market and developed one of its strongest products of that period, the IBM 1401. Introduced in 1959, the IBM 1401 series used magnetic tape and punched cards for its input/output, ferrite-core for its main memory, and a transistorized processor. Designed for commercial data-processing tasks, the 1401 was available with a basic assembly language, SPS or Symbolic Assembly Language, and an assembler called "Autocoder." Various report program generators were also made available for both the 1401 and its subsequent series, the 1440, 1460, 1410, and 7010. Approximately 14,000 of the 1401 systems were installed, and the success of this system propelled IBM into a leadership position in the commercial digital computer market.

IBM competed against a number of other firms throughout the late 1950s and early 1960s for a share of the growing market for computers. USA-based firms such as General Electric, Honeywell, Bendix, Philco, CDC, RCA, UNIVAC, and Burroughs developed competitive products for both the commercial and scientific markets. Computer companies were also formed in Europe. Only a few of the early entrants were able to gain a significant profitable market share.

Timesharing, Networks, and Real-time Applications

As large-scale computer installations became more prominent within business organizations, the task of managing these investments became a critical issue. One solution to the problem that received considerable attention involved the emergence of timesharing techniques in the 1950s and 1960s. Prior to this period, most computers operated in batch mode in which applications and data were processed serially, one "batch" at a time at a centralized computer center. Such techniques were inconvenient for users and complicated the debugging of new applications. The initial concept of timesharing was articulated in 1959 by Christopher Strachey at the National Research Development Corporation in England and John McCarthy at MIT. Some of the earliest implementations of time-sharing occurred in MIT's Compatible Time Sharing System and its Project MAC effort, the JOSS System developed at the Rand Corporation, and the development of timesharing systems at Dartmouth College.

A related development of the 1960s involved the creation of some of the first computer networks. In 1968, for instance, the Defense Advanced Research Projects Agency (DARPA) started development of the ARPANET. Based on packet-switching technology, the ARPA-NET eventually demonstrated that a heterogeneous network of different hardware, software, and data resources could operate successfully.

The early 1960s also witnessed the development of "real-time management systems" by some of America's leading corporate computer users. American Airlines began this movement with their collaborative effort with IBM to develop the SABRE airline reservation system. Similar systems were installed by other US-based airlines, and eventually became strategically important computer applications for these firms.

Quest for Compatibility

While higher-level languages had eased the task of developing efficient programs, one of the persistent problems in early computing concerned the incompatibility of different processors even within the same product line. In 1964, IBM announced its S/360 family of upwardly compatible computers (Pugh et al., 1991). The fourteen models that eventually made up the 360 family featured a standardized input/output interface and subsequently spawned a separate peripheral devices industry. The IBM 360 series allowed users to run both character-based business applications and word-based scientific applications on the same machine. The IBM 360 was also part of a movement toward the use of integrated circuits, developed by Jack Kilby, at Texas Instrument, and Robert Noyce, at Fairchild Semiconductor, in computer design (Braun & Mcdonald, 1982). This was followed by the IBM 370 in 1970. By all accounts, the IBM 360 was a complete success, and by 1970 more than 18,000 installations of this machine were in operation. Some of IBM's competitors, like RCA with its Spectra Series, developed rival lines of 360 compatible computers, but the success of IBM's product series continued throughout the 1960s and 1970s.

Minicomputers

By the mid-1960s business organizations could lease an IBM mainframe or one of its competitors' products. While these systems were fast and expandable, they also were expensive, physically large, and required a team of specialists skilled in their operation and maintenance. Minicomputers rose to the fore in the late 1960s as a low-cost, small-sized alternative for many organizations. They resulted from continued technological development of circuit design, component packaging, and the shifting requirements of computing.

Digital Equipment Corporation was founded in 1957 by Ken Olson and Harlan Anderson and emerged as one of the most successful developers of minicomputers (Rifkin & Harrer, 1988). Originally oriented toward large-scale mainframe, DEC's engineers turned to the problem of designing inexpensive, small computers. Beginning with the highly successful PDP-8 minicomputer (1965), DEC produced a series of minicomputers that included the PDP-11 (1968) and the VAX-11 in 1976. DEC's success spawned a series of other minicomputers, like Interdata's model-1, Prime's 200 mini

(1972), and General Automation's SPC-8 and SPC-12 (1968). One of DEC's primary competitors in the minicomputer market was Data General. Data General developed their NOVA minicomputer in 1969, Eclipse in 1980 (Kidder, 1981). IBM also introduced its System 38 and AS/400 series of minicomputers.

The Personal Computer Revolution

Personal computers emerged in the 1970s as the cost of electronic components declined and people recognized a need for inexpensive, powerful, small systems. Initially, all of the established computer companies considered the potential market for personal computers to be too small to merit product development. Innovations in electronic component technology, particularly the development of the Intel 8080 microprocessor in 1974 by Marcian "Ted" Hoff, provided an opportunity for experimentation in small computer design. Electronics hobbyists were among the first to attempt to construct and operate small computers, building kits like EDP Company's System One (1973), Scelbi Computer's Scelbi-8h, and the MITS Altair 8800 computer (1975). These amateurs demonstrated that inexpensive, personalized computers were feasible. By the later 1970s, firms like Commodore and Radio Shack started to produce personal computers as either extensions of their hand-held calculators or electronics businesses.

Working off a few thousand dollars of venture capital, Steve Wosniak and Steven Jobs developed their Apple II in 1977 (Butcher, 1987). Unlike many of the hobbyist machines, the Apple featured a full-sized keyboard and a separate floppy drive and monitor. The availability of software, particularly the program Visicalc written by Daniel Bricklin and Bob Frankston in 1979, made the Apple II an overnight success and accelerated the move to personal systems. After visiting Xerox's Palo Alto Research Center (PARC), Steve Jobs initiated a development project that ultimately resulted in the Macintosh computer in 1984. The Macintosh's user-friendly, graphically oriented system software created a paradigm for personal computing that has been widely emulated.

The growing popularity of personal computers prompted IBM to develop its own personal computer in 1980. Led by Philip Don Estridge, the IBM design team used outside contractors for many of the PC's components and system software. Bill Gates and Paul Allen, for instance, were contracted in 1980 to write the disc operating system or DOS for the PC. IBM's decision to create a PC with an open architecture, that would allow outside firms to develop peripherals and other system components, has had a lasting impact on the course of PC development.

Bibliography

Aspray, W. (Ed.) (1990). *Computing Before Computers*, 1st edn. Ames, IA: Iowa State University Press.

Bashe, C. J., Pugh, E. W., Johnson, L. R. & Palmer, J. H. (1986). *IBM's Early Computers.* Cambridge, MA: MIT Press.

Braun, E. & Macdonald, S. (1982). *Revolution in Miniature: The History and Impact of Semiconductor Electronics*, 2nd edn. New York: Cambridge University Press.

Butcher, L. (1987). *Accidental Millionaire: the Rise and Fall of Steve Jobs at Apple.* New York: Paragon.

Ceruzzi, P. E. (1983). *Reckoners: The Prehistory of the Digital Computer, from Relays to the Stored Program Concept, 1935–1945. Contributions to the study of computer science, vol. 1.* Westport, CT: Greenwood Press.

Cortada, J. (1993). *The Computer in the United States: From Laboratory to Market, 1930 to 1960.* New York: M. E. Sharpe.

Kidder, T. (1981). *The Soul of a New Machine.* Boston: Little, Brown.

Norberg, A. L. (1990). High-technology calculation in the early 20th century: punched-card machinery in business and government. *Technology and Culture*, 31, 753–79.

Pugh, E. W. (1984). *Memories that Shaped an Industry: Decisions Leading to IBM System/360.* Cambridge, MA: MIT Press.

Pugh, E. W., Johnson, L. R. & Palmer, J. H. (1991). *IBM's 360 and Early 370 Systems.* Cambridge, MA: MIT Press.

Redmond, K. C. & Smith, T. M. (1980). *Project Whirlwind: the History of a Pioneer Computer.* Bedford, MA: Digital Press.

Rifkin, G. & Harrer, G. (1988). *The Ultimate Entrepreneur: the Story of Ken Olsen and Digital Equipment Corporation.* Chicago: Contemporary Books.

Stern, N. B. (1981). *From ENIAC to UNIVAC: an Appraisal of the Eckert–Mauchley Computers.* Bedford, MA: Digital Press.

Swade, D. (1991). *Charles Babbage and his Calculating Engines.* London: Science Museum.

ERIC S. BOYLES

human–computer interaction To accomplish tasks using a computer, a dialog usually occurs between the user and the computer. This dialog is an iterative cycle of bi-directional communications with the user issuing instructions to the computer and the computer presenting the results (feedback) of carrying out those instructions. The field of human–computer interaction (HCI) is concerned with the study and design of this dialog. An understanding of both the technological artifact and the user are needed in order to design the structure of the dialog between the user and the computer. HCI draws on such diverse fields as computer science, psychology, artificial intelligence, linguistics, anthropology and sociology.

In early computer systems, the technology was relatively more expensive than the personnel who used the system. As a result, engineering considerations dominated designs and users were forced to adapt to the system. As technology has become relatively inexpensive and more powerful, there has been an increasing emphasis on fitting the system to the user. Although the emphasis is shifting, human–computer interaction is essentially a situation of mutual adaptation or accommodation (Norman & Draper, 1986).

To accommodate the user, the designer must employ (either explicitly or implicitly) some theory or model of user behavior. Much of the research in human–computer interaction is aimed at building such a theory or theories (Card et al., 1983). System design involves constructing a conceptual model of how the system is to function. In adapting to the system, the user also develops a conceptual model of the system as a guide to his or her interaction and dialog with the system.

Inconsistencies between the designer's model of the system and the user's model of the system create potential for error. Such inconsistencies arise because the primary means for communicating the designer's model to the user is through the physical system (and its accompanying documentation). Thus, inconsistencies can arise when the system fails to accurately reflect the designer's model (i.e. the system has bugs), or when the user's experience with the system results in a misinterpretation of the model embodied in the system. From this perspective a good system not only has few bugs but also has a conceptual model that is clearly evident in the technological artifact itself. The use of metaphors, such as the desktop metaphor popularized by Apple Macintosh, is a useful means of conveying a conceptual model of the system to users (Gerlach & Kuo, 1991).

In addition to having a conceptual or mental model of the system, the user also has a model of the task. It is the user's task knowledge that determines *what* functions or operations the user will require the computer to perform. The user's conceptual model of the system informs the user as to *how* to get the system to carry out the desired operations. From the standpoint of a human–computer interaction, a system should reflect a good understanding of the task domain. Without such an understanding, a system may still provide the functionality a user requires for a given task, but it may be inconsistent with the way the user thinks about accomplishing the task. In a well-designed system, the system model and the user's task model should be consistent, thereby enabling the user to work almost entirely in terms of the task domain. In such situations, the technology becomes virtually transparent.

There are several common design principles and guidelines that can aid HCI design. The use of a good metaphor as a basis for the system model is an important design principle. Consistency both within and across applications is another important design goal. Consistency is desirable both in the manner in which an operation is initiated by the user, such as in the keystrokes required to carry out similar actions within or across applications, and also in the presentation of information to the user.

Visibility is also an important design objective (Norman, 1988). A good design makes clearly visible the actions that are available to the user and the state of the machine. The on-screen buttons that pervade modern graphical user interfaces are designed to make clear the actions available to the user. Similarly, disk drive access lights and flashing cursors are examples of visible cues to the current state of the computer.

While it is valuable to make the possible actions available to a user visibly obvious, it is also important to provide the user with feedback about the success or failure of an attempt to carry out some action. The beep that the computer makes when the user presses the wrong key is an example of such feedback. The beep is, however, not complete feedback; it merely signifies that an attempted action was erroneous. A better design not only signifies to the user that the action failed, but describes how or why it failed. It may provide guidelines on how to appropriately execute the desired action.

Human–computer interaction is also facilitated by placing appropriate constraints on both user and system behavior. Constraints can be physical, such as in the design of the 3.5 inch floppy disk which cannot be inserted into a disk drive other than in the correct manner. User actions can also be constrained by software. Many software-imposed constraints are protection mechanisms intended to prevent user error. Examples include confirmation of critical actions such as file deletion and disk formatting. None the less, errors can still occur so it is also important to provide the ability to reverse or undo mistaken operations.

Providing a natural mapping between the logical action a user wishes the computer to perform, and the physical action required by the user to get the computer to carry it out, is also an important factor in system design. The popularity of the mouse as an input device owes much of its success to the fact that it exploits a natural mapping. To move the cursor in any direction the user simply moves the mouse in that direction.

Within the bounds of these various design principles, the possible styles of interaction and interface devices vary. In terms of styles, the possibilities include simple command languages, question and answer dialogs, menu selection, on-screen forms (appropriately mapped to their paper equivalents), and "direct-manipulation" (Shneiderman, 1992) or icon-based user interfaces. Common devices include keyboard, mouse, and monitor. Other emerging devices and methods are speech synthesis and recognition and virtual reality gloves and helmets. The appropriate design choice in all cases depends on the user and the task to be accomplished with the computer.

Bibliography

Card, S. K., Moran, T. P. & Newell, A. (1983). *The Psychology of Human–Computer Interaction.* Hillsdale, NJ: Lawrence Erlbaum.

Gerlach, J. H. & Kuo F.-Y. (1991). Understanding Human–Computer Interaction for Information Systems Design. *MIS Quarterly*, **15**, 527–49.

Norman, D. A. (1988). *The Psychology of Everyday Things.* New York: Basic Books.

Norman, D. A. & Draper, S. W. (1986). *User-centered System Design: New Perspectives on Human–Computer Interaction.* Hillsdale, NJ: Lawrence Erlbaum.

Shneiderman, B. (1992). *Designing the User Interface: Strategies for Effective Human-Computer Interaction.* 2nd edn, Reading, MA: Addison-Wesley.

MICHAEL J. DAVERN

humans as information processors   Information processing is an innate human capacity. Several models of human information processing have been proposed. Newell and Simon's (1972) model of the human information-processing system is patterned after the computer and it incorporates a central processing unit (CPU) along with three kinds of memory: short-term, long-term, and external. The speed and operation of the CPU are not only bounded by its incapacity to engage in parallel processing of data but also by upper bounds on the speed of information retrieval from memory and the operating constraints of each kind of memory.

Short-term memory holds the rather small set of symbols that are immediately available to the CPU for information processing. The upper bound on the number of symbols available in short-term memory was identified by Miller (1956) as being about seven (plus or minus two). Although each symbol in memory might be equivalent to one piece of information or data, each symbol might also be a pointer to a larger (and topically grouped) set of data, known as a "chunk," that is resident in long-term memory. The speed of the retrieval of these symbols or chunks from short-term memory is much more rapid than from long-term or external memory. Further constraining the operation of short-term memory is the limitation that its contents begin to decay within a short time, particularly if the attention of the human information processor is being distracted by a new stimulus.

Long-term memory has a very large storage capacity but its data storage and retrieval operations are governed by the constraining principle of associativity. As humans acquire information through learning and experience, the information is organized associatively into patterns or chunks. Storage of information into long-term memory (i.e. memorizing) takes much longer to effect than retrieval from it.

External memory consists of the patterns or chunks of symbols that are stored by the human information processor in the external environment for later access and retrieval. Typically, this is written text, but it can also include objects, the configuration of objects, or even a network of people and things meaningful to the human information processor.

Also included in the Newell and Simon (1972) model is a description of how human information processors solve problems confronting them. Human behavior occurs within a task environment of a problem. The task environment is mentally represented as a problem space. The structure of a problem space is what informs the human information processor as to how to achieve a solution to the problem. The contents of the problem space are manifest as knowledge states. These are a combination of either knowledge about how to search for other knowledge that can generate a solution and/or knowledge that can be directly applied to generate a solution (Newell, 1990).

Beyond the Newell and Simon model, the fields of psychology and decision science have found that human heuristics (judgmental rules of thumb) are quite limited in respect of handling decision-oriented information for tasks of judgment and discrimination, and may even introduce biases. For example, when engaged in making a judgment of a situation, humans will typically establish an initial assessment of the situation and then subsequently make adjustments to that assessment in response to further data. The problem with this anchoring and adjustment heuristic (Tversky & Kahneman, 1974) is twofold: the final decision too closely resembles the initial assessment and that assessment may well have been flawed. Parallel to this is the representativeness heuristic that humans apply to assess the likelihood of an event. They assess how similar the properties of the event are to the

most generally encountered and perceived properties of the type of event to which it belongs (Kahneman & Tversky, 1972). A third constraining heuristic is the concreteness bias, the preference of humans to evaluate only the most readily available information about the surface properties of alternatives presented to them. Humans also tend to mistake association or correlation between two events as implying a causal relationship, particularly when the events fit established patterns of expected sequences (Yates, 1990).

The tendency to fit experienced or perceived events into expected sequences of events is part of a larger feature of human information processing known as scripts. These are prototypical combinations of events, actions, and objects that people expect to encounter during the course of specific processes (such as an expected sequence of *ordering* some *food* listed on a *menu* from a *waiter* in a *restaurant*). Closely related to the notion of scripts as sources of organization for human information processing is that of narratives, which have been proposed (Bruner, 1990) as the basis for human experience and thought in that they both precede and underlie human language comprehension. The causal relations between facts are embedded by humans into narratives. These are fundamental building blocks used by people to create mental models or representations of their experiences. Narratives and scripts are quite advantageous because they provide cognitive economy by embodying a relatively. small number of significant categories for understanding the world. Humans employ them in order to cope with an almost infinitely large number of potential relationships between objects in different categories.

Scripts and narratives also underlie a key form of human information processing known as case-based analogical reasoning (Riesbeck & Schank, 1989). This type of problem-solving approach occurs when humans recall from long-term memory a past instance of a problem solution with features similar to the presenting problem at hand. The recalled solution is then adjusted according to those features that are different from the presenting problem and the modified solution is applied to the problem at hand. Narratives and scripts facilitate the analogically enacted recall operation.

Scripts and narratives further serve to counterbalance the intrinsic cognitive constraints of short-term memory (decay and limited space). Also assisting to overcome cognitive constraints is the tendency for humans to perceive objects in the world as instances of types and super-types arranged as hierarchies. This tendency is highly congruent with the storage of information as "chunks" in both short-term and long-term memory. However, it is so pronounced that if objects or entities in the world do not fit into some hierarchical grouping, they may be simply ignored by human information processors (Simon, 1988).

The use of theories and findings about human information processing has not been limited to the level of analysis of the individual problem-solver or decision-maker. In fact, several theories of organizational decision-making and organizational function have taken facets of information-processing theory into account. Perhaps the most famous has been that of Simon (1976), who argued that human decision-making is based on "bounded rationality." Humans make decision choices that are rational but based on a limited set of alternatives and a limited set of decision criteria supporting those alternatives. This occurs because humans, when functioning in real task environments, have a bounded cognitive capacity to fully determine the available alternatives and the appropriate decision criteria to employ. Cyert and March (1963) extended this idea and proposed that

1 Organizations can only scan limited aspects of their external environment.
2 Organizations usually contain multiple and often conflicting goal-sets based on the desires of competing subunits.
3 Organizations typically execute decision-making by engaging in serial attention to goals and problems, as well as following established operating procedures.

Galbraith (1974) proposed that even the internal structure of an organization is largely determined by how it chooses to cope with the additional information-processing burden imposed by uncertainty in its external environment.

Situated cognition is a more recent perspective in cognitive science. It rejects the idea that human information capacity is generally functional across task domains (Lave, 1988). Those who subscribe to this perspective propose that features of the external environment afford and constrain the possible set of actions by human problem-solvers and are thus the primary determinants of human information processing.

Human limits as information processors are important in the design of information system applications and in the creation of user interfaces for those applications. For example, applications can be designed to minimize memorization and to assist recall, or even to present data in a way that decreases the employment of human biases in decision-making. Indeed, superior applications of information technology can assist humans to identify hierarchies of objects or classes of relationships between objects in the world. Awareness of human information-processing limits at the organizational level can help teams of systems designers as they implement new information systems for public and private organizations.

Bibliography

Bruner, J. (1990). *Acts of Meaning.* Cambridge, MA: Harvard University Press.

Cyert, R. & March, J. (1963). *A Behavioral Theory of the Firm.* Englewood Cliffs, NJ: Prentice-Hall.

Galbraith, J. (1974). *Organization Design: An Information Processing View.* Reading, MA: Addison-Wesley.

Kahneman, D. & Tversky, A. (1972). Subjective probability: a judgment of representativeness. *Cognitive Psychology,* 3, 430–54.

Lave, J. (1988). *Cognition in Practice: Mind, Mathematics and Culture.* New York: Cambridge University Press.

Miller, G., A. (1956). The magical number seven, plus or minus two: some limits on our capacity for processing information. *The Psychological Review,* 63 (2), 81–97.

Newell, A. (1990). *Unified Theories of Cognition.* Cambridge, MA: MIT Press.

Newell, A. & Simon, H. (1972). *Human Problem Solving.* Englewood Cliffs, NJ: Prentice-Hall.

Riesbeck, C. & Schank, R. (1989). *Inside Case Based Reasoning.* Hillsdale, NJ: Lawrence Erlbaum.

Simon, H. A. (1976). *Administrative Behavior: A Study of Decision-making Processes in Administrative Organization,* 3rd edn. New York: The Free Press.

Simon, H. A. (1988). *The Sciences of the Artificial.* Cambridge, MA: MIT Press.

Tversky, A. & Kahneman, D. (1974). Judgment under uncertainty: heuristics and biases. *Science*, 185, 1124–31.

Yates, J. F. (1990). *Judgment and Decision Making*. Englewood Cliffs, NJ: Prentice-Hall.

DAVID BAHN

hypermedia/hypertext   Hypertext is a method for linking documents (nodes) to each other through a network of semantic links. The term "hypertext" was coined by Ted Nelson in 1965 to refer to non-linear text. Nelson defined hypertext as "a body of written or pictorial material interconnected in a complex way that it could not be conveniently represented on paper." The power of hypertext lies in its ability to create a "virtual document" composed of several other documents. By adding MULTI-MEDIA to hypertext, *hypermedia* can be constructed. Using hypermedia, the user can be presented with a document which, while it appears to be a single entity, is actually composed of many different parts. The parts may be located separately on a single computer or on different computers (in some cases in different parts of the world).

Hypertext is extremely useful for combining information in a non-linear way. Humans think non-linearly, so providing these linkages supports human cognition. As an example, hypertext is an excellent tool in manuals. By clicking on a link, the user is transferred to the document it represents. This makes it extremely easy to navigate between references, and related material can be linked to each other.

The basic concepts in hypertext are *nodes* (documents or concepts) and *links* (the relationship between the nodes). Hypermedia is created when nodes which contain media other than text are linked together. For example, a document can have pictures, video, and sound integrated so that it appears as though it were one document. By selecting a video, for instance, the user is able to see the video on the computer screen.

Hypertext is implemented through the use of a standardized language. The most common hypertext language today is the HyperText Markup Language (HTML), which is used in the WORLD WIDE WEB (WWW) of the INTERNET. HTML is a simple derivative of another language, the Standard Generalized Markup Language (SGML). HTML works by enclosing text within tags in order to explain how that text should be treated by a browser (an application interpreting HTML). For example, <b>This text would be bold</b> when the browser sees the <b> (starting tag) and </b> (ending tag). Likewise, documents can be linked, like this link to the <a href="http://www.w3.org/pub/WWW/">World Wide Web Consortium Homepage</a>. When the browser sees the text <a href=". . . "> it knows that this is a link. Anything after the first > sign becomes what the user sees when viewing the document in a browser, and the </a> marks the end of the link. Thus, from the previous excerpt, the user would see "World Wide Web Consortium Homepage." These kinds of links, whether to other hypertext documents, or other media, can be combined into a seamlessly integrated page. By implementing the simple set of semantics available in HTML, very powerful documents can be produced.

Bibliography

Nelson, Ted (1965). A file structure for the complex, the changing, and the indeterminate. *Proceedings of the ACM Twentieth National Conference*. New York: ACM Press.

JESPER M. JOHANSSON

——— I ———

ICIS The International Conference on Information Systems is an annual international conference for information systems academics (*see* ASSOCIATIONS AND SOCIETIES FOR INFORMATION PROFESSIONALS). Begun in 1980, it is considered the leading international conference for academics in information systems.

IFIP Begun in 1960, membership of the International Federation for Information Processing comprises national information processing societies (*see* ASSOCIATIONS AND SOCIETIES FOR INFORMATION SYSTEMS PROFESSIONALS). Its technical activities are performed by Technical Committees. The most important Technical Committee for Information Systems is TC8 (Information Systems).

image processing Image processing is the use of an exact digital electronics representation of a document. It involves the electronic capture, storage, retrieval, display, processing, distribution, and printing of digital images of documents in a computer system. Image processing has widespread applicability in business, government, and education. These users are heavily dependent on processes that require many individuals to create, read, modify, file, retrieve, distribute, and approve documents.

Processing paper documents is a significant problem in an organization. They are accessible to only one individual at a time unless multiple copies are available. Paper documents are easily lost or misplaced and they are expensive and time consuming to file, store, and retrieve. Transportation from one individual to another adds time delays and cost to business processes.

Paper documents provide many important characteristics that are incorporated in image processing applications. These include portability, ability to modify and annotate, legal requirements for original and certified copies, and coding via color and notations.

Conventional data processing involves entering the information from a paper document into a computer system by keying in the data. The data, when presented by the computer system, usually does not visually match the original document in format or completeness. For example, the logo on the letterhead, penciled notes in the margins, the paper stock, and the format of the data are either missing or appear differently in the computer representation.

Image processing provides a number of important characteristics that can significantly improve business processes. Document images can be accessed simultaneously by several individuals in seconds. This permits business processes to be executed in parallel rather than in serial. Document annotations and signatures can be electronically filed with the document image. Document retrieval can be by index, title, author, date, etc. as well as by text content. This aids retrieval and reduces the incidence of lost documents. The digital images can be used for business processes; the original paper documents can be in a secure place for retrieval if needed for legal and other requirements.

Digital Images

Image processing depends on a digital representation, digitizing (converting) a document, such as a memorandum on paper, into digital form via use of a Fax or scanner. Digitizing converts an analog image into a two-dimensional grid of picture elements (pixels) represented as sets of bits. The lowest resolution form of a digital image is to represent each pixel with one bit (1 or 0 representing dark or light). Levels of gray can be represented by up to 8 bits for each pixel (256 levels of gray), and levels of color can be represented by up to 8 bits for each of red, green, and blue for each pixel (16,700,000 levels of color). A Fax or scanner that results in high visual quality will typically use a grid of 300 × 300 pixels per inch.

Digitizing a document results in a very large number of bits, many of which are visually redundant. For example, a page of text with 1,000 words contains large areas of contiguous "white space." Compression is a technique to reduce the quantity of bits by a short-hand representation of the redundant bits, typically resulting in a reduction factor of 10 to 25. Decompression reverses the process to display the original image.

Physical Components

The physical components of image processing can be described in terms of an information system model of input, processing, output, storage, and communications. Input into document processing comes from scanners or facsimile machines that digitize documents, stored images, magnetic and optical disk media, and electronic communication. Processing includes a computer, general software, and optical character recognition hardware or software. Output devices include magnetic and optical disk media, laser printers, facsimile machines, microform, and computer and television displays. Storage devices include magnetic and optical disk media, microform, and paper. Electronic communication includes a wide variety of computer and communication networks.

Functional Capabilities and Benefits

Indexing and retrieval provide easy and rapid multiple concurrent access to document images and support workload balancing, resulting in improved productivity, reduced cost, and enhanced service. The capability to simultaneously process images and data provides access to needed information significantly faster than paper.

The user views an exact digital copy of the document plus notes, commands, and action taken by others using the document. The familiar document image reduces training time and encourages use of the system. Ease of use is enhanced with a combination of textual and visual document description and the ease of finding documents through retrieval options. Processing is accelerated and scanning is more accurate than manual processing. Online help is available.

Workflow reporting is facilitated by document imaging, which allows better administration of information, distribution and redistribution of workload, management of items in a work queue, productivity and cost measurement automation, operational efficiencies, performance feedback, centralized supervision of decentralized services and increased caseload while maintaining standards.

Annotations, audit trail, and editing provide the ability to capture information that was heretofore "lost" in conventional data processing systems. Annotations in written and voice form allow notes to be written on a document without changing the content of the original. Information added to the image facilitates workflow. Digital approval added to images reduces time required for approvals and allows identification of those who approve the transaction. Explanation of actions taken can be dated and traced, making case research and investigation easier. Quality tracking can be by annotation by person and department, with elimination of paper for audit trails and real time update of files.

Data collection standards are enhanced via improved accuracy of data entry whether by key entry, recognition technology, or machine-readable turnaround document. Use of a universal source document minimizes transaction processing costs, reduces rejects by restricting extraneous input and content, and ensures consistency of data across the enterprise.

Applications

Image processing applications are defined from the perspective of what the application does, rather than the physical or functional capabilities required for the application. Audit applications involve retrieval of indexed document images along with other database information in support of an audit function. Examples are airline ticket revenue accounting, and product and material data safety sheets. Case management applications support maintaining a file, for tracking and resolution of a "case," with judgment, some predetermined rules and steps, often over a long time period. Examples include social services cases, insurance claims, client file folder, patient medical file and mortgage loans.

DESKTOP PUBLISHING applications permit generation of documents containing text with images and graphics, with emphasis on professional presentation quality. Examples include newspaper copy preparation, marketing presentations, and preparation of advertising copy from a library of graphics images. Electronic publishing applications involve distribution of professional quality documents mixing text, graphics, images, and color. Examples include newspapers, distribution of product manuals, and modular textbooks and cases. Image mail applications allow individuals or groups to freely route, annotate, index, file, and retrieve document images in a multi-user electronic mail environment. Examples are multimedia browser and e-mail systems over the Internet.

Medical, scientific, and engineering applications involve image generation, enhancement, and manipulation using very high resolution. An example is sending radiographic imaging of X-rays to an expert for analysis. The analysis can involve simultaneous examination of the X-ray by the attending physician and the remote expert.

Retrieval applications support multiple concurrent access to document images by index, document content, or visual image. Examples include maintenance manuals, government records, land and real estate records, reference library material, and research and technical files. Training, teaching, and testing applications include delivery of individualized training or education via MULTIMEDIA, with student interaction. Examples include language courses, job skills, competency testing and remediation, and performance-based teaching modules. Workflow automation applications support processing of documents through a predetermined sequence of steps, with automated scheduling and routing. Examples include order entry, invoice processing, and credit card collections.

LESTER A. WANNINGER JR

implementation of information systems

Implementation processes for information system projects focus on the diagnosis and resolution of concerns that individuals and groups have about changes that an information system project will produce in their work life. The discussion of implementation processes is organized around three topics: (a) the change process; (b) the diagnosis of implementation problems; and (c) management actions for implementation. These three components are illustrated in figure 1.

The Change Process

To be successful, an information systems project must move a work system from its current state to a desired new state. This movement involves passing through three phases: (a) unfreezing; (b) moving; and (c) refreezing (Lewin, 1952). The length of time for a phase depends upon the nature of the system being built, the nature of the organization for which the system is being built, and the management actions used to manage the transition. Failure of the project can occur at each stage.

Implementation involves all the stakeholders to an information systems project: those various groups of people, inside and outside the organization, whose methods of work will be affected by the project. In addition, stakeholders are also groups of people whose actions can affect the success of the project. For an improvement in an order entry system, for example, the stakeholder groups include personnel from credit and collections, distribution, manufacturing, and information systems, plus general managers and owners. Outside of the organization, the stakeholders would include customers, competitors, and suppliers.

Unfreezing involves gaining recognition and acceptance from the stakeholders of the project that changes to the work system are needed. The data used to achieve unfreezing successfully arises at two organizational levels. For the upper management and suppliers of capital to the organization, the required data revolves around projected improvements in organizational performance and increase in value that the project will bring to the organization (e.g. increases in sales, gains in market share, reduction in costs, and improvements in

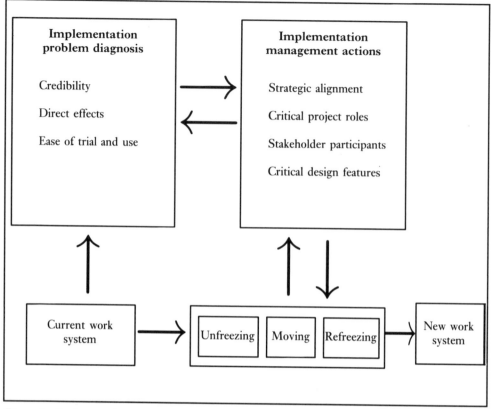

Figure 1   Implementation management process

quality). For others, such as mid-level managers, front-line workers, sales people, as well as customers, competitors, and suppliers, interest focuses on what benefits and costs the project will produce for them personally, not for the organization in general.

Moving involves the functionality of the system. Functional requirements are implemented in hardware, software, management policies and procedures, and education and training specifications for the stakeholder groups. Approaches to developing these specifications fall within the domain of SYSTEMS ANALYSIS AND DESIGN. It is through the successful completion of the systems development process that the projected, as well as unforeseen, benefits and costs used as evidence in the unfreezing stage are achieved.

Refreezing involves ensuring that the new work systems become institutionalized standards of work behavior for the stakeholder groups. The focus is on demonstrating that the

benefits and costs, projected in unfreezing and captured by the analysis and design efforts, are delivered to the various stakeholders.

Diagnosis of Implementation Problems

Research on innovation in general, and innovation and information technology, has identified three broad categories of factors to judge the value and acceptability of a proposed project: (a) the credibility of the project proposers and developers and the technology being employed; (b) the direct positive and negative effects of the proposed system; and (c) the ease of trial and use of the proposed system. While each individual stakeholder evaluates a proposed system in terms of these three categories, implementation problem diagnosis focuses upon identifying the typical beliefs about the systems held by different groups of stakeholders. For example, the evaluation of a proposed new order-processing system is done in terms of the beliefs of sales personnel, customers, distribution personnel, and others.

Credibility of proposers, developers, and technology is important because it influences *a priori* perceptions of the implementation project. For example, if the system is being recommended by sales management, the credibility of the sales management in the eyes of the various stakeholder groups is critical. In information systems projects, the reputation of the specific system developers involved in the project, as well as the general credibility of information systems groups, are important. The reliability of the hardware and software employed in the project is important. If the technology being employed (e.g. voice recognition in an order-processing system) has been used successfully elsewhere, credibility is acceptable. Conversely, if there has been a failed implementation of the technology, credibility will be unacceptable.

Direct effects of the proposed system consist of incremental benefits, incremental costs, and failure consequences. *Incremental benefits* may be monetary or non-monetary. As an example of monetary benefits to a stakeholder, a new sales support system may directly lead to an increase in sales and sales commissions. Most stakeholders do not receive monetary payment; they receive benefits such as the ability to complete a task faster with higher quality. *Incremental costs* for most stakeholders are not monetary. Rather, the costs may be the incremental effort to learn to use the proposed system and pressure to perform at higher levels of productivity with the new system. These incremental costs may be transitory or continuing. *Failure consequences* are encountered if a stakeholder adopts the new system and it temporarily or permanently fails. If, for example, a sales force moves to an electronic customer information database system and the system fails, it will affect sales effort.

Ease of trial and use of the proposed system focuses on five issues. The first two are *physical and intellectual ease of use* and *ease of conversation about the system*. If, for example, stakeholders can talk about and use a new system without learning complex technical procedures and terminology, they will be more likely to view the system favorably. The importance of these two issues explains the significance of graphical user interfaces in END-USER COMPUTING. The

third issue is *compatibility* with other parts of the stakeholders' work processes. The more localized the effects of a proposed system, the more favorably it will be viewed. The fourth and fifth issues are ability to test a system *on a limited basis* before committing to full-scale use and ability to reverse the *usage decision*. The ability to try a proposed system on a limited, experimental basis and the ability to discontinue use if the actual system does not live up to expectations increase the likelihood that the system will be viewed favorably.

The three evaluative categories and the issues in them define measures that the proposers and developers of a new system should monitor during the three phases of the change process. Positive responses across key stakeholder groups increase the likelihood that the project will succeed. When a proposed project scores poorly on several issues, a prototyping approach may be used. Extensive training may be required. *Incremental benefits* are critical. Stakeholders will be willing to work to overcome a number of problems if they see a clear benefit in the system. Perception of no benefit or limited benefits by a stakeholder group is almost certain to cause implementation problems and may lead to outright failure of a project.

Management Actions for Implementation

Implementation problem diagnosis for stakeholders defines implementation management problems. There are four broad categories: (a) the alignment of the proposed system with the strategy of the organization; (b) critical roles within each project; (c) participation by representatives of stakeholder groups; and (d) the critical system design features.

Strategic alignment focuses on the relationship between the proposed system and the strategy of the organization. It explains why the system is important to the *success factors* of the organization. While the systems analysis process builds this linkage as it defines the information requirements and capability, the implementation management process assures that all stakeholder groups understand the reasons for the proposed system. Although not all stakeholders will see personal *incremental benefits*, the strategic alignment explanation provides a legitimate reason for the system.

Critical project roles refer to positions and activities of sponsor, champion, and project leader. The sponsor is a senior-level manager in the organization who can legitimize the spending of resources and time on the proposed project. The sponsor is the person who, by his or her support, communicates the alignment of the project with the organization's strategy. The project must also have a *champion*, usually an upper-level manager in the functional organization that will use the system. The champion is usually organizationally above the directly affected organizational stakeholders. From this position, he or she commits the time and energy to manage the negotiations and resolve the political issues that evolve with an information systems project. Champions are usually at some political risk in the organization if the project fails. The *project manager* is the person responsible for managing the day-to-day activities of the project. For information systems, the project manager usually comes from the systems development group in the organization. There should also be a co-project leader from the main user area. This dual project manager approach is necessary to ensure that both the business issues and the technical issues are addressed during the development process.

Stakeholder participation refers to the active and appropriate involvement of the stakeholder groups in the systems analysis and development process. If there is a positive level of trust between the stakeholders and the project proposers and developers, stakeholder involvement can increase the quality of input concerning the functionality required in the system. The involvement of stakeholders also helps to obtain their "buy-in" concerning the changes in work processes that will be required. In terms of the implementation problem diagnostic dimensions discussed in the previous section, involvement is a productive way of achieving favorable perceptions among the various stakeholder groups. In cases where there is little trust between the stakeholders and the proposers and developers, participation can be an alternative to the control process that stakeholders may require before proceeding with the project.

Critical design features refer to system functionality and system user interfaces. These features are necessary to the success of the project, but they are not sufficient. The degree to which they will contribute to the success or failure of the project often depends on how well *strategic alignment*, *critical project roles*, and meaningful *participation* are executed.

Bibliography

Lewin, K. (1952). Group decision and social change, in E. E. Maccoby, T. M. Newcombe and E. L. Hartley (eds), *Readings in Social Psychology*, pp. 459–73. New York: Holt.

NORMAN L. CHERVANY and
SUSAN A. BROWN

inference engine An inference engine performs reasoning in a knowledge-based system. It applies formal logic to a set of facts to derive valid conclusions, which provide the basis for further reasoning. This continues until the goal is reached or all possibilities are exhausted. Inference engines perform forward reasoning, backward reasoning, or both.

See also **Expert systems**

AMIT DAS

information concepts Processing, delivering, and communicating information are essential objectives of the management information system of an organization. The system employs information and communications technology in achieving these objectives. The concept of information is therefore fundamental to the design of an information system.

In the context of information systems, information is data that has been processed into a form that is meaningful to the recipient and is of real or perceived value in current or prospective actions or decisions. Underlying the use of the term are several ideas: information adds to a representation, corrects or confirms previous information, or has "surprise" value in that it tells something the receiver did not know or could not predict. Information reduces uncertainty. It has value in the decision-making process in that it changes the probabilities attached to expected outcomes in a decision situation. It has value in motivation and building expertise about the organization and its processes and values.

The relation of data to information is that of raw material to finished product. An information-processing system processes data into information. Information for one person may be raw data for another. For example, shipping orders are information for the shipping room staff, but they are raw data for the vice president in charge of inventory. Because of this relationship between data and information, the two words are often used interchangeably.

Information resources are reusable. When information is retrieved and used, it does not lose value; in fact, it may gain value through the credibility added by use. This characteristic of stored data makes it different from other resources. Since management information systems deal with information, it would be useful to be able to measure the information provided by the systems and how much comes from informal information channels. There is no adequate method for measuring the information provided by an information system. However, several concepts are useful in understanding the nature and value of information in organizations. These are (a) information theory; (b) message reduction concepts; (c) information quality; (d) the value of information in decision-making; and (e) the non-decision value of information.

Information Theory

The term "information theory" refers to a mathematical theory of communication. The theory has direct application in electronic communication systems. It focuses primarily on the technical level of accuracy in information communication. It is limited in its practical application to management information systems, but it does provide useful insights into the nature of information.

Information theory was formulated by Norbert Weiner, a well-known mathematician, in connection with the development of a concept that any organism is held together by the possession of means for acquisition, use, retention, and transmission of information. Claude Shannon of Bell Laboratories developed and applied these concepts to explain telephone and other communications systems.

The purpose of a communication system is to reproduce at the destination a message selected at the source. A transmitter provides coded symbols to be sent through a channel to a receiver. The message that comes from a source to the transmitter is generally encoded there before it can be sent through the communications channel and must be decoded by a receiver before it can be understood by the destination. The channel is not usually a perfect conduit for the coded message because of noise and distortion. Distortion is caused by a known (even intentional) operation and can be corrected by an inverse operation. Noise is random or unpredictable interference.

As used in the mathematical theory of communication, information has a very precise meaning. It is the average number of binary digits that must be transmitted to identify a given message from the set of all possible messages to which it belongs. If there is a limited number of possible messages that may need to be transmitted, it is possible to devise a different code to identify each message. The message to be transmitted is encoded, the codes are sent over the channel, and the decoder identifies the message intended by the codes. Messages can be defined in a variety of ways. For example, each alphanumeric character may be a message, or complete sentences may be messages if there is a limited, predefined number of possible sentences to be transmitted. The size of the code is dependent on the coding scheme and the number of possible messages. The coding scheme for information theory · is assumed to be binary (only 0 or 1 as values).

The information content (or code size in bits) may be generalized as:

$$I = \log_2 n$$

where n = the total number of possible messages, all equally likely. Some examples for a message selected from 8, 2, 1 or 27 possible messages illustrate the formula. If there are eight messages, a code with only three bits can be sent to distinguish among them, i.e. there are three combinations of 0s and 1s in three bits ($n = 8$, $I = \log_2 8 = 3$). If there are only two outcomes, a single bit (0 or 1) value can identify which of the two is intended ($n = 2$, $I = \log_2 2 = 1$). If there is only one message to select from, there is no need to transmit anything because the answer is already known by the receiver ($n = 1$, $I = \log_2 1 = 0$).

If the set of messages is the alphabet plus a space symbol, the number of bits required will average 4.75 per letter, assuming all letters to be equally probable ($n = 27$, $I = \log_2 27 = 4.75$). However, all letters are not equally probable. The probability of an A is 0.0642 but for J is 0.0008. When probabilities are unequal, the average information content is computed by the following formula:

$$I = \sum_{i=1}^{n} p_i \log_2 \frac{1}{p_i}$$

A computationally equivalent form is

$$I = \frac{-\sum_{i=1}^{n}}{} p_i \log_2 p_i$$

A communication is rarely if ever completely composed of information. There are usually redundant elements. Redundancy reduces the efficiency of a particular transmission because more codes are transmitted than are strictly required to encode the message. However, some redundancy is very useful for error control purposes. A message may not be received as sent because of noise in the communication channel. The transmission of redundant data allows the receiver to check whether the received message is correct and may allow the original message to be reconstructed.

Message Reduction Concepts

The mathematical theory of communication deals with the information content of messages that are assumed to be objective. However, the richness of language by which humans communicate, and the constraints on humans and organizations as information processors, means that humans typically receive too much information, and the interpretation of received messages are subject to misunderstanding. Information concepts for information systems therefore also include concepts of message reduction, either by sending or receiving efficiency or by selective distribution.

Two methods for reducing the quantity of information are summarization and message routing. Within organizations, message *summarization* is commonly utilized to reduce the amount of data provided without changing the essential meaning. Formal summarization is illustrated by accounting classifications. The president of an organization cannot normally review each sale to get information for decisions. Instead, the accounting system summarizes all sales into a "sales for the period" total. The system may provide more meaningful information for decision purposes by summarizing sales by product group, geographical area, or other classification. The level of summarization is dependent on the organizational level of the decision-maker. For example, the president may need only the total sales by area, but the sales manager for the area may need sales by sales representative and sales by product.

In *message routing*, there is a reduction in communication volume by distributing messages only to those individuals or organizational units that require the information for some action or decision. This is illustrated by the transmission of copies of purchase orders to only those departments (production, distribution, billing) that take direct action based on the information on the order. The efficiency of message routing is often thwarted by individuals who have little or no use for information but require their own record of it "just in case."

In addition to message routing, individuals or organizational units exercise some discretion over the content and distribution of messages to control their workloads, to control distribution that may have perceived undesirable effects to the individual or unit handling the message, or as part of a presentation format. Messages may be delayed, modified, or filtered before being sent to a recipient. For example, customer complaints may be delayed, modified, or filtered as the information moves up the organization. Serious indicators of customer dissatisfaction may be blocked.

The way that data is presented will influence or bias the way it is used and the interpretation of its meaning. Three examples of presentation bias are (a) order and grouping in the presentation; (b) exception selection limits; and (c) selection of graphics layout. Order and grouping of data influence the perception of importance and affect the comparisons a user is likely to make. The selection of exceptions to be reported also causes presentation bias. In exception reporting, only those items that vary from an "acceptable level" by a fixed deviation are presented to the decision-maker. The choice of a limit automatically introduces presentation bias. A third example of potential presentation bias is the layout of graphics. Examples of ways in which bias is introduced are choice of scale, graphic, size, and color.

Information Quality

Even if information is presented in such a way as to be transmitted efficiently and interpreted correctly, it may not be used effectively. The quality of information is determined by how it motivates human action and contributes to effective decision-making. Andrus (1971) suggests that information may be evaluated in terms of utilities that, besides accuracy of the information, may facilitate or retard its use.

1 *Form utility.* As the form of information more closely matches the requirements of the decision-maker, its value increases.
2 *Time utility.* Information has greater value to the decision-maker if it is available when needed.
3 *Place utility* (physical accessibility). Information has greater value if it can be accessed or delivered easily.
4 *Possession utility* (organizational location). The possessor of information strongly affects its value by controlling its dissemination to others.

Given a choice, managers have a strong preference for improvement in quality of information over an increase in quantity. Information varies in quality because of bias or errors. If the bias of the presenter is known to the receiver of the information, he or she can make adjustments. The problem is to detect the bias; the adjustment is generally fairly simple.

Error is a more serious problem because there is no simple adjustment for it. Errors may be a result of incorrect data measurement and collection methods, failure to follow correct processing procedures, loss or nonprocessing of data, wrong recording or correcting of data, use of wrong stored data, mistakes in processing procedure (such as computer program errors), and deliberate falsification.

The difficulties due to bias may be handled in information processing by procedures to detect and measure bias and to adjust for it. The difficulties with errors may be overcome by controls to detect errors, internal and external auditing, adding of "confidence limits" to data, and user instruction in measurement and processing procedures, so they can evaluate possible errors in information.

Value of Information in Decision-making

In decision theory, the value of information is the value of the change in decision behavior caused by the information less the cost of obtaining the information. In other words, given a set of possible decisions, a decision-maker will select one on the basis of the information at hand. If new information causes a different decision to be made, the value of the new information is the difference in value between the outcome of the old decision and that of the new decision, less the cost of obtaining the new information. If new information does not cause a different decision to be made, the value of the new information is zero.

The value of perfect information is computed as the difference between the optimal policy without perfect information and the optimal policy with perfect information. Almost no decisions are made with perfect information because obtaining it would require being able to foresee or control future events. The concept of the value of perfect information is useful, however, because it demonstrates how information has value as it influences (i.e. changes) decisions. The value of information for more than one condition is the difference between the maximum value in the absence of additional information and the maximum expected value with additional information, minus the cost of obtaining it. The maximum expected value can change by a change either in the probabilities for the conditions or in the payoffs associated with them.

The quantitative approach suggests the value of searching for better information, but decisions are usually made without the "right" information. Some reasons are that the needed information is unavailable, acquiring the information is too great an effort or too costly, there is no knowledge of the availability of the information, and the information is not available in the form needed.

Non-decision Value of Information

If the value of information were based only on identified decisions, much of the data that organizations and individuals prepare would not have value. Since the market for information suggests that it does have value, there are other values of information such as motivation, model building, and background building.

Some information is motivational; it provides the persons receiving the information with a report on how well they are doing. This feedback information may motivate decisions, but its connection is often indirect. The information may reinforce an existing understanding or model of the organization. It may provide comforting confirmation that results are within allowable limits. It also aids in learning as individuals receive feedback on the consequences of actions.

The management and operation of an enterprise function with models of the enterprise within the minds of the managers and operations personnel. The models may be simple or complex, correct or incorrect. Information that is received by these individuals may result in change or reinforcement in their mental models. This process is a form of organizational learning and expertise building. Since the models are used in problem-finding, a change in the models will have an influence on identification of problems. The information also communicates organization values and culture, thereby providing a frame of reference for future decisions.

In decision theory, the value of information is the value of the change in decision behavior (less its cost), but the information has value only to those who have the background knowledge to use it in a decision. The most qualified person generally uses information most effectively but may need less information since experience has already reduced uncertainty when compared with the less-experienced decision-maker. Thus, the more-experienced decision-maker may make the same decision for less cost, or a better decision for the same cost, as the less-experienced person. The value of the specific information utilized in a decision cannot be easily separated from the accumulated knowledge of the decision-maker. In other words, much of the knowledge that individuals accumulate and store (or internalize) is not earmarked for any particular decision or problem. A set of accumulated knowledge allows a person to make a better decision, or the same decision at less immediate cost, than one who lacks this expertise.

Application   of   Information   Concepts   to Information Systems

Information theory, although limited in scope, provides useful insights about the surprise value and uncertainty reduction features of some information. It emphasizes the value of information in changing decisions. The idea that information has value only in that it alters a decision provides a useful guideline for parsimony of information. A common mistake in information system design is to produce volumes of data in the form of reports because they are easy to produce. In many cases, the actual value of the additional information is zero.

The theory explains that not all communications have information value, but there is value in redundancy for error control. In management information systems, there is substantial noise in the information being communicated due to the unknown but differing backgrounds of humans, their differing frames of reference, varying prejudices, varying levels of attention, physical differences in ability to hear and see, and other random causes. Redundancy can be effectively used to overcome noise and improve the probability of messages being received and interpreted correctly.

Concepts of message reduction suggest ways to improve sending and receiving efficiency and reduce bias. Summarization and message routing reduce information being communicated. Filtering, inference by use of statistics, and presentation choices may improve efficiency but may also introduce bias. The quality of information received is not directly measurable. However, design can focus on achieving utilities associated with information and on processes to reduce bias and errors.

In decision theory, information is associated with uncertainty because there is a choice to be made and the correct choice is uncertain. The reason for obtaining information is to reduce uncertainty so the correct choice can be made. If there were no uncertainty, there would be no need for information to influence choice. Information received will modify the choice by altering the subjective estimate of the probability of success. The decision theory approach focuses the attention of the information system designer not only on the value of information in decision-making but also on the fact that the cost of obtaining more information may not be worthwhile.

Much data is received and stored without reference to decisions being made. However, the data is meaningful to the recipient and is of real or perceived value in current or prospective decisions. It has value in building mental models and expertise that will be useful in future analysis and decision-making.

Bibliography

Andrus, R. R. (1971). Approaches to information evaluation. *MSU Business Topics*, Summer, 4046.

Cherry, C. (1957). *On Human Communication*. Cambridge, MA: MIT Press.

Gilbert, E. N. (1966). Information theory after eighteen years. *Science*, **152**, 320.

Shannon, C. E. & Weaver, W. (1962). *The Mathematical Theory of Communication*. Urbana, IL: University of Illinois Press.

Weiner, N. (1948). *Cybernetics, or Control and Communication in the Animal and the Machine*. New York: Wiley.

GORDON B. DAVIS

information economics   A management method for evaluating company investments in information technology (IT), it consists of an information technology business value philosophy and a management approach for determining the value of existing IT investments and prospective IT development projects.

The business issue addressed by information economics is how much to invest in information technology (as compared with marketing, new products, or new business acquisitions), and which IT investment will produce the greatest business impact. This is not a new problem. IT investments may include cost-saving automation, management information systems, customer-focused systems, and electronic commerce. In every case, the central problem is to express in business terms how an enterprise can achieve maximum business impact from its investment in information technology.

Traditionally, IT investments and development projects have been assessed with return-on-investment and cost-benefit analysis methods. These work well when the assessment applies to a single organization and the benefits are tangible and easily measured as, for example, when benefits are primarily cost reductions in a single department. Many information technology applications, especially distributed and infrastructure systems, affect multiple organizations, integrate activities across the enterprise, and significantly change how the enterprise does business. As a result, many of the benefits derived from IT projects are intangible relative to cost-benefit analysis.

Traditional cost-benefit analysis is especially difficult when an enterprise must make fundamental IT infrastructure investment decisions. The investments in infrastructure – for example, in networks and databases – are one step removed from the actual business activity that causes reduced cost, improved customer service, or new products and services. For example, a communications network needed to support an automated teller machine (ATM) network for a financial institution by itself cannot reduce operating cost or improve customer service. The network is simply one component of the overall business activity needed for an ATM service. How much should be invested in it? What alternatives should be considered? Should a network be built in-house or outsourced?

Information itself has similar attributes. For example, from a manager's perspective, it is important to have the full customer history available when making decisions in a financial institution. A loan officer can use the history to assess a proposed loan transaction. The IT investment issue is the value of this information and how much the financial institution should invest in providing it.

Information economics evaluates the impact information technology has on the enterprise in four domains:

1 *Financial performance improvement*, such as increased profitability, productivity, and earnings.

2 *Business performance improvement*, based on business measures such as customer satisfaction, product quality, time to market, time to process orders, inventory turns. Management expects that improvements in performance of this type will ultimately be reflected in improved financial performance.

3 *Management's intent to improve business and financial performance*. These are management's goals, objectives, or agendas that must be accomplished for a business unit to meet its business and financial performance measures. Such items can often be stated as critical success factors. Managers expect that achieving their management agendas will ultimately produce improvements in financial performance.

4 *Risk and uncertainty* include items that can affect the cost of the investment (for example, uncertainty or disagreement about development project objectives, or risky new technology) or that can cause conditions leading to project or investment failure (for example, unknown project requirements). When applied to installed IT systems, the items include factors leading to prospective failure or higher than necessary operating costs.

Information economics defines IT investment value in terms of IT contributions to business objectives in the four domains. Managers define specific management factors in each domain. These factors are applied consistently to each IT investment project for the enterprise. Each project is compared to every other project in terms of impact on the business. A business value prioritization of all projects results.

By applying the factors from the four domains to all projects, information economics connects each investment and proposed development project to the management factors for the enterprise in a consistent way. Information economics asks what the effect of each project will be on each management factor (for example, on financial performance) if the investment is made.

Robert J. Benson

information overload Information overload is one extreme of the construct of information *load*. Information load is a continuum in which both underload and overload are detrimental to human performance. When there are too few stimuli, *information underload* ensues and human attention is not maintained. Typical problems studied include those faced by night guards or submarine sonar operators. The other extreme is *information overload*. In these situations, information load is higher than the capacity to cope. Information overload has been researched in the management literature. The main focus of this literature has been decision-making behavior, such as purchasing in marketing and the relationship between amount of information available and satisfaction/performance in management. The implications of information overload for design, operation, and use of some specialized information systems, such as electronic mail, have also been searched.

Psychologists have investigated the construct of information load and not limited research to information overload. They have adopted the term "human mental workload" to include tasks that, besides processing information, pose other demands on the individual. "Mental workload refers to that portion of the operator's limited capacity actually required to perform a particular task" (O'Donnell & Eggemeier, 1986, p. 4). In other words, mental workload is the portion of one's available information-processing resources demanded to accomplish a task. The concepts of underload and overload are important in the design of information system applications. To avoid underload, the task division between the computer and the human should give sufficient stimulus and activity to the human to maintain attention. To avoid overload, systems should be designed with human limits on amounts of information to be processed, and there should be structures, such as hierarchies, to facilitate human processing.

To research information load, the three main workload measurement methods are (a) secondary task method; (b) physiological measures; and (c) subjective ratings. The *secondary task method* requires the subject to perform a second task concurrently in order to assess process demands on the primary task. The most serious drawback of such a method is the intrusive aspect of the secondary task. Certain physiological functions usually show changes when an individual is under higher mental workload. Several functions have been investigated. These include sinus arrhythmia (heart beat rate changes), mean pulse rate, pulse rate variability, respiration rate, and pupil diameter. Although objective and hard to refute, physiological data is difficult to collect in the field or in large quantities in the laboratory. Moreover, special equipment is necessary. Subjective ratings provide generally valid and sensitive measurement. Two validated measurement scales are the subjective workload assessment technique (SWAT), sponsored by the US Air Force and developed by Eggemeier and associates (Eggemeier, 1981), and the NASA-TLX (Task Load Index), developed by Hart and associates (Hart & Staveland, 1988). A review and assessment of these methods can be found in Nygren (1991).

Bibliography

Eggemeier, F. T. (1981). Current issues in subjective assessment of workload, *Proceedings of the Human Factors Society 25th Annual Meeting*, pp. 513–17. Santa Monica, CA: Human Factors Society.

Hart, S. G. & Staveland, L. E. (1988). Development of NASA-TLX (Task Load Index): results of empirical and theoretical research, in P. Hancock and N. Meshkati (eds.), *Advances in Psychology*, vol. 52, pp. 139–84. Amsterdam: North Holland.

Nygren, T. (1991). Psychometric properties of subjective workload measurement techniques: implications for their use in the assessment of perceived mental workload. *Human Factors*, 33, 17–33.

O'Donnell, R. & Eggemeier, T. (1986). Workload assessment methodology, in K. Boff, L. Kaufman and J. Thomas (eds), *Handbook of Perception and Human Performance*, Vol. II, ch. 42, New York: Wiley.

ROBERT EVARISTO

information retrieval   Critical to the research process are those activities in which existing, published information is gathered, analyzed, and used in some manner. The process of transferring information through various formal channels – from book or journal publication to speeches at conferences or preprint reports of research - is well understood today. Now, these various options or channels for collecting and reporting information are being challenged by the increasing use of informal methods of sharing information: self-publishing or use of the INTERNET listserves, for example, which may result in a destabilizing impact on this system.

Traditional information transfer processes begin with the generation of research or data: from the government, private groups or publicly funded sources such as higher education or government departments. As a critical part of traditional research, reports of work are shared with colleagues at various stages in the research process (as preprints, seminars, speeches at conferences, etc.) for critiques and input. Much of the information is accessible to subsequent researchers through indexes, databases, conference proceedings, etc. Primary publication in the form of journal articles, research reports or other mechanisms follows. Secondary publication – summaries in books or research review sources – follows, usually at about a year after primary publication. At this point, indexes, bibliographies, library catalogs and other organizational means are available to help identify and access these works or ideas.

Today, online databases, the Internet, and other channels have collapsed this process and have made the identification of research-in-progress much easier. Databases of stock data or corporate activities can help identify organizational shifts or anticipate product announcements when used by trained specialists. Full-text versions of major newspapers, industry newsletters, government reports, securities filings, journals, and even press releases have grown with the shift to an information-centered economy. This results in much more information being made easily available, but increases the need for sound judgment and careful study to avoid unnecessary work or to overlook critical information.

Analyzing Information Needs

Given the glut of information available today, finding intelligent ways to navigate through all this data to gain the information needed is essential. The following questions may be asked. Do you need a particular document/resource/specialist or are you looking for a specific piece of information instead? Do you need background information or only a particular statistic? Are you looking to ultimately develop a perspective or make a decision concerning some issue or are you hoping, more generally, to scan the environment for new developments in some particular area? Is this comprehensive, retrospective information that you need or a time-bound update (e.g. everything in the past two weeks)?

In order to get the information needed, an individual must clearly understand the dimensions of information need. Formulating a search strategy may be done by an individual, possibly aided by an information professional who assists in framing search questions.

What Information Sources are Available

A second critical area is understanding what information may be available to help you answer a question. Does the information already exist? Is this something that some industry group or the government might track? Are the companies involved private or public? Would some of the information be mandated and kept by the government or other agencies? If trend data is needed, perhaps industry analysts or trade publications would be good sources. This is another area in which working closely with subject experts or information professionals can be helpful.

Data Gathering

Much data today is available in electronic format, making the process of gathering and organizing information much easier; however, many critical resources, including human experts, still require other methods of contact. Sophisticated database and information management programs can help to index information, create spreadsheets or to give free-text searching access to huge files. Many source databases are still very expensive to access and the use of subject experts or information professionals at this stage is often critical.

Analyzing and Valuing Information

Analyzing the information that is found will help in identifying gaps for further research, make initial conclusions about your subject and may point out disparities or problems with available information. For example, estimates and projections from industry analysts may vary greatly, requiring an investigator to carefully re-examine what and how each expert evaluated their subjects. Often information is given by un-named or unknown sources so that the validity of the data cannot be carefully checked.

Current Awareness or Selected Dissemination of Information

In the past 15 years a common service of database vendors and information centers has been the on-demand, ongoing provision of regular updates of information on specified topics. This allows researchers to get updated information from specified resources or databases on a regular basis. This is generally done once an initial, comprehensive search has been performed so that subsequent searches can target those points/issues/questions most critical and use only those databases or other resources deemed to be most relevant. Public libraries in major cities, research libraries and private information brokers all provide information services today and should be contacted for information before starting any major research effort involving secondary or published information.

Bibliography

Brownstone, D. M. (1979). *Where to Find Business Information: A Worldwide Guide.* New York: Wiley.

Daniells, L. M. (1993). *Business Information Sources,* 3rd edn. Berkeley, CA: University of California Press.

Encyclopedia of Business Information Sources (1995–6). Detroit: Gale Press.

Kantor, P. B. (1994). Information retrieval techniques. *Annual Review of Information Science and Technology,* **29**, 53–90.

Lancaster, F. W. & Warner, A. J. (1993). *Information Retrieval Today.* Arlington, VA: Information Resources Press.

Salton, G. & McGill, M. J. (1983). *Introduction to Modern Information Retrieval.* New York: McGraw-Hill.

Stanfill, C. & Waltz, D. L. (1992). Statistical methods, artificial intelligence and information retrieval, in P. S. Jacobs (ed.), *Text-based Intelligent Systems: Current Research and Practice in Information Extraction and Retrieval,* 215–25. Hillsdale, NJ: Lawrence Erlbaum Associates.

Strauss, D. W. (1988). *Handbook of Business Information: A Guide for Librarians, Students and Researchers.* Englewood, CO: Libraries Unlimited.

NANCY K. HERTHER

information system methodologies   An information system development life-cycle (SDLC) establishes a structured set of activities for developing and implementing information system applications. The set of methods to be applied are termed a "methodology."

Information System Life-cycle

In common with other complex artifacts, an information system goes through a life-cycle (a term adopted from biological sciences). While the life-cycle view is widely accepted, there are varying opinions about the breakdown of this life-cycle into stages (or phases). One example of the breakdown of an information system life-cycle has been used by an international task group (IFIP Working Group 8.1 Design and Evaluation of Information Systems) (Olle et al., 1991). This life-cycle identifies the following twelve stages.

1 Strategic study
2 Information systems planning
3 Business analysis
4 System design
5 Construction design
6 Construction and workbench test
7 Installation
8 Test of installed system
9 Operation
10 Evolution
11 Phase out
12 Post mortem

In an attempt to be more specific, broad terms such as "development" and "implementation" are not used in this breakdown. Development covers roughly the stages from 3 to 6. Implementation covers either the stages 5 and 6 or else 7 and 8, depending on the use of the term.

A *strategic study* is the preliminary stage in which it is determined whether new information systems are needed at this time and if so how to proceed. *Information systems planning* is a stage which covers a large business area (possibly the whole enterprise) and includes a broad analysis of information requirements. On the basis of this stage, it is possible to subdivide the business area for more detailed analysis.

The *business analysis* stage is the one in which the business is analyzed in detail to determine which business activities are performed and the detailed information requirements of each. Business analysis is more concerned with the

business than with considerations of computer hardware and software. *System design* covers the specification of the external features of the system (the users' view). It is independent of any considerations attributable to the construction tools that are to be used to build the system.

Construction tools may not be selected until the system design is completed. *Construction design* is concerned with the system internals (which the users do not see). Furthermore, construction design depends heavily on the construction tools to be used. The term construction is used in preference to programming because, with recent advances in technology, programming is only one of a number of alternative ways of constructing the computerized part of an information system. It is already commercially viable for a system to be constructed automatically from the system design specifications.

The *evolution stage* is being recognized as of increasing importance and various distinct approaches exist for changing a system after it has been in the operational stage for some time. Typical distinct approaches are referred to as restructuring, re-engineering, and reverse engineering.

Information Systems Methodology

Just as there are many different views of the information systems life-cycle, so there are many different views on how one should progress through the life-cycle toward an operational information system. Many approaches have been the subject of considerable formalization (usually not in the mathematical sense). The term *methodology* is used to refer to such an approach. It is noted that this term is etymologically incorrect since "methodology" strictly speaking means "a study of methods." For this reason, some approaches carry the name "method", but the majority prefer "methodology."

Most methodologies cover only a few stages in the information systems life-cycle. The stages in the above information systems life-cycle which have received the most attention from methodology designers are business analysis, system design, and construction design. However, the information systems planning stage and the evolution stage are also supported in some methodologies.

Each information system methodology uses a number of techniques. Examples of techniques are data flow diagraming and data structure diagraming. It should be noted that the term methodology is occasionally applied to a single technique. Many methodologies are referred to as system development methodologies. This usually indicates that the methodology covers the construction design stage and an activity preceding that which is often labeled "requirements definition" or "requirements specification." This view of the life-cycle either combines (or fails to differentiate between) the business analysis stage and the system design stage.

Information systems methodologies have their origins in different aspects of data-processing technology. Some methodologies spring from a programming language background and emphasize the processing that needs to be carried out by the computerized information system. Others have evolved from the use of DATABASE MANAGEMENT SYSTEMS. These methodologies focus more heavily on the data used in the business area and on a database that is central to the design of the system. Techniques based on preparing models of the data (see DATA MODELING, LOGICAL) are extensively used in this context. More recently, there have been claims that representations of events in the business and events that happen in the computerized system must be incorporated in a successful methodology. These various views are now converging and it is increasingly recognized that a good methodology should be able to support all of the three perspectives of data, process, and events.

Bibliography

Olle, T. W., Hagelstein, J., Macdonald, I. G., Rolland, C., Sol, H. G., van Assche, F. M. J. & Verrijn-Stuart, A. A. (1991). *Information Systems Methodologies: A Framework for Understanding*, 2nd edn. Reading, MA: Addison-Wesley.

T. WILLIAM OLLE

information system stage hypothesis The stage model for information systems was first published in the early 1970s (Nolan, 1973;

Gibson & Nolan, 1974). This model was presented as a description of information systems growth in organizations. Nolan initially hypothesized that an organization moves through four stages in the development of its computing resource. This hypothesis was based on Nolan's observation that the computing budget over time for three firms was approximately S-shaped. He stated that the points of inflection in the curve indicate the transition between stages. The four stages were named initiation, contagion, control, and integration.

Stage 1, *initiation*, is the introduction of computing into the organization, where the computing investment is treated like any other capital investment, and there is usually excess computing capacity *vis-à-vis* the initial computing applications. Stage 2, *contagion*, is a period of unplanned, rapid growth as users become aware of the potential benefits from computing. As there are few formal controls over the computing resource at this point, the result is a steep rise in computing expenditures for hardware, software, and personnel. Senior management concern about burgeoning IS costs results in stage 3, where formal *controls*, such as budgets, charge-out and project management, are implemented. Often an overemphasis on control occurs and there is a failure to exploit information systems fully. Eventually, the organization reaches stage 4, *integration*, where it has settled many of the issues for managing the computing resource. Growth in the computing budget begins to level off.

In subsequent papers, Nolan modified the model in a number of ways. He noted that the growth in the computing budget did not level off at the integration stage, but that it continued to grow. He included two additional stages after integration: data administration and maturity, to accommodate the then new database technology (Nolan, 1979). In this expanded model, stage 4 (*integration*) marks the transition from management of computing resources to management of organizational data resources. At the beginning of stage 4, database and data communications have transformed key applications, and users experience significant increase in benefits from computing. User demand for information systems again escalates. Stage 5, *data administration*, therefore sees rapid growth in the computing budget, which eventually levels off in stage 6, *maturity*, when the applications portfolio is completed.

Benchmarks for characterizing each stage were also proposed. In addition to IT expenditure, there were also benchmarks for technology, applications portfolio, data processing (DP) organization, DP planning and control, and user awareness (Nolan, 1979). The model also evolved from being primarily descriptive to being used for prescription as well. For example, Nolan proposed using the model to identify the organization's stage of computing development, and to apply the appropriate amount of management slack or control.

The model has, however, been the subject of several critiques (Benbasat et al., 1984; King & Kraemer, 1984). A major criticism has been the lack of empirical support. Empirical studies by other researchers have not supported the existence of an S-shaped budget curve, nor the benchmarks for each stage. It appears that the maturity criteria do not always move together; for example, "mature" IS organizations did not have more formalized data administration procedures, while increased user awareness did not correlate with reduced problems.

None the less, the Nolan model was popular, particularly with practitioners, as it boldly and broadly framed the complex phenomenon of computing development within organizations. It is also noteworthy for proposing testable hypotheses, and for generating debate within the field.

Bibliography

Benbasat, I., Dexter, A. S., Drury, D. H. & Goldstein, R. C. (1984). A critique of the stage hypothesis: theory and empirical evidence. *Communications of the ACM*, **27**, 476–85.
Gibson, C. F. & Nolan, R. L. (1974). Managing the four stages of EDP growth. *Harvard Business Review*, **52**, 76–88.
King, J. L. & Kraemer, K. L. (1984). Evolution and organizational information systems: an assessment of Nolan's stage model. *Communications of the ACM*, **27**, 466–75.
Nolan, R. L. (1973). Managing the computer resource: a stage hypothesis. *Communications of the ACM*, **16**, 399–405.
Nolan, R. L. (1979). Managing the crisis in data processing. *Harvard Business Review*, **57**, 115–26.

CHRISTINA SOH

information theory   Information theory is usually used to refer to the mathematical theory of communication. It is a much narrower concept than the common use of information (*see* INFORMATION CONCEPTS). Information theory was developed by the mathematician Norbert Weiner in connection with his study of cybernetics. Claude Shannon of Bell Laboratories developed and applied these concepts to the telephone system. As used in the mathematical theory of communication, information has a very precise meaning. It is the average number of binary digits that must be transmitted to identify a given message from the set of all possible messages to which it belongs. If there is a limited number of possible messages, a different code may be used to identify each message. Messages can be defined in a variety of ways. An alphanumeric character may be a message, or complete sentences may be messages if there is a limited, predefined number of possible sentences to be transmitted.

The size of the code is dependent on the coding scheme and the number of possible messages. The coding scheme for information theory is assumed to be binary. This means that one bit (with a value of either 0 or 1) can distinguish between two messages. If there are eight possible messages, three bits must be transmitted, since there are eight combinations of 0 and 1 for the three bits. These examples assume that all messages are equally likely. If the messages, such as letters of the alphabet, are not equally likely, then codes of differing lengths may be used.

The information content of a message is the minimum number of bits that must be transmitted in order to identify the message being sent from all possible messages that could be sent. In the theory, information reduces uncertainty. Given a set of messages, the receiver does not know which one is to be selected until information is received. The theory also indicates the value of redundancy. Additional codes not required for the essential message can be used to reconstruct the message when part of the coding is lost in communication.

Although information theory is most directly applied to the development of codes for communications, the underlying concepts can be useful in information processing systems. For example, information tells the receivers something they did not know, information has surprise value, and redundant coding prevents misunderstanding by the recipient losing or not receiving some of the coding.

GORDON B. DAVIS

innovation and information technology

An *innovation* is something new to the adopter. It may be a new idea, a new thing, or a new method. Organizations search for innovations because (a) something needs to be changed; and (b) the change is directed at improving performance. Here, the target of the information technology (IT) innovation is assumed to be the improvement of work and management processes in organizations. An IT innovation proceeds through stages.

The General Stages of IT Innovation

Based upon more than 3,000 studies, Rogers (1983) identified five general stages through which all innovations proceed: (a) knowledge; (b) persuasion; (c) decision; (d) implementation;

Table 1   The Information Technology Innovation Process

Stage	*Definition*
Initiation	
Process	Scanning of organizational challenges and IT solutions occurs. Change arises from need-based pull or technology-based push
Product	A match between an IT solution and organizational need is found
Adoption	
Process	Rational and political negotiations are undertaken to obtain organizational backing for implementation of the IT application
Product	A decision is made to invest organizational resources in the IT application
Adaptation	
Process	The IT application is developed and installed; work and management processes are revised; training in the new processes and IT application is provided
Product	The IT application is available for use in the organization
Acceptance	
Process	Organizational members are encouraged to commit to the usage of the IT application
Product	The IT application is employed in the work of the organization
Use	
Process	Usage of the IT application within the new work and management processes is encouraged as a normal activity
Product	The IT application is no longer perceived as out of the ordinary
Incorporation	
Process	Increased organizational effectiveness is obtained by using the IT application in a more comprehensive and integrated manner to support work and management processes that are beyond the initial goals of the application
Product	The IT application is used to the fullest potential within the organization

and (e) confirmation. Rogers' definition was developed from the perspective of the individual adopter. It also provides a reasonable description of innovation at organizational level.

To understand Rogers' process, consider a voice-recognition technology for data encoding and how this potential innovation goes from an unknown entity to a functioning part of organizational processes. At the outset (*knowledge*), an individual must become aware of the existence and operational characteristics of the voice-recognition technology. *Persuasion* occurs as an individual forms favorable or unfavorable attitudes toward the technology. *Decision* occurs when an individual engages in evaluative activities required to make an adoption or rejection decision about the technology. Assuming adoption has occurred, *implementation* starts when the technology is put into continuous use. Finally, in *confirmation*, the individual seeks reinforcement of the adoption decision from others in the organization. If the value of the technology is confirmed, continued usage follows; if not confirmed, the individual may reverse the adoption decision.

The Specific Stages of IT Innovation

Starting with the work of Kwon and Zmud (1987), information systems researchers have further articulated the IT innovation process. As defined in table 1, this work modifies Rogers' process in four ways. First, it explicitly recognizes that IT innovations involve both organizational and individual behaviors. Secondly, it provides more details about each stage. Thirdly, it recognizes that there is a process and a product associated with each stage. The process describes the activities that occur within a stage; the product, the outcome of each stage.

The fourth modification redefines and extends the stages from five to six. The revised stages are: (a) initiation; (b) adoption; (c) adaptation; (d) acceptance; (e) use; and (f) infusion. *Initiation* combines Rogers' stages of *knowledge* and *persuasion*. This recognizes that the acquisition and interpretation of basic facts about a potential IT innovation are integrated activities. Rogers' *decision* stage is equivalent to *adoption* and *adaptation*. This change emphasizes that an IT innovation requires political support and resource allocation, as well as technical development and process re-

engineering. *Acceptance* and *use* equate with Rogers' *implementation* and *confirmation* stages. The logic is that the change process, including organizational confirmation, should be managed. Finally, *infusion* is added to recognize that an IT innovation often has many applications beyond the initial *adoption* and *adaptation*.

Bibliography

Kwon, T. & Zmud, R. W. (1987). Unifying the fragmented models of information systems implementation in R. J. Boland and R. A. Hirschheim (eds), *Critical Issues in Information Systems Research*, 251–67. New York: John Wiley.

Rogers, E. M. (1983). *The Diffusion of Innovations*, 3rd edn. New York: Free Press.

NORMAN L. CHERVANY
and SUSAN A. BROWN

input devices   Input devices accept data or information from outside the computer and convert it to a form the computer can manipulate. Input devices and their counterpart output devices typically do not include storage devices, such as disks and tapes, that allow the storage of data that is external or secondary to the central processing unit (CPU) and its primary memory. Secondary storage devices must perform input and output (I/O) operations, but because their primary purpose is to store data, they are typically considered separately (*see* COMPUTER STORAGE, TELECOMMUNICATION). Other devices that perform input and output functions are communications devices.

In the early days of data processing most input was done using a keypunch machine and 80 column computer cards. Data entry clerks transcribed the data from a source document onto the cards by using a keyboard similar to that of a standard typewriter. The cards were then fed into a card reader, which converted the data into machine-readable form. While the cards have become obsolete, the keyboard remains a primary input mechanism.

Today, most data is entered directly into the computer by using the keyboard. The basic keyboard layout is virtually unchanged from that of the first manual typewriters. This type of keyboard is also known as the QWERTY keyboard, based on the first six characters on the left of the top row of letters. A modern keyboard is generally divided into five different areas. The first area, alphanumeric keys, includes all the letters of the alphabet, as well as the numerical digits from 0 through 9. It also includes punctuation mark keys and operational keys such as Tab, Backspace, Shift, Caps Lock, Enter (or Return), and the Spacebar. Many keyboards also have a variety of "Shift" keys that change the operation of the standard keys. For example, pressing the "E" key along with the "Ctrl" key creates a keystroke or character that is different from the upper or lower case "E". The "Alt" key is a similar shift key.

The second area consists of the function keys, usually located across the top or to the left of the keyboard. These keys enable the user to perform a specific function by pressing the appropriate key. Most of the functions performed are controlled by the application software, and vary from program to program. However, there are a few standard function keys which perform the same action independent of the application software (e.g. Escape). For example, combining the Shift key with the F7 key creates the Shift-F7 keystroke which in Microsoft Word invokes the Thesaurus, while the same keystroke in WordPerfect prints the document.

The numeric keypad is laid out similar to a 10-key adding machine. This facilitates the entry of large amounts of numerical data. It is generally located on the right side of the keyboard, but may be a keypad separate from the rest of the keyboard. The layout of the telephone keypad and the 10-key are different, so that the integration of the telephone and the computer will require some compromises.

The fourth section of the keyboard contains the cursor-movement keys. These keys, as the name implies, permit the user to move the cursor up, down, left, or right around the screen. Depending on the key selected, the cursor can move as little as one character or as much as one page or more. Finally, indicator (or toggle-switch) lights show the status of certain features which can be set by specific keys. These include the Num Lock, Caps Lock, and Scroll Lock keys.

There is an increasing number of specialized keyboards available for individuals who find it difficult to use the traditional keyboard. This includes those who incur repetitive stress injuries or carpal tunnel syndrome from long periods of time spent at the keyboard. Ergonomically designed keyboards that fold or split in the middle offer a more natural position for the hands and those with wrist rests provide additional support. One-handed keyboards, keyguards, and keyboards equipped with sip-and-puff straws are other examples of available assistive technologies.

While the keyboard gives the user a powerful and flexible tool for working with the computer, it can also be cumbersome, especially if the user is a slow or inaccurate typist. To increase the speed and effectiveness of user–computer interaction, a variety of pointing devices have been developed. These devices generally allow the user to execute commands by literally pointing at the screen and pressing a button. Common pointing devices include the mouse, trackballs, light pens, and joysticks.

Perhaps the most familiar pointing device is the mouse. It is standard equipment with almost every personal computer sold today. The mouse is a small, handheld device that is linked to the cursor on the screen. As the mouse is moved around, the cursor moves also. By manipulating the mouse, the user can position the cursor (or some other object) to the desired location. One or more buttons on the mouse increase the range of options available to the user. Depending on the application program, a mouse can be used to select and execute a large number of actions. With the proliferation of graphical user interfaces (GUI) the mouse has become a required tool. Selecting an item on the screen can be done by moving the cursor to that location and clicking a mouse button.

Similar in function to the mouse is a device called the trackball. The trackball is basically an upside-down mouse. It is a small ball, fixed in position on or near the keyboard. The cursor moves as the ball is rotated in place. Trackballs tend to be used with portable or laptop computers. Another pointing device is a light-sensitive tool shaped like a pen. Called light pens, these devices are placed directly on the screen at the desired location. By pressing a button on the pen, the user can select an item, highlight a menu choice, manipulate graphic objects, or even draw on the screen. Light pens are useful in graphic-intensive work or in situations where a keyboard would be impractical, such as dirty or dusty environments. Generally found with personal computers, joysticks are used like a mouse to position the cursor on the display screen and select items or commands. Initially developed for use with game applications, joysticks are also used more and more in industrial and medical applications.

The slowest link in data entry has historically been the human entering the data. One method used to speed up this process is source data automation which uses a variety of input devices to capture the desired data related to an event in machine-readable form at the time and place the event occurs. Common methods of source data automation are magnetic ink character recognition, magnetic tape strips, and optical character recognition.

Magnetic ink character recognition (MICR) begins with documents being encoded with characters printed in a special magnetic ink. By processing these documents through MICR readers, the information can be captured and entered directly into the computer. MICR technology is used mainly for high-volume document processing, such as check processing by financial institutions. The checks are pre-printed with identifying information (the bank's routing and transit number, the customer's account number, and the check number). When the bank receives a check the amount is then printed on the check in magnetic ink. As the check is processed, this information is used to update the customer's account and the bank's records. Magnetic tape strips are short lengths of magnetic tape encoded with data. The strips are passed through devices which read the data and forward it for processing. The most common examples of this technology are the magnetic strips on credit cards and ATM cards.

Optical character recognition (OCR) devices scan images and translate the data into machine-readable form. The three general types of OCR devices are scanners, bar codes readers, and digitizer tablets. Scanners transform images, either print or pictures, into digital form that the computer can process. This is done by converting areas of light and dark into digits. By literally mapping the digits (bitmapping), the computer can recreate, store, and manipulate or edit data from the source document being scanned. There are two main types of scanners:

flatbed and handheld. Flatbed scanners are similar to office copiers, with the source document being fed into the scanner. Handheld scanners must be moved manually over the source document. Companies that handle large amounts of documents or correspondence, such as insurance companies or law firms, find scanners are particularly useful when used in conjunction with document imaging systems. These systems create digitized images of documents, significantly reducing paper-shuffling by allowing firms to store, retrieve, and edit the document images through computer terminals or networks. This also allows multiple users access to the same document, eliminating time spent requesting, searching, and transferring a paper document.

Bar codes are specially designed patterns of lines which are typically used to identify an item or product. By varying the width of the bars and the distance between them, a large amount of data can be represented. One example of bar codes is the universal product code (UPC), which is used on items in grocery and retail stores. By reading the bar codes with a special scanner, inventory, movement, and price data can be captured and processed. Other uses of bar codes include railroad cars, library books, inventory, and next-day delivery packages.

Digitizer tablets, or pen-and-tablet devices, transform handwritten data into machine-readable form. A special pen is used to write on a sensing surface which digitizes the input. These devices can be used to write, draw, or manipulate the screen cursor. They are useful in graphics applications and some inventory control and tracking situations. Substantial improvements have been made that allow the computer to convert the handwritten information into the appropriate corresponding computer character.

There are other devices used to input data into a computer system. With touch screens, a user touches a video monitor to enter commands or retrieve information. By touching the screen, the user's finger interferes with a fine mesh of light beams that crisscross the computer screen thereby allowing the computer to determine where the user is touching the screen. Touch-screen systems are used often in retail stores and financial institutions in devices called kiosks where users make queries.

Voice input devices change the spoken word into machine-readable form. These devices are still in their infancy, have limited though growing vocabularies, and often require the user to "train" the computer to recognize certain words. Still, voice input provides a quick, simple, and natural way to input data. It is also very useful for individuals who cannot use more traditional input devices.

Analog/digital sensors are becoming more commonly used as input devices. Used in a variety of, scientific, industrial, and medical applications, sensors can monitor environmental or other conditions and feed the data directly to a computer for storage and analysis. The analog inputs, such as temperature or time, are converted to digital signals and processed by the computer.

With the advent of MULTIMEDIA computers, video and audio sources can be used as input. Using the appropriate software, laser disks, VCRs, audio cassettes, and CDs can be used as input sources. The VCR or audio player becomes the input device and transmits the data to the computer.

Virtual reality (VR) systems, while still in their infancy, are becoming more sophisticated. VR systems employ advanced technology to heighten HUMAN–COMPUTER INTERACTION by giving the user the feeling of immersion in a simulated environment. Input devices include data gloves, motion detectors, and pressure sensors which communicate user movement and actions to the computer. Areas using VR applications include airlines and the military (flight simulators and training), medicine (video fibers and microtools can be inserted into a body, allowing doctors to internally examine and treat patients without large incisions), and the entertainment industry.

As computer technology becomes part of consumer products and services, more natural and easy-to-use user interfaces will be needed. Input devices will become more sophisticated with less entry from keyboard and mouse and more entry with microphones and touch screens. Interacting with a computer will become more natural for users.

DENNIS ADAMS and TIM GOLES

insurance industry use of computers An insurance company accepts funds in exchange for a promise to return even more later if specified conditions occur. This process requires information on risks in order to set premium rates and record keeping for policies.

Traditional uses of computers in insurance company operations range from the standard payroll and accounting systems to highly specialized actuarial programs. Property and liability insurers use automated systems to assist with policy processing of automobile, home, and commercial lines of business. The entire policy life-cycle of underwriting and issuing a policy to sending bills through processing claims is supported by specialized computer systems. In addition, the determination of what to charge for coverage and the classification of insureds into risk classes are done with the assistance of computers. The large amount of raw data that must be processed to develop effective rating information is ideally suited for computer processing.

With policies that are in force for the lifetime of an insured, life insurance companies use computer systems to maintain information about insureds and their policies, process premium receipts, and pay claims. Since investment income is a significant portion of the profit for insurance companies, computer systems are used for monitoring investment portfolios. Besides individual life insurance policies, life insurance companies process annuities, retirement accounts, and group policies.

Health insurers use computer systems to support health insurance policies for groups and individuals. With prompt, efficient, and correct claims payments as an important company goal, computer systems are used for determining the validity of medical claims, monitoring for overcharges and unnecessary medical expenses, and issuing claim checks when appropriate. Many health insurers take advantage of ELECTRONIC DATA INTERCHANGE (EDI) and are processing claims in a paperless fashion. The doctor or hospital electronically submits the patient's bill through a service company to the insurance company. The company processes the claim and provides payment for covered costs directly to the medical provider. Some insurers monitor claims and other health care bills submitted through the use of an EXPERT SYSTEM or similar computer system that checks the claims for unnecessary or duplicate charges.

Insurance agents, whether associated with only one insurer or independent of a specific insurance company, are heavy users of computer technology. Agents use computer systems to provide potential customers with insurance cost quotes and policy illustrations. A database of existing customers and potential customers may be kept. This can then be used for "prospecting" to help people identify additional insurance needs and provide service. Agents serve as the customer's main contact point with the insurance company and are usually called upon to provide customer service. Some insurers provide agents with a system that will allow them to collect application information online, process the application, and issue the policy immediately.

Expert systems are being used to speed up processing in several areas of insurance company operations. Beyond their usage in evaluating health claims, expert systems are used to underwrite auto, property, life, and health insurance. Based on information from the application, the system requests additional information if needed. In most cases the system can determine automatically whether the policy should be issued and its pricing. Expert systems are also used in risk assessments for large commercial accounts. Using questions from an expert system, risk managers analyze exposures and identify steps to eliminate or reduce them. Insurance applications can require that customers provide answers to a detailed collection of questions. However, the questions to be answered vary depending on the answers to previous questions. Expert systems are used to automate the application process and ensure that all necessary questions have been answered before the application is submitted to the underwriters.

Insurance companies are among the most successful users of imaging and workflow management technology. By using these technologies, the use of paper is reduced, document tracking is improved, and processing cycles are reduced. An insurance company must build and maintain a file of all information received or sent about a policy or claim. Through the use of imaging technology, access is improved and storage space reduced.

The Internet and the World Wide Web are used by some insurance companies. Home pages on the Web provide information about the company and its products, and furnish name, address and phone number of local agents.

KEVIN STOLARICK

integrated services digital network   ISDN is a digital communications service over the telephone network. It provides higher transmission rates than an ordinary telephone service. An ISDN can, for example, support two voice connections or simultaneous transmission of voice and data. Narrow-band ISDN operates over existing telephone systems; broad-band ISDN requires higher-capacity fiberoptic systems. A narrow-band ISDN provides two 64 kilobyte per second "B channels" for data or voice and one "D channel" for signaling. ISDN is important in information systems because it provides higher transmission rates between computers and also allows online applications between users communicating by voice and working with displays of data being transmitted.

GORDON B. DAVIS

interface   The intersection between two systems or two subsystems. For example, in computer applications, the display screen is an interface between the application and the user.

Internet   Defined as a *network of networks*, in essence the Internet is used to link computer networks with other computer networks, with few limitations on the distance between networks, the number of computer networks linked together, or the number of computers on each linked network. From a functional perspective, people frequently think of the Internet in terms of the services it provides, e.g. ELECTRONIC MAIL, file transfers, or browsing the WORLD WIDE WEB. In order to understand the Internet, it is necessary to understand a bit about its history, its present, and what many people think is its future.

The Internet has grown tremendously over the past decade, particularly over the past few years. In 1995 it was estimated that 10 million Americans used the Internet. It was further estimated that the number would grow to 16 million by 1996. These figures are in stark contrast to the Internet of the 1980s, which was used by a few research universities and companies for communication purposes.

The Internet evolved as a result of a number of factors. In the late 1970s there occurred a growing use of smaller, less expensive computers to meet business needs instead of the larger, more expensive mainframes. Over time, networks of smaller computers (called LOCAL AREA NETWORKS or LANs) began to service small businesses or business units. Communication across greater distances (beyond the technical capabilities of LANs) was handled by the wide area network (or WAN). Unfortunately, LAN software was frequently designed for particular types of computers, and two different types of LAN software would not talk with one another (termed incompatibility). In addition, WANs and LANs did not speak the same language. Thus, while companies were saving money through the use of less expensive technology, communication problems among and between businesses were common.

During the 1970s and 1980s, the US Department of Defense also was interested in this problem for a number of reasons, not the least of which was a means for military installations to share information reliably in the event of a nuclear war (even if some computers on the network were inoperable). The Advanced Research Projects Agency (ARPA) was given the task of coming up with a network technology which would reliably allow for the efficient communication and exchange of information across great distances. As a result of this research, ARPA developed a technology called packet switching which allowed information to be routed across a network in the form of small addressed packets which were then reassembled into a coherent whole on the receiving end. This differed dramatically from the way information was traditionally sent, i.e. setting up a temporary circuit established for the duration of the communication. With packet switching, multiple messages could be sent to different locations at the same time over one or several communication routes without confusion. A key component of the packet switching software was a set of protocols termed TCP/IP, which was short for transmission control protocol/internet protocol.

By 1982, a network prototype was established which serviced a few dozen corporate and academic research sites. Since this time, many types of Internet software have evolved, including e-mail, File Transfer Protocol, Gopher, Telnet, and the World Wide Web. In all instances, these types of software are concerned with the transmission of information or files. As the Internet has evolved, the type and form of this information has become increasingly complex. Now, using modern Internet applications, information as rich and complex as full motion videos with sound can easily be transferred across vast distances.

The original set of Internet users were primarily scientists and researchers, and the Internet applications reflected this user group. Primary functions were directed at sending simple messages between locations, as well as documents or other files which were then opened or used at the recipient's end. From this beginning, the Internet has evolved to include applications such as online journals and magazines, interactive catalogs, electronic banking, database retrieval, financial reporting, inventory tracking, career placement services, as well as online entertainment such as games and movies (and this list is far from inclusive). As bandwidth increases (that is, as the pipe for carrying the data gets larger), and computer applications associated with the Internet become more powerful, more Internet functions will become possible.

MARK A. FULLER

interorganizational systems Traditionally, information systems were constructed to serve the needs of a single organization. Opportunities soon emerged for companies with information systems to tie trading partners together in new and innovative ways (Kaufman, 1966). Such systems are called *interorganizational systems* (IOS). The popularity of ELECTRONIC DATA INTERCHANGE (EDI) in most major industries and in many government operations is part of the reason for the interest in IOS, but EDI is just one form of IOS.

In 1989, Peter Drucker envisioned a future wherein "businesses will integrate themselves into the world economy through alliances." Drucker cites, as one of the reasons for this, that technology is moving so quickly that it is impossible for businesses to keep up with it without forming strategic alliances with other businesses, as well as with noncommercial entities such as universities and governments. Later, he notes that businesses in the future will follow two new rules: "One: to move work where the people are, rather than people to where the work is. Two: to farm out activities that do not offer advancement into fairly senior management and professional positions" (Drucker, 1989). He points out that neither of these two important trends would be reasonable options without the enabling and facilitating effects of computer and communication technologies.

Strategic Outsourcing

The second of Drucker's new rules is termed "strategic outsourcing" by Quinn and Hilmer (1994, p. 43). They suggest that if firms concentrate on their own unique "core competencies" and strategically outsource those for which the firm has neither a strategic need nor special capabilities, managers can leverage their firm's resources and skills for increased competitiveness. They cite examples such as Nike Inc., which outsources 100 percent of its shoe production. Nike prospers, they say, by focusing on research and development and marketing, distribution and sales, with all functions coordinated by a state-of-the-art marketing information system. They note that while many companies look at outsourcing only as a way of reducing short-term direct costs, a strategic outsourcing (or partnership) approach can yield significant additional benefits such as lower long-term capital investments and a leveraging of core competencies.

Some of the new management approaches necessary to obtain the benefits of strategic outsourcing arrangements include a much more professional purchasing and contracting group to deal with supplier selection, relations and management, and a greatly enhanced logistics

information system "to track and evaluate vendors, coordinate transportation activities, and manage transactions and materials movements from the vendors' hands to the customers" (Quinn & Hilmer, 1994, p. 54). Quinn and Hilmer demonstrate that business partnerships and alliances can come into being as a result of a "strategic outsourcing" decision and be supported and facilitated by EDI and other techniques of electronic commerce.

McGee and Prusack (1993) label the approach "pursuing cooperative advantage in a world of electronic commerce." They note that one approach to cooperative systems is to attempt to "lock in" customers by making it difficult or expensive to switch from one technologically supported business process to another. On the other hand, they note that EDI systems are more often pursued by trading partners in a cooperative mode, in an attempt to obtain mutual benefit from streamlining the business processes that their companies share.

Information Partnerships

Konsynski and McFarlan (1990, p. 114) identified the potential for "information partnerships." They describe several forms of information partnership beyond the typical customer–supplier relationship, including joint marketing partnerships such as the airline coalitions of Amadeus and Galileo, intra-industry partnerships such as the ATM banking networks or MEMA's Transnet system, which connects manufacturers and thousands of retailers. This research suggests five key ingredients to successful information partnerships:

1 *Shared vision at the top.* Underscoring the notion that successful information partnerships are likely to be strategic in nature, top executives in the partnering companies must agree on the objectives of collaboration, whether it be cost reductions, obtaining new customers, or cross-selling of services.

2 *Reciprocal skills in information technology.* Partnerships work better when both partners possess the necessary skills to manage the complex technologies that may be involved: databases, communications networks, and the like. Additionally, both must have high standards of data integrity and quality control. The authors note that

"many companies that have initiated electronic data interchange agreements have been shocked to find partners unable to assimilate even modest data technologies and applications" (Konsynski & McFarlan, 1990, p. 118).

3 *Concrete plans for an early success.* Early successes give employees in the partnering companies confidence in the venture. This is important because the cultures of most organizations do not view outsiders as partners. Arms-length relationships have been the norm, and in many cases it has been adversarial.

4 *Persistence in the development of usable information.* Attention must be given to packaging shared data in a way that is useful to partners. In most cases, data has been developed and organized with no thought given to the possibility that it would someday be shared with trading partners. Ways of organizing, formatting and presenting data may need to be analyzed in order to make it useful to trading partners.

5 *Coordination of business policy.* Information partnerships go beyond merely sharing data. True information partnerships are supported by information systems that ignore normal organizational boundaries between companies. Operating in such an environment requires intercompany working groups or task forces to deal with such issues as common business processes and standard methodologies for information systems development and maintenance.

IOS Process Re-engineering

Venkatraman (1994, pp. 79, 83) notes that "Benefits from business process redesign are limited in scope if the processes are not extended outside the local organizational boundary to identify options for redesigning relationships with the other organizations that participate in ultimately delivering value to the customer . . . I strongly believe that the real power of IT for any firm lies not in streamlining internal operations (efficiency enhancements) but in restructuring the relationships in extended business networks to leverage a broader array of competencies that will deliver superior products and services."

The idea of partnership, and the potential payoffs from partnership, should be foremost in the benefits of IOS presented to general managers. Partnerships clearly seem to be an important strategic trend, and they can be facilitated by the electronic technologies of the world of electronic commerce: EDI, e-mail, imaging, bar coding, etc.

Bibliography

Drucker, P. (1989). The futures that have already happened. *The Economist,,* October 21, 19–24.

Kaufman, K. (1966). Data systems that cross company boundaries. *Harvard Business Review,* **44**.

Konsynski, B. R. & McFarlan, F. W. (1990). Information partnerships – shared data, shared scale. *Harvard Business Review,* **68**, 114–20.

McGee, J. V. & Prusack, L. (1993). *Managing Information Strategically.* New York: John Wiley.

Quinn, J. B. & Hilmer, F. G. (1994). Strategic outsourcing. *Sloan Management Review,* **35** (2), 43–55.

Venkatraman, N. (1994). IT-enabled business transformation: from automation to business scope redefinition. *Sloan Management Review,* **35** (4), 73–87.

DONALD J. McCUBBREY

K

knowledge Accumulated information and aggregations or summaries thereof. Additional information can often be inferred from explicit information or facts, with varying degrees of confidence. This can be formalized in rules of inference or production rules which is the domain of EXPERT SYSTEMS. Such a set of rules is often called a KNOWLEDGE BASE (which may or may not be considered to include the underlying database of explicitly stored facts).

GORDON C. EVEREST

promising rule for further processing becomes difficult. Also, some rules in a large knowledge base may contradict one another and need to be reconciled. Checking for consistency becomes especially critical (and difficult) as new rules are added to an already large knowledge base to improve its problem-solving performance. Maintaining the integrity and performance of a large knowledge base can be an exceedingly difficult task.

AMIT DAS

knowledge base Knowledge-based systems (also called EXPERT SYSTEMS) differ from traditional computer programs in that they maintain a clear separation between the domain knowledge and reasoning procedures used to solve a problem. The domain knowledge used by a knowledge-based system is stored in a knowledge base designed for efficient storage, retrieval, and updating.

Domain knowledge may be represented in several different ways in a knowledge base. The most common representation takes the form of *if–then* rules. Each rule has two parts – a set of conditions necessary for the rule to *fire* (the *if* part), and a set of actions or consequences resulting from the application of the rule (the *then* part). Other representations of domain knowledge, such as frames or semantic networks, are much less common than rules.

To perform complex tasks, such as medical diagnosis, a large amount of domain knowledge may be required. This translates to a large number of rules in the knowledge base and gives rise to several problems. During problem-solving, many rules may have their *if* conditions satisfied at the same time, and selecting the most

knowledge work The terms *knowledge work* and *knowledge workers* are commonly used to describe the kind of work and workers critical to organizational success in post-industrial society. Today KNOWLEDGE is considered a primary resource for organizations (Drucker, 1988) and a source of wealth and competitive advantage for nations (Porter, 1990). Work increasingly involves the processing and production of symbols rather than physical materials. Knowledge work requires employees who can (a) use their own KNOWLEDGE BASE; (b) acquire new information; (c) combine and process information to produce and communicate new information outputs; and (d) learn continuously from their experiences. Information technology provides support for these basic knowledge work functions and has had some unanticipated impacts on knowledge workers and their productivity.

Use of Personal Knowledge Base

In order to perform knowledge work successfully, individuals must employ their own *intellectual capital*: a personal base of knowledge that includes both factual and procedural information. Knowledge workers build their intellectual capital through education and experience. Information technology can supplement the knowledge base stored in a knowledge worker's memory. For example, DATABASE MANAGEMENT SYSTEMS enable knowledge workers to store more information and retrieve and combine it in more ways than information stored in memory or in paper-based systems. Knowledge workers can build their own personal knowledge base by entering data directly or by importing data extracted from corporate databases and external sources. The personal database becomes a unique, external archive of the intellectual capital of the knowledge worker.

Acquisition of New Information

Acquisition of new information from print resources is facilitated by bibliographical data storage and retrieval systems that provide references to (or, in some cases, full text of) books, articles, and other printed materials. New information about one's own company can be retrieved from corporate databases, and information external to an organization pulled from a variety of commercial online services (e.g. Dow Jones). This new information can be stored in the personal database of the knowledge worker (as previously described) and/or manipulated (as described below).

Combine, Process, Produce, and Communicate Information

Knowledge workers use a variety of information technologies to manipulate information. Systems like word processing and desktop publishing support combinations of information from a variety of sources and of different types (text, numeric, graphic) to produce new documents. Processing of information may be accomplished by specialized applications (e.g. tax preparation software) in which decision and processing rules are already included and data can be entered or imported from other systems. Processing may also be accomplished via software that allows users to develop their own applications (e.g. spreadsheet programs). Technologies such as electronic mail, groupware, and information networks enable knowledge workers to share information with both individuals and groups. Portable computers equipped with Fax/mod-

ems, supported by worldwide networks, allow knowledge workers to compute anytime, anywhere and to keep in constant contact with their office and colleagues.

Continuous Learning from Experiences

A key advantage of using information technology for knowledge work is the ability of information systems to capture task data and processes. Once a knowledge worker bears the cost of learning how to use a technology and/or builds a system to perform a task, a record of task inputs, processes, and outputs can be made. These computerized records can be recalled for subsequent task performance. When tasks are complex and repeated, but are not performed again for some time interval, the computer files can help knowledge workers remember what they learned from the last time they performed the task.

For example, suppose a manager uses a spreadsheet program to support budgeting. The manager will need to enter the data for that year in the appropriate categories, enter formulae that represent the relationships between the categories, and enter text that labels the categories and calculated data. The spreadsheet may be formatted so that a final document can be printed. Some benefits from using the spreadsheet program are realized immediately, since it enables the manager to consider many more budget alternatives than are feasible via hand calculations. Additional benefits are realized when the budget spreadsheet is retrieved at the next budget cycle, since the spreadsheet contains the content, rules, and format for the budgeting task. Only new or changed data or rules must be entered. The spreadsheet is a stored recipe for budgeting that the manager or others can recall and reuse. This helps prevent individual knowledge workers and the organization from "losing the recipe" for important tasks.

The organization can also benefit from using expert system technology to capture the intellectual capital of knowledge workers. EXPERT SYSTEMS can make an individual's expertise available even after that person has left the firm, and also can make it possible to extend that expertise to other, less knowledgeable, employees in the firm.

Impacts on Knowledge Workers and their Productivity

It seems logical that information technology support for the main functions of knowledge work would lead to increased productivity. Computer systems equipped with a variety of software and communications capabilities are standard tools for knowledge workers, and as common as telephones in offices. The seemingly insatiable demand for more hardware with additional capabilities in increasingly smaller packages, and for software to support new and existing tasks, would appear to reflect the value of information technology for knowledge work.

However, economic data from the 1980s indicates that productivity in knowledge work-intense sectors has not improved with increased investment in information technology. Many top managers question whether they have realized performance benefits commensurate with the large and continuing costs of information technology acquisition and support. There are several possible reasons for this "missing technology payback" in knowledge work. One central reason may be that knowledge-worker productivity is not accurately measured. While the benefits from information technology that replaced workers was easy to measure in reduced labor costs, information technology support for knowledge workers is intended to assist and enhance task performance. Higher-quality information products may not be captured by productivity measures. When technology speeds task performance, the knowledge worker may "use up" that efficiency gain in striving for non-measured improvements in task processes or outputs. Or, as described above, many of the benefits from technology use may accrue in the future, when a task is repeated. Poor or no productivity gains may also be caused by changes in the division of labor, since knowledge workers may be assigned a larger task set because they have computer support. For example, some companies eliminate or drastically reduce the number of secretaries because the professional workers have tools such as word processing and electronic mail. Another reason for the missing technology payback is the high, continuing costs of using information technology: the organization experiences increased back office costs to build and keep technology systems working and the individual bears costs to learn and use information technology.

Bibliography

Drucker, P. F. (1988). Management and the world's work. *Harvard Business Review*, **66**, 65–76.

Porter, M. E. (1990). *The Competitive Advantage of Nations.* New York: Free Press.

ROSANN COLLINS

L

local area networks A local area network (LAN) consists of several different devices that have been connected together in relatively close proximity for the purpose of communicating and sharing files and other resources with one another. Generally, a LAN will serve the individuals in a department, building, or cluster of buildings in close proximity with one another. The early motivation to create LANs was to facilitate the sharing of files and expensive hardware resources, like laser printers, tape backup drives, and large hard drives. Today, those motivations still exist, but the uses of LANs have evolved to include the support of work group computing and connecting users on one LAN to other networks through a wide area network, or through the INTERNET. To fully understand the topic of local area networks, it is necessary to discuss several related topics: network topologies, protocols, communications media, and network operating systems.

Topologies

A network topology is the physical arrangement of the nodes (devices) along the cable that connects the nodes with one another. There are three dominant topologies for LANs in use today: star, ring, and bus. A *star network* (figure 1) consists of a centralized host computer which is linked individually to each of the other computers in the network. Data is sent from one computer to another through the host computer. Additional computers, or nodes, are added at the host computer, thus minimizing the impact on the network as a whole. Therefore, a star topology is easier to maintain than other topologies. The major disadvantage of a star network is that if the host goes down, the entire network is disabled.

In a *ring network* (figure 2) each node on the network is physically connected to the two

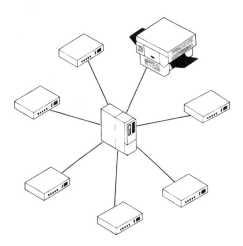

Figure 1 Star network topology

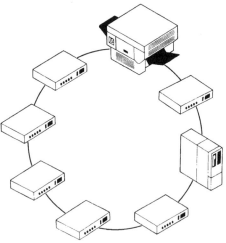

Figure 2 Ring network topology

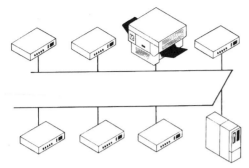

Figure 3   Bus network topology

adjacent nodes, forming a complete circle. Information is sent around the ring in one direction, from one computer to the next, until it reaches its destination. The final network topology is the *bus topology* (figure 3), which is also the most common. The bus topology uses the least amount of cable, but the cost savings from the initial cabling is offset by higher support costs. If an error occurs anywhere along the network, the entire network is shut down.

Protocols

A protocol is a set of rules that govern how a device gains access to the cable in a LAN. There are two important protocols used extensively on LANs today: token passing and carrier sense multiple access with collision detection (CSMA/CD).

A network that uses a token-passing protocol requires a device to control the token before it can have access to the network. An empty token passes from one device on the network to the next. If a device has some data to transmit, it must wait until an empty token passes. The device may take the empty token, attach its data to the token, then send it back out on the network. Once the token completes the circuit of the ring and returns to the original device, a new token is generated and passed, empty, back on the network. In that way, each device has equal access to the network, and there is no chance that more than one device will be using the network at a time. Token passing is typically utilized in a ring topology, and is most commonly implemented today as an IBM token ring, which can support up to a maximum of 260 nodes on the main ring, and a total length of the main ring of 1,200 feet. This protocol

supports transmission speeds of 4 million bits per second (Mbps).

When a network utilizes the CSMA/CD protocol, each device must contend for access to the network. If a node has data to transmit, it listens to the network. If no traffic is detected, it begins to transmit. Of course, it is possible that two or more devices may try to transmit at the same time, which would lead to collisions between the packets of data. If a collision is detected, both stations stop transmitting, and wait a period of time before beginning the process again. Ethernet (developed by Xerox) is a protocol associated with the CSMA/CD protocol. Networks utilizing this protocol have a maximum transmission rate of 10 Mbps, but as the number of users increases, the transmission speed degrades because the number of collisions increases.

Communications Media

Most local area networks today operate on one of three different media: twisted pair, coaxial, or fiberoptic cable. Twisted pair is similar to the wiring that is used in most telephone systems. It consists of two insulated copper wires that are twisted together to minimize electrical interference from other nearby wiring. The data transmission speeds vary widely for twisted pair, with speeds ranging from 14,400–28,800 bps over typical telephone lines to speeds of 56,000–144,000 bps possible on specially conditioned lines. These latter speeds make twisted pair useable in LANs. This feature, coupled with the low cost and ease of installation of twisted pair relative to coaxial or fiberoptic cable, makes twisted pair the media of choice for many new networks.

Coaxial cable consists of a heavy copper wire at the center and a braided copper conductor separated by insulating material. This type of wiring is widely used in LANs, and in other applications like cable television. There are two kinds of coaxial: baseband and broadband. Baseband is much easier and cheaper to install. It provides a single digital transmission channel which makes it ideal for LANs. Broadband coax uses analog transmission, and can be divided into multiple transmission channels. However, installation of broadband coax typically requires the services of an engineer to design the network, since the signal will need to be amplified at various points. The advantage of coaxial cable over twisted pair is the greater transmission speeds possible. Baseband coax is capable of transmission speeds of 10–264 Mbps, while broadband is capable of speeds of 10–550 Mbps.

Fiberoptic cable consists of one or more strands of optical fiber, surrounded by insulation and reinforcing material. Instead of using electronic signals to transmit data, light is used. Relative to twisted pair or coaxial cable, fiberoptic cable is capable of much greater transmission speeds, but costs more to purchase and install. Transmission speeds can range from 0.5 Mbps to 10 billion bps.

Network Operating Systems

Just as every computer must have an operating system to control its operations, each network must also have an operating system to control access of individual nodes to the resources on the network. The services typically provided by network operating systems include file services to allow the sharing of data and application programs, print services to facilitate sharing of expensive printers and other output devices, security services to limit access to certain network resources to particular users, and communication services to support LAN-to-LAN, LAN-to-host, and remote-to-LAN communications. Leading network operating systems today include Windows NT, AppleTalk, and Novell NetWare.

JONATHAN K. TROWER

M

macro program   A macro is a program consisting of a few instructions that invoke underlying functions. Historically, a macro is a "super instruction" because a single instruction results in a large program segment. The term "macro" is now widely used in computing to refer to a set of commands and menu selections stored in a file and executed (played) by a few keystrokes or a mouse stroke. A macro may be programmed by macro recording or by writing macro instructions provided by an application package.

Macro recording is a method of programming by doing. The user performs the sequence of activities that are to be automated, and the macro facilities create a program of instructions to perform the activities. For example, a user may perform a set of spreadsheet operations to create a heading, set fonts, define borders, establish row and column headings, etc. If these same operations are to be repeated frequently, they may be automated using a recording macro. The user specifies a name for the macro, turns on the macro recorder by an instruction, performs the activities to be automated, and turns off the recorder. The macro is stored. Subsequently, when the macro is "played," the activities are performed in exactly the same way. The advantages of macro recording is that the user need not understand the macro programming language; programming is by doing the activities. The main disadvantage is that only a sequence of actions may be programmed. No program logic to select from alternatives can be recorded. Because it is a fairly easy approach to automating a sequence of actions, macro recording is an important capability for improving productivity in using computer software.

The second approach to macro development is writing macro program instructions. Macro instruction languages resemble conventional procedural programming languages. Such languages are designed to write the procedures the computer is to execute and the logic to govern the execution of the computer actions. A generalized software package may have a macro language that is unique to it, or it may employ a macro language that is used across a suite of generalized packages.

Macros are programs. However, they tend to be short and limited in scope. They are developed and executed within a software package. The macro will not work without the software package. Although most macros tend to be short, many large, complex applications have been developed using a macro language. Spreadsheet macros have been used for complex applications based on spreadsheet processes. In the case of database packages, the macro language is designed as a development language for the development of applications that use the facilities of the database package for data storage and retrieval.

Many software packages include a set of pre-written macros for common functions. For example, a word processing package may include a macro that displays a common memo format or performs operations such as printing envelopes.

Pre-written macros are not limited to those included with the packages. Independent software vendors often offer macros for widely used packages. User groups share macros, and magazines for users of packages include them.

GORDON B. DAVIS and J. DAVID NAUMANN

maintenance Software maintenance is the modification of an existing software system by information systems professionals. It applies to both system software and applications. It involves three types of activities: repairs, improving technical performance, and enhancement. Repairs are required when incorrect or incomplete software code renders the system defective. Changes to software features, such as rewriting the code to take advantage of processing efficiencies, may be made to improve technical performance. Enhancements are additions, changes, or deletion of software functionality. Repairs tend to dominate the maintenance activity for the first few months of operation of a new software system. Later, most of the maintenance is enhancement. Sometimes maintenance is performed by the system developers, but often it may be the responsibility of a separate maintenance group.

Productivity in Software Maintenance

Software maintenance is an expensive activity. At least half of information system resources in organizations are devoted to software maintenance activities. On a life-cycle basis, more than three-quarters of the investment in software occurs after it has been implemented. It is thought that many problems in software maintenance are caused by inadequacies in the initial software design (Schneidewind, 1987). Poor choices in software development may result in low-quality software that is difficult to modify. A particularly problematic aspect of the software that ensues from bad design is software complexity. Software complexity refers to the characteristics of the data structures and procedures in the code that make the software hard to understand. There have been several studies that suggest the importance of software complexity for performance in software maintenance. Experimental studies by Curtis et al. (1979) and Gibson and Senn (1989), as well as others, indicate that software complexity is a major factor in software maintenance performance.

Software complexity is believed to interfere with the critical maintenance activity of software comprehension. Software that is large in size or that has complicated data interactions or logic paths is difficult to understand. There are several measures of software complexity. The most

noted are Halstead's (1977) software science metrics, which measure software volume, and McCabe's (1976) cyclomatic complexity metric, which counts the number of decision paths in the software. These measures, as well as others, can be used to assess the quality of software design. Such assessment is important to ensure that maintainability is built in to the software when it is initially constructed.

Maintenance Management Concerns

There are several managerial issues related to software maintenance. A critical task is to effectively manage the system portfolio, or set of systems. As software systems age, they tend to become more complicated, with frequent modifications and enhancements. In addition, there may be few information systems personnel and users familiar with these systems. Thus, a key maintenance management decision concerns whether to continue to repair a system or replace it entirely. Another maintenance management concern is how to organize the software maintenance function. Software maintenance can be organized together with software development, so that IS personnel work on both development and maintenance tasks. Another alternative is a life-cycle arrangement where there are separate development and maintenance staffs. While this arrangement has potential advantages for quality assurance and user service, it may have disadvantages of coordination and political costs. Motivation of maintenance personnel is a final important managerial concern. Studies by Couger and Zawacki (1980) and Swanson and Beath (1989) indicate that information systems personnel may not consider maintenance work to be sufficiently interesting or challenging. Especially when technological obsolescence is prevalent, information system workers may fear that unless they are continuously involved in development work, their skills will deteriorate, and this will not only affect their future earning power, but also their ability to do work they enjoy.

Future of Software Maintenance

Several software development innovations, such as structured programming techniques, computer-aided software engineering, software reuse and object-oriented programming, promise to reduce the software maintenance burden. In addition, there have been tools and techniques developed to improve software maintenance performance. Some of the most prominent maintenance aids include software code analyzers, code restructurers, and reverse engineering tools. These software development and maintenance practices may lower the need for maintenance and increase the maintainability of systems.

Bibliography

Couger, J. D. & Zawacki, R. A. (1980). *Motivating and Managing Computer Personnel.* New York: John Wiley.

Curtis, B., Sheppard, S. B., Milliman, P., Borst, M. A. & Love, T. (1979). Measuring the psychological complexity of software maintenance tasks with the Halstead and McCabe metrics. *IEEE Transactions on Software Engineering*, **SE-5 (2)**, 96–104.

Gibson, V. R. & Senn, J. A. (1989). System structure and software maintenance performance. *Communications of the ACM*, **32 (3)**, 347–58.

Halstead, M. (1977). *Elements of software science.* New York: Elsevier North-Holland.

McCabe, T. J. (1976). A complexity measure. *IEEE Transactions on Software Engineering*, **SE-2 (4)**, 308–20.

Schneidewind, N. (1987). The state of software maintenance. *IEEE Transactions on Software Engineering*, **SE-13 (3)**, 303–10.

Swanson, E. B. & Beath, C. M. (1989). *Maintaining information systems in organizations.* New York: John Wiley.

SANDRA SLAUGHTER

make or buy for software   A key decision in an information system development project is how to acquire the SOFTWARE for the new system. The three options are to write the software code internally, hire external contract programmers to write the programs, or purchase a software package.

If the system development team chooses to develop the software internally, programmers employed by the company use the system specifications developed during the systems analysis and design phase to write, test, and debug the program code. The decision to produce software internally is typically based on a need for application programs that are unique or that must be tailored to specific company requirements and, as a result, cannot

be found in the marketplace. In some instances, a company's search for a competitive advantage through sophisticated proprietary applications may lead to a decision to produce software internally. The primary advantage of producing software internally is that it can be designed to fit the specific, and perhaps unique, needs of the company. The major disadvantages are that it requires significant programming staff, takes notably longer than to purchase, and has a higher risk of cost overruns if problems arise during testing that require significant debugging and rework.

An alternative to internal software development that retains the advantage of tailoring the code to unique organizational needs is to hire, or "outsource," the programming activities to external contract programmers. These contractors may work independently on an individual basis, or they may work for an organization that specializes in providing system development staff. In either case, the contracting company provides the system specifications to the outsourcing programmers who write, test, and debug the code, and then provide the finished software product on a "turnkey" basis. In addition to enabling the code to be tailored to the company's particular needs, another major advantage of the contractor alternative is that the code is written by highly qualified programming staff, yet the company does not have to take on the responsibility of hiring, training, and supervising them. This lack of direct supervision over the programming staff can also be a disadvantage, however, since it transfers some control over the system development process to parties outside the organization. Although it depends on the nature of the contract, another potential disadvantage of this alternative is that the contractor may obtain the experience to develop and sell similar software to other companies (including competitors of the contracting company), and perhaps at even lower prices since the development costs have already been recovered under the original development project.

The third major option for acquiring software is to purchase a software package directly from a software vendor. This approach is applicable if the company can apply a standard set of software capabilities found in packages. The company has little or no need for unique or tailored system requirements. The company does not need a proprietary system that will provide significant strategic advantage. Given the reduced time, cost, and risk, companies believe that these advantages more than offset any software tailoring or potential competitive advantage they may forgo.

WILLIAM D. NANCE

management information system   The terms management information system (MIS), information system (IS), and information management (IM) are synonyms. They refer both to an organization system that employs information technology in providing information and communication services and the organization function that plans, develops, and manages the system.

Definition of MIS as a System

The *management information system* is a system within an organization that supplies information and communication services and resources to meet organization needs. The system consists of information technology infrastructures to provide information processing and communication capabilities and application systems for delivery of specific information resources and services.

The infrastructures are core technology systems, databases, and information management personnel. The infrastructures provide capabilities and services for applications. Application systems deliver information resources and services for specific organizational functions or purposes. Types of applications include systems embedded in products or services, transaction processing, communications, cooperative work support, reporting and analysis, decision support, and management support. The applications employ both automated and manual procedures. They are human–technology systems because the results are obtained through an interaction of human users with the technology. The applications are model-based, i.e. the designs reflect models of decision-making, human–machine interfaces, social interaction, organization behavior, customer service, and so forth.

The objectives of the MIS infrastructures and applications are to meet an organization's information and communication needs, improve productivity in organizational activities, add value to organizational processes, and assist the organizational strategy. The systems apply information technology and information resources to functionality and performance in products and services, quality and scope in analysis and decision-making, communication and sharing in cooperative work, and improved, faster operational and management processes at all levels. In a well-designed MIS, the different applications are not independent; they are interconnected subsystems that form a coherent, overall, integrated structure for information and communication services.

Definition of MIS as an Organization Function

The management information system *organization function* plans, develops, implements, operates, and maintains the organization's information technology infrastructures and the organization's portfolio of applications. It also provides support and advisory services for systems developed and operated by individuals and departments.

The function employs, trains, and manages personnel with specialized knowledge and expertise for these purposes. The system development processes of the information management function include methods, techniques, and technologies for analyzing business processes, identifying system requirements, developing and implementing systems and related organization changes, and maintenance of systems. The management processes of the function include interaction with organizational strategic planning to identify ways information technology systems may be used to achieve competitive advantage and other strategic goals, planning of infrastructures and applications, management of information system projects, operation of systems, consultation services to users, and evaluation of MIS performance.

The MIS function is needed by an organization because of organizational reliance on information technology, the size of the investment, the need for organizational coordination and standards for the information system, and the need for expertise in processes for planning, development, and management of the information and communication infrastructures and applications for an organization. The reliance on information technology is pervasive in transactions and other business processes; few organizations could operate competitively without it. The investment in information technology has, in recent years, been a significant part of the investment budget of organizations. The need for a function to coordinate information technology in the organization is increased as information technology innovation is diffused across all functions. Information technology use in business functions depends on an information technology infrastructure, organization-wide applications, and standards for systems that cross functional and organizational boundaries. The MIS function performs this important role. A fourth reason for the MIS function is the expertise required for planning, developing, operating, and managing the information technology infrastructure and organization applications.

Body of Knowledge Associated with MIS

The use of information technology is so pervasive that a certain level of expertise must be distributed broadly across the organization. Individuals and workgroups within other organization functions may have significant responsibility for their own information management activities or local systems involving information technology. However, the management information system function has responsibility for maintaining expertise sufficient to assist individuals, groups, departments, and functions in their information management, to provide integration across the organization, and build and maintain the corporate information infrastructures and standards necessary for integrated information processes. The expertise associated with the MIS function consists of:

1 *Information strategies and structures.* Information system strategies and structures provide an organization with the capacity and capability for obtaining and using information, for applying information technology in its processes and systems, and for using information and systems in its competitive strategy. The MIS function applies expertise in strategy and structures in the process of PLANNING FOR INFORMATION SYSTEMS.

2 *Business process and information system development.* The information management function has special expertise in the design and implementation of business processes and systems. Information technology is a key element in most designs. Although all organization functions have some responsibility for their systems, the information management function has an ongoing expert role with primary technical responsibility for SYSTEMS ANALYSIS AND DESIGN, development, and integration.

3 *Organization and administration of the information management function.* This area includes organization of responsibilities for the functioning, hiring, and training of information systems personnel, budgeting and planning of activities, and ASSESSMENT OF MANAGEMENT INFORMATION SYSTEM performance. Information system specialists are expected to have expertise to perform advisory and consulting services to users, build and maintain technical infrastructures, analyze requirements, and acquire or build solutions that employ information technology.

4 *Information management operations.* The operations within the domain of MIS include the operation of organization-wide systems for information processing and communications. The activities include scheduling, operating, and controlling information and communications facilities, organization applications, and organization databases.

The body of knowledge for planning, implementing, and operating the MIS for an organization rests upon a number of underlying disciplines or bodies of knowledge. As examples, it relies on the software engineering principles and computational algorithms of computer science, the organization behavior and management principles of the field of management, the concepts and principles of human behavior in human–technology systems from cognitive psychology, principles of co-operation and communication from the field of communications, SYSTEM CONCEPTS and INFORMATION CONCEPTS from a variety of fields, and analysis of costs, benefits, and productivity from economics. From these reference disciplines, MIS has built a body of knowledge about the design, implementation, operation, and evaluation of information system infrastructures and applications in organizations.

Evolution of the MIS Concept

When computers were applied to business data processing in 1954, the first applications were document and report preparation based on batch input of transactions. Payroll checks, customer order documents, inventory analyses, and related reports are examples. In large part, computer technology was employed in early applications as a substitute for clerical labor and electromechanical devices. The systems were often referred to as electronic data processing (EDP) systems. Innovative organizations soon applied the computer to management reporting and analysis. The files that had been prepared for transaction document processing and transaction reporting provided the basis for more timely, analytical management reports. The computer made possible the use of quantitative modeling in support of business decisions. To reflect this change in emphasis from data processing to management support, the systems and function began to employ the term *management information systems*. The term included support for various levels of management and for decision-making.

The concept also included data as an organization resource. The data resource concept was implemented with DATABASE MANAGEMENT SYSTEMS. Prior to computers, transaction data files were viewed as being "owned by" or the responsibility of a single business function. The marketing files were the responsibility of the marketing department, the accounts receivable records were the responsibility of the accounting department, and so forth. Database management systems and databases freed the organization from functional constraints on the use of data. Data was defined as an organization resource to be managed for broad organization use. Retrieval software was made available to selectively search and retrieve from the databases. Any authorized person could employ the software to access the databases.

Data could be organized, analyzed, and alternatives modeled in order to support decision-making. Since many models are applicable across the organization, a model base of analytical tools was developed to support decision-making and decision-making access to data. Software was provided as part of the MIS to support individual modeling of decisions and access to data for the model. Software was added to the system to support group decision-making and cooperative work (*see* COMPUTER-SUPPORTED COOPERATIVE WORK; DECISION SUPPORT SYSTEMS; EXECUTIVE INFORMATION SYSTEMS; GROUP DECISION SUPPORT SYSTEMS).

An extension of the MIS concept was the STRATEGIC USE OF INFORMATION TECHNOLOGY to improve the competitive position of the organization and achieve competitive advantage. The MIS planning process became more closely tied to the strategy of the organization. The MIS function is expected not only to respond to requirements as defined by other business functions but interact in the planning process to suggest innovative uses of information technology to improve products, services, and business processes. This new set of applications includes interorganizational applications that apply information technology to reduce cycle time and improve communications and transaction handling between the organization and its suppliers and customers.

The Structure of an MIS

The structure of an information system may be visualized as infrastructures plus applications. The applications have a conceptual structure based on the purposes or needs being met and the functions of the organization that employ them. The three infrastructures that provide the general capacity and capabilities for information access and processing are technology, data, and personnel. The infrastructures enable specific applications and activities.

1 The *technology infrastructure* consists of computer and communication hardware, system software, and general purpose software systems. The computer hardware consists of computers and related storage, input, and output devices. The communications hardware contains devices to control the flow of communications within internal networks and with external network provi-

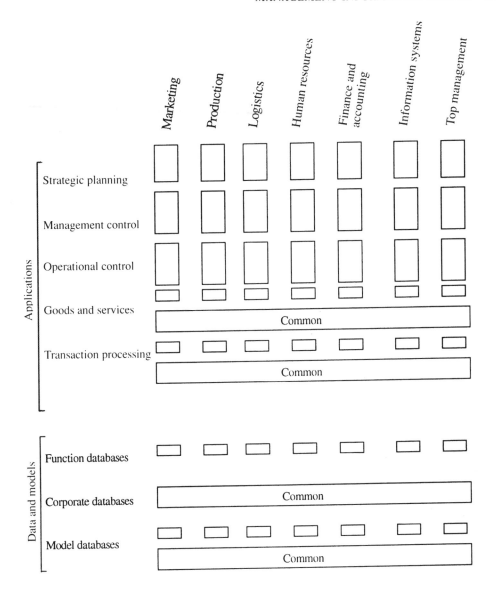

Figure 1   Organizational MIS applications, data, and models

ders. Computer hardware is made opera- tional through system software that provides generalized functions necessary for applications. COMPUTER OPERATING SYSTEMS, communications software, and network software are examples. Generalized software is not specific to a single application but provides facilities for many different applications. An example is a database management system to manage databases and perform access and retrieval functions for a variety of applications and users.

2 The databases form a *data infrastructure*. They provide for storage of data needed by one or more organizational functions and one or more activities. There will be a number of databases based on organization activities. Planning of the database infra- structure involves determining what should be stored, what relationships should be

maintained among stored data, and what restrictions should be placed on access. The result of database planning and implementation with database management systems is a capacity to provide data both for applications and *ad hoc* needs. Comprehensive databases designed for *ad hoc* use may be termed DATA WAREHOUSES.

3 The information systems *personnel* can be viewed as a third infrastructure, which includes all personnel required to establish and maintain the technology and database infrastructures and the capacity to perform user support, development, implementation, operation, and maintenance activities. The personnel may be divided between an MIS function and functional areas. There may be, for example, general purpose user support personnel in the MIS function and functional information management support personnel in the functional areas of the organization.

The application portfolio provides the specific processing and problem-solving support for an organization. It consists of the application SOFTWARE and related model bases and KNOWLEDGE BASES. The application software consists of applications that cross functional boundaries and applications identified with a single function. Although there is significant integration of applications because of the use of common databases and use of the same application by more than one function, the application portfolio reflects a federation of systems rather than a totally integrated system. A single, integrated system is too complex; the selective integration by interconnections among the federation of systems is more manageable and robust. A visualization of the MIS based on the application portfolio consists of applications in direct support of each business function (marketing, production, logistics, human resources, finance and accounting, information systems, and top management) plus general-purpose applications and facilities. Although the database management system provides general-purpose support, it also supports databases common to many functions and databases unique to a function. The applications can also be classed as being associated with transaction processing, products and services, and manage-

ment. The management applications can be classified as related to operational control, management control, and strategic planning. This conceptual structure is illustrated in figure 1.

In terms of the use of technology and the frequency of use of the software, the applications in figure 1 differ in several respects. The transaction processing and goods and services applications tend to support lower-level management and operating personnel. The applications tend to incorporate programmed decision processes based on decision rules and algorithms. Applications supporting higher-level management processes are less structured and require human interaction to specify the decision process and data to be used. Because of these differences, the application structure of a management information system is often described as a pyramid (figure 2).

Information System Support for Management Activities

In addition to its use in transaction processing, business processes, and within products and services, information systems support management processes such as planning, control, and decision-making. This use of information technology can provide significant value to the organization. The Anthony framework is used by both academic researchers and business practitioners to model and classify the information system support for management. The three levels of the Anthony hierarchy define the nature of the management support applications.

1 *Operational control* ensures that operational activities are conducted efficiently and effectively according to plans and schedules. Examples of applications in support of operational management are scheduling, purchasing, and inquiry processing for operations. The decisions and actions cover short time periods such as a day or a week. An example of processing in support of operational control is the sequence of operations to authorize an inventory withdrawal. The balance on hand and on order is examined to determine the need for a replenishment order. The size of the replenishment order is based on reorder quantity algorithms to control inventory

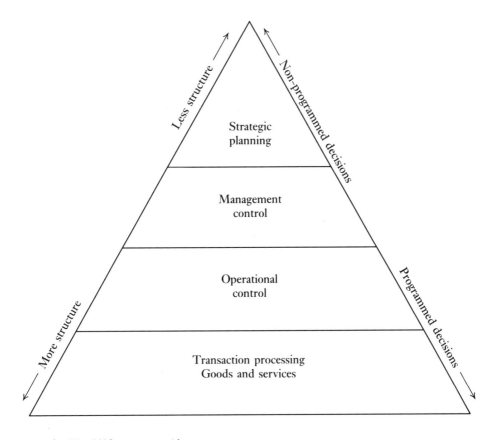

Figure 2   The MIS as a pyramid

levels. An order document is prepared automatically for review and acceptance or modification by a purchasing analyst before it is released.

2 *Management control* focuses on a medium-term time period such as a month, quarter, or year. It includes acquisition and organization of resources, structuring of work, and acquisition and training of personnel. Budget reports, variance analysis, and staffing plans are typical of management control applications.

3 *Strategic management* applications were designed to assist management in doing long-range strategic planning. The requirements include both internal and external data. The emphasis is on customer trends and patterns and competitor behavior. Market-share trends, customer perceptions of the organization and its products and services, along with similar perceptions for competitors, and forecasts of technology changes, are examples of information useful in strategic management.

A set of applications and retrieval/report facilities within an MIS designed especially for senior executives has been termed an EXECUTIVE INFORMATION SYSTEM (EIS). It focuses on the unique needs of senior management. These include an ability to formulate executive-level inquiries, construct special information requests, explore various alternative analyses, and so forth. The databases used for an EIS include portions of the corporate transactions databases, selected summary and comparative data, and relevant external data.

Information System Support for Decision-making

The decision-making support provided to an organization by its information system can be described in terms of Simon's three phases of the decision-making process: intelligence, design, and choice. The support for the intelligence phase of discovering problems and opportunities consists of database search and retrieval facilities. For example, an analyst investigating collections policy can use retrieval software to obtain data on customers, sales, and collections for a representative period. The decision design phase in which decision alternatives are generated is supported by statistical, analytical, and modeling software. In the collections example, the decision design might involve correlation of collection times with customer characteristics and order characteristics. The support for the choice phase includes decision models, sensitivity analysis, and choice procedures. A choice procedure for a collections policy might involve the use of models to compare collection policies on various dimensions and rank order the policies.

EXPERT SYSTEMS support decision-making by rule-based or knowledge-based systems. The most commonly used rule-based systems incorporate decision procedures and rules derived from the decision-making processes of domain experts. Data items presented to the rule-based system are analyzed by the expert system and a solution is suggested based on the rules derived from experts. The decision may be supported by an explanation facility that details the rules and logic employed in arriving at the decision. Unlike expert systems based on rules, NEURAL NETWORKS are a decision-support procedure based on the data available for a decision. The neural network is established (or recalibrated) by deriving the factors and weights that will achieve a specified outcome using an existing set of data. The factors and weights are applied to new data to suggest decisions. An example of neural network use is decision-making relative to credit worthiness for a loan or credit approval for a transaction.

The term DECISION SUPPORT SYSTEM (DSS) refers to a set of applications within an MIS devoted to decision support. Although some writers distinguish between MIS and DSS, the MIS concept is typically defined to include a DSS. The concept of a DSS incorporates the Anthony framework and the decision-making categories of Herbert Simon (1977). The classic description of the concept is by Gorry and Scott

Morton (1971). Their framework for a DSS classifies decisions as structured, semi-structured, and unstructured within the three levels of management. Structured decisions can be incorporated in the programmed procedures of computer software, but unstructured (and many semi-structured) decisions are best supported by analytical and decision models and analytical and modeling tools. These facilities aid human decision-makers to deal with difficult problems that cannot be solved with algorithms. The concept of a DSS incorporates human–system interaction as the human decision-maker formulates scenarios, models alternatives, and applies analytical procedures in order to explore alternative solutions and evaluate consequences.

The Future of the MIS System and Function

Systems based on information technology have become an integral part of organization processes, products, and services. The data available for analysis and decision-making has increased with the capabilities for computer-based storage and retrieval. The infrastructures have become more complex as more information technology is distributed to individuals and departments. The planning, design, implementation, and management of information resources have become more complex and more vital to organizations. The need for a specialized MIS function has increased. Although some routine functions may be outsourced, the critical functions that affect competitive advantage are likely to remain part of an MIS function in the organization.

Information technology is still changing rapidly, and new opportunities for business use continue to emerge. The rate of innovation and change and the investment implications also underlines the need for an MIS function to support organizational use of information technology for information access, processing, and communication.

Bibliography

Anthony, R. N. (1965). *Planning and Control Systems: A Framework for Analysis*. Cambridge, MA: Harvard University Press.

Davis, G. B. & Olson, M. H. (1985). *Management Information Systems: Conceptual Foundations, Structure, and Development*, 2nd edn. New York: McGraw-Hill.

Gorry, G. A. & Scott Morton, M. S. (1971). A framework for management information systems. *Sloan Management Review*, **13** (1).

Simon, H. A. (1977). *The New Science of Management Decision*, rev. edn. Englewood Cliffs, NJ: Prentice-Hall.

GORDON B. DAVIS

manufacturing resource planning *see* MANUFACTURING USE OF INFORMATION TECH-NOLOGY.

manufacturing use of information technology   The backbone of information technology for planning and controlling a manufacturing company involves a manufacturing resource planning (MRP) system. An MRP system provides the common database and communicates needed actions that coordinate operations across different functional areas. The major information flows involved in an MRP system are shown in figure 1 and explained below. Other applications of information technology integrate with and build on the MRP application.

Business planning.   The business planning process results in annual budgets that establish the baseline for financial planning and measurement purposes. An MRP system defines budgets by general ledger account and tracks actual versus budgeted costs. Spreadsheet simulations can be used to develop budgets, drawing on informa-

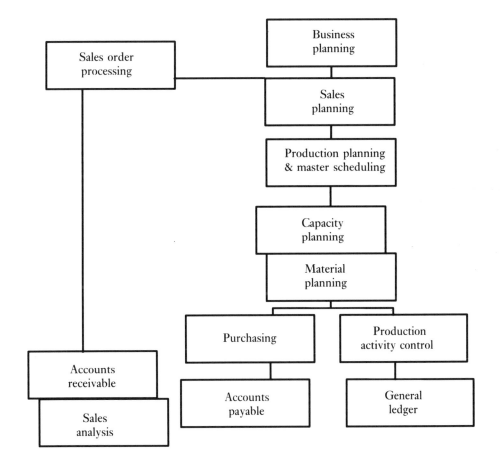

Figure 1   MRP information flow

tion in the database and also updating the database with new budget data.

Sales planning.   Sales planning identifies independent demands for the company's products/ services, such as customer orders and forecasts, and establishes an inventory (or backlog) plan as a buffer against forecast inaccuracy and demand variations. Forecasts and inventory plans are generally expressed for items at the highest possible stocking level, such as finished goods for standard products and intermediates for assemble-to-order custom products. They may also be defined for purchased materials with long lead times or supplier availability problems. Forecasts can be projected from sales history information about bookings, shipments, and/or invoices, or from information about leading indicators. Forecasts by product family provide aggregate planning, with planning bills to disaggregate the forecast based on product mix percentages.

Sales order processing.   Sales order processing starts with entry of the sales order and ends with shipment and invoicing. Basic variations in sales order processing stem from differences between standard and custom products.

1 *Standard products*: item availability can be checked against finished goods, or against scheduled receipts, for promising delivery dates/quantities. Pricing may be based on customer contracts or quotes, or the customer and product types.
2 *Custom products*: the sales order defines the custom product configuration of what should be built. The bills/routing for the custom product can be directly defined, copied from a previous order and modified, or created by selecting from a predefined list of options. Item availability can be checked for the parent item (against its production plan) or for the components. Pricing may be based on a cost-plus-markup or rolled-price approach.

A quotation may initially be developed and subsequently converted to a sales order. Credit policies are typically enforced during order entry. Order acknowledgments (and quotations) may be communicated to customers. Customer schedules can be used to indicate planned/firm sales orders, and ELECTRONIC DATA INTERCHANGE can be used to communicate customer schedules/orders electronically. A multi-site operation may require centralized order entry, in which a customer order includes shipment from several sites. The ship-from plant may also need to be overridden as a result of production planning.

Customer order activities generate actions that need to be communicated to other functional areas. For example, an MRP system needs to communicate planner actions to produce make-to-order products, buyer actions to procure non-stock items, credit management actions to review orders placed on hold, and stockroom actions to ship material. Shipping personnel can print picking lists, packing lists, box labels and bills of lading. Shipment transactions update the general ledger for inventory and cost of sales, and pass information to accounts receivable for creating invoices. Shipments provide the basis for tracking warranty periods, reporting return goods authorizations, and analyzing historical sales.

Production planning and master scheduling.   The production plans and master schedules represent the company plan for satisfying demands identified in the sales plan. A master schedule identifies production for a specific item, whereas a production plan identifies production for a product family, typically consisting of items with common material, production processes and/or a custom product configuration. A production plan also defines the limits of a final assembly schedule through a common process, where customer orders for make-to-order products drive the final assembly schedule. An MRP system generates planned supply orders which "chase" demands, and provide the starting point for production plans/master schedules. A "level load" strategy can be employed by firming up the production plan and master schedule over a time horizon (referred to as the planning fence) which covers an item's cumulative manufacturing lead time. An MRP system provides capacity planning to highlight overloaded periods that require adjustments in capacity or load, and material planning to highlight anticipated shortages. Simulations can be used to analyze various alternatives.

Capacity planning.   Capacity planning compares work center load to available capacity to highlight overloaded periods. A work center's calendar and efficiency/utilization factors determine available capacity. A work center's load reflects routing operations for planned/firm/released work orders, which have been scheduled based on infinite or finite scheduling logic. Drilling down to a period's load identifies the work orders and operations that can be rescheduled.

Material planning. Material planning calculates supply/demand schedules for each item in the product structure and generates recommended actions to meet the production plan/master schedule and final assembly schedule. Recommended actions identify the need to release, reschedule, cancel and/or follow up orders. They are grouped by make items and purchased items. Recommended actions also apply to interplant transfers in a multi-site operation when sites operate as feeder plants to other manufacturing or distribution sites.

Purchasing. Purchasing executes the materials plan through periodic negotiation of vendor agreements (buyer activities) and daily coordination of deliveries (vendor scheduling activities). In support of buyer activities, an MRP system identifies approved vendors, generates requests for quotes, defines price quotes and blanket purchase orders, specifies requisitions, tracks approvals, and measures vendor performance. In support of vendor scheduler activities, an MRP system generates vendor schedules, identifies recommended buyer actions, defines purchase orders, enforces receiving procedures, tracks material through inspection, and handles returns to vendor. Purchase orders can be defined for different types of items, such as normal material, expense items, and outside operations. Receipt information is passed to accounts payable for matching receipts to invoices and to general ledger for updating inventory and unvouchered payables.

Production activity control. Production executes the materials/capacity plan by coordinating production activity through work center dispatch lists and recommended planner actions. A work center dispatch list (or production schedule) lists work order operations in priority sequence, such as operation due date or order priority. Infinite or finite scheduling can be used to schedule work order operations. Additional coordination tools include a router/traveler of detailed work instructions (typically for custom product operations) and/or a visible scheduling system such as KANBAN tokens (typically for repetitive standard product operations).

A work order defines the quantity and start/complete dates for manufacturing the parent item and the version of the item's bill and routing to be used in manufacturing. The item's bill and routing, copied to the work order, can be modified to reflect material substitutions or alternative operations. This order-dependent bill forms the basis for picking components, although designated components can be automatically deducted (backflushed) upon reporting work order receipt or unit completions at paypoint operations. The order-dependent routing forms the basis for reporting labor by operation, although labor can also be backflushed. Labor and material transactions can be reported through a data collection system using technologies such as bar code readers. An MRP system tracks actual against planned costs, highlights variances, and generates corresponding financial transactions for updating the general ledger.

The MRP information flows utilize several key master files in the common database. These master files include information about product/process design, customers, vendors, locations, and employees.

Product/process design. The item master and bills of material define product design with engineering changes managed by date or serial number effectivity. The work center master and routings define process design. Standard operations minimize routing maintenance. The bills and routings can be used to calculate product costs.

Customers. Customers can have different bill-to and multiple ship-to locations. Customer policies can be established for credit (such as credit limits and terms), applicable tax authorities (by ship-to location), and sales person. Contracts and/or quotes can specify and summarize sales and receivables activities for each customer.

Vendors. The system summarizes purchasing and payables activities by vendor. It specifies approved vendors for items and specifies vendor quoted prices with quantity breakpoints and effectivity dates.

Inventory locations. An item's inventory can be stocked in multiple locations, typically identified by warehouse/bin within a plant. Inventory can also be uniquely differentiated by lot and serial number.

Employees. The employee master is used for payroll and personnel application purposes. Employees are identified on labor transactions, so that pay-rates can be used to track actual manufacturing costs.

Manufacturers have significant similarity in the need for information to manage their resources. They have the same information flows and key master files to perform aggregate planning – business, sales, and production planning – and coordinate detailed plans for execution in purchasing and production. Two other types of operations illustrate the similarity in information flows:

1 Distributors have similar information flows to manufacturers; the major difference is the lack of production activity. Production planning (for families of end items) and master scheduling (of purchased material) still apply, and capacity planning may focus on warehouse space/personnel.

2 Project manufacturers require additional functionality in an MRP system. Using a project master file, business planning focuses on budgeting/estimating by project. Project budgets are frequently developed by using cost/schedule reporting capabilities to define the budgeted cost of work scheduled (with subsequent comparison to the budgeted and actual cost of work performed) by cost account and work package. Projects get identified in sales forecasts and customer orders, with MRP exploding requirements by project through the product structure. Actual costs are tracked by project, along with performance against work packages (such as work order completions).

Other Uses of IT in Manufacturing

Sales Planning. Information technology has expanded the availability of external information useful in forecasting sales and identifying potential customers. Portable computers are used for doing proposals, presentations, and sales order entry. Expert systems have been employed for automated product configuration to meet customer specifications. The shipping function can use a variety of information technologies (such as bar-code readers) to record shipments and returns. Electronic communication of customer orders and shipments improves coordination with customers.

Product/process design. Information technology has been applied to schedule R&D efforts for product/process design, to directly design products via computer-aided design (CAD), and to simulate a product's performance.

Inventory and production control. Information technology has been employed for automated material handling systems and storage/retrieval systems. Data collection applications use a variety of devices (such as bar-code readers) to minimize data entry efforts for reporting labor and material transactions. Expert systems are used for scheduling and assignment of workers/machines (e.g. based on skill attributes) to optimize utilization, throughput, or sequencing.

Quality. Quality management uses information technology to perform failure analysis, record and diagnose test results, and suggest corrective action. Lot and serial control are enforced and tracked through the MRP system.

J. SCOTT HAMILTON

metrics for assessment of information systems   Information systems (IS) assessment is concerned with collecting accurate and meaningful indicators or metrics about software systems. It is important to measure information systems for a number of reasons. Information systems providers and users are under increasing pressure to improve productivity and quality. Measures can be used as a learning tool to monitor and evaluate the performance of software systems as well as their developers, maintainers, and users. They can also be employed to control the process of developing and maintaining software systems. Measurement information may reveal problems in the software process. This information can provide insight into the process and can be used to improve performance. Finally, metrics can enhance communication among information system stakeholders including top management, software management and staff, users, and external stakeholders.

Types of Metrics

Information systems metrics can be grouped into four major types: (a) internal performance; (b) growth and learning; (c) user/client perspective; and (d) business contribution. Many organizations first implement internal performance measures and gradually evolve to the use of more sophisticated business contribution measures.

An *internal performance* view focuses on the performance of the IS function relative to industry and organizational standards. Typical types of metrics include productivity, quality, and delivery rates. Productivity indicators measure the software delivery rate and the ability to support software. A key example is the function point metric that assesses the size of software functionality implemented. Quality metrics measure the technical quality of the software produced and maintained, and the quality of the software engineering process as practiced by the information systems function. A primary example is defects per line of software code. Delivery metrics measure the information systems organizational ability to meet time and cost commitments. An example is the number of elapsed days required to process a request for information services.

Growth and learning measures focus on assessing the capabilities of IS personnel and improving them. An important example is the maturity level of the information systems organization. This is measured using the Capability Maturity Model developed by the Software Engineering Institute (SEI). Another example of a growth and learning metric is the number of training days per information systems employee.

User/client measures are concerned with assessing the relationship between the IS function and its customers. These measures indicate the extent to which business needs are met. An example is customer satisfaction metrics that measure whether users are satisfied with the system's functionality, ease of use and availability, and with the system development process.

Business contribution measures link the information systems function to the success measures used by the business to gauge business performance. Financial return, or business value of information technology, may be measured as the business benefit resulting from the use of the technology less the costs to develop or acquire the technology. Another example is strategic impact. This may be assessed by determining the amount of IS resources devoted to strategic business areas.

SANDRA SLAUGHTER

microcomputer The term "microcomputer" originally referred to a class of computers with significantly less processing power and memory than mainframe or minicomputers. Microcomputers today are often referred to as "personal computers," as a reflection of their orientation toward selection and use by individuals. They include computers that will fit on a user's desktop and portable or laptop computers. Powerful machines in their own right, they are now capable of performing many tasks that could previously only be handled by higher-level machines. Workstations may be of a similar size, but are generally characterized by more powerful mathematical and graphical processing capabilities. As the price of powerful processing and display capabilities drops, the distinction between workstations, minicomputers and microcomputers is likely to blur even further.

Minicomputer and mainframe systems may have terminals that physically resemble personal computers, yet do not have the same capabilities. The major distinction between a microcomputer and a "terminal" used to access a mainframe or minicomputer is the ability to control computer processing of text or data within the machine that is being operated directly by the user. The terminal serves only to accept input (i.e. typed commands) and display output (i.e. a menu of options available from the program on the mini- or mainframe computer).

Microcomputers are typically comprised of several different pieces of computer hardware. These include a central processing unit (a processor), memory, some form of disk storage (usually a hard disk drive), a monitor and related peripherals. Common peripherals include a mouse, to control the movement of a cursor in a machine using a graphical interface such as Windows, Macintosh, or X-windows for UNIX; a printer; a CD ROM reader; and a modem, to communicate with other microcomputers or computer systems via phone lines. The processor, disk drives, CD ROM reader and modem may all be housed in one "box," and therefore be perceived as a single unit by many users.

Microcomputers may be part of a larger networked system as well as being used as an independent, stand-alone system by a single user. When used as a stand-alone system, the software used is contained completely on the single system and all peripherals that may be used are attached directly to the box containing the processing unit and storage drives. Stand-alone systems may also be attached via network cabling or modems to other computer systems, provided that the hardware and software connections are compatible.

If a personal computer is used to connect to another system, it may be used as a terminal to access the other system, continue to be used primarily as a stand-alone system, or do some combination of the two in a shared processing activity. If it is used as a terminal, most data processing will be controlled by the "host" machine (see LOCAL AREA NETWORKS). This places the processing burden on the remote system, tying up mainframe or server resources but providing capabilities that may not normally be available on the local microcomputer.

Alternatively, it may also be used as a "client," retrieving files or programs from a "server," and retaining control of their processing in their local machine (see CLIENT/SERVER ARCHITECTURE). This client/server type of operation relieves the stress on shared network or mainframe resources. It may also result in better performance (i.e. faster processing) if the personal computer that is acting as the client has more memory or a faster processor.

The relative inexpensiveness and ease of acquiring microcomputers has led many individual users to select and set up their own systems either for work or for personal use. Most software that has been written for personal computers is easy to set up and learn. This combination has led to a huge growth in the use of microcomputers as many new users discover the gains that can be had in using a personal system. Personal computers can typically correspond more closely to an individual user's needs because of the wide variety of hardware and software options available.

This freedom to customize is not without drawbacks, however. The needs of individuals within organizations may not coincide with the more general concerns of their organization. Personal computer systems typically do not consider strong security measures, may lack compatibility in communication among systems, and may lead to widely varying expertise and standards between users within an organization. Users who seek a system for personal use may find similar frustrations as they attempt to accomplish their personal work on other, incompatible, machines or to share files or programs with other users.

Personal computer users must be concerned with their own security and backup of the programs and data. If a personal computer is attached to a network, it may be possible to have the network system read and backup the information on the microcomputer's storage devices, but backups are typically considered the responsibility of the user. Most microcomputers are not equipped with any extensive security protection; typically, any one can sit down, turn on, and operate a personal computer without the need for a password to verify their authorization to do so.

There are a few major operating systems that are used by most microcomputers today. The use of a common operating system has helped the problem that occurred frequently with early microcomputers that could not communicate at all with each other. In addition, most of the major and most widely used applications for microcomputers today incorporate the ability to save files in formats other than the original one used by that application. Some hardware manufacturers are also designing their products to handle multiple standard formats. Apple

Computers, for example, ships disk drives that are capable of reading DOS formatted disks.

However, there are many application packages that do not create "portable" files. They may be capable of saving a user's work in a standardized format, but the process may remove or make unusable special features such as graphics in a word-processed document or macros that perform calculations in a spreadsheet. Unless an organization has and enforces some policy of standardization of software selection among users, it is still relatively easy to end up with incompatible files that cannot be shared among users or between different personal computer systems.

HEATHER E. CARLSON

model management systems   A model management system is a component of a DECISION SUPPORT SYSTEM (DSS) that helps managers and analysts to construct, maintain, execute, and interpret decision models. Model management systems are similar to data management systems (*see* DATABASE MANAGEMENT SYSTEM), except that the information objects are models instead of files.

The early work on model management, which began in the mid-1970s, consisted of extending the CODASYL framework for data management to include decision models. This was supplemented by a relational view of model management in which models were viewed as virtual relations (*see* RELATIONAL DATABASE). The relational operations of selection, projection, and join were applied to these virtual relations. For example, a logical join of two models is accomplished by the physical operation of entering the output of one model into another model (*see* DATA MODELING, LOGICAL; DATA MODELING, PHYSICAL).

More recent work on model management has been directed to the use of ARTIFICIAL INTELLIGENCE (AI) (*see* EXPERT SYSTEMS; KNOWLEDGE BASE) in modeling. There are two principal areas of application here. The first is in the use of AI to help a user to construct models. One of the early systems of this type was a prototype system that helped a user to construct queuing simulations. The user entered a description of the queuing problem,

the system attempted to construct a simulation program, and it interrogated the user if additional information was needed. More recently, several prototype systems have been developed to help users to construct linear programming models. Most of these are domain-specific; that is, they require the problem to be of a certain type (product planning, production scheduling, etc.). The user enters a description of the problem and the system attempts to identify the decision valuables, objective function, and constraints.

The second application of AI to model management is in the interpretation of model outputs, especially when an anomaly, or counterintuitive result, appears in the output. As an illustration, a system called ANALYZE identifies anomalies in linear programming models, such as an unbounded solution, the absence of a feasible solution, or the use of apparently costly resources in a cost-minimization problem. (In the latter case, the less expensive resources may be explicitly or implicitly constrained, and the constraint may not be apparent to the user.) Another illustration is a system called ERGO that explains anomalies in spreadsheet outputs (*see* EXECUTIVE INFORMATION SYSTEMS). These will occur when two cases being compared for sensitivity analysis purposes have similar inputs but quite dissimilar outputs. ERGO searches for a simple explanation. Both of these systems contain expert knowledge in the form of heuristics for analyzing model outputs.

Model management systems are seldom stand-alone systems; rather, they are embedded in systems that contain two other important types of information for decision support: stored data and expert knowledge. This should not be surprising. The trend in single-user DSSs is toward the integration of stored data, decision models, and expert knowledge, and this is being supplemented with systems (*see* GROUP DECISION SUPPORT SYSTEMS) in which other people are information sources as well (*see* HUMANS AS INFORMATION PROCESSORS). Model management systems are one part of this trend.

ROBERT W. BLANNING

multimedia   The use of combinations of data, text, pictures, sound, animation, motion video, and graphics on a computer system. Multimedia comes at the intersections of analog and digital representations of information and of computing, TELECOMMUNICATION, consumer electronics, and media industries. It brings together very different technologies, approaches, and people. The blending of the underlying technologies and industries offers the computing abilities to index, store, and randomly retrieve information, the media abilities to create and deliver content that affects many of our senses, the wide availability and familiarity of consumer electronics devices, and the availability and access of the telecommunications and television infrastructures to transmit content between locations.

Digital Images

Multimedia involves the processing, storage, retrieval, and transmission of large amounts of data. A typical typed page of text contains 1,000 characters. That document, when "digitized," as in a Fax or with a scanner, is represented by about 1–10 million characters depending on whether it is stored as simple black and white or in full color. Recognizing that much of the document is contiguous white space, the computer software "compresses" the digitized data by indicating the number of consecutive white or black dots rather than storing all of them. Compression reduces the amount of data to represent the digitized page of text to in the region of 50,000 characters. Full motion video typically shows 30 "frames" per second to represent the motion fluidly. Motion video would require about 30 million characters of data per second without compression. Compression to represent full motion video reduces the data to 300,000 characters per second.

Physical Components

The physical components of multimedia come from the media, consumer electronics, computer, and telecommunications fields. Media and consumer electronic devices include microphones and electronic amplifier/speaker systems, professional and home video cameras, television technology, home and professional still cameras, audio CD players, VCRs, laser disc players, audio tape players, radios, and the

tape, disc, and film media that contain the creative content displayed by the devices. These devices and storage media have all traditionally been analog, although digital forms of most of the players have been introduced in the past few years.

Computer devices and storage media include magnetic and optical disks, magnetic tapes, digital monitors, room display devices such as LCD panels and digital TV-type display projectors, portable and desktop microcomputers, scanners, Fax, software, laser printers, modems for telecommunications, and LOCAL AREA NETWORKS (LAN). The computer devices are digital, although interfaces exist in terms of hardware cards and software drivers to integrate the analog media devices into computer systems. Computer devices convert analog inputs such as full motion video into digital form. Software capabilities include optical character recognition, which recognizes or converts a scanned page into text characters, and voice recognition technology which converts speech into text and text to speech.

Telecommunication includes the transmission facilities of the communications companies, satellite transmission, television, microwave, and LANs plus the software and protocols that transmit the varieties of data between a wide range of devices.

Functional Capabilities and Benefits

Functional capabilities of multimedia include the ability to generate, store, manipulate, retrieve, transmit, and present "images" from the physical devices. Scanned, faxed, written, voice, motion video, and still camera images can be used as input, processed, and presented as output, or communicated across geography via telecommunications and portable storage media such as optical and magnetic disk. Multimedia supports use familiar forms and formats of information in a computer and communications system.

Multiple party audio-video conferencing is a common, basic, and dominant multimedia capability, having broad applicability. Conventional telephone communication, while simultaneous among the parties, is often viewed as suitable for highly personal or social communications or group meeting situations, which therefore requires the parties to meet face to face for that discussion or communication. ELECTRONIC MAIL, even when simultaneous, has similar shortcomings. Video conferencing adds the important common capability of "looking the other person in the eye," and thus offers the potential to significantly change the way we work, become educated, and conduct transactions.

Indexing and electronic retrieval of multimedia audio and video clips and images is another basic capability that provides a foundation for many applications. In education, this supports remote access to multimedia libraries and videos of classes. In communication, it supports multimedia mail. In transactions, the purchaser can access a multimedia catalog. In entertainment, it supports remote access to video libraries.

Multimedia can be employed in GROUP DECISION SUPPORT SYSTEMS to support groups in local and remote meetings. The addition of multimedia to games and simulations enables the situation to be represented in a manner that is very familiar to the users. Business games and simulations are used in class lectures, in labs, and at home to teach basic business processes and data uses. The use of multimedia in simulations allows the comparison of a variety of situations and operating modes, and can also be used as a tutor.

Applications

The applications of multimedia can be grouped into four general categories: educate and inform; exchange and transact; entertain; and communicate. The functional capabilities of audio-video conferencing, indexing and retrieval of multimedia content, group decision support technology, and multimedia games and simulations provide the basis for specific applications. Following are examples of specific applications of multimedia to the education category, which also translate to the other application categories.

Multi- and two-way interactive and real-time distance learning for remote students, faculty, and guests to become an active part of the in-class delivery, is an important example of video conferencing. Implementation of distance learning, although difficult, offers significant opportunity to deliver courses differently and to a different mix of students. Video conferencing can also support remote individual or small group tutoring and grading.

Indexing and retrieval applications offer significant potential in education, in the classroom, in labs, and in remote access. Case discussions are widely used to relate conceptual material to actual situations. Cases are typically presented in written form. A multimedia case includes written case materials prepared by the faculty author, many of the materials used in developing the case, audio-video clips of case principals in a question/answer mode, and audio-video clips of pertinent products and facilities. Student preparation and the class discussion of the case can be enhanced by random access to motion video clips of principles of the case discussing certain points, and a "clip library" to illustrate or explain concepts, places, people, etc. Similarly, lectures can be enhanced by access in the classroom to multimedia content; for example, video clips of questions and answers, experts, specific situations, and instructor access to libraries of multimedia files, databases, etc.

Group meetings are typically limited to one person speaking at a time, by the listening and writing ability of the recorder, and by the ability of the meeting facilitator. Group decision support systems using multimedia allow simultaneous brainstorming input in the words and writing of each individual. This both speeds up the meeting and moves more easily to consensus. Video conferencing and retrieval applications also facilitate the group being separated in both time and place.

Simulations of very complicated or dangerous situations are typically mathematically based and as such difficult for most people to interpret. The use of multimedia allows people to examine the simulation using more of their senses. Video conferencing and retrieval applications can also provide interpretive help for simulations.

LESTER A. WANNINGER JR

N

neural networks   A neural network is a software system that learns. Assume a data set with n pieces of input data, m pieces of output data, and k examples specifying input–output pairs. It is possible to analyze the data to come up with an algorithm specifying input and output relationships. A program can be written to execute the algorithm. Alternatively, the data can be used to train a neural network, a general-purpose analytical program, to arrive at an algorithm. The factor weights, which are internal parameters of the general-purpose programs, will be adjusted to suit the given problem. This produces a tailored neural network. With the input data from one of the k examples, the system will reproduce the corresponding output data. With a new set of input data, it will produce a set of output data based on some relationship criteria. It is also a system that is massively parallel. The nodes in the network can perform simple computations independently. Since the computations are simple, it is assumed that they are completed at the same time. It is not necessary to check and make sure that other nodes have completed their job. This simplifies the algorithm and allows the system to arrive at a solution quickly.

The information stored in a neural network is distributed. If asked to remember ten pictures that the software should recognize, it does not store the bit patterns of these pictures. It learns the pictures to be recognized by using the picture bit patterns to calculate weights. These weights can be considered as a kind of weighted average of the bit patterns. When a noisy picture with some missing parts is presented as input, a degraded picture is output. The degradation is distributed throughout the picture instead of concentrating on the missing part. This is known as gradual degradation.

Internally, a neural network consists of a large number of interconnected processors called nodes. Each connection is represented by an arrow that points from a parent node to a child node. The nodes are classified into three types: input, output, and hidden. An input node has arrows radiating from it but no arrow pointing to it. The opposite is true of an output node. A hidden node is connected to both types of arrows.

The nodes are usually arranged in layers. Connections are allowed only between nodes in adjacent layers. For the purpose of computation, each node is characterized by a quantity called its *activation*, and each arrow is associated with a quantity called the *weight*. A parent node uses a transfer function to convert the activation into a message and sends it along the connections to its children nodes. The receiving node uses the message and the weights to perform simple computations to get its own activation. The process is repeated and the information is modified and passed along through the network. The network is essentially the algorithm for producing outputs from inputs.

There are two types of users of the neural network: the application programmer and the end user. The application programmer needs to know the structure of the neural network. Decisions are made about the number of layers, the number of nodes in each layer, the learning algorithm and the transfer function to be used. K examples are used to train the network and test and make sure that the system produces the correct output when the k sets of input are presented. The end user sends new input to a tailor-made network and obtains output from the output nodes.

A neural network has its limitations. There is no proper theoretical basis for most of the models. The conditions for the learning process to converge are not known. When it converges, we do not know whether it reaches a global minimum or a local minimum. A few applications illustrate its use.

1 *Information retrieval*. Using a neural network, records can be retrieved from a database with over-specified condition or with conflicting information. In these cases, the system provides a prioritized list of answers.
2 *Logical inference*. Implementing EXPERT SYSTEMS by using a neural network as its INFERENCE ENGINE allows learning by examples. It is not necessary for the domain expert to provide rules. The neural network does not work by rules. The expert provides examples. This approach has been applied to systems based on classical, three-valued, probabilistic, and fuzzy logic.
3 *Financial forecasting*. A neural network can be used for time series prediction. Examples are stock market, foreign currency market, and various other financial indices.

LOKE SOO HSU

O

object-oriented database management systems OODBMS represent a new breed of DATABASE MANAGEMENT SYSTEM (DBMS). These grew out of a marriage of object-oriented programming languages and conventional DBMSs. They represent the next generation of database management systems.

OODBMSs are intended to handle more complex data in increasingly complex application systems. This includes heterogeneous multimedia forms of data such as text, graphics (bit mapped and vector), three-dimensional graphics, moving video, audio, etc. They are also designed to handle complex object composition and complex inter-object processing. As such, they can produce substantially better performance compared to traditional relational DBMS. Relational DBMSs are optimized to process one or a small number of large files, whereas OODBMSs are optimized for complex inter-entity processing. Typical applications include computer-aided design/computer-aided manufacturing (CAD/CAM), geographic information systems (GIS), document description, CASE repositories, and others characterized by complex object descriptions and relationships.

The essential characteristic of an OODBMS is the encapsulation of objects or entities and the procedures used to access and process those objects. The system provides a formal mechanism which separates the referencing, accessing and manipulation of objects from the methods which implement those actions. Thus the method of implementation is hidden from the outside world, that is, the world of users and programmers which access and modify objects. The object-oriented approach provides for levels of abstraction in the design and implementation of systems.

OODBMSs differ from relational DBMSs in several significant ways. Object (entity) identifiers must be immutable, that is, unchanging, whereas in a relational DBMS they are defined by users and can be changed by users. An OODBMS depends upon immutable object identifiers to maintain inter-object relationships. Good design in a relational environment requires records to be in third normal form. This means record decomposition. Then it is necessary for the user to perform JOIN operations to bring together the data pertaining to an object. Relational database design breaks down records and formally defines the result to the DBMS. However, relational systems provide no formal mechanism for defining record (re)compositions to get back to how end users actually think about objects. In contrast, OODBMSs provide formal mechanisms for defining inter-object relationships and complex object compositions.

OODBMSs are used primarily in environments where system developers write their own programs. Hence, the emphasis is on providing an application programming interface (API) to object-oriented programming languages such as C++ and SmallTalk. There has been less emphasis on providing a human interface for interactive processing and high-level query languages.

Initially, the main players in the marketplace for OODBMSs were new names. However, traditional DBMS vendors will eventually enter the marketplace as well with revised or new versions of their packages. Some OODBMSs are built as extensions of existing object-oriented programming languages, some are built from scratch, and some are hybrids of a relational system and an object-oriented system.

GORDON C. EVEREST

object-oriented programs and systems
Object-orientation (OO) is a philosophy of software development based on the concept of autonomous *objects* providing services for each other through requests (*messages*). The metaphor for object-oriented programming is assembling a set of objects and coordinating their behavior with a script of messages to meet the application requirements. Object-oriented systems support object-oriented programming by providing a language and development environment.

Smalltalk, originally developed at Xerox Palo Alto Research Center (PARC), is among the purest and most influential object-oriented systems. It incorporates a programming language and an interactive development interface. It includes an extensive set of system classes and objects capable of providing services such as object creation, window management, user interaction, data conversion, arithmetic, string manipulation, and iteration.

An object is an *instance* capable of providing services. It is the fundamental building block of an object-oriented program. Everything in an object-oriented program is an object. Objects can be as simple as numbers and characters and as complex as window managers and jet engines. Every object has a system-supplied *object identifier* (OID). Services are obtained when a *client* object sends a message to a *server* or *receiver* object. Services can be as simple as answering itself and as complicated as analyzing an entire engineering design.

An object provides services by using its data (*variables*) and procedures (*methods*). Only an object has access to its variables. Clients request a server to execute one of its methods by sending it a message with the same name as the method (termed the method's *signature*) and providing appropriate parameters, if necessary. The client only knows the method's signature and what to expect as an answer. It does not know how the service is provided, i.e. the implementation is *hidden* from the client. This insulates objects from changes in other objects.

Provided its signature and answer remain constant, a method can be changed without affecting its clients.

Objects are composed of other objects (an object's variables contain other objects) and are organized into *classes* according to their services. Classes are organized into a class structure. In Smalltalk, the class structure is a superclass/subclass hierarchy with the class *Object* as the root. All other classes are *subclasses* of it (i.e. children in the hierarchy). All subclasses *inherit* the variables and methods of the superclass. Classes can be viewed as containers for variable and method definitions.

Smalltalk differentiates *class* variables and methods from *instance* variables and methods. Class variables and methods apply to the class. Instance variables and methods apply to the objects in the class. A class method is executed when the corresponding message is sent to the class. An instance method is executed when the corresponding message is sent to an object of the class. Class variables and methods are inherited by subclasses. Instance variables and methods are inherited by objects in the subclasses.

Consider the following Smalltalk code segment.

'Smalltalk is Object-Oriented' size.

Enclosing the words, Smalltalk is Object-Oriented, in single quotes causes Smalltalk to create an object of the class String (a character string). This object is sent the message *size*. In the Smalltalk class hierarchy the path from Object to String is: Object, Collection, SequenceableCollection, ArrayedCollection, CharacterArray, String. String inherits all of the variables and methods from all of these classes. In particular, an object of class String inherits the instance method *size* from Collection (a string is a collection of characters). Hence, this string can respond to the message *size*. It answers 28, an object of the class Integer.

Since the answer from a message is an object, messages can be sent to answers. In

'Smalltalk is Object-Oriented' asSet size

the message *asSet* is sent to the String object, 'Smalltalk is Object-Oriented' which answers an object of the class Set containing the unique characters in the string. The message *size* is sent to this object which answers 18.

Collection is an ancestor of String and Set. Both inherit the method *size* from it. This illustrates the concept of code *reuse*. All subclasses of Collection can use the same method to respond to the message *size*. Inheritance facilitates the design of systems that minimize new code by reusing existing code. Of course, subclasses can *reimplement* methods if it is more efficient to do so.

Surprising results can be obtained from this definition of messaging. Consider the following code segment.

$$5 + 6 * 3.$$

This answers 33 rather than the expected 23! The message + is sent to the object 5 with the parameter 6 (an object). 5 answers the object 11 to which the message * is sent with the parameter 3 (an object). 11 answers the object 33. Precedence can be altered by using parentheses.

Applications are developed in Smalltalk by extending the class hierarchy. New variables and methods can be added to existing classes to extend their capabilities. New classes can be inserted into the class hierarchy to take advantage of inheritance. One of the most important prerequisites for developing applications in Smalltalk is learning the capabilities of the class hierarchy. One of the major management issues is *control* over the class hierarchy. A *reuse engineer* identifies commonality among applications so that classes and methods developed in one application can be reused in other applications rather than redeveloped in them.

The capabilities of the class, Number, can be extended by adding the following method, *alignRight:*, to it. This method answers a string of specified size containing the number aligned to the right or *s if the specified size is too small. The colon in the method signature indicates that it has one parameter (the size of the string).

alignRight: stringSize

"Answer a String aligned to the right of the field"

| n str |

str := self printString

n := str size

(n > stringSize)

ifTrue: [^String new: stringSize with All: $*]

ifFalse: [^(String new: stringSize withAll: $)

changeFrom: stringSize −n + 1 to: stringSize with: str]

n and *str* are temporary variables; *self* refers to the receiver; all messages are defined in the class hierarchy; ^ precedes the object answered.

This method is executed by sending the message *alignRight:* with an integer parameter to any object of the class Number (or any of its subclasses), e.g.

453.87 alignRight: 10

453.87 would answer a String object containing four blank spaces and the characters 453.87

As a simple example of defining new classes for an application, the class Employee can be added as a subclass of Object.

Object subclass: # Employee
    instance VariableNames: 'eno ename ssn exemptions'
    class VariableNames: 'FICARate FitPerExemption FitRate MaxFICAGross'

Class methods specific to Employee would include methods to assign and access its class variables (parameters for the calculation of federal taxes). Instance methods would include methods to assign and access instance variables and to calculate gross pay and deductions for payroll. Employee would inherit the class method *new* from Object to create Employee objects.

One of the complexities of payroll production is that different types of employees calculate their gross pay in different ways, e.g. hourly, salaried, and commission employees. To address this, subclasses of Employee can be created, e.g. HourlyEmployee, SalariedEmployee, and Commission Employee, each having an instance method called *calcGross* to calculate gross pay in the appropriate way. Having different methods with the same name is termed *polymorphism*. Methods for common calculations, e.g. taxes, would be defined in Employee and inherited by the subclasses. This reuse reduces the amount of code that needs to be developed and simplifies the application design.

SALVATORE T. MARCH

object role modeling   Object role modeling is a database design modeling technique based upon NIAM (Nijssen Information Analysis Method). The extensions and refinements to NIAM were primarily due to Terry Halpin (1995). NIAM/ORM modeling has also been called Binary Relationship modeling.

Object Role (OR) modeling builds a data model using two constructs: objects and relationships. This is in contrast to record-based data modeling techniques such as relational or entity relationship (ER) modeling. Record-based modeling uses three constructs: entities, attributes, and relationships. In OR modeling, entities and attributes are both treated as objects (this use of the term objects has no relationship to object-orientation). In OR modeling, objects obtain attributes by virtue of being related to other objects.

OR modeling is more expressive than ER modeling, particularly in the expression of constraints on a data model. OR modeling does not cluster attributes into records. Building records should be the next step in the database design process. If done prematurely (and often incorrectly), building records can lead to a violation of normal forms. In record-based modeling, proper record design demands that records be in third normal form, that is, not containing any multiple, partial, or transitive dependencies. A violation of third normal form is remedied by further decomposing the records in the design. OR modeling achieves the ultimate end of record decomposition, where each record has at most one non-key domain. Hence, normal form violations can never occur.

OR modeling views the world as objects playing roles in relationship with other objects. It begins with an expression of facts made up of nouns and verbs. The nouns are the objects and the verbs are the roles played by the objects in relationships. Facts are expressed in sentences. In an object role model, these are *elementary* (or irreducible) sentences. For example, an elementary unary fact might be "Jane smiles". This is

an instance of the general fact type "the person named Jane smiles". An example of a binary fact might be "Bob likes Jane". At the type level, this is expressed "person named Bob likes person named Jane". It is possible to express higher order facts. For example, employee with name — possesses skill — with proficiency rating of — is a ternary fact type.

These elementary sentences can be represented diagrammatically with circles for objects and arcs for relationships. The circle contains the name (noun) of the object. On the arc, a box is drawn with one or more parts. A line connects each part of the box to exactly one object. In each part of the box, a verb is used for the role the connected object plays in the relationship with the other object(s). For example:

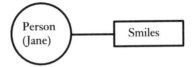

For the ternary fact type above, the diagram would appear as:

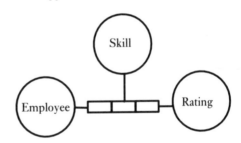

In a ternary relationship, if only two of the roles are needed for uniqueness, they can be separated out and made into a nested or objectified object, to which is attached the third object. In the above example, employee and skill could be together in one box, and then have that become another object by drawing a circle around the box with two parts and connecting that with another box to the rating object. Object types can be divided into subtypes relating to a supertype.

To any data model diagram, the following types of constraints are added:

- *Uniqueness* to specify the multiplicity (or cardinality) on the relationship, such as one to one, one to many, many to many

- *Dependency* when it is mandatory that all instances of an object participate in the relationship (sometimes called the totality constraint)

- *Reference* scheme for naming or referencing objects

- *Value set* for valid ranges or ennumerated sets of values

- *Set constraints* such as IF (conditional), IFF (if and only if), subset, etc.

There are other types of constraints.

Bibliography

Nijssen, Shir & Halpin, Terry (1989). *Conceptual Schema and Relational Database Design.* Prentice-Hall International (Australia). Second Edition, Terry Halpin, 1995.

GORDON C. EVEREST

office automation   A term applied to a wide variety of equipment and software for automating or supporting clerical and professional activities in an office environment. The technology for office automation includes hardware and software for communications, data and text management, and image processing. Communications support includes voice mail, electronic mail, fascimile (Fax), and teleconferencing. Examples of data and text management include optical character recognition, copier and printing systems, storage and retrieval systems, and access to external information sources. Image processing includes scanners and graphics packages.

OLE   Object linking and embedding (OLE) is a method for linking or embedding an object from one application into another application. For example, a spreadsheet or part of a spreadsheet can be embedded in a document and linked to the spreadsheet source. When the source object is changed, the embedded object is also changed automatically. The automatic change may, however, be disabled. Object linking and embedding is important for information processing because many applications use data or analyses from other files. OLE reduces the need to re-enter changes when documents or spreadsheets are interconnected. OLE is a proprietary standard developed by Microsoft. A competing standard is Open Doc, developed by a consortium of other vendors.

online analytic processing   OLAP is the acronym for a set of tools and a form of information processing that allows end users to access, analyze, and represent organizational data in ways useful for management decision-making, control, and forecasting. OLAP tools allow end users to explore the historical databases of an organization, looking for patterns and anomalies that can lend insight into managerial decision-making and forecasting. OLAP addresses search and representation problems that highlight the difference between data and information. The problems are caused by the combination of the constraints inherent in the human cognitive processing system and the current functional architecture of relational database management systems or online transaction processing systems.

OLAP tools use a multidimensional representation of aggregated, summarized, and statistically manipulated data to make possible pattern recognition by end users. A typical example of this multidimensional representation might be a spreadsheet depicting the mean number of items sold by a distributor, by region of the country, by month of the year, with rankings within product groupings. This multidimensional representation (time, location, and product type are the dimensions) extracts patterns and trends in the data that are meaningful to the user instead of the row-by-column representation of raw data contained within the transaction data. These tools allow pattern extraction by the end user to operate in an intuitive and iterative fashion. Users create one form of summary or statistical analysis, the results of which naturally lead to "drill down" to a greater level of detail, "roll up" to a higher level of aggregation, or view the data along another dimension.

CHRIS CARR

online systems   Applications with immediate data input and processing. Users interact with the computer to enter data and obtain results (*see* PROCESSING METHODS FOR INFORMATION SYSTEMS).

open doc   A method for object linking and embedding (*see* OLE).

optical character recognition   OCR is a technology for reading and interpreting machine-printed or hand-written symbols. Optical character recognition can also include technology to read optical marks and magnetic ink characters. Examples of optical marks are the universal product code (*see* BAR CODE) and the United States Postal Service bar code for zip codes. Magnetic ink characters are used on bank checks and similar bank documents.

Optical character recognition systems are used to read machine-printed fonts. Standard stylized fonts are available for optical character applications (OCR-A and OCR-B), but most machine-printed fonts are readable. In a typical business application, a customer returns a part of the billing form containing customer information, such as account number and amount due, printed on it. The turnaround document is read with an OCR reader.

Hand-printed characters can also be read. In order to achieve reasonable accuracy, the characters must be carefully printed. To aid users in entering data, forms typically provide a marked space for each character.

GORDON B. DAVIS

organization of the information system function   Information systems (IS) have traditionally been organized by function. For example, a typical IS functional organization would have units for systems analysis, programming, computer operations, technical support, and user support. Some managerial, financial/planning, and administrative support would also be present. There are variations to this functional model. For example, some information system groups have combined systems analysis and programming; others have organized systems analysis and programming by business function. Some application groups within IS have combined applications maintenance with new development; others have split such groups apart. In some cases, development projects are under the direction of information systems; in other cases, projects have a cross-functional team structure including users. In a number of cases, application developers or user-support employees have also been transferred to user departments.

These basic and variant IS organizational structures are examined using the perspective of Henry Mintzberg (1979). Three primary aspects of internal IS structure are considered: the design of IS positions; the combining of IS positions into groups; and coordination among IS groups. Two structural issues from outside the IS group are also addressed: decentralization and outsourcing.

The Design of IS Positions

Positions entail sets of task-related roles. Four broad types of IS positions may be identified. The first three positions are technical in nature: system developer, technical support specialist, and computer operator. The fourth position is that of a managerial/clerical person. The managerial/clerical positions are much like those in any organization. IS is unique in that its technical positions are typically filled by quasi-professionals.

The first issue in designing positions is job enlargement. This issue addresses how specialized each IS position should be, and how much discretion the worker in the position should be given. For example, should a computer operator only monitor one type of system, and how much discretion should the operator have in resolving system problems? These questions relate to two types of job enlargement: horizontal and vertical. Horizontal job enlargement (opposite of job specialization) is the degree to which a job contains many tasks. Vertical job enlargement (i.e. worker discretion or absence of management control) means the degree to which the worker controls how the task is done. The design of vertical and horizontal job enlargement depends on three types of factors: task, people, and organizational constraints.

Effective job enlargement requires consideration of task factors. IS tasks that are complex or unstructured (e.g. large system development) tend to have high horizontal job enlargement. Tasks that are routine or well structured (e.g. computer tape locating) are likely to have low horizontal job enlargement. Similarly, complex and unstructured tasks are hard to control except by the person working on them; hence, vertical enlargement is typically high. System developers fit this criterion. In routine tasks, vertical enlargement (worker control) would be low.

Human factors should also be considered. Human cognitive limitations tend to lower horizontal enlargement (e.g. no one can be an expert in all technologies). This leads to specialized technical positions within IS. Individual preferences for the amount of control over one's task affect vertical enlargement. For example, a quasi-professional system developer, given the complex and unstructured nature of the task, will want more discretion over the work to be done. This may become a motivation issue as well, since decreased task discretion tends to destroy intrinsic motivation and leads to reliance on sanctions for motivation. These extrinsic motivators may work well for routine positions, where behaviors and/or outcomes are easy to measure; but those performing complex roles are not easily measured. Hence, extrinsic rewards will often not be practical for those with complex and unstructured jobs. An example is system development. Further, quasi-professionals who start with high intrinsic motivation may become less motivated overall if given extrinsic motivation. Worse still, they may become motivated only to do those things on which their compensation depends, leaving other important matters not done. There is also an interaction between task and human factors. The fit of the task to the individual becomes key, since one person will be motivated by one task and its rewards, while another person will be motivated by a very different task and reward set.

The third factor to consider in job enlargement is organizational constraints. A number of organizational constraints on job design may be present. Constraints include, for example, a need for high productivity (low unit costs), or a need for better employee satisfaction. For routine jobs, such as data entry, low horizontal and vertical job enlargement tend to lead to high productivity but low satisfaction. However, such outcomes will depend on how constraints interact with task and human factors.

In addition to job enlargement, designing positions requires consideration of behavior formalization. Behavior formalization means the standardization of work, which can be done by job and task descriptions, rules, or workflow specifications. The issue is the extent to which IS tasks can be standardized. Behavior is formalized to maximize control and predictability over the work process (and thus the work outcome). In the IS context, behavior formalization may be very appropriate to computer center operations where assurance of continued operation is critical. Formalization is also key to assuring productivity and quality for stable, repetitive work, such as installing computer devices. However, high levels of behavior formalization will be futile or even dysfunctional when tasks are complex or unstructured, such as system development or technical support. The nature of the system development task is such that it is very difficult to pre-specify analyst behavior. Hence, attempts to formalize only create a set of procedures that are put on the shelf but rarely followed. Further, improperly applied behavior formalization can make interpersonal communication and behavior rigid and defensive, harm creativity, and hurt the relationships between superiors and subordinates. Some levels of behavior formalization are desirable when the following are urgent: high productivity, need to display order, need for precise coordination, and need to show fairness to clients.

Combining IS Positions into Groups

The next consideration is how to group positions into units (i.e. groups) and how to place small units within larger units. This question may be applied to such issues as whether to group all maintenance programmers together or whether to keep them with development programmers, who are organized by user group. Positions may be grouped by technical work function (functional grouping, e.g. by system operator versus developer); market/client (e.g. systems development supporting finance); time (first, second, third shift); or geographical place. Many large organizations use combinations of these types of groupings. Use of time groupings will depend on the use of shifts. Use of geographical groupings will be done if the location-related differences (e.g. language or time zones) create significant coordination issues. Functional and market groupings have advantages and disadvantages.

Functional grouping encourages specialization, socialization, and coordination between similar people. Hence, a functional grouping benefits IS to the extent that it is important that:

- coordination takes place smoothly within the group (e.g. for self-contained project teams)

- individuals socialize and train one another in highly specialized functions (high need for technical excellence, specialization, career satisfaction)

- individuals are supervised by one of their own (high need for hierarchical coordination/control or technical excellence)

- economies of scale are gained via utilization of functional specialists on cross-market initiatives (high need for productivity/low costs)

Several of these needs are typically displayed in parts of IS. For example, technical specialists and programmer/analysts may learn more from each other than from outside training. The disadvantages of the functional grouping include:

- an increased difficulty in coordinating work between functional groups

- a tendency for workers to be more interested in design elegance than in cost-effective, customer-oriented solutions

- less flexibility in changing tasks

- difficulty in using user-oriented outcome controls for some tasks

Market grouping (e.g. organizing programmers by user group) encourages smooth workflow coordination, since market groups can often contain all the major work-related interdependencies. Coordination can then be done without behavior formalization, because two other key coordination mechanisms (informal mutual adjustment and direct supervision) reside within the unit. Market group outcomes, such as satisfaction, may be measured at the client or product level. This grouping type enables a unit to independently perform a wider variety of tasks than a functional unit. It is therefore more flexible to task changes. Market grouping is also effective when the group needs to focus attention on its markets or improve rapport with its clients by being more responsive. The disadvantages of market grouping are:

- lower ability to do specialized tasks well

- lower sense of professional worth/satisfaction because the evaluation of work takes place outside specialist peers

- resource utilization inefficiencies

From this discussion of factors favoring functional versus market grouping, it is clear that the tradeoffs to consider in IS organization design are complex and situational. If technical excellence and cost efficiency needs are preeminent (e.g. for system development tasks), the functional grouping should be used, but only if workflow interdependencies can be effectively addressed through coordination mechanisms such as liaison positions or standardization. Market groupings should be chosen if workflow coordination or customer-specific flexibility needs are predominant, but it will be ineffective to the extent that technical sophistication or efficiency needs are also salient. The tendency to organize system development groups both functionally and by client is an indication that, for this function, both sets of needs are often important to address.

Coordination among IS Groups

Beyond grouping by function or market, it is important to address the interdependencies between groups. The issue is how IS groups should coordinate interdependent needs. Highly interdependent manager groups (e.g. mainframe system hardware and software operations) should report to the same director group, where possible. The type of interdependence can help determine unit grouping (Thompson, 1967). Groups that are reciprocally interdependent (i.e. they must frequently interact and mutually depend on each other's work) should be grouped in the organization closest to each other.

The multiple complex needs of an organization sometimes create residual interdependencies, which means that task, process, or social coordination needs are not being met by the formal organization structure. Informal coordination (mutual adjustment) mechanisms fill the gaps. In order of their increasing ability to provide mutual adjustment, coordination devices include liaison positions, task forces, integrating managers and matrix structure. In IS, these structures may take the form of user liaisons, project teams, engagement managers, or dual reporting relationships. Liaison devices can help make up for the deficiencies of market or functional structures. For example, coordination problems between two functionally separate but interdependent units can be addressed by liaison positions. When this structure needs more mutual adjustment, additional methods are a task force and an integrating manager. For example, such devices may be applied to computer operations to meet the needs of customer groups. The market organization that needs the benefits of specialization (e.g. a system development group) can use a functional manager to help its team members to retain their quasi-professional identity, update their skills, and make clear their career path. Matrix structures may be used if critical interdependencies remain.

The matrix structure tries to strike a balance between market and functional groupings. Some matrix structures, such as large, cross-functional system development teams, are created for the project duration only. During the project, user and IS team members report both to their functional unit leaders and to the project leader. Another example is the dual reporting of a maintenance programmer, who may report both to a functional manager accountable for efficiency and a market manager accountable for relations with the functions using the applications. The matrix structure embodies a very difficult balance to maintain. Also, it eliminates unity of authority and creates ambiguities for workers. Because no one has final authority, each side must work out its differences through informal peer-to-peer negotiations. Other problems with matrix structures include stress, higher coordination costs, and the difficulty of maintaining a balance of power between functional- and market-oriented managers.

Decentralization

The next consideration is the extent to which IS functions should be decentralized (done within the firm, but outside the centralized IS group). Decentralization primarily depends on interdependencies between task groups. The principles discussed above regarding combining IS positions into groups apply here. For example, users and system developers may need to be grouped together because of strong reciprocal interdependencies, especially during development projects. Decentralization is also done because of the trend toward microcomputing and client/server infrastructures and the general industry trend toward decentralizing organizations. Decentralized IS often offers greater flexibility and better customer support. Drawbacks include those discussed for market grouping of IS. The exception to the decentralization trend is with large mainframe environments that serve multiple organizational constituents.

Outsourcing

The final issue is the extent to which IS functions should be done outside the organization (*see* OUTSOURCING). The choice to use internal or external providers can either be framed as a market issue or a strategic issue. The market perspective primarily examines the costs of contracting and administering workers. Internalized IS workers most likely consist of those with organization-specific skills. Externalized workers tend to be those with less organization-specific, more rapidly obsolete, skills. Rapid evolution of technology may quickly erode particular technical skills. For example, by the time an organization invests in and trains its IS staff in a certain technology, that technology may already be obsolete. Hence, keeping internal people trained may be too costly.

The strategic perspective assesses strategic value or benefits of the IS function. Strategically, organizations should develop a core set of corporate skills and capabilities internally, and, at the same time, contract out activities that support the core. Hence, internalized IS workers would consist of those involved in activities deemed critical to the firm's survival.

Organizations sometimes outsource because of the scarcity of particular skills. Such arrangements have been legitimized by major organizations. IS often faces severe skills shortages because the industry is relatively new, highly specialized, and growing. Skills scarcity increases when organizations reduce investment in training IS personnel. High turnover rates mean organizations may not recover training investment.

Bibliography

Mintzberg, H. (1979). *The Structuring of Organizations: a Synthesis of the Research.* Englewood Cliffs, NJ: Prentice-Hall.

Thompson, J. D. (1967). *Organizations in Action.* New York: McGraw-Hill.

D. HARRISON MCKNIGHT and
SANDRA SLAUGHTER

output devices   For an information system to be useful, a user or another information system must be able to use the results or output of the information processing. Output devices take processed data or information from the computer and convert it to a form that the user can understand and use. Logically, output is the inverse of input, and both are required to integrate information systems into human systems. There are devices that perform both input and output. These are called secondary or external storage devices and telecommunications devices and, although vital to the effective use of the information system, they are considered separately from the output devices discussed here.

Computers interact with the outside world using devices called *ports*. A port is an electronic gateway through which signals pass to and from the computer to the user and the world outside. Output devices typically use either parallel or serial ports. A *parallel port* sends multiple bits of data from the computer to the output device, while the *serial port* sends only one bit at a time. There are several different standards for ports

and, with the increasing need for more data and more sophisticated output devices, more are being developed.

Output can be divided into two very general classes: hard copy and soft copy. Hard copy, usually printed material (text or graphics), is more tangible and permanent than soft copy, which is usually displayed on the monitor screen or heard and is not considered a permanent record. There are two basic types of printers: impact and nonimpact. As the name implies, impact printers operate by impacting, or physically striking, the paper. Impact printers have two advantages over nonimpact printers. They are generally less expensive, and they can print on multicopy forms such as invoices, shipping labels, and receipts. However, their print quality is usually not as good as nonimpact printers; they are generally slower and noisier. The two types of impact printers are dot-matrix printers and daisy wheel printers.

The matrix in a dot-matrix printer consists of a rectangle filled with very small pins. Different combinations of the pins are used to represent different characters. As the pins are activated they strike a ribbon, similar to a typewriter ribbon, which is pushed against the paper. Ink is transferred from the ribbon to the paper, resulting in the printed character. Dot-matrix printers may be classified by the number of pins in the matrix (e.g. a 24-pin printer). The more pins, the better the print quality. Daisy wheel printers are becoming less common. They use a wheel or disk which spins at high speed. As the wheel rotates, the desired character is brought into position, where it is struck by a piston or hammer. The force of the blow causes that portion of the wheel with the character on it to impact the ribbon, transferring the character image to the paper.

Nonimpact printers use a variety of methods to print characters. The three most common types are thermal, ink-jet, and laser. Thermal printers share the same basic design concept as dot-matrix printers. They have a rectangular matrix filled with heated rods. As the ends of the selected rods touch the paper, they literally burn, or brand, a character into the paper. Early thermal printers required special heat-sensitive paper, but modern ones can use regular paper. As with dot-matrix printers, the more rods in the matrix, the higher the print quality.

Ink-jet printers use a nozzle to shoot a stream of extremely small droplets of ink through electrically charged plates. These plates arrange the ink particles into the required characters. The quality of ink-jet printers is usually superior to that of dot-matrix, daisy wheel, or thermal printers. Certain ink-jet printers can also print in color (red, green, blue, and black ink is combined to create the desired color). Care must be taken when selecting paper to be used in ink-jet printers, however. A soft grade of paper may absorb the ink, resulting in fuzzy looking print.

Laser printers use a beam of light focused through a rotating disk containing a character set. The laser beam, now shaped like a character, is projected on a photosensitive drum. Powered ink (toner) is then fixed to the paper with heat. Laser printers are capable of higher print quality and faster speeds than other printers, but with higher cost. Laser printers able to print in color are available.

Print quality is generally defined as either letter quality or near-letter quality. Letter quality is comparable to typewriter or published print. Near-letter quality is less sharp. Impact and thermal print is usually considered near-letter quality, although some dot-matrix printers with a high number of pins can approach letter quality. Most ink-jet and laser printers are letter quality. Another measure of print quality is the number of dots per inch (dpi). This comes from the number of pins per inch in a dot-matrix printer. Once again, the higher the number, the better the print quality. Letter-quality print is considered to begin at around 300 dpi. Higher dpi is required for high-quality reproduction.

Printer speed can be clocked two different ways. Dot-matrix and ink-jet printers, which print one character at a time, are measured in characters per second (cps). These printer speeds can range from approximately 50 cps to over 400 cps. Because laser printers use a drum that prints line by line, their speed is measured in pages per minute (ppm). Using general approximations, laser printers operate between 4 and 25 ppm. Most laser printers used with personal computers are capable of around 6 ppm. By contrast, most ink-jet printers are rated in the neighborhood of 3 ppm, and dot-matrix printers are about half as slow as ink-jet printers. These speeds are for printers generally used with microcomputers. There are large-scale commercial printers which can generate over 20,000 lines per minute, or approximately 400 ppm.

Monitors, sometimes called video display terminals (VDT) or cathode ray tubes (CRT), are devices that display output on a video screen, similar to a television. Like a television, a monitor uses an electron gun to shoot a beam of electrons onto the inside, or backside, of a specially coated piece of glass. When the coating (phosphor) is struck by the electrons, it glows. The coating is organized into tiny dots, called picture elements, often called pixels. Since this glow quickly fades it must be refreshed, or restruck, by the electron stream. The refresh rate is measured in hertz (Hz) or cycles per second. If the refresh rate is too slow the screen will appear to flicker, which can lead to eyestrain and headaches. To avoid this, most monitors have a refresh rate of at least 60 Hz. Another technique used to reduce or eliminate flicker is by noninterlacing the screen. Televisions refresh every other row of pixels on each pass of the electron gun. Noninterlaced (NI) monitors refresh every row of pixels on every pass of the gun. This requires more processing capability, but has become the *de facto* standard for monitors.

Monitor resolution, or sharpness, is primarily determined by the distance between pixels (dot pitch, or dp). The lower the dp, the better the resolution. Dot pitch is expressed in millimeters, and is usually around 0.28 mm. The number of pixels on the screen can also be an indicator of resolution. The more pixels, the better the resolution, all other things being equal. The number of pixels is usually shown by expressing the number of pixels per row, and the number of rows (e.g. 1024 × 768, or 1024 pixels per row, and 768 rows). Monitor size usually refers to its diagonal measurement with 14 inches being the generally accepted standard, although the number of readily available and comparably priced 15 inch and larger monitors is increasing. Monitors come in black and white (monochrome) or color, although monochrome monitors are slowly disappearing. Monitors typically display 80 columns and 24 lines of text data.

One disadvantage of VDT or CRT monitors is their size and weight. This makes them impractical for portable or laptop computers. These PCs use flat-panel monitors. The most common type of flat-panel display is the liquid crystal display (LCD). This is the same technology used in some digital watches and calculators. There are three types of LCD monitors: passive matrix, dual-scan matrix, and active matrix. The basic difference between the three is the number of times the screen is refreshed and the size and shape of the matrix elements. Active matrix has the highest refresh rate and uses matrix elements that generate sharp, clear images that can be seen from almost any orientation of the screen. Passive and dual-scan matrix screens are more difficult to read.

Plotters are often used when a hard copy of a graphic image is required. Charts, blueprints, maps, and drawings are some of the items a plotter can produce. Plotters use multicolored pens to draw, rather than print, graphic images. They are slower than printers, but capable of much more detail. While laser and ink-jet printers have all but replaced smaller plotters, large plotters are still required to create large documents such as maps and schematic drawings.

There are several assistive output devices that enable handicapped users to use computers. Such a specialized printing device is a Brailler, which produces output in Braille format for the visually impaired. Voice synthesizers, or voice response units, convert digital output into versions of the spoken word. Output can be either mechanically synthesized or actual human speech that has been prerecorded and stored. Telephone information systems are one example of voice response units. Another is speech output devices for the voiceless or visually impaired.

Computer output microfilm (COM) is used to reduce images of hard copies to microfilm or microfiche. This reduces the amount of space needed to store documents, and is commonly used in the insurance and banking industries. However, this is a mature technology and is gradually giving way to optical disk technology.

Output devices can also extend beyond the printer and monitor into the 3D world. Drilling, milling, and machining devices associated with computer-aided design and computer-aided manufacturing (CAD/CAM) can convert data into finished or semi-finished products. Virtual reality (VR) systems use output devices such as head-mounted displays, large projection screens, and headphones or speakers to enhance simulations.

As more and more emphasis is placed on using computers in our work and leisure activities, users will demand more natural means for interacting with these devices. Effective input and output devices are essential elements of information systems today and in the future.

DENNIS ADAMS

outsourcing of information systems Outsourcing of information systems refers to the contracting out of some or all of the IS services of a firm. Although "outsourcing" came into common parlance only in the late 1980s, the concept of contracting out for IS services is not new. Even in the early 1960s, when computers were first introduced to businesses, outsourcing was characterized by the presence of service bureaus that offered application-specific transaction-processing services to firms. A notable example is ADP which provided payroll processing to a wide variety of businesses. In the 1960s and 1970s, outsourcing was restricted to a small number of standard applications within a firm's application portfolio. These applications included payroll, inventory control, general ledger, etc.

IS outsourcing of the late 1980s represented a new twist. Taking Kodak as a model, firms embraced a "total outsourcing" approach, characterized by high dollar value deals (ranging from $100 million to $3 billion) and long-term contracting (e.g. 10-year contracts). Under such contracts, firms relinquished the entire IS function, including data center operations, network and communications management, disaster recovery, and PC acquisitions and maintenance, to vendors. In extreme cases, systems development was also contracted out. In total outsourcing, a firm legally transfers IT assets and human resources to the vendor. For example, in the $2 billion IS contract between General Dynamics and Computer Services Corporation, General Dynamics recovered $20 million from IT assets sold to CSC.

By the mid-1990s, the total outsourcing approach has given way to "selective outsourcing." Companies adopt a more conservative approach to outsourcing by retaining the ownership and control over IS function and contracting out only for one or a few IS services. Common IS services to outsource include production-oriented activities, such as data center operations, network management, and PC acquisitions and maintenance. Design-oriented activities such as systems development are commonly retained in-house.

Variations of Outsourcing

According to Apte and Mason (1995), companies have three options for IS outsourcing: co-location outsourcing; domestic multi-location; and global multi-location. The Kodak–IBM arrangement is an example of co-location outsourcing, where IBM built a data center facility locating physically on Kodak's premises. The Chevron's US data networking contract with AT&T is an example of domestic multi-location where the network operations are managed out of AT&T's facilities; while GE Appliances outsourcing of some of its programming projects to Infosys, a software house in India, is an example of global outsourcing.

Rationale for Outsourcing

Two primary reasons jointly drive a firm toward outsourcing one or all of its IS services. First, a company will outsource if it does not deem IS to be a core competence of the firm, or if it does not deem IS to have strategic value to the organization. The firm will outsource IS so that it can channel its resources into other activities that are more central to the firm's business. Secondly, a company will outsource its IS function if vendors are more efficient in performing the services in-house. To the extent that vendors can offer the quality services more efficiently, firms should outsource to reap the economies of scale and scope of the vendors.

Managing Outsourcing Contracts

The key to successful long-term IS outsourcing is the management of relations between the client organizations and the vendor. Turnover and rapidly declining price–performance ratios of IT products and services threaten to make obsolete initial contractual agreements (McFar-

lan & Nolan, 1995). Sufficient flexibility and control structures must be embedded in the initial contractual agreement to ensure a smooth working partnership between the client and the vendor even as technologies and prices change. According to Ang and Beath (1993), any IS outsourcing contract must include five major elements:

1 *Authority structures* where rights and responsibilities are assigned to either the client or vendor to make discretionary decisions, issues orders, or demand performance. Examples of these decisions include identifying and changing key personnel; making price adjustments; and changing the scope of the contract as price–performance ratios of IT drop.

2 *Rule-based incentive systems* where rewards and punishments are tied to vendor performance, and not to the market. Market incentives work well under conditions of certainty, where all performance contingencies are considered prior to contractual agreement. Rule-based incentive systems dissociate compensation from market-determined forces. They reflect locally determined inducements for desirable future performance. For example, if timely delivery is vital, penalties for delays beyond agreed completion date and bonuses for early completion may be incorporated into the contract.

3 *Standard operating procedures* where routines are followed by parties in the contract to ensure that the contract progresses as planned. Examples of routines include requiring the vendor to produce formal progress reports; to conduct regular face-to-face meetings with clients; and to bring to the attention of the client potential IT operational problems and project delays.

4 *Nonmarket-based pricing systems* where pricing algorithms are designed to accommodate cost uncertainties in long-term IS contracts. Nonmarket-based systems are market-price established by competitive bidding but modified by cost-recovery procedures. A combination of market pricing and cost-recovery algorithms is designed to ensure a reasonable balance

between price risk for the client and compensation risk for the vendor.

5 *Informal mechanisms for resolving disputes* where procedures are developed to settle conflicts without direct referral to court sanction. Unlike any typical arms-length contractual arrangement, a series of private and informal appeals is embedded in the contract to ensure that parties survive disputes. In the event of any disagreements, parties should agree to discuss and resolve the dispute informally and privately between top management of the client and vendor organizations. In the event that such negotiation is not successful, parties should submit the dispute to mediation by a third party arbitrator – a mutually agreed-upon computer professional. Only if the arbitration fails, formal legal litigation commences.

The act of outsourcing is not a panacea for all IS problems. The success or failure of out-sourcing depends in large part on how one manages the relationship between the client and the vendor. Flexibility and control structures must be in place at the beginning of the long-term contractual arrangement to ensure that partners to the contract survive technological changes, declining price–performance ratios, personnel turnover, and other environmental jolts.

Bibliography

Ang, S. & Beath, C. M. (1993). Hierarchical elements in software contracts. *Journal of Organizational Computing*, 3 (3), 329–62.

Apte, U. M. & Mason, R. O. (1995). Global disaggregation of information-intensive services. *Management Science*, 41 (6), 1250–62.

McFarlan, F. W. & Nolan, R. L. (1995). How to manage an IT outsourcing alliance. *Sloan Management Review*, Winter, 9–23.

SOON ANG

P

performance evaluation for computer systems Computer systems are designed to perform certain functions. Computer systems performance evaluation refers to the process of determining how well a computer system performs its functions. Computer system performance is evaluated in order to select a system from given alternatives, to evaluate design alternatives of a proposed system, or to improve the performance of a given system. To be acceptable to users of a computer system, the system must meet certain performance specifications. The performance of a computer system is specified or determined by system characteristics such as:

- responsiveness: time to perform a given task or set of tasks

- throughput: rate at which the service is performed

- utilization: resources consumed while performing the service

- reliability: probability of error while performing the service

- availability: fraction of time the system is available to perform service

The three basic performance evaluation techniques are measurement, simulation, and analytic modeling.

1 *Measurement*. This is a requirement of all performance evaluation studies since it is used to determine the system characteristics and calibrate simulation and analytic models.
2 *Simulation*. Performance of computer systems can be evaluated by representing the system (with mathematical relationships or

equations) as a network of queues. A computer system is represented as a collection of servers with differing service times. These different service times require that data or messages must be stored in buffer areas or queues between the servers. A simulation model uses measured or generated events as inputs or initial conditions and evaluates the relationships numerically over time intervals of interest. The results are statistical distributions or estimates of system characteristics.
3 *Analytic modeling*. This approach solves a set of equations exactly giving as results average values for server utilization, service time, and response time.

A computer system is an organization of hardware and software components. The complexity of the organization influences the performance evaluation since the hardware and software components interact. The total performance of the system is determined by the performance of the various components. The performance of hardware components, such as central processors, input–output devices, storage or memory, interact with the software components, such as the operating system and user programs. Both of these may interact with human operators (to mount a device or reply to a program condition). Computer performance evaluation determines the contribution of the various system components to the total performance of the system. This decomposition can be used to detect bottlenecks (the component with the highest response time or utilization) which can then be remedied and performance improved, or as input to a capacity study to determine if increased volume will require a hardware upgrade or design change and if so to which component.

BARRY PIEPER

personal computer   *see* MICROCOMPUTER

planning for information systems Information systems (IS) planning is an organizational administrative process that involves the consideration of alternative methods for employing information, computing, and communications resources in furtherance of the organization's objectives and its overall "business" strategy. IS planning takes place at a number of different levels in the organization. At the highest level of strategic IS planning, the relationship between the organization's objectives and strategy and its IS resources is articulated. At a much lower level, IS project planning involves the specification of the activities, resources, and relationships that will be required to develop a new computer system, install and implement new hardware and software, or perform any other complex task involving computer resources.

Strategic IS Planning

Strategic IS planning is the core of IS planning since it directly involves the translation of organizational objectives and strategy into data, applications, technology, and communications architectures that can best support the implementation of that strategy and the achievement of the organization's overall objectives. It also involves the assessment of the "product-market" opportunities that may be supported by existing and planned information resources (i.e. identifying whether the organization's information resources and competencies may suggest opportunities for it to carry on its activities in ways that may make it more competitive in the market).

Figure 1 shows these two major elements of strategic IS planning in terms of two arrows that connect an "organizational strategy set" and an "information resources strategy set." The former represents the organizational mission, objectives and strategies that have been developed through a strategic "business" planning process. The right-facing arrow shows that the information resources strategy set (composed of the information resources strategy and information infrastructure) is derived from the organizational strategy set. The left-facing arrow describes the assessment of information resources that may be conducted to identify important changes in the organizational strategy set.

Evolution of IS Planning

Tracing the development of IS planning can serve to describe its various levels, since the forms of IS planning that represented its highest and most sophisticated level in past eras are still conducted today. Higher (more strategic) levels of planning have been added to the previously existing planning activities in each era as the IS planning field has evolved. This approach also offers the opportunity of identifying the underlying concepts and techniques associated with each planning paradigm.

The pre-strategic planning era
In the early computer era, the most sophisticated level of IS planning involved assessing the

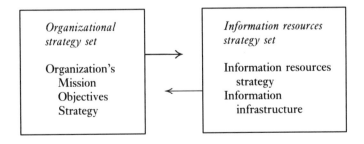

Figure 1   Strategic IS Planning

future computing needs of the enterprise and ensuring that adequate and appropriate computing capacity was available to fulfill those needs. An associated planning task was that of evaluating and selecting the applications and systems development projects that would be funded and implemented by the enterprise. At the project level, project plans were developed to ensure that appropriate milestones were identified and that specific activities and tasks were assigned to appropriate IS professionals.

The systems development life-cycle (SDLC) was the primary conceptual basis for planning in this era. The SDLC for information systems evolved from the basic SDLC for complex systems. The SDLC postulated that the development of all complex systems naturally evolved through a sequential series of phases that were most appropriately managed in different ways, and which demanded different mixes of resources to complete effectively and efficiently. An extremely simplified version of the SDLC is shown at the center of figure 2 where it is labeled "Traditional SDLC."

In this era, the multi-project levels of planning (capacity planning and project selection and evaluation) were based on the concepts of forecasting and project selection, respectively. Capacity planning involved the forecasting of computing requirements and planning for the acquisition, installation, and testing of new generations of hardware and software. Project evaluation and selection were conceptually based on the project selection methodologies that had largely been previously developed and used in the research and development (R&D) context.

Because "cost avoidance" was the major criterion for project evaluation in this pre-strategic era, this project selection procedure was relatively straightforward, primarily involving the estimation of the costs that could be avoided if manual systems were to be automated. This criterion usually resulted in the approval of projects that were at the operational or operational control levels. Those projects that substituted computer systems for human operatives or those that measured and controlled the performance levels of operations were accepted as being cost-effective. Projects whose rationale depended on the sometimes intangible benefits that they might produce were difficult to justify because of the emphasis on the cost-avoidance criterion and the relatively greater ease of forecasting costs versus benefits.

The highest level plan that came into being in some organizations during the latter part of this pre-strategic era was the "IS master plan." This plan demonstrated the intended relationships among the various systems and subsystems that the organization operated or planned to develop. The need for a master plan was recognized by organizations that had developed independent and incompatible systems. While such systems may well have been individually effective to operate, they could not be readily integrated to provide information that might be of use to higher-level management. Illustrative of this situation were the many banks that had developed expensive and operationally effective product-oriented computer systems. Their checking account systems, loan systems, and trust systems, for example, had databases that were not readily cross-referenced to enable a

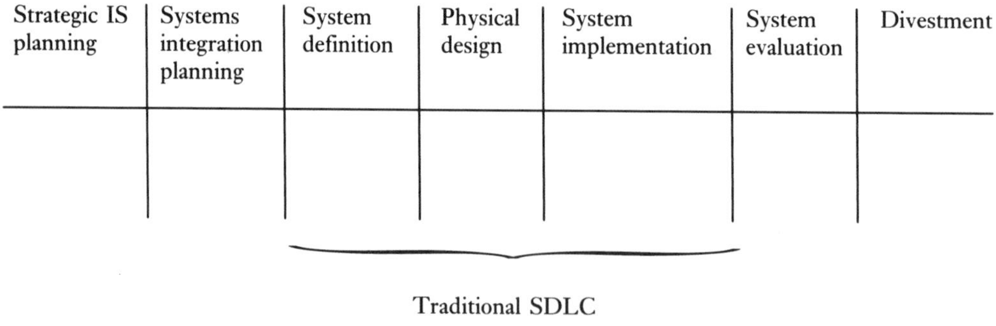

Strategic IS planning	Systems integration planning	System definition	Physical design	System implementation	System evaluation	Divestment

Traditional SDLC

Figure 2   Expanded systems development life-cycle

marketing manager to readily determine which of the bank's many products and services were utilized by a given customer. The master plan was intended to ensure systems integration. The adoption of this notion was the precursor to the IS strategic planning era.

The early strategic IS planning era

The simple idea of deriving the IS strategy directly from the overall organizational strategy, and thereby of developing the IS resources that best supported the organization's strategy, had profound effect on IS planning and on IS development activities (King & Cleland, 1975; King, 1978). When IBM incorporated the notion into this widely known business systems planning (BSP) methodology, strategic IS planning came into widespread use (IBM, 1981).

This expanded domain for IS necessitated a change from the simple, cost-avoidance IS project selection criterion that had been in common use to more sophisticated criteria that gave greater consideration of the potential benefits that might result from an IS project. Because cost remained a necessary consideration and benefits were often intangible and difficult to quantify, the net result was a multidimensional criterion that was conceptually similar to those that had been in use in R&D project selection for some time.

For the first time in the history of many firms, IS applications whose benefits were intangible, and/or more difficult to forecast than was cost avoidance, came to be given higher priority. The result was that top managers developed a greater appreciation of the IS function as a potential contributor to business value rather than viewing IS merely as a service function.

The expanded planning horizons of IS and the emphasis on assessing and evaluating systems in more sophisticated ways have been conceptualized in terms of the expanded life-cycle shown in figure 2 (King & Srinivasan, 1983). Figure 2 shows a simplified version of the "traditional SDLC" embedded in a broader life-cycle that also includes strategic planning, systems integration planning, evaluation, and divestment phases. These phases serve to extend the traditional SDLC, which applies to a single system, to a broader organizational context. The systems integration planning phase primarily involves the sort of systems integration functions that are implicit in the earlier notion of a "master plan." The strategic planning phase involves the development of an IS strategy that is derived from, and which directly supports, the business strategy.

In figure 2, the two phases that are shown to begin after the traditional SDLC – evaluation and divestment – reflect the growing attention that has come to be paid to the formal evaluation of systems and the need to phase out systems. In the evaluation phase, other measures, such as user satisfaction and business value assessments, are commonly used to complement traditional cost, time, and technical performance measures. These two phases further recognize that an IS, like any complex system, has a finite useful life. These phases not only reflect the need to evaluate systems, but *the need to plan for the shutdown, replacement, and phasing out of systems.* In the earlier eras of IS planning, little attention was given to divestment, leading many firms to make the implicit assumption that systems would function forever. This assumption inevitably leads to decisions concerning systems maintenance, updating, and modification that might be significantly different from what they would be under the assumption of a finite useful lifespan for a system.

Strategic planning for information resources: the modern era

In the 1980s, the initial notion of strategic IS planning was expanded to include the idea described by the left-facing arrows in figure 1. This involved the recognition that information resources could become a basis for new organizational strategy as well as being supportive of existing organizational strategy. This idea, enunciated by King and Zmud (1981), has come to be a basic concept of the IS field.

The systems that have been developed as a result of the planning process described by the left-facing arrow in figure 1 are variously described as "strategic systems," and "competitive weapons" (i.e. systems that impact the "product-market" strategies of organizations). Among such systems are Merrill Lynch's Cash Management Account (CMA), a "product" whose core technology is information processing, and American and United Airlines' reservation systems, which have been employed to achieve competitive advantages in the market rather than serving merely for transaction processing.

This new view of "information resources," as contrasted with "information systems," reflects both the greater organizational importance of computer-related entities and the rapid development of a wide variety of useful communications and information technologies that greatly transcend the traditional computer hardware and software dimensions of IS. LOCAL AREA NETWORKS, wide area networks, DATABASE MANAGEMENT SYSTEMS, word and document processing, EXPERT SYSTEMS and many other technology-based entities are now physically and/or conceptually integrated into an overall set of information resources that must be jointly planned for and managed. Moreover, in the modern information era, the important role of data *per se*, without regard to the technology that is used to collect, process, and disseminate it, has also increasingly been recognized. An organization can utilize these entities much as it has traditionally employed its human, financial, and physical resources to create business value.

The evolution of the criteria used to evaluate and select systems has moved toward a focus on "sustainable competitive advantage" in the era of strategic systems. Systems that have the potential to produce an identifiable advantage over competition, sustainable over time, are those that will be given highest priority (e.g. Sethi & King, 1994). Systems that promise cost avoidance or temporary competitive advantage will generally be less highly valued (unless, of course, in the former case, cost leadership is a strategy that is intended to produce an advantage in the market).

Current Trends in IS Planning

At least three major trends in IS planning are readily identifiable: (a) the integration of IS planning into overall organizational planning; (b) the integration of planning for various communications and information technologies; and (c) the development of planning for business process re-engineering as an element of IS planning.

Integration of IS planning and organizational planning

The recognition of strategic planning for information resources as a "free-standing" administrative activity may be beginning to reach the limits of its value. With the emerging view of information resources as one of the important kinds of resources that a general manager can employ to achieve organizational objectives, many organizations have embarked on the integration of IS planning with overall strategic "business" planning processes. Although this trend is not universal, it is clearly identifiable and, if successful, will undoubtedly become a major theme of future developments in the area.

When strategic planning for information resources becomes a process conducted under the aegis of the organization's general manager with the heavy involvement of non-IS personnel, it will have emulated the evolution of IS from a backroom technical service function to one that is not only important to the organization but also includes the significant involvement of non-IS personnel in its management.

Integration of communications and information technology planning

At the same time as IS planning is being integrated into overall organizational planning, its scope is being expanded because of the physical and conceptual integration of technologies. As ELECTRONIC DATA INTERCHANGE (EDI), TELECOMMUNICATION systems and a wide variety of other technologies become less distinguishable from computer systems, and as the requirements for organizations to employ these various technologies in an integrated manner becomes clear, information resources planning has expanded to address a broad range of communications and information systems and technologies.

Planning for business process re-engineering

Planning for business process re-engineering (BPR) is also one of the important trends in IS planning. The redesign of business processes has become a major organizational activity that usually has a high information systems and technology content. As such, BPR projects must be designed, selected, and implemented just as any other IS project. Since BPR is potentially of great strategic importance to the enterprise, in some organizations BPR planning is treated as an element of strategic IS planning.

Conclusion

Planning for information resources has become a complex and sophisticated administrative process. Its increasing integration into overall organizational strategic planning processes parallels the increasing regard of information resources as one of the most important varieties of resources that are at the disposal of managers in the pursuit of their organizational objectives. This development vividly contrasts with earlier eras when computer systems were backroom service functions of relatively limited importance to business and when information systems planning was a straightforward capacity and requirements-driven process.

The increasingly important and visible role of the IS function and of communications and information resources represents both opportunity and challenge for the field. In earlier eras, failures of computer systems to perform in the manner that was expected were often not of enormous significance to overall organizational performance. Therefore, IS planning was not usually instrumental in determining long-run overall organizational success. Now, we can, with increasing frequency, identify situations in which organizational success is primarily based on the ability to develop and exploit information resources. In the future, such situations are likely to proliferate as are situations in which the decline and fall of organizations can be explained by their failure to do so. In such an environment, IS planning is of fundamental importance.

Bibliography

IBM (1981). *Business Systems Planning: Information Systems Planning Guide.*

King, W. R. (1978). Strategic planning for management information systems. *MIS Quarterly*, **2** (1), 27–37.

King, W. R. & Cleland, D. I. (1975). A new method for strategic systems planning. *Business Horizons*, **18** (4), 55–64.

King W. R. & Srinivasan, A. (1983). Decision support systems: planning, development and evaluation, in R. Schultz (ed.), *Applications of Management Science*, vol. 3. JAI Press.

King, W. R. & Zmud, R. (1981). Managing information systems: policy planning, strategic planning and operational planning, *Proceedings of the Second International Conference on Information Systems*. Boston, MA, December.

Sethi, V. & King, W. R. (1994). Development of measures to assess the extent to which an Information Technology application provides competitive advantage. *Management Science*, **40** (12), 1601–27.

WILLIAM R. KING

privacy in information systems   Privacy is comprised of two separable parts: *physical* privacy and *information* privacy. When one's physical space is intruded upon, this is a violation of one's physical privacy. When information about someone is collected, used, or shared inappropriately, this is a violation of someone's information privacy. Our concern here is with information privacy, a significant and growing issue for information systems managers. As corporations find their data management activities receiving more scrutiny from a privacy perspective, information systems managers should be aware of exposure and be accountable to their organizations (Straub & Collins, 1990).

Dimensions of Information Privacy Concern

Individuals often indicate that they are "concerned" about their privacy. Public opinion polls in the United States and Canada show that such concerns are at record levels (Equifax Inc., 1992, 1993). It is surprisingly difficult to dissect these concerns and to ascertain exactly what is troubling respondents, since the factors contributing to such concerns are fairly complex. In fact, the research of Smith et al. (1995) indicates that there may be four primary dimensions of information privacy concern and two secondary dimensions. The primary dimensions are as follows:

1 *Collection.* Individuals often perceive that large quantities of data regarding their personalities, background, and actions are being accumulated, and they often resent this. Laudon (1986) coined the term "dossier society" to describe our increasing reliance on personal data and the increasing collection of such data. While few individuals dispute an organization's right to

collect data which is pertinent to a particular decision (e.g. household income on a credit-card application), many resent being asked for personal data not clearly tied to a specific transaction.

2 *Unauthorized secondary use.* Sometimes, information is collected from individuals for one purpose but is used for another, secondary, purpose without authorization from the individuals. Even if contained *internally* within a single organization, unauthorized use of personal information will very often elicit a negative response. For example, some credit-card issuers have come under attack for utilizing data about their cardholders' transactions in their own marketing campaigns. Specific examples of such secondary, internal uses include "sugging," a practice in which data is collected ostensibly for research only to be used later for marketing purposes (Cespedes & Smith, 1993). Concerns about secondary use are often exacerbated when personal information is disclosed to an *external* party (i.e. another organization). The sale or rental of direct mail or telemarketing lists often falls into this category. This concern is an important one as the number of INTER-ORGANIZATIONAL SYSTEMS increases, a trend enabled by computing and telecommunications advances.

3 *Errors.* Many individuals believe that companies are not taking enough steps to minimize problems from errors in personal data. Although some errors might be deliberate (e.g. a disgruntled employee maliciously falsifying data), most privacy-related concerns involve instead *accidental* errors in personal data. Provisions for inspection and correction are often considered as antidotes for problems of erroneous data, but many errors are stubborn ones, and they seem to increase in spite of such provisions. Also at issue are questions of responsibility for spotting errors: does a system rely on individuals to monitor their own files, or is there a structure for such monitoring in place? Although errors are sometimes assumed to be unavoidable problems in data handling, whether controls are or are not included in a system represents a value choice on the part of the system designers.

4 *Unauthorized access.* Who is allowed to access personal information in the files? This is a question not only of technological constraints (e.g. access control software) but also of organizational policy. It is often held that individuals should have a "need to know" before access to personal information is granted. However, the interpretation of which individuals have, and which do not have, a "need to know" is often a cause of much controversy. Technological options now exist for controlling such access at file, record, or field level. But how those options are utilized and how policies associated with those uses are formed represent managerial judgments.

The secondary dimensions are:

1 *Reduced judgment.* As organizations grow in size and data-processing capabilities, they tend to rely more often on "standard operating procedures" than on individual decisions. Their use of automated decision-making processes may lead people to feel that they are being treated more as "a bunch of numbers" than as individuals. Laudon (1986, pp. 3–4) has noted that "decisions made about us . . . rely less and less on personal face-to-face contact, on what we say, or even on what we do. Instead, decisions are based on information that is held in national systems and interpreted by bureaucrats and clerical workers in distant locations." As systems are increasingly designed so that these decisions are automated, and when there are few provisions for referring decisions to human beings at appropriate times, concerns about this dimension of decision-making increase. While privacy advocates often claim that "reduced judgment" is a privacy concern, it is actually somewhat tangential and can be viewed as an issue of organizational design.

2 *Combining data.* Concerns are sometimes raised with respect to combined databases which pull personal data from numerous other sources, creating what has been termed a "mosaic effect." Even if data items in disparate databases are seen as innocuous by themselves, their combination into larger databases appears to some to be

suggestive of a "Big Brother" environment. This is a somewhat tangential dimension of information privacy, since the concerns associated with combined data are actually subsumed by the "Collection" and "Unauthorized secondary use" dimensions.

Corporate Approaches to Managing Privacy

In a study of banks, insurance organizations, and a credit-card issuer, Smith (1994) reported that a consistent policy-making cycle can be observed as corporations grapple with information privacy issues. The cycle contains three parts: drift, external threat, and reaction. By delegating decisions about management of personal data to mid-level managers, and by allowing different organizational units to establish different sets of practices, which sometimes conflict with one another, corporations allow their privacy policies to *drift*. Corporations may experience an *external threat* in the form of negative media attention, legislative scrutiny (e.g. congressional committee hearings), or a competitive threat (e.g. consumer complaints or a competitor's use of privacy protection as a marketplace weapon). In response to an external threat, corporation executives become involved in a defensive *reaction* period of assessment and official policy-making. Often, task forces are convened to deal with such crises. Differences in practices across the organization are then confronted. In many cases, more conservative approaches to managing personal data are embraced, and these new approaches are codified in new policies.

At one health insurer, the *drift* period was characterized by the creation of a variety of practices across organizational units in which individuals' medical claim data were either protected with rigid controls or were provided to outsiders with varying degrees of discretion. Internal access controls also varied widely during this period, with some individuals being allowed to see medical data inappropriately. The *external threat* was in the form of a new state law which regulated the collection and use of AIDS test data. This prodded a *reaction*, an extensive reassessment of the existing practices at an executive level and a codification of a new, omnibus policy.

Fair Information Practices

The most widely quoted guidelines for "fair" management of personal data are found in the 1973 Code of Fair Information Practices developed by the US Department of Health, Education, and Welfare (as presented in CPSR, 1989):

- There shall be no personal data record-keeping systems whose very existence is secret.

- There must be a way for a person to find out what information about the person is in a record and how it is used.

- There must be a way for a person to prevent information about the person that was obtained for one purpose from being used or made available for other purposes without the person's consent.

- There must be a way for a person to correct or amend a record of identifiable information about the person.

- Any organization creating, maintaining, using, or disseminating records of identifiable person data must assure the reliability of the data for its intended use and must take precautions to prevent misuse of the data.

Smith (1994) suggested that the Fair Information Practices should be updated to also include:

- There must be no deception in data-collection practices.

- A person should be given the opportunity to "opt out" of any information practices he or she finds inappropriate.

- Only individuals with a legitimate "need to know" should have access to personal data.

- Disparate data files should not be combined unless the conditions regarding data collection and "opt out" have been met.

Privacy Regulation

Many different models of privacy regulation exist around the world. While overall legislative activity regarding information privacy is flourishing internationally, no single, standard policy regarding privacy issues has emerged. As

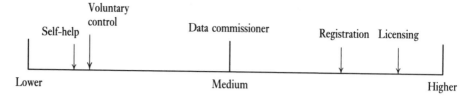

Figure 1   Regulation models: lower, medium, and higher refer to the level of government regulation in corporate privacy management
Source: Milberg et al. (1955)

described in Milberg et al. (1995), the predominant models appear to be those represented in figure 1. The models vary significantly in terms of governmental involvement in day-to-day corporate operations. At the low government involvement side (left end) of the continuum, the government assumes a "hands-off" role and allows corporations to monitor themselves, with reliance on injured individuals to pursue their own remedies in the court system. At the high government involvement side (right end) of the continuum, the government assumes authority to license and regulate all corporate uses of personal data, including the right to conduct inspections inside corporations and to examine all proposed applications of personal data before they are implemented.

The models can be described as follows:

1 *The self-help model* depends on data subjects' challenging inappropriate record-keeping practices. Rights of access and correction are provided for the subjects, but they are responsible for identifying problems and bringing them to the courts for resolution.
2 *The voluntary control model* relies on self-regulation on the part of corporate players. The law defines specific rules and requires that a "responsible person" in each organization ensures compliance.
3 *The data commissioner model* utilizes neither licensing nor registration, but relies on the ombudsman concept through a commissioner's office. The commissioner has no powers of regulation but relies on complaints from citizens, which are investigated. The commissioner also is viewed as an expert who should offer advice on data handling; monitor technology and make

proposals; and perform some inspections of data-processing operations. This model relies to a great degree on the commissioner's credibility with legislature, press, and the public.
4 *The registration model* acts much like the licensing model with one exception: the governmental institution has no right to block the creation of a particular information system. Only in a case where complaints are received and an investigation reveals a failure to adhere to data-protection principles would a system be "deregistered." Thus, this model provides more remedial than anticipatory enforcement of principles.
5 *The licensing model* creates a requirement that each databank containing personal data be licensed (usually upon payment of a fee) by a separate government institution. This institution would stipulate specific conditions for the collection, storage, and use of personal data. This model anticipates potential problems and heads them off, by requiring a *prior* approval for any use of data.

The United States is usually described as intermingling the self-help and voluntary control models. Germany is often viewed as a good example of the data commissioner model, the United Kingdom as the registration model, and Sweden as the licensing model. Some countries have no data protection laws at all (*see* Bennett, 1992; Madsen, 1992, for additional details).

Bibliography

Bennett, C. J. (1992). *Regulating Privacy: Data Protection and Public Policy in Europe and the United States*. Ithaca, NY: Cornell University Press.

Cespedes, F. V. & Smith, H. J. (1993). Database marketing: new rules for policy and practice. *Sloan Management Review*, **34 (4)**, 7–22.

Computer Professionals for Social Responsibility (1989). *The CPSR Newsletter*, **7 (4)**, 16.

Equifax Inc. (1992). *Equifax Canada Report on Consumers and Privacy in the Information Age.* Quebec: Equifax Canada.

Equifax Inc. (1993). *Harris–Equifax Health Information Privacy Survey 1993.* Atlanta, GA: Equifax Inc.

Flaherty, D. H. (1989). *Protecting Privacy in Surveillance Societies.* Chapel Hill, North Carolina: University of North Carolina Press.

Laudon, K. C. (1986). *Dossier Society: Value Choices in the Design of National Information Systems.* New York: Columbia University Press.

Linowes, D. F. (1989). *Privacy in America: Is your Private Life in the Public Eye?* Urbana, IL: University of Illinois Press.

Madsen, W. (1992). *Handbook of Personal Data Protection.* New York: Macmillan.

Milberg, S. J., Burke, S. J., Smith, H. J. & Kallman, E. A. (1995). A cross-cultural study of relationships between values, personal information privacy concerns, and regulatory approaches. *Communications of the ACM*, **38 (12)**, 65–74.

Smith, H. J. (1994). *Managing Privacy: Information Technology and Corporate America.* Chapel Hill, North Carolina: University of North Carolina Press.

Smith, H. J., Milberg, S. J. & Burke, S. J. (1995). Information privacy: measuring individuals' concerns about corporate practices. Unpublished working paper, Georgetown University.

Reindenberg, J. R. (1992). The privacy obstacle course: hurdling barriers to transnational financial services. *Fordham Law Review*, **60 (6)**, S137–S177.

Rule, J. B. (1974). *Private Lives and Public Surveillance: Social Control in the Computer Age.* New York: Schocken Books.

Rule, J. B., McAdam, D., Stearns, L. & Uglow, D. (1980). *The Politics of Privacy: Planning for Personal Data Systems as Powerful Technologies.* New York: Elsevier.

Straub, D. W. & Collins, R. W. (1990). Key information liability issues facing managers: software piracy, proprietary databases, and individual rights to privacy. *MIS Quarterly*, **14 (2)**, 43–6.

Westin, A. F. (1967). *Privacy and Freedom.* New York: Atheneum Publishers.

H. Jeff Smith and Detmar W. Straub

processing methods for information systems   Processing methods are generally associated with transaction processing. Transaction processing is a basic organization activity. Without transaction processing, business transactions would not be completed. Without it, bills would not be paid, sales orders would not be filled, manufacturing parts would not be ordered, and so on. Without it, data for management activities would not be available.

Transaction Processing Cycle

The transaction processing cycle begins with a transaction that is recorded in some way. Although hand-written forms are still very common, transactions are often recorded directly to a computer by the use of an online terminal. Recording of the transaction is generally the trigger to produce a transaction document. Data from the transaction is frequently required for the updating of master files; this updating may be performed concurrently with the processing of transaction documents or by a subsequent computer run.

The capturing of data on documents or by direct entry is a necessary first step preceding other activities in processing the transaction. For example, a sales order is manually prepared on a sales order form by a salesperson, a telephoned order is entered in a computer by a telephone salesperson, a cash withdrawal is entered in an automatic teller machine by the customer, and a reservation is entered by a travel agent using an online reservation terminal.

When a transaction is recorded manually, a copy of the document is usually used for data preparation. The transaction is keyed into a file using a terminal or data entry computer. The records of the transactions are used for processing. Many times, the documents involved are partially or completely coded. A bank check is precoded with the customer number and bank number; the amount of the check must be added. A turnaround document may be coded with much of the transaction data. An example is the part of the invoice returned with the payment; the turnaround portion may often be read with optical scanning.

Data validation is the testing of input data records to determine if they are correct and complete. This cannot be accomplished with complete assurance, but reasonable validation is usually possible. Validation tests applied against each data item or set of items may include tests for missing data, valid field size for each data item, numerical data class test, range or reasonableness test, valid or invalid values test, and comparison with stored data. Identification numbers and processing codes are very sensitive to errors. They can be validated for size, range, and composition of characters. An additional, very effective, validation technique for codes is a check digit. It is a redundant digit derived by computations on the identification number and then made a permanent part of the number. During data preparation and input validation, the check-digit derivation procedure is repeated. If the procedure results in a different check digit, there has been an error in recording or entering the identification number.

When input data items have been validated, the transactions are processed. Subsequently, two major activities occur during transaction processing: updating of machine-readable stored data (master file) related to or affected by the transaction, and preparation of outputs such as transaction documents and reports. In both of these activities, control information is also produced.

Transaction data output can be classified as to its purpose. There are three major reasons for producing transaction documents or other transaction output: (a) informational to report, confirm, or explain proposed or completed action; (b) action to direct a transaction to take place or be completed; and (c) investigational for background information or reference by the recipient. Action documents include shipping orders, purchase orders, manufacturing orders, checks, and customer statements. These documents instruct someone to do something. For example, a purchase order instructs a vendor to ship, a check instructs a bank to pay, etc. When action is taken, the completed action (or lack of completion) is reported back to the organizational unit initiating the action. A sales order confirmation verifies receipt of an order. Lists of checks not paid by banks represent a confirmation of completed action (if not on list, checks have been paid) and lack of completed action (by being listed as unpaid). A single document or different copies of it may serve both action and informational purposes. For example, one copy of the sales order confirmation may be sent to the customer to confirm the order; a second copy may be used as

an action document to initiate filling of the order.

Some transaction records are distributed to other departments in the organization to provide background information for recipients in the event that they need to respond to inquiries or need them for other reference. With online systems, a reference copy of the transaction can be stored in a computer file and may be retrieved via a terminal by anyone who is authorized and has need of the information. Transaction documents may also be used for managerial information or control scanning, as when a purchasing manager scans all purchase orders to spot unusual occurrences. In general, however, managerial information purposes are better met by reports or analyses which summarize transactions.

When transactions are processed, a listing of data about each transaction is usually prepared. The listing includes control totals for the number of transactions processed, total dollar amount of transactions, etc. The listing represents a batch of transactions or, for online processing, processing during a period of time. It provides a means of processing reference and error control.

Methods for Processing Transactions

There are three different methods commonly used for processing transactions and updating master files: (a) periodic data preparation and periodic batch processing (usually termed batch processing); (b) online entry with subsequent batch processing; and (c) online entry with immediate processing (termed online processing). The choice of methods should reflect the underlying process being supported. If the underlying process is transaction-oriented with immediate completion of the transaction desirable (as with order entry), online processing is indicated. If the process is periodic (as with payroll), batch processing is adequate.

Batch processing involves the accumulation of transactions until a sufficient number has been assembled to make processing efficient or until other considerations, such as a report cycle, initiate processing. The processing of batches can be daily, weekly, or monthly, depending on the volume of transactions and other considerations.

Batch processing of transactions can be very efficient in terms of data preparation and processing of transactions. One major disadvantage of periodic batch processing is the delay in detecting and correcting errors. This is an especially serious problem for errors that can be found only when the transaction is compared against the master file. For example, if a transaction is coded with an apparently valid customer number for a nonexistent customer, the error will not be detected until processing is attempted against the customer file. The delay makes it difficult to trace the transaction back to the origination point and identify the correct customer.

With a batch system, the user prepares data input as a batch of transactions recorded over a period of time such as a day or week. A user responsible for processing data in a batch system must prepare input data in the exact format and with the exact codes required by the processing program, prepare control information used to ensure that no records are lost or remain unprocessed, and check output received for errors (including checking against the control information prepared with input data). The user is also responsible for reviewing error reports, preparing corrections, and submitting corrections for processing.

When *transactions are entered at an online terminal*, the transaction is entered directly into the computer and validated immediately. The processing itself may be performed immediately or at a subsequent time as with periodic batch processing. One important advantage of online entry over periodic data preparation and input is that most of the validation may be performed while the transaction is being recorded. Many errors can therefore be corrected immediately while the person entering the transaction is available for correction. Often the user or customer originating the transaction is still available to make appropriate changes. In addition, the master files can be accessed for the detection of errors such as nonexistent master file records. In online entry with subsequent batch processing, the computer is used for direct data entry and validation, but valid transactions are stored for later periodic batch processing.

In *online entry with immediate processing*, the transaction is validated online and then pro-cessed immediately if valid. A response with the result of processing or a confirmation of completion of processing is generally provided to the user at the input terminal. The advantages of this approach are the same as direct entry with subsequent processing (i.e. immediate validation with opportunity for immediate corrections by the person doing the input) plus the additional advantage of immediate processing with immediate results. The master files are always up to date. For instance, after an item is sold, the inventory master file reflects the actual state of the inventory for that item. The disadvantages of immediate processing are the somewhat higher cost of online processing versus periodic batch processing (requires greater computer power and often data communications) and the extra procedures required to produce adequate control information and to safeguard the files against accidental or deliberate destruction during online updating.

In online processing, the user has a terminal or microcomputer for the input of transactions and output of results. The terminal is connected by communication lines to a remote computer where processing actually takes place. Transactions are entered and processed one at a time as they occur (in real time). The user generally has to be identified to the system as an authorized user before transactions are accepted. System sign on and authorization usually uses a password protection scheme. Users may have different authorization levels which determine what types of transactions they may perform. For instance, a user may be authorized (via his or her password) to process certain update transactions (e.g. a sale) but not others (e.g. alteration of payroll data). The mode of operation is a dialog. The dialog may be extensive and provide tutorial and help information for entry of data, or it may be very limited and require the user to understand what data to enter and how it should be entered. A user responsible for processing data in an online system must enter transactions in the proper format based on a dialog, a visual form, or instructions in a manual; respond to error messages (since the system should reject any invalid data) with corrected input; and review control information. At the end of a period of processing transactions, the user signs off, so that an unauthorized user may not subsequently enter data.

Retrieval in Transaction Processing

Many online systems use data retrieval software to support transaction processing. Even in applications where batch updating is appropriate, the capability to access related records during transaction preparation is often desired. For instance, a bank may install online terminals so that customers may inquire about the status of their accounts. A customer complaint department in a retail catalog company may check the status of an order when a customer calls. In these examples, online inquiry into master files is required.

Inquiries associated with a transaction-processing system tend to be fairly structured, so that they may be programmed to use a standard set of commands that can be mastered fairly easily. In some systems, commands can be assigned to special function keys on the keyboard so that the operator needs only to press a single key rather than type in a command. Terminals that are only to be used for inquiries, such as terminals for customer use on a bank floor, may be specially designed with only function keys.

Information Processing Controls

Control of transaction processing begins with the design of the document for initially recording the transaction. If the document is manually prepared, it should be designed to minimize errors in completing it. This requires adequate space, unambiguous directions and labels, and a sequence of recording that is natural to the preparer. Boxes, lines, colors, labels and menus of alternatives are some of the methods used to aid the preparer. One serious problem is how to make sure every transaction is recorded and entered into processing. Interruptions or carelessness may cause a transaction to not be recorded or the source document to be misplaced. To prevent or detect such errors and omissions, the transaction processing system may have one or more controls such as the following: (a) prenumbered source document; (b) record anticipating a transaction (such as payment due); (c) document produced as a byproduct; or (d) comparison with related transaction controls.

The use of a terminal to enter the original transaction has the advantage that a machine-readable record is produced at the same time as source documents needed for the transaction. If a source document is misplaced or lost, the computer record permits the tracking or reconstructing of the missing record. Accuracy and completeness considerations for source document design also apply to input screen design for the visual display terminal. Since online entry may also be performed without a source document (as with order entry by telephone), the machine record may be the only "document."

In the flow of control in batch processing, it is best to establish a control total of documents before data preparation. The control total can be a record count, a financial total, or a "hash total" of numbers such as account numbers, which are not normally summed (hence the total is meaningless except for control purposes).

During the data-preparation process, the control totals are checked to verify that no transactions are missing and that items used in control totals have been entered correctly. The control total is input with the data and checked by computer as part of data validation, processing, and output. The control totals appear on batch reports and on other control reports. The output (after adjusting for rejected transactions) should match the control total for the input batch. Computer programs and control personnel make control total comparisons during processing; users check controls on output against control totals for data they submitted for processing. This checking provides a simple but powerful control procedure to ensure that all transactions in the document batch are processed.

In the case of online input from documents, there is no control total of transactions prior to entry. However, if there are reasonable control procedures to enforce entry of all transactions, control totals can be developed for logical batches of input (transactions that are logically grouped by some common feature). The logical batches provide a basis for listings for reference, follow-up, comparison with physical evidence, and so on. For example, the log of all transactions entered is sorted, and logical batches of transactions are prepared by terminal, by operator, by type of transactions, etc.

There are special control considerations with online processing. The files change continuously, and therefore any error can disrupt a file and create additional errors as subsequent transactions are processed. The straightforward preprocessing batch control totals cannot be used to check batches before updating. Some examples of controls illustrate how control in online processing is handled. Restart procedures tell input personnel which transactions were lost if a system goes down. A separate backup file copy and transaction log are used for making file correction.

Processing Reference Control

The audit trail (or a processing reference trail) is the trail of references (document numbers, batch numbers, transaction references, etc.) which allows tracing of a transaction from the time it is recorded through to the reports in which it is aggregated with other transactions, or the reverse, tracing a total back to amounts on individual source documents. The processing trail is required for internal clerical, analytical, and management use because of the frequent need to examine the details behind a total or to trace what happened to a transaction. It is also needed by external auditors and is required by certain tax regulations for tax-related records.

An audit trail should always be present. Its form may change in response to computer technology, but three requirements should be met:

1 Any transaction can be traced from the source document through processing to outputs and to totals in which it is aggregated. For example, each purchase of goods for inventory can be traced to inclusion in the inventory totals.
2 Any output or summary data can be traced back to the transactions or computations used to arrive at the output or summary figures. For example, the total amount owed by a customer can be traced to the sales and payments that were used to arrive at the balance due.
3 Any triggered transaction (a transaction automatically triggered by an event or condition) can be traced to the event or condition. An example is a purchase order triggered by a sale that reduced inventory below an order point.

GORDON B. DAVIS

production and operations use of information technology *see* MANUFACTURING USE OF INFORMATION TECHNOLOGY

productivity from information technology The interest in productivity from information technology (IT) arises from the rapid growth in IT expenditure. In the United States, for example, in the decade 1980–89, expenditure on information processing and related equipment grew at a rate of 8.58 percent, faster than any other category of durable equipment (Thachenkary, 1991). As a result, by the end of the 1980s, annual expenditure on information processing and related equipment accounted for about a third of all durable equipment expenditure.

Productivity, in a general sense, is the relationship between inputs (resources such as capital and labor) and outputs (goods and services). In calculating productivity from IT, output may be measured in physical or financial units. For comparability across time and units of analysis, output has usually been measured in financial terms such as gross domestic product at the national level, or in terms of sales at the organizational level. There is more variation in the measurement of IT. It has been measured in terms of computer capital, which consists largely of computing equipment, and in terms of IT expenditure, which consists of expenditure on hardware, software, and IT labor.

How might IT contribute to productivity? One obvious example is the deployment of transaction-processing systems, such as check processing in banks or sales processing in many organizations. Such systems automate repetitive and voluminous clerical work and reduce the number of clerical staff needed, while increasing the organization's capacity for processing routine transactions. IT that provides managers with information and decision-making support may also help to increase the firm's output if it enables managers to better deploy organizational resources and to better identify and respond to market opportunities.

Surprisingly, macro-level studies have been unable to show a strong link between IT and productivity. They have shown that while IT expenditure has grown at a rapid rate, productivity growth has been sluggish. Output per hour of labor, for example, grew only between 1 and 2 percent in the 1980s. Roach (1991) has attributed most of the poor productivity to white-collar workers, citing statistics that show that output per white-collar worker decreased by 6.6 percent from the mid-1970s to 1986, while output per blue-collar worker increased by 16.9 percent in the same period. Productivity studies of samples of firms have also not shown strong positive relationships between IT and productivity. The persistent lack of evidence about productivity from IT in the face of rising expenditure on IT has been termed the "productivity paradox."

A number of reasons has been offered for the productivity paradox (Brynjolfsson, 1993). The first is that inputs and outputs have been mismeasured. IT can increase the quality and variety of outputs offered, and also the speed and convenience to customers. However, these important results from the deployment of IT are not captured by traditional methods of national income accounting. A second reason is that there is a lag between expenditure on IT and the occurrence of benefits. This is because benefits arise only after necessary complementary investments have been made, and users have had sufficient time to learn by using. Thirdly, aggregate productivity statistics may not reflect returns to IT because IT may be helping to redistribute the share of the economic pie rather than enlarging the overall pie. If this were true, then firm-level studies would show a positive relationship between IT and productivity. However, firm-level studies have not provided consistent support for such a relationship. Finally, it is possible that organizations are mismanaging their IT investments. Agency theory, for example, suggests that information system managers, as agents, may make IT investments which are not in the best interests of the firm's owners, the principals.

More recently, another explanation has been offered for the lack of evidence regarding IT productivity from studies using aggregated data. This explanation states that not all firms benefit from their IT expenditure because firms differ in their ability to obtain productivity and other benefits from IT (Weill, 1992). Documented cases of firms that have had unusual success with IT also suggest that IT spending does not confer the same level of benefits on all firms. Firm ability to benefit from IT depends on a number of factors such as the quality of its management processes, prior experience with IT, user skills, and competitor responses (Markus & Soh, 1993). Management processes, such as the integration of IT and business planning, and appropriate project selection, development and implementation procedures, influence the benefits that firms receive from IT. The large amount of literature on appropriate IT management practices affirms that it is not how much firms spend on IT but what they do with it that matters.

Bibliography

Brynjolfsson, E. (1993). The productivity paradox of information technology. *Communications of the ACM*, **36**, 67–77.

Markus, M. L. & Soh, C. (1993). Banking on information technology: converting IT spending into firm performance, in R. D. Banker, R. J. Kauffman and M. A. Mahmood (eds), *Strategic Information Technology Management: Perspectives on Organizational Growth and Competitive Advantage*. Harrisburg, PA: Idea Publishing.

Roach, S. S. (1991). Services under siege – the restructuring imperative. *Harvard Business Review*, **69**, 82–91.

Thachenkary, C. S. (1991). Information technology expenditure and US productivity: on the fundamentals of an information economy. *EDI Europe*, **1**, 153–68.

Weill, P. (1992). The relationship between investment in information technology and firm performance: a study of the valve manufacturing sector. *Information Systems Research*, **3**, 307–58.

CHRISTINA SOH

programming languages A computer program is a set of instructions that direct the computer to execute operations. Writing a set of instructions is termed "coding." The computer executes machine language instructions, but programs are not written in this form because they are expressed in some binary form that is difficult for human use. A symbolic assembly language was used in the early development of computers to allow programmers to code machine-level instructions using mnemonic names for instructions and symbolic names for storage locations. The difficulty with symbolic assembly languages is that they require one symbolic instruction for each machine instruction. Most programming is now done in a higher-level language. There are different types of high-level languages, but a common characteristic is that the program is written in instructions that describe the procedures or problem-solving steps to be performed. The high-level instructions are converted to a machine-level program by a computer program called a "compiler."

High-level languages used in information processing can be categorized by their orientation. The classification below is useful in thinking about the orientation of languages, but often programming languages do not fit exactly into any one category.

1 Algebraic, formula processing languages.
2 Business data processing languages.
3 Specialized languages.
4 General purpose languages.
5 Fourth-generation languages (4GL).
6 Screen-oriented languages.
7 Object-oriented languages.

Algebraic languages are oriented toward computational procedures for solving mathematical and statistical problems or problems that can be expressed in terms of formulas or numerical solution procedures. Algebraic languages have good facilities for expressing formulas, for describing computational procedures and for specifying common mathematical functions. Typically they are less useful for complex input and output and manipulation of non-numeric data. The most commonly used algebraic languages are FORTRAN (FORmula TRANslator) and BASIC (Beginners All-purpose Symbolic Instruction Code). FORTRAN has developed through a number of versions and is supported by standards efforts. BASIC was developed as a language for student use but is now widely used as a simplified language. Other well-known algebraic languages are ALGOL (ALGorithmic Language) and APL (A Programming Language).

Business data processing languages emphasize information processing procedures involving manipulation of non-numeric data, large files, and high volume of input and output. They also have extensive formatting capabilities for reports. The processing procedures do not usually require extensive mathematical manipulation. COBOL (COmmon Business Oriented Language) is the most widely used of these languages. A language often used with smaller business computers was RPG (Report Program Generator). In the development of business-oriented data processing, existing languages have been expanded to include user screen design and screen object operations. Database packages include programming facilities for retrieval of data and formatting of reports. A standard language, SQL, is the most common query language. Many database packages have graphical user interfaces for formulating queries, but the underlying instructions are generated in an SQL-like language.

Specialized languages are used for situations requiring functions that are not common to algebraic or business processing. An example is simulation languages, which are used to simulate operations involving queues. These can be quite complex and difficult without a specialized language. For example, a simulation of the operation of a job shop will involve many processing stations, many waiting lines of jobs to be processed, etc. Other specialized languages are used to write programs to control machine tools, do computations unique to engineering, etc.

General purpose languages are designed to support both algebraic and business data processing plus some common specialized functions. An example is ADA, a general purpose programming language. It is especially suited for the programming of large, long-lived systems with a need for ongoing maintenance. It supports modern programming structured techniques and concurrent processing.

Fourth-generation languages (4GL) are languages that produce programs based on high-level specifications rather than detailed procedural code. Fourth-generation languages are used both by professional programmers and by experienced users to access data and build reports. Complete applications can be built using fourth-generation languages. This is frequently the case in applications that depend upon database use.

Screen-oriented languages are designed to assist in programming applications that are run by a user employing a GRAPHICAL USER INTERFACE to select operations from a menu, by a mouse operation to activate a screen object, or by keyboard entry.

Object-oriented languages are designed to assist in programming with reusable objects rather than writing extensive procedures. Each element of an object-oriented program is an object. Each object consists of data structures plus the operations, called methods, that can be performed on its data. Objects are activated by messages that come from other objects or are triggered by external events. Objects interact only by exchanging messages (that can include data). This characteristic of data and methods contained within an object is called "encapsulation", one of the main principles of the object-oriented approach. The effect of encapsulation is that data can only be affected through the methods of the object containing it. Another important characteristic of objects is inheritance. Once an object has been defined, a descendant object may be created that automatically inherits the data structures and methods of the original object. The two most widely used object-oriented languages are Smalltalk and C++. Each of these language systems provide complete development environments tailored to the needs of object-oriented implementation.

The type of language or its orientation is useful in selecting the programming language that best fits the characteristics of an application. However, because most information processing functions can be programmed in almost any language, a programmer will often select a language that is known rather than the language that has the best functionality for the problem.

GORDON B. DAVIS

protocols   When two devices are communicating, there must be agreement as to the meaning of control information being sent with the data, and agreement as to how the control information and data will be packaged. This agreement is the protocol. There are a number of standard communication protocols. The most widely known communications protocol is the OSI (Open Systems Interconnect) reference model developed by the ITU (International Transport Union). It has been standardized as the X.25 seven layer model. In this model, separate sets of rules (protocols) are defined for different communication conditions and needs.

There are other models or collections of protocols. These models are often called communications architectures. Examples include IBM's SNA (Systems Network Architecture) and TCP/IP (Transmission Control Protocol and Internet Protocol, two key elements of the protocol architecture). Communication on networks using a single protocol architecture are simpler and more efficient that communication involving multiple architectures.

GORDON B. DAVIS

prototyping   There are two schools of thought concerning the use of prototyping during systems analysis and design. The first view maintains that prototyping is a rapid development approach that replaces the traditional systems development life-cycle (SDLC). The second view suggests that prototyping is useful chiefly as a REQUIREMENTS DETERMINATION FOR INFORMATION SYSTEMS technique within the conventional design methodologies.

Sometimes managers and systems analysts refer to prototyping as an alternative methodology that has supplanted the SDLC. This approach, however, may be rife with problems if the skills of the analyst and programmer have not evolved to handle this approach. It may be true that through prototyping a system can be built more rapidly than when traditional SDLC methodologies are used, but good modular design may be sacrificed. A patched-up prototype might work, but it may be inefficient.

Prototypes can be developed and tested in a limited way. A prototype might be tested in one corporate branch or division and, if successful, might be implemented for use in the entire corporation. This kind of prototype is often used in manufacturing when an innovative product, such as a new model of an automobile, is developed.

When analysts use prototyping as a data-gathering technique, they interview, observe, and listen to feedback from users who make suggestions for improving the final system. Just as an architect builds a scale model before the actual building is constructed, a systems analyst may present a nonoperational prototype that reveals the new designs for input, output, and user interfaces.

A systems analyst may choose to develop a prototype that only presents key features of the system. Users may suggest that additional features, such as help screens, might be incorporated into the revised prototype. Using feedback in this way permits users to become deeply involved with the information system they will soon be using. Prototyping goes through successive iterations until the user is satisfied.

Most CASE: COMPUTER-AIDED SOFTWARE/SYSTEM ENGINEERING tools used for systems analysis and design possess functions supporting the development of input and output design. These programs use information stored in the data dictionary (for example, the field lengths of all data elements) to aid a systems analyst in creating balanced and uncluttered input and output screens. User-interface design is typically left to the imagination of the systems analyst, with little automated support presently available.

There are three main advantages of using prototyping within traditional systems analysis and design approaches. By gathering data about use of the prototype, the analyst increases the potential for improving the system early in its development. Furthermore, the analyst gains valuable information that may become useful in the event that development must be halted.

Thirdly, the final system is more likely to meet the needs of the users who desire valid input, meaningful output, and an appropriate user interface.

Bibliography

Alavi, M. (1984). An assessment of the prototyping approach to information systems. *Communications of the ACM*, **27**, 556–63.

Kendall, K. E. & Kendall, J. E. (1995). *Systems Analysis and Design*. 3rd edn. Englewood Cliffs, NJ: Prentice-Hall.

Naumann, J. D. & Jenkins, A. M. (1982). Prototyping: the new paradigm for systems development. *MIS Quarterly*, **6**, 29–44.

JULIE E. KENDALL and
KENNETH E. KENDALL

punched cards   Developed in the 1890s for use in the United States census, punched cards are important historically in information processing. Each card encoded information about a person, using punched holes. The information could be tabulated by a machine that sensed the pattern of punched holes. Although there were several punched-card formats, the most common measured $7\frac{3}{8} \times 3\frac{1}{4}$ inches with 80 columns and 12 rows. This was often referred to as the Hollerith or IBM card. The 80-column design of the punched card influenced the design of forms and early computer screens. Punched cards dominated large-scale data processing until the advent of computers in the 1950s. Punched cards continued to be used for data entry with computers until the early 1980s when other data entry methods supplanted them.

GORDON B. DAVIS

— Q —

quality 'in information systems *see*
ASSESSMENT OF MANAGEMENT INFORMATION
SYSTEMS

R

re-engineering and information technology Business process re-engineering (BPR) is an analysis and design approach for achieving significant breakthroughs in important organizational performance indicators such as cycle time, quality, service, and cost. The scope for change may be limited to one function within an organization, may include processes across several functions, or may extend to external processes linking separate organizations. Re-engineering often leads to radical change not only in core business processes, but also in job requirements, organizational structure, management systems, culture, and values (Hammer, 1990).

An organization creates customer value and other desired business results through its business processes. In advanced manufacturing firms, nonproduction processes may account for up to 75 percent of total product value. In service firms, such as banks and hotels, business processes describe virtually every step to meeting customer needs. Business process examples are the *order–delivery–payment cycle* in distribution, *customer account management* in financial services, and the *systems development life-cycle* in software firms. The structure of a business process refers to the way that tasks are differentiated according to knowledge and skill requirements, and how the tasks are coordinated to achieve integrated outcomes that are of value to customers. Traditionally, tasks are divided into narrow specialized duties and then coordinated in an assembly-line manner by supervisors and staff units organized in a hierarchy of authority relationships.

Re-engineering is *not* about speeding up or automating existing processes. BPR *is*:

1 The fundamental rethinking of what must be done to meet organizational goals.
2 Starting from a clean sheet to design new processes to achieve this.
3 Using information technology to enable such processes.
4 Institutionalizing dynamic new ways of doing business based on these processes.

Re-engineering seeks to change process structure by empowering motivated front-line workers to make decisions that have outcomes that are aligned to organizational mission and by providing access to relevant information that enables workers to make the best possible decision in a timely manner. BPR links worker motivation to performance by aligning each process to explicit goals, and by informing and rewarding workers according to desired results. Many re-engineering solutions employ case-management techniques such as case worker, empowered customer representative, and self-managing teams.

Successful BPR efforts require a change in mindset affecting five critical dimensions of organizational culture. Organizational change along these five dimensions distinguishes successful applications of BPR. Altered information flows accompany each shift, from:

1 *Convention to innovation.* BPR improves performance by challenging traditional practices, as in the invoice-less accounts receivable system developed by the Ford Motor Company. The efficacy of rules and assumptions underlying existing business practices were questioned and re-evaluated to determine their validity. New rules that better reflect current business reality were used as the bases of new process designs.

2 *Independent to interdependent processes.* The logic of integrated logistics, rapid replenishment in distribution, and value-added partnerships among independent firms substitute information for expensive resources such as capital, space, inventory, people, and time. A centralized database may be used to coordinate and communicate information among organizational units without undermining autonomy to decide and act.

3 *Sequential to integrated processing.* Re-engineering shifts the organization from dependence on a fragmented series of process steps to an integrated set of processes performed by a case worker or by a cross-functional team. The integrated case team processes all the tasks required for a major category of business transactions with access to the information necessary to do the job without the need for time-consuming hand-offs or approvals.

4 *Equal misery to differentiated service.* Re-engineering shifts process design from one-size-fits-all to custom-tailored processes that serve more finely defined groups of customers. A triage is usually designed to filter customers into differentiated processes designed to better meet their needs.

5 *Bureaucratic control to entrepreneurial initiative.* New process designs are aimed at transforming rigid bureaucracies based on central command and control into dynamic organizations of informed workers guided by performance measures that are aligned with goals.

Information technology (IT) plays a crucial role in enabling the re-engineering of business processes by overcoming basic limitations to performance, such as time differences, geographical dispersion, social distances, and organizational boundaries. Fundamentally, IT capabilities enable time compression and non-hierarchical communications across social barriers and geographical distances to add value in the performance of business processes. IT facilitates process innovation by changing the manner in which business processes traditionally capture, manipulate, store, present, communicate, and use information as a complement to the performance of physical activity. Data may be automatically captured at source via bar-coding, validated by programs in handheld computers, and transmitted to a shared database by radio. Unlike paper documents, a shared database simultaneously distributes information to many uses simultaneously. Unlike human experts, an EXPERT SYSTEM provides a co-worker with consistent advice round the clock. Unlike catalogs, a videodisk helps customers or trainees to interact with content. And unlike a typical trip log, automatic identification and tracking means mobile assets, such as vehicles or containers, tell dispatchers where they are now, instead of forcing the dispatcher to find the location. Developments and applications in workgroup computing, enterprise-wide integrated systems, and INTERORGANIZATIONAL SYSTEMS will enable organizations to take greater advantage of IT in re-engineering the way that work is structured to deliver value to customers and other stakeholders.

When firms should consider initiating BPR depends on the driving force for re-engineering and whether the BPR target is to resolve performance issues or to exploit new opportunities. BPR is driven by the twin forces of upheaval in the business environment and dramatic improvements in the price–performance ratio of IT. The four common sets of circumstances triggering considerations of BPR are depicted in table 1.

Table 1   When to re-engineer

Driving force for re-engineering	Focus on re-engineering	
	Resolving issues	Exploiting opportunities
Business imperatives	Major performance shortfalls	Business start-ups
Technological change	Major systems development	Technological breakthroughs

Many BPR efforts in North America have been triggered by *major performance shortfalls*. On the other hand, many Singapore BPR projects started because of government-led efforts to *develop new IT systems* to support major sectors of the economy. *Business start-ups* present natural opportunities for BPR because such organizations can design the new business with a clean slate, as opposed to a conceptual clean slate for BPR in existing organizations. *Technological breakthroughs* present yet another opportunity since they give organizations new capabilities for overcoming the limitations of human cognitive abilities, physical constraints of geography, and differences arising from separate time zones. New developments in ARTIFICIAL INTELLIGENCE, document IMAGE PROCESSING, interactive videodisk, MULTIMEDIA, and wireless communication technologies can be exploited.

Although re-engineering may be carried out without the use of IT, it is highly unlikely that new process designs can be implemented efficiently without enabling information systems. At the same time, re-engineering is not merely process automation, as speeding up broken processes cannot result in major performance improvements. Re-engineering seems to have the best results when it applies out-of-the-box thinking to traditional business practices, together with creative uses of IT capabilities in developing new process designs that enable more competitive performance.

Bibliography

Hammer, M. (1990). Re-engineering work: don't automate, obliterate. *Harvard Business Review*, **68**, 104–12.

BOON-SIONG NEO

relational database   The most common type of database across all classes of computers, ranging from mainframes to personal computers. In this type of database, the data structure is based on the relational data model introduced by E. F. Codd in 1970.

A relational database is a collection of relations. The relation is the uniform structure of the relational data model. A relation can be thought of as a table consisting of rows and columns of data. Each row of the relation is called a *tuple*, representing a collection of related data values. These tuples are facts describing a real-world object or relationship. The relation's columns are its attributes. The values of an attribute are drawn from a *domain*, which specifies the valid set of values for one or more attributes. The relation names and attribute names are used to help in interpreting the meaning of data in a relation.

A relational database can be created and maintained by a software package, the DATABASE MANAGEMENT SYSTEM (DBMS). The relational DBMS is a general-purpose software system that facilitates the creation, modification, and updating of the database, the retrieval of data, and the generation of reports.

See also **SQL**

ROGER H. L. CHIANG

report generators   Facilities for producing reports by specifying data to be included and the format of the report. Report generators are included in some programming languages; they are an integral part of DATABASE MANAGEMENT SYSTEMS. Report generators allow a user to specify headings, groupings of data, subtotals, totals, etc; they simplify report preparation.

requirements determination for information systems   There are three levels at which information requirements need to be established in order to design and implement computer-based information systems:

1 *Organization-level information requirements.* These requirements are used to define an overall information system architecture and to specify a portfolio of applications and databases. Often termed "enterprise analysis," the process of organization-level information requirements determination obtains, organizes, and documents a complete set of high-level requirements. The requirements are factored into databases and a portfolio of applications that can be scheduled for development.

2 *Organization database requirements.* These arise both from applications and *ad hoc* queries. User *ad hoc* query requirements and application requirements are referred to as conceptual or logical requirements because the user views of data are separated from the organization of data in physical storage. Requirements for physical database design are derived from user requirements and hardware and software environments.

3 *Application-level information requirements.* An application provides information processing for an organizational unit or organizational activity. There are essentially two types of information system application requirements: social and technical. The social or behavioral requirements, based on job design, specify objectives and assumptions such as work organization and work design objectives, individual role and responsibility assumptions, and organizational policies. The technical requirements are based on the information needed for the job or task to be performed. They specify outputs, inputs, stored data, and information processes.

There are different strategies for determining information requirements. One of these strategies, asking indirectly, is used when requirements cannot be obtained by asking directly or by a study of an existing system. Because of its importance and value in information requirements determination, the asking indirectly strategy will be our focus in this discussion.

Strategies for Determining Information Requirements

There are three broad strategies for determining information requirements:

1 *Asking directly.* In this strategy, the analyst obtains information requirements from persons in the business processes by asking them to describe their requirements. From a conceptual standpoint, this strategy assumes that users have a mental model (or can build one) to explain their information requirements. These conditions may hold in very stable systems for which a well-defined structure exists or in systems established by law, regulation, or other outside authority.

2 *Deriving from an existing information system.* Existing information systems that have an operational history can be used to derive requirements for a proposed information system for the same type of organization or application. The types of existing information system that are useful in deriving requirements for future systems are the system to be replaced, a system in a similar organization, and a proprietary system or package. In this strategy, users and analysts start with (anchor on) an existing system and adjust from it. If the information system is performing fairly standard operations and providing fairly standard information for business processes that are stable, the use of an existing system as an anchor may be appropriate.

3 *Asking indirectly by eliciting characteristics of business processes.* Requirements for information stem from the activities of the business processes. In eliciting requirements, questions focus on the activities and responsibilities that lead to the need for information. This approach is therefore especially appropriate when the business processes are changing or the proposed information system is different from existing patterns (in its content, form, complexity, etc.), so that anchoring on an existing information system or observations of information needs will not yield a complete and correct set of requirements.

When an initial set of requirements has been elicited by one of the methods, the requirements may be extended, modified, and refined by using a prototype of the application to allow users to adjust initial requirements through experimentation with an evolving information system.

Improving the Process of Eliciting Requirements Indirectly

Four recommendations for improving the process of eliciting information requirements indirectly are to (a) consider cross-functional requirements and sharing of information; (b) use group interviews for stakeholders; (c) use sets of questions that elicit different patterns of thinking about requirements; and (d) use a

Table 1 Decision centers involved in order processing

Decision center	Activity	Examples of major decisions
Sales staff	Selling merchandise	Which major customers to call What to sell customers What is available to sell
Credit department	Accounts receivable management	Which customers to allow credit How much credit to allow Which customers need past-due notices Which customers' credit should be discounted
Warehouse	Inventory management	What inventory to stock How much inventory to stock When to reorder stock When to unload slow-moving stock Which customers to allocate available inventory
Shipping department	Packing and shipping orders	What merchandise to sell to what customers What orders can be shipped together to save delivery cost When trucks should depart

prototype of the system to elicit user refinements and extensions to requirements.

Elicit cross-functional requirements
Many users and analysts view systems as functional as opposed to cross-functional (Wetherbe & Vitalari, 1994). This perspective is too narrow. For example, when developing a new budgeting system, a focus on the information needed by the budget managers or budgeting staff members is not sufficient. People other than budgeting staff make use of budgeting information.

Order processing illustrates the need to develop systems cross-functionally. To process orders, sales people have to decide which customers to call on, what to sell them, and what is available to sell. Credit must decide which customers can have credit and how much, which customers need past-due notices, and which customers' credit should be discontinued. The warehouse must decide what and how much inventory to stock, when to reorder, when to unload slow-moving inventory, and which customers to allocate limited inventory to. Shipping must decide such things as what merchandise to send to which customers, what orders can be shipped together to save delivery

costs, and when trucks should depart. These decisions are summarized in table 1.

A system should provide information so that all decisions can be improved. In eliciting requirements ts to improve the quality of the decision, cross-functional factors that should be considered include customer importance to the business, customer need for prompt delivery of the order, the profitability of each order, credit status of customer, shipping schedule for delivery to each customer, and customer reaction if a previous order was late.

For example, consider the last decision listed for the warehouse department in table 1 of allocating available inventory to customers. If the warehouse has five orders but only enough inventory to fill three, it must make a resource allocation decision. Typically, this decision is made on a first-in-first-out (FIFO) basis. That seems equitable and fair, given the information they have available to them. This rule can result in a bad decision. What if a customer who does a lot of business with the company needs this shipment promptly, recently received an order late and was furious about it, is paying a high profit margin on the order, pays bills promptly, and a truck is routed to deliver a shipment to another customer nearby the same afternoon. A FIFO decision may cause the inventory to be allocated to someone who hardly ever does business with the company, to whom the order is not urgent, who yields a low profit margin, does not pay bills on time, and a truck is not going into the vicinity for the next three weeks, during which time inventory could have been re-stocked. Note that the information needed to improve the decision-making in the warehouse comes from outside the warehouse. For example, customer need, importance, and profitability come from sales, credit worthiness comes from credit, and shipping schedule comes from shipping.

Use group interviews

In the determination of information requirements, the system design team usually interviews managers individually instead of using a group process (also known as joint application design). Doing each interview separately places cognitive stress on a manager and hinders his or her ability to respond adequately to questions.

A second reason for a joint application design is that different functional areas of an organization have different agendas in developing a new information system. For example, in the order-processing system portrayed in table 1, each decision center is likely to emphasize different design criteria. Sales may view the primary importance of order processing as ensuring prompt and correct delivery of orders to customers. Credit, on the other hand, may view the agenda as primarily ensuring that the company receives full payment for all orders. Those responsible for inventory management

are, of course, interested in facilitating good inventory management, reducing inventory costs, etc., while those responsible for shipping are interested in ensuring good routing of trucks to minimize delivery costs. It is difficult to achieve this overall perspective if each manager is interviewed individually.

Use questions that elicit different patterns of thinking

System developers often ask the direct question: "What information do you need from the new system?" Such a direct question is not helpful to managers desiring better information for problem-solving, decision-making, and business processes. The reason the direct question may not work well is that managers think in terms of the need for information and not the list of information needed.

Good problem-solvers creatively elicit answers to requirements through indirect questions. For example, in determining what lawn mower someone needs, questions such as "How big is your yard? How steep is it? Do you have fences or trees?" are indirect questions that determine appropriate blade width, horsepower, or the need for a rear or side bagger. Those designing information systems need to follow the same approach, and executives should request that they do so.

A straightforward, useful indirect question approach to interviewing executives (instead of simply saying "What information do you need?") to determine information requirements has been developed at the MIS Research Center at the University of Minnesota (Wetherbe, 1988). The technique is based upon three

Table 2   Comprehensive interview approaches, implementations and developers

Comprehensive approach	Information system implementation	Developers
Specify problems and decisions	The executive interview portion of business systems planning (BSP)	IBM
Specify critical factors	Critical success factors (CSF)	Rockart
Specify effectiveness criteria for outputs and efficiency criteria for processes used to generate outputs	Ends/means analysis (E/M analylsis)	Wetherbe and Davis

different but overlapping sets of requirement determination questions as shown in table 2. By combining questions from these three different approaches, a comprehensive, reliable determination of conceptual information requirements can be achieved. This method is explained in more detail in the next section.

Use a prototype to elicit user refinements

After providing an initial set of requirements, users should be allowed to extend and refine their conceptual requirements and provide detailed information requirements through trial and error. Trial and error, or experiential learning, is an important part of problem-solving. It is also a part of determining detailed information requirements. It can be incorporated into the system design process through the use of a prototype or mock-up of the system. Using state-of-the-art technology, a prototype of a new system can usually be constructed quickly. As in manufacturing, much can be learned about final requirements through a prototype before "building the new factory."

Users should be able to observe and experience a prototype within a few days of being interviewed. This prototype can then be shaped into a final design within a few weeks. Once the prototype is accepted, a realistic schedule and budget can be established for building the system. Although systems must evolve over time and should be built with evolution in mind, a system that is initially "right" will not need substantial immediate modifications. Evolutionary change of such a system is therefore much more manageable.

The Eliciting Process in Asking Indirectly

Before conducting the interview, an agreement on the overall purpose of the business activity should be established in a joint application design session. For example, for the order-processing system discussed above, the objective of the system could be to ensure prompt, correct delivery of orders to customers, maintain credit integrity, facilitate inventory management, and ensure good shipment routing and scheduling. Once this has been established, questions can be asked that determine information needed to ensure that those objectives are accomplished. As explained earlier, a robust approach employs questions that overlap in

their coverage (table 2). The three sets of questions trigger different patterns of thinking.

Elicit problems and decisions

These questions define information requirements by asking indirect questions about problems and decisions. Example questions are:

1 What are the major problems encountered in accomplishing the purposes of the organizational unit you manage? For example, in an order-processing system, problems include being out of stock too often, allocating limited inventory to the wrong customers, and sending off trucks unaware that another order going to the same destination will be arriving at the dock within an hour.

2 What are good solutions to those problems? For example, to solve the problem of being out of stock too often requires better inventory management. To solve the problem of incorrectly allocating orders requires letting the warehouse know the importance of customers and the importance of orders to specific customers. It would also be helpful to know customer credit status. To solve the scheduling of truck departure problems requires letting shipping know the destination of orders that are being processed but have not yet arrived at the shipping dock.

3 How can information play a role in any of those solutions? For example, to improve inventory management, out-of-stock and below-minimum reporting could be provided electronically. Also, an automatic reordering system could be implemented. Electronic access to customer importance, importance of order, and credit status could allow the warehouse to make appropriate allocation decisions when inventory is limited. If the shipping department has access to orders received and in process, it can make better decisions over routing and scheduling trucks.

4 What are the major decisions associated with your management responsibilities? Major decisions for order processing include which customers to call on and what to sell them, credit, inventory, reordering, allocation of limited inventory, and scheduling and routing deliveries.

Table 3   Decisions elicited for order-processing system

Decision	Information
Which customers to call on and what to sell them?	Customer-order history; inventory available
Credit for whom? How much? When to discontinue?	Credit rating; current status of account, payment history
What and how much inventory to stock? When to reorder?	Inventory on hand; sales trends on inventory items; market forecasts
How to allocate limited inventory?	Priority of order; importance of customer; credit status of customer; shipping schedule
When to unload slow-moving inventory?	Sales trends
Destination of ordered inventory?	Customers' addresses
What orders can be shipped together to save delivery costs?	Shipping schedule and customers' destination for orders awaiting shipment

5 What improvements in information could result in better decisions? Table 3 illustrates the way decisions relate to information requirements.

Elicit critical success factors (CSF). A second line of questions is based on critical success factors. Table 4 provides an illustration of critical success factor/information results.

1 What are the critical success factors of the organizational unit you manage? (Most managers have four to eight of these.) For example, critical success factors for order processing include adequate inventory to fill

customer orders, prompt shipment of orders, high percentage of customer payments made, and vendors (suppliers) promptly filling reorders.

2 What information is needed to monitor critical success factors? For example, to determine if adequate inventory is available, management needs summary and exception reports on percentage of orders filled on time. In addition to overall reports, orders should also be categorized by customer and product. To determine if orders are being shipped promptly, management needs to have summary and exception reports on

Table 4   Critical success factors and information requirements

Critical success factor	Information
Adequate inventory to fill customer orders	Percentage of orders filled on time – overall and also categorized by customer and product
Prompt shipment of orders	Deliver time – overall and also categorized by customer
High percentage of customer payments	Delinquency report on nonpaying customers
Vendors (suppliers) promptly fill reorders	Exception report on vendor reorders not filled on time

Table 5   Eliciting effectiveness information for order-processing system

Ends	Effectiveness	Information
Fill customer orders	Customer orders delivered as ordered, when expected, and as soon or sooner than competition	Summary and exception reports on customer deliveries; number of order corrections made; comparative statistics on delivery service v. competition
Provide customer service	Promptly provide credit to qualified customers	Customer credit status and payment history
	Quick response to and reduction of customer complaints	Report of number and type of complaints by customers and average time to resolve complaint
	Customers are satisfied	Customer attitudes toward service perhaps determined by customer surveys

delivery time, including reports categorized by customers.

Elicit effectiveness and efficiency (ends/means)
Effectiveness measures relate to the outputs or ends from a process whereas efficiency measures relate to the resources (means) employed. Ends/means questions elicit requirements by getting managers to think about both effectiveness and efficiency and information needed to monitor it (Wetherbe, 1988). Questions to elicit this thinking are:

1 What is the end or good or service provided by the business process?
2 What makes these goods or services effective to recipients or customers?
3 What information is needed to evaluate that effectiveness?
4 What are the key means or processes used to generate or provide goods or services? For example, means for order processing include processing orders, processing credit requests, and making shipments.

5 What constitutes efficiency in the providing of these goods or services? For example, efficiency for order processing is achieving low transaction costs for orders and credit checks. It is also minimizing shipment costs.
6 What information is needed to evaluate that efficiency? Examples of information needed to assess efficiency include cost per transaction with historical trends, and shipment cost categorized by order, customer, region, and revenue generated.

Tables 5 and 6 illustrate the use of effectiveness and efficiency questions in an ends/means analysis for order processing.

The method of using these three sets of indirect questions as a basis for obtaining a reasonably correct and complete set of information requirements is both simple and powerful.

Table 6   Eliciting efficiency information for order-processing system

Means	Efficiency	Information
Process orders	Low transaction cost	Cost per transaction with historical trends
Process credit request	Low transaction cost	Cost per transaction with historical trends
Make shipments	Minimize shipment costs	Ship cost categorized by order, customer, region, and revenue generated

It is simple because it consists of components that can be learned by an analyst and a manager in a relatively short time. It is powerful because it overcomes human limitations in thinking about information requirements.

The redundancy in the questions increases the reliability of the structured interview results. For example, note that the set of problem questions may identify poor allocation of limited inventory to customers. The need to allocate limited inventory may also be identified as a *decision* that must be made. In other words, if the concept of allocating limited inventory is not recalled as a problem, it can still be identified as a decision, and so forth.

Bibliography

Wetherbe, J. C. (1988). *Systems Analysis and Design*. St Paul, MN: West Publishing Company.
Wetherbe, J. C. & Vitalari, N. P. (1994). *Systems Analysis and Design*. St Paul, MN: West Publishing Company.

JAMES C. WETHERBE

S

security of information systems The objective of information systems security (computer security, data security) efforts is to protect the computer and its information from accident and disasters and intentional security breaches (abuse). Information system security in the 1970s and 1980s dealt with hardware, programs, data, and computer service abuse. PCs introduced a concern about securing system assets against viruses. Computer communications networks, the INTERNET, and the WORLD WIDE WEB have added authentication and encryption issues.

Information Security Policies

Policies serve to set the tone for how security is viewed within an organization. Useful security policies have widespread management support and are detailed enough to give an organization a clear sense of direction. Good policies also include guidelines for implementing disaster recovery plans, designing security controls into applications, establishing system-user access capabilities, carrying out investigations of computer crimes, and disciplining employees for security breaches.

In creating information security policies, it is critical that policies are well matched to the corporate culture. Consciously or unconsciously, employees will resist policies that conflict with the corporate mores or "ways of doing things." Moreover, policies that conflict with basic, underlying beliefs, attitudes, and values of the organization are likewise unlikely to be effective. Ultimately, mismatches result in policies that are either completely ignored or suboptimal in their impact.

There are at least four attitudes that can be adopted with respect to creating organizational security policies. Adapted from Bryan (1995), they are:

1 *Secretive.* This attitude, internalized by military organizations, can be simply stated as "you know only what you must." Organizations adopting this stance would seldom be inclined to connect to the Internet, for example.
2 *Prudent.* This method specifies that only connections and operations explicitly granted are permissible.
3 *Permissive.* This lenient approach allows everything that is not explicitly forbidden.
4 *Laissez-faire.* Organizations either explicitly or implicitly adopt the policy that "anything goes."

Extent of Security Losses from Intentional Abuse

The extent of losses due to computer system abuse is uncertain, but is estimated to be substantial. It has been reported that between 25 and 50 percent of US firms discover at least one serious abuse a year. It is possible that 50–90 percent have lost money through breaches in security (Hoffer & Straub, 1989). In 1994, Ernst and Young reported that over half of surveyed firms reported losses in the past two years due to computer abuse (Bryan, 1995). Given that possibly only 5–10 percent of computer abuse cases are actually reported to the authorities (Straub & Nance, 1990), the extent of abuse is very likely to be much greater. The magnitude of the problem is such that British banks reportedly fire 1 percent of their employees each year for computer fraud (Anderson, 1994).

Intentional Security Violations

Traditionally, computer abuse has been characterized as: (a) unauthorized use; (b) abuse of data; (3) abuse of programs; and (4) abuse of hardware (Straub, 1986; Hoffer & Straub, 1989). Unauthorized use, usually by employees, has been reported to be the most common form of abuse. This category, which includes activities such as exploiting organizational resources by playing computer games or creating and running personal databases, may account for about 40 percent of reported cases. Abuse of data, for example, the actual stealing of funds or data, may amount to about 20 percent of reported cases, while abuse of programs, such as theft or unauthorized copying of copyright routines, may explain 25 percent of reported cases. Hardware abuse, such as stealing the hardware, accounts for only about 5 percent of the total.

Abusers are overwhelmingly insiders: programmers, clerical personnel, users, students, and managers. Only about 2 percent were outsiders (most often hackers). In spite of belief that a large number of users, or a large number of privileged users, will result in vulnerable systems, there is no empirical evidence that this is the case (Straub, 1986; Hoffer & Straub, 1989). The reasons why people abuse computers are: personal gain (25 percent), ignorance of proper conduct (27 percent), revenge (22 percent), and misguided playfulness (26 percent).

PCs added a new security problem of protecting against viruses. Viruses (and so-called worms) are computer programs that invade a system and have the capability of damaging the host computer system either by changing and deleting data or by wasting computer resources. Viruses usually are introduced into computer systems through contaminated diskettes that contain the virus. When such a diskette is accessed, the virus attaches itself to the host computer and, depending on the type of virus, begins to multiply and disseminate itself. In this privileged position within the host computer, it has the ability to virtually destroy its host. Some viruses begin to activate themselves immediately, while others lie in wait for special dates. The origin of many viruses is uncertain, but hackers are suspected of much of this antisocial activity. Commercial software packages have been written to locate and protect systems from virus. Anti-virus packages are currently in use by 91 percent of

organizations surveyed by Ernst and Young (Bryan, 1995).

Inadequate security is thought to be the main hindrance to the INTERNET becoming a viable commercial marketplace. Network information security has four main issues:

1 *Access control and authorization.* This area of security deals with questions of who is allowed into a network and for what purposes. However, the interdependence of authorization processes among networks and among host nodes complicates control and authorization.
2 *Information authenticity.* This area deals with identifying the source of information, i.e. the originator of the message. When an organization's network is connected to many others, it is impossible to identify network users with the traditional login and location method used in mainframes. Eavesdroppers can copy these and impersonate legitimate users. One of the proposed methods of overcoming this problem is the use of digital signatures.
3 *Information integrity.* Ensuring the integrity of information means ensuring that the data has not been altered. When information enters the organization's network from other networks, it is much harder to ensure that information has not been lost. Special protocols have been created for this purpose.
4 *Information privacy.* Privacy in networks generally means that personal and confidential information is not subject to eavesdropping. Privacy is often achieved using cryptography or cryptosystems.

Information Security and Accidents/Disasters

Information is also exposed to damage from events other than computer abuse. Accidents and disasters, such as damage due to human error or natural acts like hurricanes, are often dealt with through well-defined and tested contingency plans. These plans include automatic and manual database backups, uninterrupted power supply (UPS) systems, and offsite computer backups. In addition, many current hardware components like routers (telecommunications switches) are designed with redundancy so that if any one element fails, the system can continue to operate. Such characteristics are essential for many communication-intensive systems, such as teller machines and bank transaction processing systems.

Contingency plans include backup and recovery in the event of the computer-processing site being destroyed ‚by fire, natural disaster, or other event. Site backup provisions may include:

1 *Hot backup*. This method ensures that a fully operational redundant site is ready to take over immediately a disaster occurs at a primary site.

2 *Warm backup*. This method is similar to hot backup, except that the auxiliary site becomes operational within a matter of hours.

3 *Split site*. In this method, organizational computing is performed at two sites so that when one site is disrupted, the other can take over critical applications.

4 *Cold backup*. In this method, a facility equipped with cabling and network connections is ready for rapid installation of new hardware and software and databases from backups.

Security Techniques

The effectiveness of security techniques depends upon the deterrent effect of having administrative policies in place, management commitment to good security, and user security awareness. To prevent losses from insecure systems, security software can also be used. Methods to detect abusive activities involve monitoring system use, suspicious systems activity, and security violations. Through use of these kinds of methods, management delivers the message that security is important to the firm and that there are penalties for violating security.

Methods that deal with specific aspects of security include:

1 *Physical security*. These measures are primarily aimed at protecting system assets from theft. They include locks, alarms, and embedding the company logo in hardware. In addition, restricted entrance to sensitive departments is often used and combined with automatically monitored entrance and departure recordings. Other useful measures include administrative regulations ensuring that removable disks with secured data be locked up and that sensitive data be kept only on secure disks.

2 *Backup*. Disk and tape backups are used to deal with data loss due to faulty devices and human errors. It is often suggested that companies utilize backups to assure their chances of survival in the event of data loss.

3 *Redundancy*. Redundant data, input–output devices, and processors ("shadowed," "mirrored," or synchronized machines) can be used as a method of fault management in crucial network management systems. These mechanisms provide fault-free operations by detecting, isolating, and resolving faults. Built-in redundancy methods often use EXPERT SYSTEMS.

4 *Passwords*. The first line of defense in maintaining data security is enforcing a sign-in and password verification procedure (login). This procedure can be augmented by administrative policies that require that power be turned off whenever a PC is not in active use. An extended defense can be achieved by using available security software that forces a login and automatically encrypts protected subdirectories so that, if the login is bypassed, the files are not available.

5 *Authorizing access*. Once a user has entered the system using a password, many database management systems come with built-in authorization mechanisms that enable the systems administrators to authorize different types and locations of access to data according to user identification or group. Authorization control and security policy enforcement are also available as stand-alone software security tools.

6 *Encryption*. Even when a user has access to certain data, encryption can be used to ensure that the authorization process in a DBMS or a network is not circumvented. This method is often used to secure both data and communications. There are two types of cryptographic methods: those applying common keys and those applying private keys. The common key methods apply the same key for both encryption and decryption. These methods are faster and are often used for bulk data. A method

frequently employed in this situation is the DES algorithm. The private key method allocates two keys to each user: a public key used for encrypting and a private one for decrypting. One of the commonly used algorithms for this type is RSA. Encryption algorithms are mostly only computationally secure, i.e. breaking the code is possible, but requires an unfeasible amount of computational time and resources. These protocols, including TMN and DSA, can be broken if the random number at the core of the method is shared; for example, if an eavesdropper follows the establishment of a communication protocol between two legitimate subscribers and uses a variation of their key to establish a session with an accomplice.

7 *Firewalls.* Firewalls are a computerized barrier that controls and prevents illicit messages and users from entering the network or parts of it. This feature is essential when companies let their customers and suppliers access their internal network. Firewalls protect resources by securing servers and sites as well as transactions. This is done by controlling authentication, message integrity, and unauthorized listening. The two currently available methods are *channel-based security* and *document-based security.* A channel-based security standard, such as SSL (secure socket layer), secures the entire channel; while a document-based standard, such as SHTTP (secure hypertext transport protocol), only guarantees that specific documents broadcast will be secure. WORLD WIDE WEB commerce already exists for users with SSL servers.

The most common types of firewalls are (Bryan, 1995):

1 *Router-based filters.* These control the traffic at the IP level of TCP/IP (level 3 of the ISO OSI model) by controlling the packets allowed into the network. This method is probably the most commonly used at present. However, it does not work well with non-packet protocols.

2 *Gateways (alias bastions).* These firewalls reside on host computers and use the host computer to log activities via security software.

3 *Isolated networks.* This method is similar to gateways, with the exception that it creates an isolated internal network that connects to the outside networks through a gateway.

4 *Electronic signatures.* The digital signature algorithm (DSA) is a digital signature and verification mechanism used for digital, rather than written, signatures. DSA enables verification of signature, message origin, and message integrity without giving away information that would make signature forgery possible. DSA achieves this by allotting two different digital keys to each signature bearer: a secret private key for encrypting the message and a public key used for decrypting it. The private key is known only to the signature bearer, while the public key is known to all the network users.

Future Security Problems

Coming advances in computation will, no doubt, produce new security problems. Free agents, for example, are software programs that travel the Internet and run independently on host computers. While providing new and powerful communication tools, they also create security hazards and viruses. One of the proposed methods for controlling security with free agents is the creation of firewalls using object-oriented encapsulation which permits each free agent access only to its own and explicitly shared data. This method can be augmented with cryptographic agent authentication (Wayner, 1995).

Although advances in technology may change some features of security, it will continue to be true that information security must be seen as a human problem as much as a technology problem. Management must be involved. Without higher-level management support, there will be insufficient budgets for and insufficient attention paid to information security. Without sufficient budgets, necessary control changes will not be made. Without sufficient management attention, control decisions that need to be made will be ignored.

Bibliography

Anderson, R. J. (1994). Why cryptosystems fail. *Communications of the ACM*, **37** (11), 32–40.

Bryan, J. (1995). Build a firewall. *Byte*, **20** (4), 91–96.

Hoffer, J. A. & Straub, D. W. (1989). The 9 to 5 underground: are you policing computer crimes? *Sloan Management Review*, **31** (2), 35–43.

Straub, D. W. (1986). Computer abuse and computer security: update on an empirical study. *Security, Audit and Control Review*, **4** (2), 21–31.

Straub, D. W. & Nance, W. D. (1990). Discovering and disciplining computer abuse in organizations: a field study. *MIS Quarterly*, **14** (1), 45–52.

Wayner, P. (1995). Free agents. *Byte*, **20** (3), 105–14.

DAVID GEFEN and DETMAR W. STRAUB

SIM The Society for Information Management is an international organization of information system executives (*see* ASSOCIATIONS AND SOCIETIES FOR INFORMATION SYSTEMS PROFESSIONALS).

smart card A plastic card with embedded, integrated chips containing information about the user of the card or its use. Smart cards are useful for information system applications because they can contain information important to an application. For example, key information about an individual's medical history can be incorporated in a smart card for use in acquiring medical treatment. A smart card may be used to store value. The card stores a cash value; when a purchase is made, the stored value is reduced.

soft systems methodologies A new discipline labeled operational (or operations) research emerged from the Second World War. It applied mathematical techniques to solving a variety of operational problems. Problems ranging from the best deployment of check-out counters in a supermarket to meta-problems relating to the world's use of nonsustainable resources appeared to be susceptible to the new mathematical treatments offered by the disciplines of operational research, mathematical programming, industrial dynamics, and systems analysis. The availability of computers enabled larger and more complex problems to be tackled.

However, these so called "hard" techniques could be useful only if it were possible to define the problem to be solved in clear and unambiguous terms. In wartime, it was often possible to define the objective of a system clearly and in terms which could be quantified. Moreover, there was an expectation that all stakeholders shared goals. In situations where there were conflicts in the desirability of outcomes, the techniques took second place to what were often political judgments. Hard approaches worked well when the problem situation was well understood and clearly defined, there was broad agreement on desirable outcomes, and outcomes lent themselves to quantification and measurement.

For many business problems, instead of a definable problem, there is a feeling of unease, perhaps triggered by some unexpected changes in performance. Human behavior is frequently unpredictable and responses to situations contradict expectations. The outcomes looked for from an action, say the introduction of a new system to monitor the performance of a group of employees, turns out to reduce rather than increase productivity. A system introduced into different branches of an enterprise, all apparently identical, nevertheless results in a wide range of outcomes, some meeting all targets, others having to be abandoned as failures. Many of the desirable outcomes from an action may be classed as intangible. They do not lend themselves to measurement or the outcomes are the consequence of so great a range of external and internal factors that it becomes impossible to relate the outcome to any single cause. Cultural and political factors may influence the actions of stakeholders. The problem situation may be unstructured.

The failure of "hard" methods to cope with this kind of situation has led to the development of so-called "soft" approaches. Peter Checkland, of the University of Lancaster in England, has developed the best-known method. He was schooled in the hard systems methodology which had so successfully helped to solve some problems, but he was dissatisfied with the limitations noted above. He observed that "human activity systems," systems in which humans participated as planners, decision-makers, and operators, did not behave as the "hard" school anticipated. He sought to develop techniques which would enable systems analysts to work on human activity systems. His methodology, now widely used in many parts of the world, is called *soft systems methodology*

(SSM) (Checkland, 1981; Checkland & Scholes, 1990).

SSM provides a way of developing insights to illuminate unclear problem situations. It guides an analyst to view an organization as a "human activity system." In SSM, the first task of the analyst is to determine the system under investigation. In information system studies, it is the part of the organization where the problematic situation lies. The analyst's study should, at its conclusion, lead to a plan of action that will improve the system's function. The analyst needs to ensure that a proposed plan of action is acceptable to the relevant stakeholders and can be implemented by the organization and by the people who work there. In other words, a

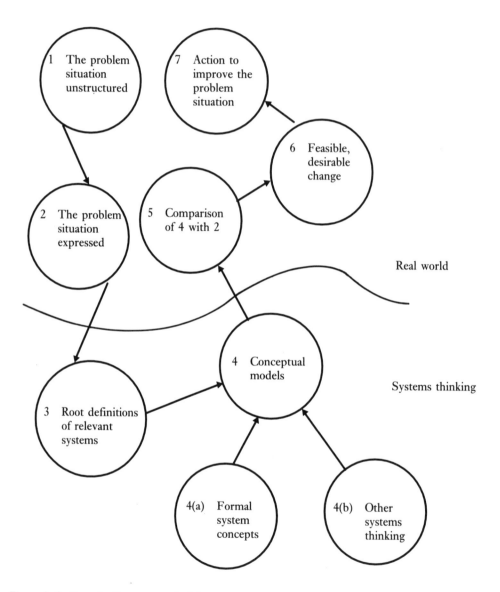

Figure 1 Outline of soft systems methodology
Source: Checkland (1981) Reprinted by permission of John Wiley & Sons, Ltd.

plan must be formulated that is not only desirable in terms of the goals of the organization, but that can be feasibly implemented in the organization in question.

Figure 1 illustrates the SSM approach (the description of how SSM is used is taken from Avgerou and Cornford, 1993). It represents SSM as a process with seven stages. In the first two stages, the analyst finds out what makes the situation problematic. To do that, it is useful to build up the richest possible picture of the situation studied by observing the processes taking place, by interviewing different stakeholders, and by examining reports and other organizational documents. It is important that the analyst gains an understanding of the functioning (and personalities) of the informal system which exists in all organizations, as well as the formal, designed system. A rich picture may be expressed in terms of structures, such as the power hierarchy and the communication patterns and processes, decision-making, and operations. It should also capture the various viewpoints from which the problem situation can be perceived. Conflicting views about a problem are likely to stem from different ways of viewing the world: the stakeholders *Weltanschauung*. Displaying the situation in a way that reveals the different points of view helps in deciding the range of possible actions to follow.

In stage 3 of SSM, the analyst uses what has been discovered about the problem situation to define notional human activity systems that seem relevant to the problem. Checkland calls these *root definitions*. Several root definitions can be developed, according to the various *Weltanschauungen* revealed in the rich picture of the situation. Each root definition must give a clear statement of the system under study. The differences in the root definitions indicate the extent to which issues such as goals and objectives are shared, as well as understanding what some of the organization processes are intended to support.

In stage 4 of SSM, the analyst forms a model of activities for each root definition. An activity model is a description of the activities that need to be carried out for the system to perform the transformation process of the relevant root definition. In stage 5, the analyst compares the conceptual activity with what actually happens in the part of the organization under study. The

objective of this stage is to tease out the complexities, contradictions, and perceived and actual inadequacies of the existing situation.

At stages 6 and 7, the analyst opens the debate about possible changes that can be made to improve the perceived problem situation. The task is to find which of the suggested changes can be implemented. The actions for change must be compatible with the culture of the organization and acceptable to its stakeholders. The analyst should seek a consensus solution: there must be agreement on the validity and utility of the proposed changes.

The wavy line in figure 1 indicates the split between two different classes of activities. Those stages lying above the line involve interactions of the analyst with the stakeholders of the organization concerned. Those lying under the line are desk work, where the analyst applies and uses systems concepts in order to formulate and structure his or her perceptions of the problem situation and to model its functioning.

The main value of SSM lies in it making the analyst aware that organizational problems are embedded in human activity systems where alternative points of view govern behavior and where successful change requires acceptance and commitment from the relevant stakeholders. It provides an approach which enables the analyst to get a better understanding of the organizational realities that determine the effectiveness of the enterprise.

SSM is just one approach to dealing with the uncertainties, informality, and unstructuredness found within most organizations (Rosenhead, 1989). Other methods tackle different aspects of the problem. Fuzzy logic provides a method for dealing with the problem of partially indeterminate relationships between the entities of a system. Multiple objective, multiple criteria evaluation methods enable the analyst to select solutions where different stakeholders have varying objectives and, even if they agree on objectives, may attach very different values to them. The analytic hierarchical process (AHP) developed by Saaty provides a way of selecting from a range of options where the characteristics of some options can be defined in quantitative forms, but that of others only in words of the form "I prefer A to B." "Soft" methods are now regarded as an important weapon in avoiding failure in systems design and development and in helping to design effective systems.

Bibliography

Avgerou, C. & Cornford, T. (1993). *Developing Information Systems: Concepts, Issues and Practice.* London: Macmillan.

Checkland, P. (1981). *Systems Thinking, Systems Practice.* Chichester: Wiley.

Checkland, P. & Scholes, J. (1990). *Soft Systems Methodology in Action.* Chichester: Wiley.

Rosenhead, J. V. (1989). *Rational Analysis for a Problematic World.* Chichester: Wiley.

FRANK LAND

software   The term *software* is contrasted with *hardware*. In computer hardware, elementary operations and functions are fixed by the equipment design and circuitry; software creates operations and functions based on a set of instructions termed a program. The software instructions make use of the hardware operations and functions to create a variety of more complex functions and sequences of operations. Software allows a single hardware design to be used for a large number of different purposes. The program of instructions is not permanently stored in the computer; it is input when needed. A program that is to be executed is brought into the main memory of the computer; when not in use, it is stored on disk or other accessible storage.

The set of instructions that comprise a computer program can be written so that it modifies itself as the instructions are executed. A program can, in essence, build the execution path as the program is run. There are usually numerous program paths that may be selected; the actual path of instructions executed depends on the data being processed, instructions provided by the user at execution, and the way the solution process was programmed. The potential number of unique combinations of instructions that can be executed by a program can easily number in the millions. This is why software is so useful in processing complex procedures required for human systems. It is also a reason why it is difficult to make sure software is correct.

All business systems that use computers are designed as *human–machine systems*. Software is used in connection with human input, human review, and human decision-making. The advantages of computers are that they are very fast and consistent. The consistency of processing is very valuable in performing procedures required by organizations. However, humans are still needed in most business processes. Even though software can be flexible with program paths to deal with different situations, it cannot innovate and respond to unanticipated inputs in the same way as humans.

Software in the information system is of two general types: *application software* and *system software*. The application software performs the information processing required by the organization; system software provides services needed by applications and supports the development of application software.

System Software

System software consists of software that provides facilities and functions to allow applications to be developed and to operate. General types of system software are the operating system, communications software, database software, and development software. System software is purchased or leased from software vendors and not developed by user organizations.

The operating system is the most fundamental system software. It is loaded in the computer prior to application programs, because it provides facilities for hardware utilization by the application program and monitors program execution for various types of errors related to hardware use. The basic operating system functions include job execution control, allocation and management of system resources, and standard methods for the use of input and output devices. For example, the application program may specify reading data from a record stored on a disk; the operating system provides the instructions to manage the physical reading of the record from disk storage. It also provides facilities for common activities such as sorting, although these are often referred to as utilities. Other system software extends the operating system concept to provide general facilities to manage user interfaces, provide database management facilities, and manage electronic communications.

The basic operating system may provide only minimal features for the user interface. Graphical user interfaces may be added to improve ease of use. The user interface software provides facilities that improve the user interaction with the operating system and allows switching among programs, transferring data between them, copying files, and other user-support facilities.

Communications software provides facilities for applications that rely on data communications. A single data communications package is installed to manage all transfer of data, deal with transmission errors, handle protocols, and so forth. In a LOCAL AREA NETWORK, the network is managed by a local area network operating system. In a wide area network, the communications software manages the communications over telephone lines or other network facilities. Database management software extends the data and file management facilities of the operating system. The DATABASE MANAGEMENT SYSTEM (DBMS) may be used by application software to manage access and storage of data.

The general category of system software includes support for application development. The development of applications requires software development tools, such as high-level software to generate programs from specifications, computer language software for writing processing procedures, and software to assist in various parts of the program development process. The database management software package that supports application programs also contains program development facilities.

Application Software

Application software is designed for specific business activities such as transaction processing, data analysis, business processes, report preparation, and so forth. Applications software can be purchased as complete packages, developed using high-level program generators, or developed using programming language facilities. The way they were acquired or developed affects how they use the operating system and facilities for user interface, communications, and database management. Application software packages are typically written to be used with a certain operating system. For example, an application package for a microcomputer may require a specific operating system and version number; a large mainframe package may require a specific mainframe operating system.

Programming Languages

Computer hardware is instructed by a program of machine-language instructions in primary storage. For all practical purposes, programmers never write computer instructions in machine language. The programmer writes instructions in a language more suited to human use and the instructions are translated to machine language. The programmer may also employ development tools that generate programs from specifications. The translation process from the source program written in a programming language to an object program in machine-level instructions uses software called an assembler for low-level languages or a compiler for higher-level languages. There are also a number of facilities in the development software to assist in linking programs, editing programs, testing programs, and maintaining programs in libraries.

A programming language consists of a syntax, command words, naming rules, and rules for constructing instructions and specifications. There are hundreds of different computer languages. Languages may be designed to support the writing of programs as a sequence of procedures (a procedural language) or as separate program objects that encapsulate the instructions and data associated with business functions (object-oriented languages). There are different levels of programming languages. The lowest level is a symbolic assembly language close to the machine level, the middle level is a language oriented to the procedures and steps in processing or problem-solving (such as COBOL), and the third level consists of problem-oriented programming facilities and very high-level language (often called fourth-generation languages or 4GLs) designed to focus on describing the output to be achieved or the problem to be solved (rather than detailed processing or solution procedures). Object-oriented programming centers program design around program objects, each of which encapsulates all the data and procedures associated with it. The most common high-level languages in business use are business data-processing languages, algorithmic languages, and database languages. As part of these languages, there may be facilities for designing and building graphical user interfaces with which humans interact with computer programs.

Data-processing languages are designed for handling business transactions and preparing business documents and reports. The dominant language is COBOL (common business-oriented language), a procedural language. More than two-thirds of all business applications are written in COBOL, although a high percentage of new applications use other languages. The dominant language for writing microcomputer programs is C, a language with some low- and some high-level features. C++ is an object-oriented language based on the C language. Algorithmic language instructions facilitate writing formulas and computational procedures. The most common algorithmic language is FORTRAN. It is used extensively in scientific and engineering work. A simplified algorithmic language for user programmers is BASIC.

There are several database query languages. The standard approach to a query language is termed SQL (structured query language) designed for programming access to a relational database. It is important because of the extent of use, the fact that it can be used across a large number of computer types and sizes, and that it has been standardized. Data can be selected with SQL, using various criteria, and combined in a number of ways. The language also provides facilities for data entry, report formatting, and other procedures. Many query languages provide simplified interfaces for users and others writing queries, but they tend to be based on the standard SQL language.

Acquisition of Application Software

There are several options to be considered in the acquisition or development of application software. Three major choices are application package, application generator, and custom development using a programming language.

Commercial application packages are written to be used by a large number of organizations for a common business processing application. They are identical in general purpose to application software written by an individual company. They are, however, written and maintained by a software company that sells or leases the software. The software vendor takes responsibility for all aspects of development and maintenance, including documentation, user instruction manuals, error corrections, and enhancements. The vendor usually provides training for users and maintains help lines to answer questions about the software. There is a growing trend toward acquisition of application packages as the preferred approach to software acquisition.

Application packages may be used without change, customized with input/output changes, and customized by adding unique features. The one chosen will depend on a number of factors. In the no-change approach, the company changes its processes and procedures to adapt to the package. This is often a useful approach to process redesign, especially if the package is based on leading-edge practices. The inputs, outputs, reports, and procedures are all defined by the package. The configuration options provide a limited number of alternatives for modeling company operations; these permit users to select the alternative that provides the best fit with company procedures. Many commercial packages have a number of options for making input/output or similar changes to the package. Examples of input/output changes include the design of inputs, reports, external documents (such as purchase orders and invoices), and the meaning of user-definable codes. The input/output changes do not change the basic logic and functions of the package.

In the customizing approach, the application software package defines the basic requirements and forms the starting point for adding unique features. The changes can be done in-house or by the package vendor. The advantage is that the basic features are well tested and meet general requirements, while the additions or changes provide unique capabilities for the company. The disadvantages are that the company may be constrained by the package's basic functionality and must take responsibility for updating the application when the basic package is altered.

In general-purpose application generator packages, much of the application is generated from simple user-defined specifications. Such packages have facilities for common tasks such as spreadsheet computation, statistical analysis, and data management. When a person uses a software package for a task, such as preparing a spreadsheet, the package does the processing based on the specification that the user has given. It is a very cost-effective way to perform. It fits the concept of END-USER COMPUTING, although such application generator packages are also used by professional developers. The packages may be used to develop applications. Simple commands create an application complete with input/output screens, editing of input data, storage and retrieval of data, computations, and other processes. Examples of application development facilities in software packages are a macro-language, user-defined menus, and user-defined error handling.

The Software Development Process

SOFTWARE ENGINEERING is a systematic approach to the development of quality software. The hierarchy of systems and relationships of subsystems in applications are the basis for a design approach termed *structured design*. The software engineering approach follows a basic engineering principle for dealing with complexity by dividing programs into modules, routines, and subroutines based on tasks, functions, and actions to be performed.

GORDON B. DAVIS

software engineering   The application of formal engineering principles, concepts, and methodologies to the task of constructing software. It involves the application of a systematic, disciplined, quantifiable approach to the development, operation, and maintenance of software systems. The focus of software engineering tends to be large software-intensive systems that have substantial performance, capacity, reliability, security, and safety requirements. The software engineering discipline addresses how such systems are built and maintained in ways that are economically viable for the producers and users.

SANDRA SLAUGHTER

software package solutions   The availability of software packages for major business processes and problem domains has introduced alternative approaches to developing software and re-engineering business processes. Software

packages are the preferred approach to software for knowledge. Information systems that have organization-wide, mission-critical, and/or competitive-advantage implications typically require serious consideration of the make/buy decision. Package solutions for some applications (such as accounting) have been widely accepted and implemented; other applications are more dependent on package evaluation.

Knowledge Worker Software Packages

Most computer users work with one or more software packages such as word processor, spreadsheet, statistical software, presentation graphics, electronic mail, numerical database management, text database and personal computer management software (such as the COMPUTER OPERATING SYSTEM). Other useful knowledge worker packages include cooperative work software, finance modeling software, scheduling and project management software, forecasting software, and possibly EXPERT SYSTEM shells. Knowledge workers in specific functional areas may have domain-specific packages such as a computer-aided design (CAD) package for engineers, a statistical process control (SPC) package for quality personnel, or an EXECUTIVE INFORMATION SYSTEM (EIS). The key issue is not make or buy because packages are the only viable option; the issue is selection among packages.

Package Business System Solutions

An application software package that fits a large percentage of a firm's system requirements has several advantages over custom-developed applications. The package has typically been written by specialists who have considered industry standards, best practices, key requirements, and integration issues. The package is typically well tested. Almost all of the costs are known in advance. The software is available for immediate use; there is no development delay. The vendor has economic incentives to keep the package up to date and running on industry standard hardware/software. The vendor (or an affiliated consultant organization) usually provides documentation, training, and professional assistance to ensure successful implementation. These advantages reduce the risks associated with a firm's ability to complete software on schedule and within budget, to maintain software and the associated documentation/training, and to retain system-knowledgeable personnel.

One disadvantage of an information system package solution is generality, so that the package cannot meet unique requirements in comparison to software developed in-house. A related issue involves the constraints that a generalized package may place on innovative applications. These disadvantages can be addressed by customizations and extensions to a package, but extensive customizations can lead to problems with future upgrades to new releases from the software vendor. In addition, customizations can be very time-consuming, expensive, and error-prone because of the complexity and/or underlying technology (such as the DATABASE MANAGEMENT SYSTEM and software development tools) of the software package. Customizations for an integrated system can have an unintended ripple effect that creates errors in other parts of the application. System complexity can also cause long and costly implementation efforts.

Multiple software packages may be employed to achieve a comprehensive information system. Manufacturing information systems, for example, may require use of manufacturing resource planning (MRP), product data management (PDM), human resources, time and attendance, and quality management application packages, in addition to database management system and software development packages.

Approaches to Using a Software Package

There are three major approaches to using application packages: (1) use without change; (2) customizing with input/output changes; and (3) customizing by adding unique features.

1 *Using package without change.* The package vendor typically offers configuration options to tailor the software to operations. The company in this situation selects options and changes its business processes and procedures to adapt to the package. This approach makes sense for a company that lacks good business practices. The software package provides a way of introducing innovative organizational changes, typically with a faster implementation cycle.

2 *Customizing inputs/outputs.* Cosmetic changes to reports, user-definable codes, external documents (such as invoices), and input screens can be made without changing the basic logic and functions of the software package. Supplementary applications can also be developed that interface with the software package using data import and export features. These changes help fit the package to the way personnel view the application, with minimal impact on ability to upgrade to new releases from the software vendor.

3 *Customizing package with unique features.* The software package can provide an integrative framework and a starting point for adding unique features. Customizations can be performed in-house, by the software vendor, or by a consulting organization. While the additions/changes can provide unique and innovative capabilities, the changes may constrain ability to upgrade to new package releases, especially when appropriate development tools and configuration controls have not been utilized. The company must take responsibility for ongoing maintenance of software, documentation, and training, and the responsibility for retaining knowledgeable systems personnel.

J. SCOTT HAMILTON

speech recognition and synthesis Speech synthesis is the generation of voice output by a computer system. Applications in information systems include systems for providing information to customers about account balances, transactions processed, status of projects, etc. For example, a bank customer connecting to an automated system may issue a request via a touch-tone telephone for account balance, recent deposits, etc. The computer system synthesizes a voice reply over the telephone.

Speech recognition by a computer program is based on an analysis of the user speech. Speech recognition has been very successful for small vocabularies of words, especially in applications where the user's hands are not available for entering data. With a small number of commands, recognition accuracy is very high.

Full text speech recognition is difficult because of the large number of variations in speech, differences in clarity of diction, lack of pauses between words, and the large number of words that sound alike or somewhat similar. Homonyms (sound same but have different spelling and different meanings) present a problem (examples are "two," "to," and "too"). Human recognition of speech is based on a complex process of recognizing words in context, so lack of pauses between words or differences in diction or accent do not prevent understanding. For example, a person may say "yabetchyalife." with no pauses between words. The listener knows the colloquial expression and interprets the meaning as "you bet your life."

Personal computer speech recognition systems are available for dictation of words, text, and numbers into cells in a spreadsheet. The software requires a period of training to adjust the software to the diction of the individual user. The user must employ discrete speech with distinct pauses between words. Background noise must be minimal. When the software has difficulty in recognition, alternative words are displayed for the user to select. Over time, the software can refine the recognition algorithms to select words the user is likely to use. For ordinary dictation with a variety of words in different contexts, current speech recognition software may misread 10–20 percent of words. The time required for correcting the errors means keyboard entry is more productive. However, with a limited vocabulary and mainly present tense, such as professional notes or memoranda, the rate of correct recognition may rise to a very satisfactory level. Successful applications include simple memoranda or notes in business and dictation of notes by users such as lawyers, pathologists, and physicians.

Full text entry by voice requires significant processing power to achieve a low error or non-recognition rate. The error or non-recognition rate is reduced by extensive processing to match a user's vocabulary, common words employed, strings of words usually used together, and grammatical usage. Speech recognition is important in some information processing applications and, with the availability of increased processing power, routine text input for reports will become more feasible.

GORDON B. DAVIS

SQL Structured Query Language (SQL) is a comprehensive database language implemented in numerous commercial DATABASE MANAGEMENT SYSTEMS. Originally called SEQUEL

Example of an SQL database

Department table

DNO	DName	Budget	Manager
001	Marketing	220000	50124
002	Operations	400000	57211
003	Accounting	100000	22054

Employee table

ENO	EName	Salary	Dept
10231	Smith, Joseph	40000	003
15342	Jones, David	55000	002
22054	Swanson, Jane	75000	003
24519	Neff, Arnold	22000	001
28332	Homes, Denise	38000	002
50124	Naumi, Susan	83000	001
57211	Young, John	71000	002

(*S*tructured *E*nglish *QUE*ry *L*anguage), SQL was designed and implemented at IBM Research in the mid-1970s as the interface for an experimental relational database system called SYSTEM R.

SQL has two components: (a) a Data Definition Language (DDL) in which the structure of the database is defined; and (b) a Data Manipulation Language (DML) in which queries on the data are specified.

Database Definition

A database is defined as a set of *tables* (relations), each having *columns* (attributes) and *rows* (tuples). Columns define the data elements in a table. Rows correspond to instances. Each row contains one data value for each column. The database illustrated below has two tables: Department and Employee. Department has columns for Department Number (DNO), Name (DName), Budget, and Manager. Each department has a corresponding row in the Department table containing the data values describing that department.

Each table has a column or set of columns designated as its *primary key*. Each row must have a unique value for its primary key. DNO is the primary key of Department; ENO is the primary key of Employee (underlined in the example).

Relationships between tables are specified using corresponding columns. The column in one table must be a primary key; the column in the related table is termed a *foreign key*. In the database illustrated, there are two relationships between Department and Employee: (1) Dept is a foreign key in Employee, containing the department number of the department to which the employee reports; and (2) Manager is a foreign key in Department containing the employee number of the employee who manages that department. For example, David Jones, employee number 15342, reports to the Operations department, department number 002. This department is managed by John Young, employee number 57211.

Data Manipulation

Query specifications in SQL are based on relational calculus. The result of a query is a table which can be saved or used in other queries. A basic query can have four clauses:

SELECT	<attribute list>
FROM	<table list>
WHERE	<condition list>
ORDER BY	<sorting list>

<attribute list> is a list of columns and column calculations; <table list> is the list of tables in which these columns are defined; <condition list> defines rows to be included in the result table; <sorting list> defines the order of the result. SELECT and FROM clauses are required. WHERE and ORDER BY clauses are optional.

The following query produces the Employee Number, Name, and Salary of all employees with salary greater than $50,000, sorted by employee name.

SELECT	ENO, EName, Salary
FROM	Employee
WHERE	Salary > 50000
ORDER BY	EName

More complex queries can access data from multiple tables (e.g., *join* and *union* queries), perform data aggregations such as sums, counts, and averages (*group by* queries), and use queries within the WHERE clause to define conditions for row inclusion (*nested* queries).

The following join query includes departments whose budgets exceed $200,000 and employees in those departments whose salaries exceed $30,000, sorted by employee name within department name.

SELECT	DNO, DName, ENO, EName, Salary
FROM	Employee JOIN Department, ON Employee. Dept=Department.DNO
WHERE	Budget > 200000 and Salary > 30000
ORDER BY	DName, EName

The *join condition*, Employee.Dept = Department.DNO is written in the fully qualified form,

<table name>.<column name>. Earlier versions of SQL have join conditions in the WHERE clause rather than in the FROM clause.

Variations of this type exist in different commercial implementations of SQL. Both American National Standards Institute (ANSI) and International Standards Organization (ISO) are developing standards to provide consistency across different implementations.

SALVATORE T. MARCH

standards for information technology
Standards can be *de jure* or *de facto*. A *de jure* standard is formally accepted as a standard because it has been authorized by a recognized standards-making body such as the International Standards Organization (ISO). A *de facto* standard is informally recognized as a standard because it is widely recognized and accepted even though it has not been through the standardization process of a formally recognized standards-making body.

It is also useful to recognize "installation standards." Organizations making use of information technology often find it convenient to adopt standards for the way information technology is used in the installation. Some of these standards may be either *de jure* or *de facto* standards. However, there are many situations for which no such standards are available and an installation using information technology may find it convenient to develop their own installation standards.

The process by which *de jure* standards are developed is lengthy and complex. The process of standardization which preceded the advent of information technology has been largely adopted and applied to information technology. Most countries in the world have a standards body, which is responsible for developing standards in that country. Some larger countries, such as the USA, may have more than one such body. The USA has an umbrella organization for standards, the American National Standards Institute (ANSI). The most significant USA technical group under ANSI for information technology standards are X3 and IEEE. Each national standards body is a member of the International Standards Organization which currently has over a hundred members. However, only a few of these bodies participate in the development of information technology standards.

Most countries involved in information technology standards tend to focus their work on the work of the ISO. After a standard has been agreed by the ISO, a country's member body may choose to issue its own standard which is usually an exact copy of the corresponding ISO standard. Since the progression of standards in the international arena has been shown to be slower than within a single country, a country's member body may choose to develop its own standard for a specific area and then submit it to ISO for progression through one of the available sets of standards procedures.

In 1986, as a result of a perceived overlap between the information technology work of the ISO and the International Electrotechnical Commission (IEC), a merging of efforts took place. One result was that the distinction between information technology standardization and other kinds of standardization was more clearly visible. This distinction was manifested by the formation of ISO/IEC Joint Technical Committee 1 (JTC1), a special committee with the name "Information Technology." The scope of this committee is quite simply "standardization in the field of information technology." One of the original ISO Technical Committees and one or two IEC Technical Committees became part of JTC1. Those not joining were considered to be concerned with standardization outside the scope of information technology.

A list of the nineteen subcommittees currently active in JTC1 provides insight into the scope of ISO/IEC. These are as follows:

JTC1/SC1	Vocabulary
JTC1/SC2	Coded character sets
JTC1/SC6	Telecommunications and information exchange between systems
JTC1/SC7	Software engineering
JTC1/SC11	Flexible magnetic media for digital data interchange
JTC1/SC14	Data element principles
JTC1/SC15	Volume and file structure
JTC1/SC17	Identification cards and related devices

JTC1/SC18	Document processing and related communication
JTC1/SC21	Open systems interconnection, data management, and open distributed processing
JTC1/SC22	Programming languages, their environments and system software interfaces
JTC1/SC23	Optical disk cartridges for information interchange
JTC1/SC24	Computer graphics and image processing
JTC1/SC25	Interconnection of information technology equipment
JTC1/SC26	Microprocessor systems
JTC1/SC27	IT security techniques
JTC1/SC28	Office equipment
JTC1/SC29	Coding of audio, picture, multimedia and hypermedia
JTC1/SC30	Open electronic data interchange

Each subcommittee has a secretariat which is typically one of the member bodies active in the work of that subcommittee. Each subcommittee also has two or more working groups which are responsible for carrying out the detailed technical work. Each member body involved in the work is expected to send a delegation to the plenary meeting of the subcommittee at which formal decisions are taken on the progression of the work.

Not all the countries represented in the ISO participate in the work of JTC1. In fact, only 26 countries participate actively. This means that each country participates in one or more of the 19 subcommittees. A further 34 countries have observer status in JTC1. The number of countries having a vote in the work of any one subcommittee may be less than 26, while the number actually participating in the work may be even less. Countries such as the USA (ANSI), UK (BSI), Japan (JISC), and Canada (SCC) play an active role in most JTC1 subcommittees.

ISO has extensive procedures which are to be used in the carrying out of the technical work. International standards are developed using a five step process: (1) proposal stage; (2) preparatory stage; (3) committee stage; (4) approval stage; and (5) publication stage. The

success of a *de jure* standard can be assessed by two criteria.

1 Are products being implemented based on these standards?
2 Are products conforming to these standards being used?

One of the major issues related to information technology standardization is whether an information technology standard should be preemptive, prepared prior to the availability of products indicating the need for the standard, or *post facto*, prepared after products have become available. In some cases, one approach is better and in other cases it is the other. The issue is complicated by the rate at which new developments in information technology are emerging.

Bibliography

Up-to-date information on ISO standards can be obtained from the ISO pages on the World Wide Web (URL is http://www.iso.ch).

T. WILLIAM OLLE

storage for information processing There is a range of computer storage media and devices that differ in technology, cost, and retrieval time. There is an inverse relationship between cost and retrieval time: faster retrieval times are obtained with higher-cost storage. This suggests that the largest volume of storage will be on the lowest-cost media, and only data needing faster access will be stored on higher-cost media.

A characteristic of storage devices is their "writeability." ROM (read-only memory) is the term used for a broad range of storage devices and media that can only have data recorded once but can be read many times. This category includes ROM chips. These semiconductor memory devices are used to store programs that will never be changed, such as the inner levels of operating systems, peripheral control devices, etc. At the other extremes of capacity and cost, CD-ROMs are machine-stamped from inexpensive plastic using a mastering process, so that copies contain exactly the data encoded on the master.

Most storage is read-and-write storage. Read-and-write storage includes internal chip memory (RAM), permanently installed large-capacity internal disk (hard disk), floppy disks and diskettes, re-writable optical disks, and magnetic tape. The primary difference between memory chips and other means of read-and-write storage is that chips are entirely electronic rather than partially mechanical.

Magnetic Disk Storage

Magnetic read/write storage is both electronic and mechanical. Physical motion, usually rotating, is used to pass the storage medium close to very sensitive read-write heads. Magnetic disks store data on concentric tracks. Read-write heads are mounted on mechanical arms that move them from one track to another. Storage capacity is determined primarily by the density of bits on each track (the space between polarized spots that can be set to represent a 0 or 1 value for a bit) and the space between tracks. The performance of rotating memory devices such as magnetic disks is determined by two factors: rotational delay and positioning delay. Rotational delay or latency refers to the average time expected for a given bit to move under the stationary read-write head. Various techniques including faster rotation and multiple heads per track are used to reduce latency. Positioning delay is defined as the time it takes the mechanical arm to move one-half the distance across the recorded surface of the disk. Most improvements in positioning have come from reducing the mass of the movable arm and read-write heads and also reducing the distance to be traveled.

Magnetic Tape Storage

Magnetic tape storage is similar to disk storage in the use of multiple tracks and tiny spots that can be polarized in one of two directions. It differs from disk storage because tape must be moved from its current position to the position of the data sought, a process that usually requires minutes. Magnetic tape storage is too slow to support real-time human activity, but its very low cost and large capacity make it useful for archival and backup storage. Magnetic tape was the first high-capacity computer storage medium. As a result, many different tape formats, specifications, and mechanisms are in use.

Optical Storage

Optical storage devices are available in all three storage modes: read-only, write-once, and read-and-write (re-writable). The read-only optical disk has emerged as the preferred low-cost approach to distributing large files (of various types). It is represented by a data disk (compact disk or CD-ROM) that follows an audio recording format. Data is stored on a CD-ROM by means of microscopic pits molded into the disk surface. A laser beam focused and aimed by a system of movable mirrors reads the pits. The advantage of CD-ROM is high capacity, high permanence, and low reproduction cost. The disks do not wear out because there is no physical contact during the reading operation. Most CD-ROMs are prepared by a vendor who records a master that is duplicated by a low-cost stamping operation. A significant limitation of the CD-ROM format standard is its base in audio technology: data bits are recorded on a single spiral track rather than the concentric tracks of magnetic disks. While this helps make CD-ROMs inexpensive, it severely limits flexibility.

Write-once optical disk (often referred to as WORM – write once, read many or read mostly) technology is closely related to CD-ROM. The difference is that write-once optical disks are written by the user, and information can be added until the disk is full. The information format is concentric tracks as used in magnetic disk storage. (This, however, makes WORM disks and drives incompatible with CD-ROM.) In the write-once mode, a write operation creates a permanent variation in the layer on the disk for each bit; the laser beam reads by detecting the difference in reflection. For example, one technology "burns" a hole into a layer of the disk. Write-once optical disks are permanent, and represent excellent archival storage. Write-once disks in the CD-ROM format are becoming a widely used archival format.

Re-writable optical disk storage is similar in concept to magnetic storage but is expected eventually to allow higher density and reliability. In re-writable optical storage, a laser beam applies enough heat to a spot to reverse polarity but not to change the surface. The spot can be read by the laser beam and can be erased or altered by writing new data at the same location. Order of magnitude improvements in speed and capacity can be anticipated for optical storage.

GORDON B. DAVIS and J. DAVID NAUMANN

strategic use of information technology

The first commercial uses of information technology (IT) often involved automating existing manual systems. Early "era 1" systems were often justified by anticipated reductions in clerical labor previously required to process business transactions. Starting in the early 1970s, firms began to make major investments in systems designed to improve both the efficiency and effectiveness of managers and other professionals. These "era 2" systems employed DECISION SUPPORT SYSTEMS, DATABASE MANAGEMENT SYSTEMS and EXECUTIVE INFORMATION SYSTEMS to improve decision-making. Simultaneous investments in office automation, including LOCAL AREA NETWORKS, wide area networks, and voice and ELECTRONIC MAIL, were the hoped-for means to quickly implement decisions and to track decision effectiveness.

Organizations continued to pursue automation and decision support, but in the mid-1980s began to invest in a third era of IT. This third era represented the strategic use of IT, in which applications were intended to provide their owners with a distinct competitive advantage over competitors. Often the justification for such systems was a hoped-for increase in sales or market share. In other cases, a competitor's strategic application of technology might motivate investment in similar systems to help recover from a strategic disadvantage.

Today, we are entering a fourth era in which a new type of strategic system is emerging. Era 3 strategic systems were typically designed to align information technology investments with the strategic objectives of the firm and they were often based on proprietary communications networks. Era 4 systems, by contrast, are often at the very heart of completely new business opportunities in which the technology impacts strategy rather than being aligned to it. Such systems will provide new marketing or distribution channels. They will largely rely on nonproprietary communications networks to reach directly to the final consumer. These new applications and businesses seem likely, over the next several years, to dramatically reshape commerce and industry as well as many other economic and social institutions.

Types of Strategic Use

In era 3, firms sometimes gained a competitive advantage by the development of a new *IT-based product or service*. For instance, Merrill Lynch, a large brokerage house, developed their Cash Management Account which allowed investors to earn a higher rate of return on cash than was possible in a bank's savings account. An era 4 strategic application, by contrast, is the attempt by Intuit to develop and sell a personal finance system, Quicken, that empowers consumers to manage their investments, bill paying, and day-to-day expenses. Quicken also provides links for home banking. A proposed merger between Intuit and Microsoft was recently denied by the US government, partly because of concerns that the combined company would be a major threat to the banking industry.

The denied merger of Intuit and Microsoft illustrates a second major opportunity to use information for strategic advantage: *control of a distribution channel*. Era 3 examples include the computer reservation systems developed by United and American Airlines, among others. Until forced to stop by legal action, the owners of the reservation systems were able to bias travel agents and passengers toward their own flights rather than those of competitors who did not have their own reservation systems. We are now witnessing the emergence of new marketing and distribution systems targeted directly at the consumer. For instance, NetScape Communications has in a very short period of time captured much of the market for the easy-to-use browser software people use to access the INTERNET'S WORLD WIDE WEB (WWW). As this browser is the first thing a user sees each time they use the WWW, it provides an excellent showcase for Netscape to highlight new products of their own or to favor those of their various business partners.

INTERORGANIZATIONAL SYSTEMS are another way to use IT strategically. Federal Express, for instance, provides corporate customers with software for preparing mailing labels for packages and summoning delivery vehicles. Such desktop applications are also being used for ordering office supplies, air travel, and so on. In the case of office supplies, such systems can provide the corporate customer with both convenience and a powerful tool for control. For instance, the prices displayed on an employee's screen can reflect discounts the firm has negotiated with the office supply distribution, constrain the amount purchased in any given month by a particular employee, or automatically inform internal auditors or management when unusual purchase behavior is detected.

Firms have also gained strategic advantage through systems linking them with suppliers, dealers, or government agencies. Large retailers, for instance, are using their influence to require suppliers to interface with them using ELEC-TRONIC DATA INTERCHANGE. In some cases they are even providing those suppliers with a direct look into information from point-of-sale terminals and then requiring the supplier to manage store inventories based on actual sales. Strategically advantageous interorganizational linkages often represent extensions of systems developed initially for the firm's own internal use. For instance, Federal Express has now made their package tracking systems accessible to customers via the World Wide Web.

Strategic advantage can also be achieved by *personalizing the service or product* to meet the unique needs of a specific customer. An illustration of a typical era 3 application is a paint manufacturer which provided its customers, the managers of large fleets of ocean-going vessels, with information on the painting requirements for each ship within the customer's fleet. The information was captured by the firm's worldwide network of dealers as ships tied up at port and was then made available for use by sales, marketing, and product development personnel. Era 4 systems will carry this personalization much further. They will permit online newspaper publishers to personalize your daily "paper", retailers to provide an electronic catalog reflecting your sizes and personal requirements, or perhaps even allow you to participate in the design of your own car, clothes, and so on.

Often, significant cost advantages can be achieved by *leveraging scarce expertise*. High-

technology manufacturers, such as Apple Computer, are beginning to make databases previously used by their support personnel directly accessible by customers. Consulting firms are developing worldwide skills databases that permit them to quickly identify individuals meeting the requirements of a particular job. Firms are also reducing costs by electronically *moving* KNOWLEDGE WORK to sources of low-cost labor. The Internet, an early version of a global data highway, provides a relatively low-cost means to partition knowledge work across country boundaries. Software developers, for instance, can significantly reduce their labor costs by using programmers in India rather than California.

Sustaining Competitive Advantage

Era 1 and 2 applications tended to be justified on the basis of hard cost savings or soft expectations of increased professional productivity or higher-quality decisions. Strategic uses often draw their justifications instead from anticipated increases in revenues and market share. Assessing these benefits requires management to carefully consider the likely sustainability of the proposed application; that is, for how long can the firm expect to achieve unusually high returns before one or more competitors effectively responds? Sustainability depends on the three questions discussed below.

How long to copy?

Some strategic applications can be quickly copied by competitors. The technology may be available for purchase, customers or others may have a good understanding of how the system operates, or the firm's own personnel may be hired away by a competitor to produce a similar system. On the other hand, some systems may be protected by patents, copyright protection, secrecy, the inherent complexity of the application, or the unwillingness of a competitor to quickly respond.

Who can copy?

Firms competing in the same industry often may use quite different strategies and technologies. If a strategic application of information technology builds on such a competitive asymmetry it may prove impossible for a competitor to duplicate. For instance, Wingtip Courier, a Dallas-based local package delivery service, installed radio communicating computer terminals in all its delivery vehicles. The despatch system they developed for the terminals permitted Wingtip to provide higher-quality service to the professional firms they served. It was an advantage that Wingtip's competitors found difficult to match. Wingtip owned its own vehicles and paid its drivers a wage, but most competitors contracted with independent drivers who worked for commission. Placing expensive computer systems in these vehicles and training the drivers was a nearly insurmountable barrier to competitive response.

Will it help to copy?
Once a competitor has duplicated a strategic system, they may discover that the "first-mover" has somehow pre-empted the challenger's response. For instance, airline frequent-flyer programs keep customers coming back because of the bank of miles they have accumulated in the past.

The answers to these three questions provide the basis for evaluating candidate strategic uses of information technology. They also can be useful starting points in seeking to identify uses of information technology that can provide competitive advantage.

BLAKE IVES

structured programming This is an approach to coding computer instructions in any procedural programming language. The fundamental idea is that programs can be constructed from a very limited set of control or decision structures. The major benefit of structured programming is to make programs understandable to humans so that they can be correctly written, modified and maintained.

Structured programming employs three basic control structures: sequence, alternation, and repetition. The *sequence control structure* is one instruction after the other, executed from beginning to end with no possibility of change. The instructions in a sequence are processing instructions such as arithmetic calculations, operations on strings of characters, retrieval of data, displaying outputs, etc.

The *alternation structure* is the way choices are controlled. The basic implementation of alternation is *if–then–else–end if*. There are a number of additional implementations of alternation. The additions are conveniences and each can be translated to the basic *if–then–else–end if* control structure. The basic alternation structure is shown below.

if conditional expression *then*
    Sequence of statements if condition is true
else
    Sequence of statements if condition is false
end if

There is a frequently occurring special case where no action is to be taken when the condition is evaluated to be false. In this special case no *else* statements are specified.

if conditional expression *then*
    Sequence of statements if condition is true
end if

Case is an extension of alternation that may be used to select among more than two possible actions. One and only one action is selected based on the value of a condition. A case statement has the following structure:

select case conditional expression
case value-1
    Sequence of statements to be executed if the expression evaluates to *case* value-1
case value-2
    Sequence of statements to be executed if the expression evaluates to *case* value-2
case value-*n*
    Sequence of statements to be executed if the expression evaluates to *case* value-*n*
case else
    Sequence of statements to be executed if none of the above apply
end select

The *repetition structure*, often termed a loop, is a way of conditionally repeating a sequence of instructions. The repetition structure evaluates a conditional expression every iteration of its loop. The statements within the loop effectively control the number of repetitions since they alter the values being tested by the conditional expression. The basic repetition structure is shown below.

do while conditional expression is true
    Sequence of statements to be executed
end while

In the *do-while* control structure, the value of the conditional expression is evaluated before any action is taken. If it initially evaluates to false, the entire sequence of statements is bypassed. If it is true, the sequence of statements is executed and control returns to the beginning, where the conditional expression is evaluated again. There are useful variants of the basic repetition structure. One repetition variant is used when a sequence of statements is to be executed a predetermined number of times. The *for* loop is often called indexed repetition because repetition is controlled by an index variable that is automatically incremented at each execution.

for index initial value *to* index ending value
    Sequence of statements to be executed
end for

An important control structure related to repetition is recursion in which modules in effect repeat themselves.

Control structures may be "nested." One control structure may be wholly contained within another. Alternation nested within repetition is shown below.

do while employee records exist
    Input employee name, status, dependents
if status = retired *then*
    Compute health benefit cost for retired
else
    Compute health benefit cost for not retired
end if
    Display employee name, status, dependents, health benefit
end while

In addition to the use of a limited set of control structures, structured programming conventions also involve the use of embedded comments, readable coding, indentations and paragraphs to clearly indicate structure. Structured programs are inherently readable and therefore easier to maintain and modify than programs lacking a regular structure.

GORDON B. DAVIS and J. DAVID NAUMANN

system concepts applied to information systems

System concepts provide a useful way to describe many organizational phenomena, including the information system, features of applications, and development processes.

Definition and General Model of a System

Systems can be abstract or physical. An abstract system is an orderly arrangement of interdependent ideas or constructs. For example, a system of theology is an orderly arrangement of ideas about God and the relationship of humans to God. A physical system is a set of elements that operate together to accomplish an objective. Examples of physical systems are the circulatory system of a body, a school system (with building, teachers, administrators, and textbooks), and a computer system (the hardware and software that function together to accomplish computer processing). The examples illustrate that a system is not a randomly assembled set of elements; it consists of elements that can be identified as belonging together because of a common purpose, goal, or objective. Physical systems are more than conceptual constructs; they display activity or behavior. The parts interact to achieve an objective.

A general model of a physical system comprises inputs, process, and outputs. The features that define and delineate a system form its boundary. The system is inside the boundary; the environment is outside the boundary. In some cases, it is fairly simple to define what is part of the system and what is not; in other cases, the person studying the system may arbitrarily define the boundaries.

Each system is composed of subsystems made up of other subsystems, each subsystem being delineated by its boundaries. The interconnections and interactions between the subsystems are termed *interfaces*. Interfaces occur at the boundary and take the form of inputs and outputs. A subsystem at the lowest level (input, process, output) is often not defined as to the process. This system is termed a *black box*, since the inputs and outputs are known but not the actual transformation from one to the other.

Types of System

Although many phenomena as different as a human and a computer program can be described in systems terms, they are still quite different. Two classifications of systems emphasize key differences. Systems are deterministic versus probabilistic and closed versus open. These concepts can be applied to the concept of the human–machine system employed in management information systems.

A *deterministic system* operates in a predictable manner. The interaction among the parts is known with certainty. If one has a description of the state of the system at a given point in time plus a description of its operation, the next state of the system may be given exactly, without error. An example is a correct computer program that performs exactly according to a set of instructions. The *probabilistic system* can be described in terms of probable behavior, but a certain degree of error is always attached to the prediction of what the system will do. An example is a set of instructions given to a human who, for a variety of reasons, may not follow the instructions exactly as given.

A *closed system* is defined in physics as a system that is self-contained. It does not exchange material, information, or energy with its environment. In organizations and in information processing, there are systems that are relatively isolated from the environment but not completely closed in the physics sense. These will be termed closed systems, meaning *relatively* closed. A computer program is a relatively closed system because it accepts only previously defined inputs, processes them, and provides previously defined outputs.

Open systems exchange information, material, or energy with the environment, including random and undefined inputs. Examples of open systems are biological systems (such as humans) and organizational systems. Open systems have form and structure to allow them to adapt to changes in their environment in such a way as to continue their existence. They are "self-organizing" in the sense that they change their organization in response to changing conditions. Living systems (cells, plants, humans, etc.) are open systems. They attempt to maintain equilibrium by homeostasis, the process of adjusting to keep the system operating within prescribed limits. Organizations are open systems; a critical feature of their existence is their capability to adapt in the face of changing competition, changing markets, etc. Organizations illustrate the system concept of *equifinality*: more than one system structure and process may achieve the same result (but not necessarily at the same cost).

Artificial systems are systems that are created rather than occurring in nature. Organizations, information systems, and computer programs are all examples of artificial systems. Artificial systems are designed to support the objectives of the designers and users. They exhibit, therefore, characteristics of the system that they support. Principles that apply to *living systems* are also applicable to artificial systems that support human or other living systems.

Information systems are generally human–machine systems; both human and machine perform activities in the accomplishment of a goal (e.g. processing a transaction or making a decision). The machine elements (computer hardware and software) are relatively closed and deterministic, whereas the human elements of the system are open and probabilistic. Various combinations of human and machine are possible. For instance, the computer can be emphasized and the human simply monitor the machine operation. At the other extreme, the machine performs a supporting role by doing computation or searching for data while the user performs creative work. An appropriate balance in the division of functions is critical to the successful performance of each component in accomplishing its objective; the division between human and machine will thus vary from application to application.

Subsystems

A complex system is difficult to comprehend when considered as a whole. Therefore, the system is decomposed or factored into subsystems. The boundaries and interfaces are defined, so that the sum of the subsystems constitutes the entire system. This process of decomposition is continued with subsystems divided into smaller subsystems until the smallest subsystems are of manageable size. The subsystems resulting from this process generally form hierarchical structures. In the hierarchy, a subsystem is one element of a suprasystem (the system above it).

Decomposition into subsystems is used both to analyze an existing system and to design and implement a new system. In both cases, the investigator or designer must decide how to factor, i.e. where to draw the boundaries. The decisions will depend on the objectives of the decomposition and also on individual differences among designers. A general principle in decomposition is functional cohesion. Components are considered to be part of the same subsystem if they perform or are related to the same function. As an example, a payroll application program to be divided into modules (subsystems) will divide along major program functions such as accumulating hours worked, calculating deductions, printing a check, etc.

The process of decomposition could lead to a large number of subsystem interfaces to define. For example, four subsystems which all interact with each other will have six interconnections; a system with 20 subsystems all interacting will have 190 interconnections. The number can rise quite quickly as the number of subsystems increases. *Simplification* is the process of organizing subsystems so as to reduce the number of interconnections. One method of simplification is clustering of systems with a single interface connection from the cluster to other subsystems or decoupling. If two different subsystems are connected very tightly, very close coordination between them is required. The solution to excessive coordination is to decouple or loosen the connection so that the two systems can operate in the short run with some measure of independence. Some means of decoupling are inventories, buffers, or waiting lines. Slack or flexible resources allow some independence. Standards of various types also reduce the need for close coordination.

System Entropy

Systems can run down and decay or can become disordered or disorganized. Stated in system terminology, an increase in *entropy* takes place. Preventing or offsetting the increase in entropy requires inputs of matter and energy to repair, replenish, and maintain the system. This maintenance input is termed *negative entropy*. Open systems require more negative entropy than relatively closed systems to keep at a steady state of organization and operation.

System Concepts Applied to Management Information Systems

System concepts are applicable to many aspects of management information systems. A few examples illustrate the application of these concepts. The information system of an organization is a system. It receives inputs of data and instructions, processes the data according to instructions, and outputs the results. The basic system model of inputs, process, and outputs is suitable in the simplest case of an information-processing system. However, the information-processing function frequently needs data collected and processed in a prior period. Data storage is therefore added to the information-system model, so that the processing activity has available both current data and data collected and stored previously. The information-processing infrastructure system has subsystems, such as the hardware system, operating system, communication system, and database system. It also has application subsystems, such as order entry and billing, payroll, and personnel. The application subsystems make use of the infrastructure subsystems.

Information systems and other artificial systems are human artifacts; the systems exist only because humans design and build them. The fact that information systems are human artifacts means that they reflect characteristics and objectives of human systems. The design and operation of living systems allows them to adapt and survive. Likewise, there is an objective of survivability in artificial systems. In order to achieve this survivability objective, information systems are designed with characteristics that simplify the system structure, reduce tight coupling, and allow system repair and change.

System concepts can be applied in the development of information-system projects. The information system is defined and overall responsibility assigned, major information-processing subsystems are delineated, each subsystem is assigned to a project, the project leader factors the job into subsystem projects and assigns responsibility for each. The structured design approach encourages definition of subsystems from the top down; at each level of the hierarchy, the interfaces between the lower-level subsystems are clearly defined. This allows development personnel to clearly define the objectives of each subsystem and provide checkpoints for its accomplishments.

The concept of *black box* is also useful when subsystems, boundaries, and interfaces are being defined: lower-level subsystems can be defined as black boxes, while the higher-level subsystems are being designed. Later in the development process a systems analyst is provided with the defined inputs and required outputs and assigned to define the rules inside the black box.

System concepts assist in understanding various features and practices of information systems. The principle of equifinality explains why many designs may work but are not equal in effort to develop and use. The principle of entropy explains why systems decay, and why MAINTENANCE to repair and update systems is vital. The human–machine nature of information systems is the basis for SOCIOTECHNICAL DESIGN that emphasizes the consideration of both human/social and technical factors.

Bibliography

Checkland, P. (1981). *Systems Thinking, Systems Practice*. New York: Wiley.

Churchman, C. W. (1968). *The Systems Approach*. New York: Dell.

Davis, G. B. & Olson, M. H. (1985). *Management Information Systems: Conceptual Foundations, Structure, and Development*, 2nd edn. ch. 9. New York: McGraw-Hill.

Emery, F. E. (1969). *Systems Thinking*. Baltimore, MD: Penguin.

Katz, D. & Kahn, R. L. (1978). *The Social Psychology of Organizations*, 2nd edn. New York: Wiley.

Miller, J. G. (1978). *Living Systems*. New York: Wiley.

Simon, H. A. (1981). *The Science of the Artificial*, 2nd edn. Cambridge, MA: MIT Press.

GORDON B. DAVIS

system software Software is often divided into system software and application software. System software enables application software to be developed and executed. Application software performs the specific processing needed by the computer users. System software, as a broad term, therefore encompasses any software with functions used by applications or by personnel who operate the computer and manage its resources. The dominant system software is the operating system. The operating system includes many functions that are also available as separate software packages. Examples of other system software include utilities to perform common processing functions, performance software to monitor system performance and assist operations in managing resources, and security software. The graphical user interface for microcomputer users is system software that may be separate from the operating system or packaged with it. System software is usually obtained from software vendors; this is contrasted with application software that is often developed by the organization or person using it.

See also **Computer operating system; Software**

GORDON B. DAVIS

systems analysis and design This is a systematic and complex endeavor that has as its goal the improvement of a business through the skillful use of computer-based information systems in an organization. Systems analysts are typically educated in universities or technical schools. Systems analysis and design demand an entire spectrum of skills, ranging from computer programming to effective interpersonal skills. Numerous categories of information systems, serving each functional area of business, as well as all different levels of management, are developed. These extend from transaction processing systems (TPS) on the operations level all the way up the organizational hierarchy to EXECUTIVE INFORMATION SYSTEMS (EIS) on the strategic management level. Complicated projects involving large amounts of financial and human resources are often directed by systems analysts.

Issues

A systems analyst approaching a new project deliberates about several issues that are important to the project's overall plan and eventual implementation. Most of these decisions are not taken unilaterally, but rather are made in consultation with management, users, and other analysts who are involved in the systems project. These issues include, but are not necessarily limited to: the scope and boundaries of the systems project; how many people are involved in the project directly; how many people ultimately will be affected by the proposed changes; assessing the level of motivation and resource commitment for the project; how to involve key decision-makers and users in the systems project; choosing a systems development methodology from both structured and other approaches; and whether it is necessary to create unique software applications for the client or whether customizing off-the-shelf software is appropriate. Many additional issues are subsumed under these broad concerns.

The issue of choosing an alternative methodology not only revolves around the systems analyst's skills and preparation, but also must reflect the way in which management and users envision their future. For instance, the enterprise might consider that it is a complex machine, working precisely toward its goals in a structured, orderly, and predictable way. Other organizations believe they are on a long journey, one beset by disorder and chaos, although a clear goal is stated. Still another company might hold that it is a family. Choosing an appropriate systems development methodology can help enrich and extend this organizational perspective.

For the most part, this entry covers the most widely taught and used approach to systems analysis and design which is embodied in structured analysis and design methodologies (some with proprietary names such as STRADIS and SSADM along with many others), and which is supported by popular CASE: (COMPUTER-AIDED SOFTWARE/SYSTEM ENGINEERING) tools.

Machine-like organizations, as well as those involved in a game mentality, are well served by structured methodologies, but if the organization houses individuals who are autonomous, and make different evaluations leading to a variety of actions, use of SOFT SYSTEMS METHODOLOGIES may be more appropriate. ETHICS, a SOCIOTECHNICAL DESIGN method, may be useful in family-like organizations. Organizations on journeys may feel PROTOTYPING is the methodology of choice.

Systems Analysis and Design Processes

There are many processes in which the systems analyst must engage, regardless of which development methodology is used. Completing these processes helps ensure that the organization will meet its goals and objectives. The processes often referred to as the systems development life-cycle (SDLC) fall into five broad phases: information requirements determination; analysis of the existing and proposed system; design, development, and documentation of the new system; implementation; and evaluation of new system performance.

Information Requirements Determination

Major processes include collecting data about existing information systems; and analyzing and documenting the data, systems, and user needs. Many methods are used to accomplish these processes. Analysts use interviewing, observation, archival data collection, and questionnaires to investigate user information requirements as well as system needs. They may also use prototyping which permits the interaction with working or nonworking models of the input, processing, or output stages of information systems. In order to document what they have found, analysts use field notes to document structured interviews with information-system users; interview forms; diagrams of offices; examples of existing forms and screens; and system specifications for the existing system (see REQUIREMENTS DETERMINATION FOR INFORMATION SYSTEMS).

Entity-relationship Diagrams

One tool a systems analyst can use to define system boundaries is an entity-relationship model. It is critical that the systems analyst understand early on the entities and relationships in the organizational system. An entity may be a person, a place, or a thing; such as a customer, the New Jersey warehouse, or a CD-ROM product. Alternatively, an entity may be an event, such as the end of the month, or a machine malfunction. A relationship is the association that describes the interaction between the entities.

Two symbols (a rectangle and a diamond) are used to draw an entity-relationship diagram as shown in figure 1. The rectangle depicts the

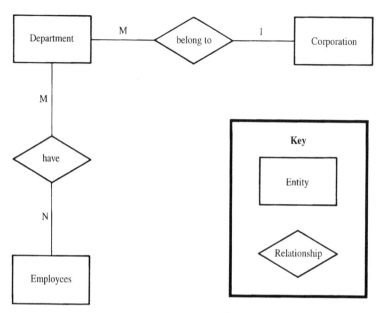

Figure 1 An entity-relationship diagram

entity, while the diamond shows the relationship between that entity and another entity. In the example one can see that many (M) departments belong to 1 corporation and many (M) departments have many (N) employees.

A systems analyst may identify many entities and relationships and then decide where the boundary will be. For example, a physician may have relationships with the patient, the health-care provider, a hospital, and pharmaceutical representatives. If the systems analyst decides that the system will include only scheduling office visits with patients, then the physician and patient would be the only relevant entities. Entity-relationship diagrams are useful in data modeling (*see* DATA MODELING, LOGICAL).

Data Flow Diagrams

Data flow diagrams (DFD) are a structured analysis technique the systems analyst can use to put together a graphical representation of how data proceeds through an organization. The data flow approach includes describing the existing system, and then describing the logical data flow as it would occur in the improved system. After the logical flow is described, a physical data flow diagram can be developed that includes not only

data movement but also hardware and manual procedures. Finally, the physical data flow diagram can be partitioned, enabling the programmers to program the system using sensible, meaningful modules.

Figure 2 is a data flow diagram using symbols developed by Gane and Sarson (1979). Four symbols describe external entities, data flows, processes, and data stores. The external entity (a company, department, customer, or manager, for example) is a main source or main destination of data, and is drawn as a double rectangle. Data flows are represented by arrows showing the movement of data from one point to another, with the head of the arrow pointing toward the data's destination. Data flows depict data in motion in the organization. Processes (the transformation of data into a different form of information) are drawn as rectangles with rounded corners. Processes always denote a change in or transformation of data; hence, the data flow leaving a process is always labeled differently from the one entering it. Data stores are drawn as open-ended rectangles. In logical data flow diagrams, the type of physical storage, whether it is tape, diskette, or other, is not specified. Therefore, the data store symbol

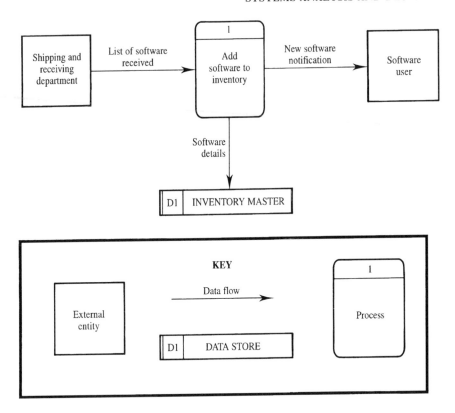

Figure 2   A data flow diagram

simply shows that data is stored for use at this point or elsewhere in the system. Data stores depict data at rest in the organization.

Data flow diagrams are usually drawn from the most general to the most specific, typically top down. The first diagram the systems analyst draws is called a context diagram that shows only the entities and one process, the system itself. This context diagram is then "exploded" to show more detail. At this point, data stores are identified and drawn. The diagram can be exploded further into child diagrams. Detailed logic, however, is not revealed in a data flow diagram. This is done in process specifications.

Data Dictionary and Data Repository

Using data flow diagrams, the systems analyst begins compiling a data dictionary, which contains data about data (meta-data) on all data processes, stores, flows, structures, and elements within the system being studied. The data repository is a larger collection of project

information. An important reason for compiling a data dictionary is to sort out the proliferation of uncoordinated names or aliases for data items that may exist if a variety of computer programs and systems are developed over time by different systems analysts. The data dictionary also serves as a consistent, organization-wide standard for data elements.

While a data dictionary should be as inclusive as possible, it is never complete. In fact, it should be updated as changes are implemented, just as other documentation is. In order to be useful, data dictionary entries should contain specific categories of information including: the name and aliases of the data item (e.g. customer or client); a description of the data item in words; data elements related to the entry (e.g. name, address, telephone, and credit card information); the allowable range of the data item (September cannot have more than 30 days); its maximum length in characters (e.g. a US social security number may never exceed nine numbers); proper encoding (e.g. Tuesday is coded as "Tue" not "Tues"); and any other pertinent editing information.

The data repository is structured to contain much more than the data dictionary including: information maintained by the system such as data flows, data stores, record structures, and elements; logic specifications; screen and report design; data relationships; project requirements and final system deliverables; and project management information, including delivery schedules, achievements, and issues that need resolving. Many CASE tools now feature automated data dictionaries and extensive data repositories that include reusable program code as well as data elements. They are valuable for their capacity to cross-reference data items, since necessary program changes can be made to all programs sharing a common element. Additionally, data repositories can help to reduce the amount of new computer program code that must be written. New CASE tools prompt and assist the systems analyst in creating the data dictionary and the data repository concurrently with the analysis of the information system. This reduces the time necessary for documentation once the system is complete.

Process Specifications and Logic

After data flow diagrams are drawn and data dictionaries are well under way, the systems analyst will need to describe the logic of decision-making in a more detailed manner. A large part of a systems analyst's work involves identifying and diagramming structured decisions; that is, decisions that can be automated if identified circumstances occur. A structured decision is repetitive, routine, and has standard procedures to follow for its solution. An example of a structured decision is approval of a credit card purchase by a credit card company. Three commonly used methods for describing structured decision processes are structured English, decision tables, and decision trees.

Structured English uses accepted keywords such as IF, THEN, ELSE, DO, DO WHILE, and DO UNTIL to describe the logic used and, when written, phrases are indented to indicate the hierarchical structure of the decision process. CASE tools tend to favor structured English to express logic in terms of sequential, decision and case structures, as well as itera-

tions. Structured English is easy to understand, and therefore is a good way to communicate simple decision processes. *Decision tables* provide another familiar way to examine, describe, and document decisions. Four quadrants (viewed clockwise from the upper left-hand corner) are used to: (1) describe the conditions; (2) identify possible decision alternatives such as Yes or No; (3) indicate which actions should be performed; and (4) describe the actions. The use of decision tables promotes completeness and accuracy in analyzing structured decisions.

A third method for decision analysis is the *decision tree*, consisting of nodes (a square depicts actions and a circle depicts conditions), and branches. Decision trees do not have to be symmetrical, so trees may be more readable that decision tables and are essential when actions must be accomplished in a certain sequence.

Modularity and Structure Charts

By using these tools, the analyst is eventually able to break apart the system into logical, manageable portions called modules. This kind of programming fits well with top-down design because it emphasizes the interfaces or relationships between modules rather than neglecting them until later in systems development. Ideally, each module should be functionally cohesive so that it is charged with accomplishing only one function in the program.

There are many advantages to modular program design. Modules are easier to write and debug (correct errors) because they are virtually self-contained. Tracing an error in a module is less complicated, since a problem in one module should not cause problems in others. Modules are easier to maintain because modifications usually will be limited to a few modules, rather than spreading over an entire program. Logic within modules is easier to understand since they are self-contained subsystems.

In order to represent the modules, the systems analyst may use a structure chart, which is a diagram consisting simply of rectangular boxes and connecting lines as shown in figure 3. Additional information noted on a structure chart includes "data couples" which show which data must pass from one module to another, and "control flags" which show which instructions must pass

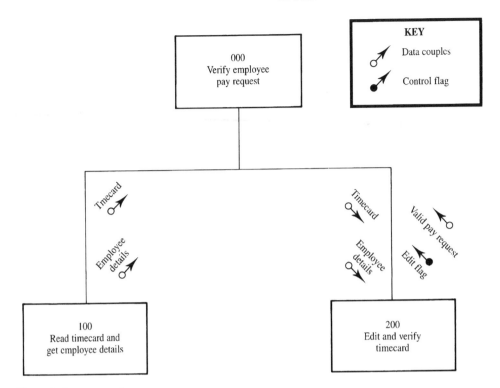

Figure 3 A structure chart

between modules. Ideally, the analyst should keep this coupling to a minimum. The fewer data couples and control flags one has in the system, the easier it is to alter the system in the future.

While structure charts are used to communicate the logic of data flow diagrams to the computer programmers, Nassi–Schneiderman Charts (N–S Charts) are used to communicate process specifications and logic. N–S Charts are similar to structured English, but use symbols to indicate processes, decisions, and iterations. Warnier–Orr diagrams and Pseudocode are similar methods useful in describing logic that is ready to be coded by programmers.

Designing Output, Input, and User Interface

There are six main objectives in designing output of information systems:

- to serve the intended purpose
- to fit the user
- to deliver the right quantity of output
- to deliver it to the right place
- to provide output on time
- to choose the right output method

Once limited in scope to paper reports, output now can take virtually any form, including print, screen, audio, microforms, CD-ROM, and electronic output such as e-mail and Faxes. Output technologies differ in their speed, cost, portability, flexibility, storage, and retrieval possibilities, and users often prefer some technologies over others (*see* OUTPUT DEVICES). The systems analyst needs to consider all of these factors as output is designed. Data that is not already stored in a database, or data that is unavailable via scanning or electronic transfer, must be captured with more traditional methods. These include paper forms and computer screens. In either case the design of the form is critical, especially with regard to the logical way in which the data is to be entered. Systems analysts can take advantage of a variety of fonts, icons, and colors to help make forms more readable and easier to fill out. Proper input design encourages more accurate and valid data.

Systems analysts must often design interfaces as well. Interfaces are the means by which the system user interacts with the machine. Some interfaces include: natural language, command language, question-and-answer, menus, form-fill, and graphical user interfaces (GUI), which is pronounced "gooey." Systems analysts also design powerful queries, which are developed to help users extract meaningful data from a database. Finally, analysts need to design *feedback* for users. System feedback is necessary to let users know:

- if their input is being accepted
- if input is or is not in the correct form
- if processing is going on
- if requests can or cannot be processed
- if more detailed information is available and how to get it

Deliverables

The term *deliverables* refers to an installed and working information system, including all of the tangible items and training needed to support and maintain the new or upgraded system, which the systems analyst agrees to deliver to management and other involved parties throughout the project and at its end.

A written systems proposal typically presents three alternatives (only one of which the analyst will recommend), given to management after some feasibility and data analysis has been performed. At this juncture, management and the systems analyst examine each alternative for costs and benefits, as well as whether they are technically, operationally, and economically feasible. Once management and the analyst have agreed on an option, they agree to go forward with the project during a specified time frame.

The systems analyst (particularly one who has chosen a structured methodology that is supported by a CASE tool) delivers logical diagrams depicting new data flows, physical data flows, a data dictionary, a data repository, and process specifications. These deliverables were described earlier. No matter what systems analysis approach is adopted, the output, input, and user interface design are critical components for which the systems analyst is responsible. No matter how completely the data flow and logic are described, if there is meaningless or unintelligible output, invalid input, and/or an ineffective user interface design, the resulting project may be unsuccessful.

It is incumbent on the analyst to provide as much assistance as possible to the programmers who will code the software for the system. Structure charts are used to promote modular program design, and N–S Charts, Warnier–Orr diagrams, and Pseudocode help transfer process specifications and logic to programmers.

When purchases of hardware and coding of software are complete, the system is installed and tested with the analyst's help. System hardware and software are among the most easily identifiable and visible deliverables provided to management. An overall plan to test the system for accuracy, reliability, and usefulness is implemented at this time.

Clearly written and thoroughly tested documentation, such as manuals and online help systems written to accompany the hardware or software, its installation, operation, and maintenance, are also deliverables for which the systems analyst is responsible. Manuals range from highly technical documents for use by maintenance programmers to online, context-sensitive, help directed at end users who must use the system as part of their daily jobs, but who are not computer experts.

Finally, as the analyst assists in getting the system into production, an evaluation plan, already written as part of the systems proposal, is implemented. This can include interviews and questionnaires designed both to assess user satisfaction with the system and to measure the actual system performance based on the benchmarks established earlier (*see* ASSESSMENT OF MANAGEMENT INFORMATION SYSTEM). Systems analysts may be involved up to a year or more after the system is installed in order to complete necessary refinements based on this feedback. The project is then officially ended.

Bibliography

Alavi, M. (1984). An assessment of the prototyping approach to information systems. *Communications of the ACM*, **27**, 556–63.

Avison, D. E. & Wood-Harper, A. T. (1990). *Multiview: An Exploration in Information Systems Development.* Oxford: Blackwell Scientific.

Checkland, P. B. (1989). Soft systems methodology. *Human Systems Management,* 8, 271–89.

Davis, G. B. & Olson, M. H. (1985). *Management Information Systems: Conceptual Foundations, Structure, and Development,* 2nd edn. New York: McGraw-Hill.

Downs, E., Clare, P. & Coe, I. (1988). *Structured Systems Analysis and Design Method: Application and Context.* Hemel Hempstead, UK: Prentice-Hall.

Gane, C. & Sarson, T. (1979). *Structured Systems Analysis and Design Tools and Techniques.* Englewood Cliffs, NJ: Prentice-Hall.

Jackson, M. (1983). *Systems Development.* Englewood Cliffs, NJ: Prentice-Hall.

Kendall, J. E. & Kendall, K. E. (1993). Metaphors and methodologies: living beyond the systems machine. *MIS Quarterly,* 17, 149–71.

Kendall, K. E. & Kendall, J. E. (1995). *Systems Analysis and Design,* 3rd edn. Englewood Cliffs, NJ: Prentice-Hall.

Mumford, E. (1983). *Designing Participatively: a Participative Approach to Computer Systems Design.* Manchester, UK: Manchester Business School.

Mumford, E. & Weir, M. (1979). *Computer Systems in Work Design: The ETHICS Method.* London: Associated Business Press.

Naumann, J. D. & Jenkins, A. M. (1982). Prototyping: the new paradigm for systems development. *MIS Quarterly,* 6, 29–44.

Yourdon, E. (1989). *Modern Structured Analysis.* Englewood Cliffs, NJ: Prentice-Hall.

KENNETH E. KENDALL and
JULIE E. KENDALL

T

task/system fit   The concept of task/system fit focuses on the "fit" or "match" between the capabilities or functionalities provided by a given information system and the information-processing requirements of the task in which the system may be used. Task/system fit models contain two key components: information-processing requirements of a given task and information-processing functionalities in a given information system. The degree to which the information system capabilities "fit" or are "aligned with" the needs of the task determines system usefulness for that task. This degree of fit, or system usefulness, in turn, influences user task performance when the system is used to complete the task.

The concept of technology fit or alignment originated among contingency theorists at an organizational level of analysis to explain organizational effectiveness as a function of the extent to which organizational variables fit the context in which the organization operates. Subsequent extensions of research on contingency fit have utilized less aggregate levels of analysis such as organizational work units, groups, jobs, and individuals. Researchers have also examined several different dimensions of fit itself. Some have assessed fit from an objective, "engineering" perspective that excludes any individual component. Other researchers have included a strong individual dimension in their evaluation of task/system fit. They focus on dimensions such as individual perceptions of an application fit for tasks and on the cognitive fit between three components: the task information-processing requirements, the capabilities of the information system, and the cognitive information-processing style of the individual completing the task.

Regardless of the level of analysis or dimension of task/system fit, a key idea is that task performance improves when the information system application used in the task provides the appropriate functionalities for the task that needs to be completed. When other factors are the same, the task performance of a user who takes advantage of the appropriate system capabilities is generally better than the performance of one who uses a system with less useful capabilities relative to the task needs.

The task/technology fit concept has implications for the development of information systems. To develop systems that are likely to improve user performance, the systems development team must understand the key information-processing needs of the task(s) the users will perform. They design into the new application the functionalities that support these information-processing requirements.

WILLIAM D. NANCE

TCP/IP   Transmission Control Protocol/ Internet Protocol is a widely used routing protocol. The Internet Protocol routes data packets across networks and the Transmission Control Protocol enables flow control and reliable transmission.

See also **Protocols; Telecommunication**

teams in system development   Central to developing information system applications is determining business requirements that such systems must address. Given the interdependent and systemic nature of the functions and processes within business organizations, the knowledge and skills required to understand completely business requirements and the complex interrelationships between them requires a number of participants. In practice, teams made up of participants from various affected business functions come together to provide necessary expertise. Cross-functional systems development teams represent the assembly of these KNOWLEDGE WORK experts from both business functions and information technology areas.

Once the business requirements have been identified, development methodologies and tools are employed in order to articulate the requirements into technical specifications. In addition, an understanding of the potential hardware, software, and networking technologies is required. Development skills are necessary to build and maintain application systems. The knowledge and skills required for development suggest an ongoing need for teams of knowledge workers.

BRIAN D. JANZ

telecommunication   The word "telecommunication" was formed by adding the word "tele" to "communication." "Tele" comes from the ancient Greek for "at a distance" and is used as a prefix to create a word which represents a new communication form made possible by using electricity. Telecommunication is, therefore, long-distance communication using electromagnetic methods. It encompasses other words that use the "tele" prefix such as telephone (speaking at a distance), television (seeing at a distance), telegraph (writing at a distance), and teleconference (conferencing at a distance).

When human beings wish to communicate, they exchange information in the form of messages. The form of the message is affected by whether the communication will be face to face or occur at a distance. In face-to-face communication, visual cues, such as facial expressions, hand gestures, and other body language messages, are included in communication. Face-to-face communication also provides the ability to share reports and drawings. In face-to-face meetings, participants regularly look at the body language of other participants and view common reports and drawings to

support the communication. When communication occurs at a distance, the number and quality of the messages are reduced. Body language, for example, cannot be viewed over the telephone, and the tone of the voice cannot be heard using e-mail. The goal of telecommunications is to provide communication systems which span long distances and deliver an optimal set of messages to support particular communication needs.

Telecommunications can be viewed either as a set of communication services or as an infrastructure to support telecommunication services. Some common telecommunication services include telephone, television, teleconferencing, ELECTRONIC MAIL, voice mail, and the INTERNET. The telecommunication infrastructure includes various public and private networks which deliver telecommunication services.

Telecommunication Services

A large and growing number of telecommunication services are offered to people around the world. Figure 1 classifies telecommunication services according to their level of interactivity and the type of messages supported. Interactivity is the ability of the receiver to reply to the sender in a particular time frame. Messages can be thought of as words, graphics, audio, and video sent electronically in various combinations.

At the low end of interactivity, the receiver cannot respond to the message and communication is one way. Radio and television are examples of the low end of interactivity. An application such as the WORLD WIDE WEB allows some navigational feedback, but it basically remains a one-way method of communication. Interactivity that is two-way can either be immediate or delayed. In delayed two-way communication, the receiver chooses when to accept the message and the sender and receiver are not required to communicate at the same moment in time. Electronic mail and voice mail are examples of delayed two-way communication. Immediate two-way communication requires the receiver and the sender to be engaged in communication at the same moment in time. The telephone is an example of immediate two-way communication.

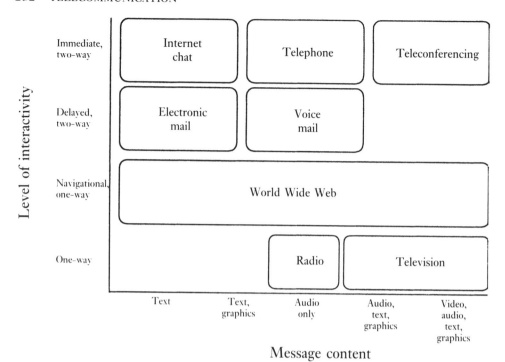

Figure 1   Telecommunication services

Telecommunication Infrastructure

Underlying telecommunication services is the technical infrastructure that permits messages to be sent and received. This infrastructure uses electromagnetic methods to encode the communication message. The most widely used electromagnetic method for representing a message involves creating a wave as shown in figure 2. This waveform can be produced by an alternating current over wires or as energy propagated through the atmosphere as electromagnetic waves.

The waveform can be varied by frequency. The frequency is the number of cycles that occurs in a second and is called a hertz. To represent large number of hertz (Hz), the words kilohertz (thousands of hertz), megahertz (millions of hertz) and gigahertz (thousands of millions of hertz) are used. The telephone system uses frequencies between 0 and 4,000 Hz to represent the human voice over telephone wires. Broadcast television uses frequencies between 30 megahertz and 3 gigahertz to send television signals through the air.

The receiver of a telecommunication message must know what frequencies the sender is using to represent the message. Thus, a basic agreement must be reached between a sender and receiver before any message can be

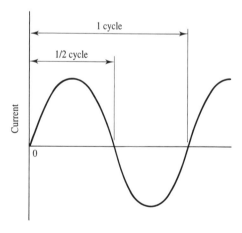

Figure 2 Electromagnetic wave

communicated. Such an agreement is called a *protocol*. When a large number of people agree on a protocol it becomes a standard. Fundamental to the entire telecommunications infrastructure is the establishment of protocols and the eventual development of standards. Standards permit the largest number of people to utilize the telecommunication infrastructure to develop telecommunication applications.

Protocols and Standards

Many protocols must be established before telecommunication services are possible. A useful approach to understanding protocols is to view them as layers. Figure 3 shows a very simple four-layer model of telecommunication protocols.

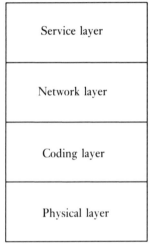

Figure 3 Four-layer model of telecommunication protocols

Physical layer

The lowest layer is labeled the physical layer because it concerns the physical characteristics of devices used to send and receive telecommunication messages. This layer includes protocols that address the physical specifications of wires, connectors, and devices that will send and receive electromagnetic frequencies. Sets of protocols which describe a particular type of wire receive names such as unshielded twisted pair (UTP), broadband coaxial cable, or single-mode fiberoptic cable. Connectors which attach wires to devices are also specified with protocols

and then labeled with names like RJ-11, RS-232, and phono jack. Protocols that govern the various devices used to send and receive microwaves, satellite waves, radio waves, television waves, and other electromagnetic waves are included in the physical layer. These devices and the frequencies of electromagnetic waves they use often involve significant government regulation so that interference with other users of electromagnetic waves is avoided.

Coding layer

Above the physical layer are protocols that address how the frequencies on the physical wires or electromagnetic waves are coded to transmit messages. Messages can be encoded using either analog or digital coding techniques.

Human senses rely on analog signals such as sound and light waves. For example, ear drums vibrate to actual sound waves and then send the resulting signal to the brain where it is heard. *Analog coding* protocols use the same technique to match electromagnetic frequencies with sound waves. The electromagnetic frequencies are transmitted over a distance and then used to reproduce the sound waves. Analog signaling, thus, uses electromagnetic waves that closely approximate the waves of sound and light.

To represent analog sound and light waves as digital signals a protocol must be established to describe how a wave can be used to represent a binary switch symbolized by the digits 0 and 1. For example, a protocol may choose one frequency to represent a 0 and another frequency to represent a 1. Other methods include using different amplitudes (height of the electromagnetic wave), or using different pulses of voltage to represent the 0s or 1s. Regardless of the method chosen, the 0s and 1s must be grouped together to represent higher-order messages such as sound, video, or data. *Digital encoding* protocols are used to represent sound on CDs, video on videodisks. Data consists of letters, numbers, and special characters. Data is usually represented by grouping binary digits (0s and 1s) together and establishing a protocol. The most common protocol to represent data is ASCII. ASCII, for example, represents the letter "j" with the binary pattern 1101010.

Network layer

The next layer is the network layer. This layer contains many protocols which address how private and public networks are developed and used to send coded signals. Networks can be grouped as either point-to-point networks or multi-point networks. In point-to-point networks, signals are transmitted between two points or nodes. Switching equipment creates a single circuit which allows for the transmission of signals between these two nodes. The telephone network is an example of a point-to-point network. Multi-point networks signal multiple nodes simultaneously. They are designed as either broadcast networks, in which the message is intended for every node, or as packet networks, in which the message is addressed to only certain nodes. The radio and television network is an example of a multi-point broadcast network. Multi-point packet networks are primarily used to transmit digital messages. The Internet is an example of a multi-point packet network.

Service layer

The service layer uses the underlying protocol layers to deliver telecommunication services. The form and type of the telecommunication service depends upon the firm selling the service. Some services are considered public services such as radio, television, and telephone. Public telecommunication services are often operated by private companies which, because of their public mission and monopolistic position, are highly regulated by national governments. Because of this regulation, public telecommunication services frequently differ among countries. This presents a significant challenge when trying to transmit messages across national boundaries.

Organizations create private telecommunication services, such as electronic mail or a system for taking customer orders. These private telecommunication services are established for the exclusive use of the organization. Private services are developed by building private networks. Portions of the private network may consist of purchased public telecommunication services. The security of the message must be protected by using encryption techniques when public telecommunication networks are used to deliver private services. Private telecommunication networks created by organizations generally transmit data and are critical to the survival of the firm. This branch of telecommunications is called data communication.

Data Communication

Data communication networks connect the computers of an organization and use digital coding to match the coding of the computers. The term *data communication* is used because data constitutes the majority of the messages transmitted over digital networks; however, data communication services also transmit audio and video. Data communication networks are generally private networks established by companies to interconnect the computers of employees, customers, and suppliers. An exception is the Internet which is a public data communication network. Data communication networks are constructed by building certain portions of the network and combining this internal network with purchased portions of the public network. The internal network covers a single geographical site, such as an office or building, and is referred to as a LOCAL AREA NETWORK or LAN. The interconnections of individual computers or of a LAN to other LANs or computers over larger distances are called wide area networks or WANs.

Local Area Networks

Local area networks interconnect personal computers. A card called a network interface card (NIC) is installed in each computer and connected using a wiring protocol such as Ethernet or Token Ring. A segment contains a group of computers that are on the same wire. Routers and bridges are used to connect segments. The data on LANs is coded in digital form and placed in packets which contain the address of the computer sending the message and the address of the computer to receive the message. NICs scan each message to see if the message contains its NIC address. Local area networks permit the sharing of common disk storage and access to common peripherals such as printers.

Wide Area Networks

Wide area networks or WANs interconnect computers over distances that can span the globe. Most WANs are constructed by purchasing the services of public telecommunication networks, but some companies own and operate their own WAN network by using their own microwave or satellite transmission devices. The services purchased from public telecommunication companies to construct WANs are specified by protocols and receive labels such as ISDN and T1. Local area networks are connected to the WAN using routers. The Internet is a familiar public wide area network.

Conclusion

Telecommunication covers a very broad and rapidly expanding array of technologies. The telecommunications industry consists of some of the largest firms in the world. Electronic communication on a worldwide basis is critical to the success of companies, governments, and society. New telecommunication services are transforming the way people work, learn, and play, by supporting their communication over large distances. Understanding protocols and standards is fundamental to the construction of telecommunication services. One area of telecommunications, data communications, which involves the transmission of data among computers is recognized as a crucial organizational asset. The telecommunication infrastructure, both public and private, and the services that are being delivered are transforming civilization.

REAGAN M. RAMSOWER

telecommuting Telecommuting refers to the substitution of computer and telecommunication technologies for physical travel to a central work location. This term, commonly used in the USA, emphasizes the substitution of "telecommunication" for "physical commuting". In Europe, the term "telework" is more popular. The main notion of telework is on "work", made possible through the use of information technology, covering a range of new ways of working outside the traditional office environment. Other terms relating to similar concepts include remote work, distance working, flexiplace, virtual office and electronic cottage. Telecommuting or telework is often associated with home-based work, but the workplace of a telecommuter can also be a satellite office, a neighborhood work center, a hotel room, or even client premises. Telecommuting offers flexibility in both the workplace and in working time.

Not all office tasks lend themselves to telecommuting. Jobs that are good candidates for telecommuting include those that can be done with relatively little face-to-face contact with other people, those that require concentration, those that can be performed without close supervision, and those with defined milestones. The business sectors most involved with telecommuting are those with a high information content such as research, software development, financial services, insurance, journalism, publishing, customer services, and sales support. Experts estimate that about 10 percent of the workforce in the USA and Europe are potential telecommuters.

The initial interest in telecommuting started in the mid-1970s when the focus was on energy conservation. Today, telecommuting is seen as an option for work with benefits for individuals, employers, society, and the environment. Telecommuting can cut business costs by making better use of available skills and eliminating the need for large central offices. Telecommuting has been shown to lead to productivity gains of between 15 and 20 percent. The telecommuter enjoys more flexible working hours and avoids the struggle of daily commuting. Telecommuting increases the quality of life and gives individuals greater responsibility and flexibility by allowing work and other commitments to be better matched. In addition, telecommuting saves energy and reduces pollution by cutting down on commuter travel and easing traffic congestion in cities. Telecommuting also boosts local employment and regional development and provides employment opportunities to those who previously found it difficult to work outside the home, such as the elderly, handicapped, and parents with childcare responsibilities.

For the telecommuter, the potential disadvantages include role conflict stemming from the merging of home and office, feelings of isolation arising from lack of social interaction, and negative implications for career advancement. For the employer, the main concerns are the start-up and running costs, data security, difficulty in supervising and evaluating the performance of telecommuters, and the loss of face-to-face communication.

Telecommuting is enabled by advances in computer and telecommunications technologies.

Telecommuters make use of a range of equipment and services to perform their work, including personal computers with modems, access to the Internet, electronic mail, telephones, mobile phones, voice mail, facsimile machines and audio- and video-conferencing. Telecommuters can work on a "dumb" terminal or a personal computer and transmit (upload) the completed task to the company's computer facilities via telephone lines or wireless means. With advanced information technology, it is possible for the telecommuter to maintain contact with and control over projects elsewhere, to communicate with colleagues in other time zones, and to gain access to resources on the Internet regardless of the time of day, the day of the week, or the weather conditions. As technologies improve and become more affordable, more organizations and individuals are likely to adopt telecommuting as a new form of work arrangement.

CHEE SING YAP

transaction processing   Transaction processing refers to applications that process business transactions such as order entry and billing (*see* PROCESSING METHODS FOR INFORMATION SYSTEMS).

V

value from information technology Organizations grapple with the question of value from information technology (IT) each time they have to make substantial investments in new systems. In some organizations, value from IT is implicitly defined in terms of financial returns, as IT projects are required to meet specified return on investment hurdle rates before they are approved. Traditional project valuation techniques such as net present value, payback period, and return on investment are applied. This approach is appropriate for systems that increase revenue, or that lower costs through improving organizational productivity. In other organizations, strict financial hurdle rates are not always applied to IT as there is recognition that the value from some IT projects are qualitative, and difficult to quantify, or that the proposed IT expenditure is a matter of competitive necessity. For example, it is often difficult to quantify the value from investment in organizational IT infrastructure because IT infrastructure does not yield value until the business applications that utilize the infrastructure are built and used, and the locus of value generation is usually diffuse as there is organization-wide sharing of the infrastructure. Organizations seeking qualitative valuation techniques usually use approaches that rely on weighting of various performance criteria and ranking of projects.

While organizations have long grappled with the question of value from specific IT projects, there has also been growing interest in the question of value from the organization's total IT expenditure. As in the question of PRODUCTIVITY FROM INFORMATION TECHNOLOGY, much of this interest was stimulated by the rapid growth in IT expenditure in organizations. Studies that sought to answer this question generally used some indicator of profitability as a measure of value. Examples of such measures are return on assets (Cron & Sobol, 1983; Weill, 1992), return on investment (Cron & Sobol, 1983); and ratio of expense to income (Bender, 1986; Harris & Katz, 1991). As in the case of studies on IT productivity, the studies of value from IT have also produced mixed results, with some showing a positive relationship between IT expenditure and performance, while others show no relationship, or a bimodal distribution, where heavy IT spenders either perform very well or very poorly.

These results are not surprising given that there are many factors, other than IT, that affect organizational profitability. The impact of IT on business profitability is often diluted by these other factors, such as competitive conditions, economic cycles, and the effectiveness of the organization's business strategy. An alternative approach to assessing the value from IT is to take a step back from firm profitability and to consider the intermediate impacts of IT. Value from IT arises from intermediate outcomes, such as improved cycle times, service quality, and product variety. If value is defined in these terms, rather than organizational profitability, the problem of dilution of IT impacts is reduced. A second explanation for the mixed results from studies of organizational value from IT is that, as in the case of productivity from IT, the amount of IT spending does not determine the amount of value received. The creation of value from IT is dependent on the portfolio of IT resources invested in, and the effectiveness of management processes such as the alignment of IT and business strategy, selection of IT projects, and the development and implementation of systems.

Bibliography

Bender, D. H. (1986). Financial impact of information processing. *Journal of Management Information Systems*, **3**, 232–38.

Cron, W. & Sobol, M. (1983). The relationship between computerization and performance: a strategy for maximizing economic benefits of computerization. *Information and Management*, **6**, 171–81.

Harris, S. E. & Katz, J. L. (1991). Organizational performance and information technology investment intensity in the insurance industry. *Organization Science*, **2**, 263–95.

Kauffman, R. J. & Weill, P. (1989). An evaluative framework for research on the performance effects of information technology investment. *Proceedings of the Tenth International Conference on Information Systems*, 377–88.

Markus, M. L. & Soh, C. (1993). Banking on information technology: converting IT spending into firm performance in R. D. Banker, R. J. Kauffman and M. A. Mahmood (eds), *Strategic Information Technology Management: Perspectives on Organizational Growth and Competitive Advantage*. Harrisburg, PA: Idea Publishing.

Weill, P. (1992). The relationship between investment in information technology and firm performance: a study of the valve manufacturing sector. *Information Systems Research*, **3**, 307–58.

CHRISTINA SOH

virtual reality Virtual reality provides a user with computer-generated, full-color, three-dimensional imagery with possible attributes of touch, sound, and motion. The virtual reality application allows a user to experience the essence of reality for a physical space, operational environment, etc. Virtual reality displays can be supplemented by virtual reality gloves so that a user can manipulate screen objects and feel weight and texture. Applications of virtual reality for information systems include walkthroughs of physical space being planned (such as a new office design), simulation of new product use, and training in new procedures.

viruses A computer virus is a computer program designed to destroy other programs, corrupt stored data, or interfere with the operation of a computer system. Virus programs can range from very benign programs that merely display a message saying that the virus exists to deadly viruses that destroy files and programs. Viruses are generally introduced along with software on diskettes or boot sectors on a diskette containing data. There are some viruses that can be sent with e-mail documents or downloaded along with data files from the Internet. There are several thousand known viruses; however, viruses tend to follow a few common patterns. Virus-protection software is available to detect the existence of viruses on diskettes or hard drives and to remove them. Organizations receiving diskettes from outside sources typically have procedures for virus checking before allowing the diskettes to be used. Users that are at risk for viruses can employ virus-detection and removal software as part of their operating procedures. The system can be tailored to automatically examine diskettes or downloaded information for viruses and to remove them.

GORDON B. DAVIS

voice recognition *see* SPEECH RECOGNITION AND SYNTHESIS

W

World Wide Web In 1993, a new function of the INTERNET was introduced termed the World Wide Web. The Web concept was developed by CERN in Switzerland and by MIT. The idea was to provide a distributed HYPERMEDIA/HYPERTEXT system. Up until this time, most people had not found the Internet to be particularly useful. While some businesses and many universities continued to use the basic functions of the Internet, i.e. message and file exchange, the ability to gather useful information from remote servers was still a reasonably complex task, beyond the skill and interest of many. While still focused on the exchange of data, the World Wide Web (WWW or Web) allowed a much richer form of information to be exchanged, in a manner more suitable for the infrequent user.

Information on the World Wide Web is organized into pages. Each page is composed of text and graphics (much like a typical publication). As the user reads through the text of a page, particular words (or pictures) can be identified as links. These links, when selected, allow the user to go to a new page, which can also have links to other resources. In addition to text and still images, other richer types of information can be retrieved when links are activated, including sound files and full motion video. In each instance, a link may be retrieving data from the same computer where the original page resides, or from a computer in another country thousands of miles away.

In addition to the types of data listed above, the World Wide Web has evolved into an interactive media as well. Scripts, or programs, running in the background of some World Wide Web pages allow the user to respond to questions on line, fill out forms, send e-mail, or enter text which prompts a search of remote databases. These new interactive capabilities have the potential to have an impact on everyday lives in the form of applications like interactive catalogs, electronic banking, database sorting and information retrieval, inventory tracking, career placement services, and online entertainment.

The concept of Web pages with embedded links is called a *hypertext* interface. As a link is clicked upon, it brings up a page located on either the same computer or some other computer. Each page and computer combination has a unique address called a uniform resource locator (URL). This addressing system enables users to find and record a particular file location for recurrent access. Web documents are created in a particular language which browsers recognize and translate. The language, termed hypertext markup language (or HTML), is reasonably simple to learn, allowing even relative computer novices to create basic Web pages in a reasonably short amount of time.

World Wide Web pages are accessed by programs called Web browsers. The earliest Web browser was designed at the University of Illinois, and was called Mosaic. Since that time, a variety of other browsers has been developed. Netscape, a browser developed by individuals from the original Mosaic development team, has been the dominant browser during 1995. However, there are many new competitors.

The success of the Web was a rapid occurrence. In 1994, one year after its inception, approximately 10 million Americans were estimated to be using the Internet. The WWW is believed to be largely responsible for that growth. While fascinating in its current form, individuals are finding ways to use the Web in creative ways. Many of these uses focus on making businesses more efficient and effective. The future of the Web is bright, yet unknown. Many believe that it will have a profound impact on our society.

MARK A. FULLER

INDEX

Note: Headwords are in bold type

abuse of computer systems
  data abuse 200
  detection 201
  extent of losses 199
  hardware abuse 200
  program abuse 200
  and unauthorized use 200
access
  and access logs 13
  authorization 176, 177–8, 181–2,
    200
  to data 22, 30, 47, 48–9, 51, 52,
    70, 123, 140, 182, 201
  direct/serial 34–5
  to images 103, 104–5
  to information 77, 189
  to information systems 12–13,
    15, 181, 200
  to information technology 13, 70,
    77
  to memory 32
  to personal data 176, 177–8
  see also hashing; index; security
access paths 48–9
  primary
    algorithmic/hashed 48
    indexed sequential 48
    sequential 48
  secondary 48
accountability, for IS use 20, 40, 175
accounting information system
  (AIS) 1–2
**accounting use of information
  technology** 1–3, 110, 124
  early systems 93, 95
  and financial management and
    reporting 2–3
  and human resources cycles 2
  information processing
    activities 1–2
  and operations cycle 2
  and purchase/procurement
    cycle 2

  and revenue cycle 2
  software 32, 209
accounts receivable, invoice-
  less 189
accuracy, of information 76, 77, 109
**ACM (Association for
  Computing Machinery)** 3,
  8
  and Management Information
    Systems group 8
ADA programming language 3, 185
addresses
  electronic mail 68
  World Wide Web 240
**advanced manufacturing
  technology**, and
  nonproduction processes 189
**Advanced Research Projects Agency
  (ARPA)**, and network
  technology 83, 96, 126
advantage, competitive see
  competitive advantage
advertising
  and electronic commerce 65, 66
  and image processing 105
agency theory 3–4, 75
  and end-user computing 3–4
  and investment in information
    technology 184
  and outsourcing 3
  and systems development 3
agents, insurance 125
AIDS, and privacy issues 177
Aiken, Howard 94
AIS (accounting information
  system) 1–2
**AIS (Association for
  Information Systems)** 4, 9
ALGOL (ALGorithmic
  Language) 185
algorithms
  compression 28
  DES 202
  DSA (digital signature
    algorithm) 202

  encoding 70
  errors 54
  genetic (GA) 85–6
  hashing 48
  in neural networks 154
  pattern-matching 79
  RSA 202
  speech recognition 211
  see also data modeling, physical
Allen, Paul 97
alphanumeric characters
  coding 26–7
  in information theory 110, 119
Amadeus 127
**American National Standards
  Institute (ANSI)** 213
  ANSI-74 COBOL 22
  ANSI X12 67, 68
  ANSI/SPARC Committee 50
  and ER model 73
  and SQL 53, 213
**American Standard Code for
  Information Interchange
  (ASCII)** 5, 27, 233
analog representation 26, 27, 94,
  152, 233
**analytic hierarchies process
  (AHP)** 205
ANALYZE system 151
Anderson, Harlan 96
Andrus, R. R. 111
Ang, S. 168
ANSI see American National
  Standards Institute
Anthony framework 142–3, 144
APL (A Programming
  Language) 185
Apple Computers 97, 150–1, 217
applications
  application programming
    interface (API) 52, 156
  development 7, 206
  evaluation 7, 11
  failure 82
  image processing 104–6

and macro recorders 33
and management information
    systems 138, 142
requirements determination 192
software 205, 206, 208–9, 222
systems architecture 73
see also spreadsheets; word
    processing
Apte, U. M. 168
arbitration, and outsourcing
    agreements 169
arithmetic logic unit 29, 30
"arithnometer" 93
ARPA see Advanced Research
    Projects Agency
ARPANET 83, 96
artificial intelligence 4, 191
    ethical issues 76–7
    and human–computer
        interface 98
    and model management 151
    see also cognitive science and
        information systems; expert
        systems; knowledge base
ASCII (American Standard
    Code for Information
    Interchange) 5, 27, 233
ASM see Association for Systems
    Management (ASM)
assembler 33, 206
assessment see information systems,
    assessment
Association for Computing
    Machinery (ACM) 3, 8
    and Management Information
        Systems Group 8
Association for Information
    Systems (AIS) 4, 9
Association for Systems
    Management (ASM) 9
associations and societies,
    professional, for information
    technology 3, 4, 7–9, 61, 103,
    203
asynchronous transmission
    mode (ATM; electronic
    communications) 9
Atanasoff, John 94
ATM see asynchronous
    transmission mode
ATM (automated teller
    machine) 14, 64, 68, 123, 179
attributes
    in data modeling 41–3, 45–7, 48–
        9, 159, 191, 212
    and data structure 50
    and ER diagrams 19, 73, 74

primary/secondary key
    attributes 48, 49, 212
audit trail 104, 183
auditing of information
    systems 9–14
    and application-specific
        programmed controls 13
    background investigation 10–11
    concurrent techniques 11
    evidence collection 11
    evidence evaluation 11
    follow-up 12
    generalized information system
        procedures 12
    generalized programmed
        controls 12–13
    and impact of change 13–14
    internal/external auditors 3, 9,
        10–11, 183
    miscellaneous controls 13
    objectives 9
    planning 11
    report 11–12
    and risks of information
        systems 9–10
Australian Computer Society
    (ACS) 8
authorization see access; password;
    security
automated teller machine
    (ATM) 14, 64, 68, 123, 179
    networks 127
    see also electronic funds transfer
automation, office see office
    automation

Babbage, Charles 93
backup and recovery processes 7,
    12, 13, 150, 183, 199, 200
    methods 201
Baldwin, Frank S. 93
bandwidth
    and asynchronous transmission
        mode 9
    and Internet 126
banking
    use of information technology 1,
        64, 167, 172–3, 179, 180,
        182, 199, 210, 216, 240
    see also automated teller machine;
        electronic funds transfer;
        magnetic ink character
        recognition
bar code 1, 15, 123
    manufacturing uses 147, 148
BASIC (Beginners All-purpose
    Symbolic Instruction

Code) 185, 208
bastions, and information systems
    security 202
batch processing 1, 2, 15, 96, 180–
    1, 182
    see also transaction processing
Beath, C. M. 136, 168
behavior
    and cognitive science 28
    employee 10
    formalization 162
benchmarking, in information
    technology 119
binary relationship modeling see
    object role modeling
bit mapping 50, 123, 156
bits 5, 15, 26–7, 103–4, 215
black box system 219, 221–2
BLOB (binary large object) 50
block, disk 48
    splitting 48
BPR see re-engineering
Braillers 167
Bricklin, Daniel 97
British Computer Society (BCS) 8
browsers 102, 105, 125, 216, 240
Bryan, J. 199
BSP see business systems planning
bugs see debugging
bulletin boards 15, 36–7
    and threading 36
    see also Usenet
Burroughs, William S. 93
bus networks 29, 133
Bush, Vannever 94
business process architecture 73
business process re-engineering see
    re-engineering
business rules, and electronic
    commerce 65–6
business start-ups, and business
    process redesign 191
business systems planning
    (BSP) 172
byte 9, 15, 26, 29

C 16, 53, 208
    and C++ 16, 156, 186, 208
cable
    coaxial 133–4, 233
    fiberoptic 134, 233
    twisted pair 133, 233
cache memory 30, 32
CAD see computer-aided design
calculation, mechanization 93
Capability Maturation Model 149
capacity planning, and information

technology use 7, 146–7, 148, 170–1, 172, 175
capital
  computer 183
  intellectual 129–30
cardinality 41, 43, 46, 74, 160
careers in information systems 16–18
  career orientations 16–17
  future directions 17–18
  types 16
carpal tunnel syndrome 122
CASE (computer-aided software/system engineering) 18–19, 136, 223, 228
  and data dictionary 41, 187, 226
  and data flow diagram (DFD) 18
  meta-model 18
  and object-oriented database management systems 156
  and prototyping 187
  and Structured English decision-making method 226
  upper/lower CASE tools 18
case-management techniques 189, 190
cathode ray tubes (CRT) 166
CD-ROM 19, 34, 214, 215
  reader 150
cellular technology 19, 65
central processing unit (CPU)
  and distributed systems 60
  early machines 95
  in human information processing 99
  and microcomputers 150
  and primary storage 30–1, 34
centralization, and information systems use 57, 60–1
chaining, backward/forward 79, 80
champion, of information systems implementation 108
change, organizational, and information systems use 189–90
change, social, and new technology 76
chargeback in information systems 19–20
Checkland, P. 203–5
Chen, Peter 73
chief information officer (CIO) 16, 20, 68
chips 29–30
  encryption 70
  memory 29, 214–15

microprocessor 29–30
  and smart cards 203
  and storage 34
CIO *see* chief information officer
circuits, computer 29, 94
  integrated 30, 96
CISC (complex instruction set computer) 30
class, in object-oriented programs and systems 157–8
client/server architecture 17, 20, **20–1**, 31
  and database management systems 53
  and enterprise architecture 72, 164
  and executive information systems 78
  and Internet 66
  and microcomputers 150
clock, in central processing unit 30
coaxial cable 133–4, 233
COBOL (COmmon Business Oriented Language) 21–6, 51, 53, 95, 207–8
  and ANSI-74 COBOL 22
  COBOL 60 22
  divisions 22
  example 23–6
CODASYL *see* Committee on Data Systems Languages
Codd, E. F. 191
code analyzers 137
Code of Fair Information Practices (US) 177
code restructurers 137
coding of data for information processing 5, 15, **26–8**
  alphanumerical characters 26–7, 109
  analog/digital representation 26, 233
  and compression 26, 28
  and information theory 109–10, 119
  pictures and graphics 27
  video and motion 27, 28, 152
  voice and sound 27
cognition
  non-linear 102
  situated 101
cognitive science and information systems 28–9, 139
  and situated cognition 101
  see also artificial intelligence; expert systems

cohesion, functional 221
College of Information Systems (INFORM-CIS) 8–9
commerce, electronic 63–7
  and barriers to innovation 66–7
  enhancement of customer service 64–5
  future prospects 64
  and new business rules 65–6
  and suitable products 65
commitment
  to employer 16
  and outsourcing 18
Committee on Data Systems Languages (CODASYL) 21–2, 151
communication
  architectures 171, 186
  cellular 19
  controls 12
  costs 60, 69
  data 234
  and information theory 109–10, 112, 119–20
  two-way 231
  see also telecommunication
communications devices, as input devices 121
compact disk *see* CD-ROM
compatibility
  software 126, 150–1
  system 96, 150
compensation, and motivation 162
competitive advantage
  and information technology use 5, 10, 67, 140, 144, 173–4, 216–17
  and knowledge 129
  and make-or-buy decisions 209
  and software development 137–8
  sustainable 174, 217–18
compiler 33, 185, 206
compression 19, 26, 28, **29**
  and image processing 104, 152
  JPEG (Joint Photographic Experts Group) standard 28
  "loss-less" 28
  LZ algorithm 28
  MPEG-2(Moving Picture Experts Group) standard 28
  space suppression 28
computer
  acceptance 95–6
  early electronic digital 94, 140
  and emergence of computer industry 94–5
  first-generation 95

laptop 149, 167
mechanical analog 94
portable 130, 148, 149, 167
see also human–computer
    interaction; mainframe
    computers; microcomputer;
    minicomputers
computer-aided design (CAD) 148,
    156, 167, 209
computer-aided manufacturing
    (CAM) 156, 167
computer-aided software/
    system engineering
    (CASE) 18–19, 228
and data dictionary 41, 187, 226
and data flow diagram (DFD) 18
meta-model 18
and object-oriented database
    manufacturing system 156
upper/lower CASE tools 18
Computer Fraud and Abuse
    Act 1986 (US) 76
computer hardware
    architecture 29–31
and basic hardware 30–1
and classes of systems 31
and hardware chips 29–30
and input/output
    management 31–2
and multiple standard
    formats 150–1
and performance evaluation 170
computer industry, emergence 94–
    5
computer operating system
    (OS) 31, **31–2,** 32, 141, 205–6
and application software 206
controls 12–13
and device management 32
and file system management 32
and hardware input/output
    management 31–2
and memory subsystem
    management 32
and microcomputers 150–1
multi-user 32
multitasking 31–2
single-tasking 31
and system software 222
and user interface 32
and user management 32
computer output microfilm
    (COM) 167
computer program 32–3, 184,
    205
abuse of 200
as artificial system 220

control structures 32–3
debugging 53–4, 75, 96, 226
as deterministic system 220
development system 33
modular (structured) design 33
modules 32, 33
object 32, 33
as relatively closed system 220
and reusability 33, 81, 136, 158,
    186
routines 32
source/object programs 33, 206
subroutines 32, 33
see also errors; languages,
    programming; macro
    program; maintenance;
    object-oriented programs
    and systems; software,
    engineering; viruses
computer science, development 95
computer storage 2, 32, **34–5**
direct access storage device
    (DASD) 34–5
direct/serial access 34–5
disk 28, 152, 206
future developments 35
in group decision support
    systems 92
magnetic 31, 34–5, 104, 152
optical 34, 104, 152
primary 30, 31, 34, 35, 206
secondary 31, 32, 34–5, 121, 165
WORM (write-once-read-
    many) 34, 215
see also byte; CD-ROM;
    compression; cost; storage
    for information processing
computer-supported
    cooperative work
    (CSCW) 35–9, 64, 130, 190
and application types 37–8, 209
and collaboration concepts 35–6
and computer systems
    design 36–7
and impact on work groups 38–9
and management information
    systems 138, 140
see also group decision support
    systems
computer systems
electromechanical 94
mainframe 31
microcomputers 17, 29–30, 31,
    149–51
minicomputers 31
performance evaluation 170–
    1

product-oriented 172
supercomputer 30, 31
computing
distributed *see* distributed systems
end-user 3–4, 6, 16, 17, 63, **70–1,**
    80, 107, 209
ethical issues 75–7, 82, 175–8
see also human–computer
    interaction
condition-action rules 79, 80, 81,
    129, 144
conferencing, computer 36, 37, 38
configuration control 12
conflict resolution, in expert
    systems 79
consent, informed 76
consequentialism 75
consistency
checks 75, 129
in system design 98, 205
constraint
cover 43, 45
exclusion 43, 45
physical 99
referential integrity 41
set 160
totality 160
construction
and programming 117
and system methodologies 117,
    118
contingency theory 230
continuity, of information
    systems 10
contract work
in information systems 17, 38
in software programming 137
see also outsourcing
contracts
and agency theory 3
long-term 17
outsourcing 168–9
control
database 13
in information systems use 20,
    71, 92, 118, 176, 199, 200
management 143
operational 142–3
output 13
and outsourcing
    agreements 168–9
of production activity 147, 148
in transaction processing 182–3
control in computer systems
application-specific program-
    med 13
concurrency 36, 53, 59–60

generalized programmed 12–13, 20
  in object-oriented programs 158
  process 31
  sequence/alternation/repetition 33, 218–19
  see also protocols
cooperation, computer-supported **35–9**, 127–8, 138, 140, 209
coordination
  and cooperative work 36, 37–8, 128
  and distributed systems 57
  and information systems function groups 163–4
  subsystem 221
copyright 76, 200, 217
Copyright Act 1976 (US) 76
core competencies, and outsourcing decisions 127, 164–5, 168
cost-benefit analysis
  and information economics 10, 20, 113, 172–3
  and systems analysis 228
cost leadership strategy 174
costs
  agency 3
  of communication 60, 69
  of data retrieval 49
  of data storage 28, 31, 49
  of information systems 10, 19–20, 60, 82, 118, 131
  of labor 131, 217
  of software maintenance 136
  of training 164
  transaction 104, 197
Couger, J. D. 136
CPU *see* central processing unit
credit cards
  and electronic funds transfer 14, 68, 106
  and magnetic tape strips 123
  and privacy of information 176
crime, computer 199
critical success factors (CSF) **39**, 107, 114, 196–7
cross-validation 45
crossover, and genetic algorithms 85–6
CSCW *see* computer-supported cooperative work
CSF (critical success factors) **39**, 107, 114, 196–7
CSMA/CD protocol (carrier sense multiple access with collision detection) 133

culture, organizational
  and applications failure 82
  and business process re-engineering 189–90
  and information partnerships 128, 190
  and information systems security 199
  and information technology use 5, 6
  and soft systems methodologies 205
  and value of information 112
Curtis, B. et al. 136
customer satisfaction 110, 114, 149
customer service
  and electronic commerce 63–5
  and information technology use 147–8, 217
Cyert, R. 101

DASD *see* direct access storage device
data **40**
  abuse of 200
  ACCESS 22
  administration 12, 36, **40**, 50, 118–19
  coding 5, 15, **21–6**
  collection 104, 116, 147, 175–7, 187
  communication 234
  compression *see* compression
  couples 226
  and datacenter professionals 16
  dictionary **40–1**, 187, 225–6, 228
  highways 64
  and information 108–9, 160
  infrastructure 141–2
  input 30, 121–4
  management *see* data, administration
  manipulation 212–13
  master 2
  organization *see* file
  processing *see* processing methods for information systems
  redundant 51, 201
  as resource 140, 173–4
  retrieval 49, 51, 83, 103, 104–5, 130, 140, 155, 182, 240
  source data automation 123
  standard data format 67
  storage *see* computer storage; data modeling, physical; storage for information processing

structure(s) 47, **49–50**, 52
  hierarchical 52
  network 50, 52
  non-record-based *see* object-role modeling
  record-based 49, 50, 159
  relational 50, 52, 191
  single/multiple file 49, 50
  see also database; information, concepts
  transaction 2, 179–80
  transmission 9, 13, 125–6, 186
  electronic 2, **9**, 28, 64, **67–8**, 234, 235
  validation 179–80
  warehousing 50, **50–2**, 142
  definition 50–1
  and information systems design 51
  tools 51–2
  see also database management systems
  see also encryption; information concepts
DATA BASE 8
data flow diagram (DFD) 118
  and manufacturing resource planning *145*
  in systems analysis and design 18, 40–1, 224–5, 228
data modeling
  and databases 52
  and generalization 43–5
  logical **41–7**, 48, 118, 151
  and entity-relationship model 41–6, 224
  and normalization 46
  physical **47–9**, 151
  and access paths 48
  and record structure 48
  semantic 41
Data Processing Management Association (DPMA) 9, **61**
data repository 18
  see also data, dictionary
data structure diagrams 118
database **52**
  combined 176–7
  controls 13
  customer 125
  definition 212
  definition language (DDL) 40, 212
  design 159–60
  and electronic commerce 66
  for executive information systems 143

macros 135
multidimensional 50
and multimedia 50
online 115
personal 200
relational 48, 49, 50, 151, 156,
160, **191**, 208, 212
requirements determination 192
schema 49–50
conceptual 50, 73
external 50
internal 50
logical 50
server 53, 58–9
shared 190
software 205
see also data, structure(s); file
database administrator (DBA) 40,
50
**database management systems
(DBMS)** 11, 13, 50, 52, **52–3**,
140–2, 216
authorization mechanisms 201
and CASE 18
classification 52–3
and data dictionary 40–1
and data modeling 41, 48
and data warehousing 51
development 53
and information systems
methodologies 118
and knowledge workers 130
object-oriented (OODBMS)
48, 53, **156–7**
and programming languages 53,
207, 208, 211–13
relational 48, 49, 52, 156, 160, 191
and report generators 191
software 206
and strategic planning 174
DBMS *see* database management
systems (DBMS)
debit cards, and electronic funds
transfer 64, 68
**debugging of computer
programs 53–4**, 75, 96, 137,
226
decentralization, and information
systems use 10, 21, 57, 63, 164
decision analysis
decision tables 226
decision tree 226
Structured English method 226
decision-making
automated 176
and bounded rationality 101
and information overload 114

and systems analysis and
design 226
tools 160
and value of information 111–12,
113
decision modeling 88, 144, 151
decision support systems (DSS)
50, **54–5**, 87, 216
data-oriented 54
and data warehousing 51–2
and decision phases 55
and management information
systems 140, 143–4, 183
and model management
systems 151
prototype model 55
and use of graphics 87, 88
see also executive information
systems; expert systems;
group decision support
systems; neural networks
decision theory
and uncertainty 112–13
and value of information 111–12
decomposition, system 18, 220–1
degradation, gradual, in image
processing 154
degree, in ER diagrams 74
deliverables, information
systems 228
deontology 75
dependency in data modeling 41,
43, 160
functional/multi-valued 46
desktop publishing 56–7
and image processing 105
and knowledge workers 130
device management 32
differentiation, and business process
re-engineering 190
Digital Equipment
Corporation 96–7
digital representation 26–7, 94, 152,
233, 234
digitizer board 6
digitizer tablets 123
direct access storage device
(DASD) 34–5
direct mail, and privacy issues 176
directory service, distributed 59
disaster recovery *see* backup and
recovery processes
discussion groups, online 15, 37
discussion management 88
disk block 48
splitting 48
disk drive 98–9, 150–1

disk storage 206, 214
magnetic 31, 34–5, 104, 152, 215
in microcomputers 34, 150
optical 34, 104, 152, 167, 214
shared 234
diskettes
contaminated 200, 239
magnetic 31, 34, 214
dispute resolution, and outsourcing
agreements 169
distortion, in information
theory 109
distributed systems 57–61
advantages 20, 60
characteristics 57
disadvantages 61
and distributed directory
service 59
and distributed file system 59–60
examples 57–9
and network 21, 57–8, 59
distribution, and information
technology use 65, 148, 190,
216
division of labor, and information
technology use 131
document, virtual 102
document analysis 45
document imaging 123
DOS (disk operating system) 97,
151
"dossier society" 175
dot pitch (dp) 166
downsizing
and executive information
systems 78
of information systems
function 17
dp *see* dot pitch
**DPMA (Data Processing
Management Association)**
9, 61
Drucker, P. 127

E-mail *see* electronic mail
eavesdropping, and security in
information systems 200, 202
Eckert, J. Presper 94
economies of scale
and functional grouping of
positions 163
and outsourcing 168
economies of scope, and
outsourcing 168
EDI *see* electronic data interchange
EDIFACT 67
education, and multimedia use 153

education in information
  technology 62–3, 76, 87
  ability, acceptance and
    productivity 63
  learning knowledge and skills 62
  and learning process 62–3
effectiveness, measurement 197,
    230
efficiency
  and agency problem 3
  and computer-supported
    cooperative work 38
  in data modeling 48, 49
  and data warehousing 51
  in information systems use 21,
    128, 241
  and requirements
    determination 197
  in resource utilization 163
EFT *see* electronic funds transfer
Eggemeier, T. 114, 115
EIS *see* executive information
    systems
electronic commerce 63–7
  appropriate products 65
  and barriers to innovation 66–7
  and enhancement of customer
    service 64–5
  future prospects 64
  and new business rules 65–6
  see also electronic data interchange
electronic data interchange
  (EDI) 64, 67–8
  and enterprise architecture 72,
    73, 174
  hub-and-spoke pattern 67
  in insurance industry 124
  and interorganizational
    systems 126–8
  organizational placement 68
  and procurement cycle 2
  and sales order processing 146
  standards development 67
  and suppliers 217
  and value-added networks 67–8
electronic data processing
  (EDP) 140
Electronic Funds Transfer
  Act 1980 (US) 76
electronic funds transfer
  (EFT) 68
  failures 10
  and fraud 66, 76
  see also automated teller machine
electronic mail (E-mail) 64, 68–
  70, 160, 216, 231
  addresses 68

  advantages 69–70, 130
  and bulletin boards 15
  and computer-supported
    cooperative work 37, 38
  and computer viruses 239
  disadvantages 153
  and image processing 105
  and information overload 114
  and multimedia 153
  public/private 69
  and telecommuting 236
  see also Internet
electronic meeting systems
  (EMS) 35, 36, 37–8
  see also group decision support
    systems
electronic publishing 105
embedding *see* object linking and
  embedding (OLE)
employees, and manufacturing use
  of information technology 148
employment
  for information systems
    professionals 17
  see also telecommuting
empowerment, employee 189
EMS (electronic meeting systems)
  see group decision support
    systems
encapsulation, in object-oriented
  programming 33, 156, 186,
  202, 206, 207
encryption 12, 13, 66, **70**, 199, 200,
  201, 234
  algorithms 70, 202
  common key method 70, 201, 202
  private key method 70, 202
end-user computing (EUC) 70–
  1
  and application generator
    packages 209
  assessment 6
  benefits and risks 71
  and database management
    system 52–3
  expansion 17, 63
  and expert system shells 80
  and graphical user interfaces 107
  management 71
  professionals 16, 17
  types 70–1
ENIAC (Electronic Numerican
  Integrator and Computer) 94
enterprise analysis 191
enterprise architecture 21, 71–3,
  174
  components 73

entertainment, and multimedia 153,
  240
entities
  in data modeling 19, 41–7, 49,
    159
  and data structure 50
  and files 83
  fragmenting 48
  nesting 48, 49
  types 41, 73
entity-relationship (ER) diagrams
  see ER diagrams
entity-relationship model *see* ER
  diagrams
entropy, system 221, 222
entry of data 30
environment, competitive, and
  information technology use 5,
  6, 7, 52
equifinality of systems 220, 222
ER diagrams 41–2, 72, 73, **73–4**,
  159, 191
  and attributes 74
  and CASE tools 18–19
  entities and entity types 73
  relationships and relationship
    types 74
  in systems analysis and
    design 223–4
ERGO system 151
ergonomics 74, 122
Ernst, 199, 200
errors
  computer program
    algorithmic 54
    logical/semantic 54
    and reusability 33
    syntactic 53–4
    see also debugging
  in information systems 74–5
    consistency checks 75, 129
    detection 75, 111, 112, 179–80,
      181, 182
    ethical issues 77, 176
    interface errors 74, 75
    prevention 75
    processing errors 74–5, 179–
      80, 181, 182–3
    redundancy checks 75, 110
    and speech recognition 211
    user 98, 99
Estridge, Philip Don 97
Ethernet protocol 133, 234
ethics of computer use 75–7
  and access to information 77
  and accuracy and reliability 76,
    77

and cost of information
    provision 77
and power 77, 82
and privacy 76, 175–8
and property 76–7
and technically induced social
    change 76
ETHICS design method 223
events, in information systems
    methodologies 118
**executive information systems
    (EIS)** 50, 51, 55, 77–8, 143, 151,
    209
  characteristics 78
  development 78, 216
  evolution 78
  and systems analysis and
    design 222
expenditure, on information
    technology 5, 183–4, 238
expert systems 78–81, 129, 190
  and cognitive science 29
  commercial applications 80
  current research 80–1
  and data redundancy 201
  ethical issues 76–7
  explanation facility 80
  and inference 53, 79–80
  in insurance industry 125
  and knowledge workers 130
  manufacturing uses 148
  and neural networks 155
  rule-based 79–80, 81, 144
  shells 80, 209
  and strategic planning 174
  see also artificial intelligence;
    cognitive science; inference
    engine; knowledge base
expertise
  leveraging 217
  in management information
    systems 139–40
explanation systems 81
  see also expert systems

facsimile
  and data transmission 28, 160
  and image processing 103–4
  and telecommuting 236
failure analysis, and information
    technology use 148
**failure of information system
    applications** 10, 62, 82, 107
  organizational culture view 82,
    175
  political view 82
  sociotechnical view 82

and soft systems
    methodologies 205
technological imperative view 82
Fair Credit Reporting Act 1970
    (US) 76
FAQs (frequently asked
    questions) 15
fault tolerance 13
Federal Paperwork Reduction
    Act 1980 (US) 77
feedback
  and decision support systems 55,
    89
  electronic 3, 99
  and prototyping 187
  and systems analysis and
    design 227
Felt, Dorr E. 93
fiberoptics
  and integrated services digital
    network 125
  and local area networks 134
file 49–50, 51, 52, 83
  distributed file system 59–60
  master 147–8, 179–82
  portability 150–1
  sharing 35, 36, 132–4
  transfer 125–6
  see also database
file system management 32
file transfer protocol (FTP) 83,
    126
  anonymous 83
finance uses of information
    technology 1–3, 22, 209, 216
  auditing 9
firewalls 202
first-mover advantage, and
    information technology
    use 218
flowchart 83
fonts, for optical character
    recognition 161
forecasting
  financial 155
  and information systems
    needs 172
  sales 146, 148
  software 209
  tools 160
Forrester, Jay W. 94
**FORTRAN (FORmula
    TRANslator) 83–4**, 95, 185,
    208
Frankston, Bob 97
fraud, computer 66, 76, 199
free agents (software programs) 202

Freedom of Information Act 1966
    (US) 76
frequency, electromagnetic 232–3
FTP see file transfer protocol
functional grouping, in information
    systems function 163
fuzzy logic 205

Galbraith, J. 101
Galileo 127
games, multimedia 153
Gane, C. 224
Gates, Bill 97
gateways, and information systems
    security 202
General Electric
  and early digital computers 95
  and outsourcing 168
generalization, in data
    modeling 43–5, 47
generation, and genetic
    algorithms 85–6
genetic algorithms (GA) 85–6
geographic information systems
    (GIS) 156
Germany, and privacy
    regulations 178
Gibson, V. R. 136
globalization, and outsourcing 168
gloves, virtual reality 99, 239
Gopher software 126
Gorry, G. A. 144
government
  and privacy regulations 66, 178
  and telecommunications
    regulation 233, 234
graphical user interfaces (GUI)
    27, 70, **86**, 206, 222
  and CASE tools 18
  design 74, 98
  in end-user computing 32, 107
  in expert system shells 80
  and file transfer protocols 83
  and input devices 122, 150
  and programming languages 185,
    186, 208
  and systems analysis 227
**graphics in information
    systems 86–7**
  coding 27
  and data structure 50
  and desktop publishing 56
  effectiveness 86–7
  and high-resolution screen 56
  and presentation bias 110–11
  software 86, 160
  statistical 86

graphs, and tables 86–7
**group decision support systems
(GDSS)** 37–8, 55, **87–92**
  and comprehensiveness 91
  and control of functionality 92
  and decision modeling 88, 90,
    140
  and decisional guidance 91
  design rationale 89–91
  and discussion management 88,
    90
  and information exchange 91–2
  and model management
    systems 151
  and multimedia 153
  operation 88–9
  private/public work 93
  and restrictiveness 91
  and software interface 91
  see also computer-supported
    cooperative work; decision
    support systems
groupware *see* computer-supported
  cooperative work

hackers, and computer abuse 200
Halpin, T. 159
Halstead, M. 136
hard copy 165
hard disk 34, 214
hard systems methodologies 203
hardware *see* computer hardware
  architecture
Hart, S. G. 114
hashing 50
  dynamic/extensible 48
hazards, workplace 76
heuristics, human 81, 100
hierarchy
  generalization 43
  information technology
    system 31, 33, 114, 220
Hilmer, F. G. 127
**history of organizational use of
  information
  technology** 93–7
  acceptance of digital
    computers 95–6
  and compatibility 96
  early calculation aids 93
  early electronic digital
    computers 94, 140, 216
  and emergence of computer
    industry 94, 95–6
  mechanical and electromechanical
    machines 94, 140
  and minicomputers 96–7

and personal computers 97
punched-card tabulation 93–4,
  95, 121, 187
and timesharing 96
Hoff, Marcian 97
Hollerith, Herman 93
home, working from 235–6
**human–computer interaction
  (HCI)** 74, **98–9**, 114, 123, 138
  and computer software 205
  and performance evaluation 170
  and system concepts 220, 222
  and virtual reality 124
human resources
  and accounting systems 2
  and software packages 210
**humans as information
  processors** 99–101
  and bounded rationality 101, 110,
    160
  and case-based analogical
    reasoning 100
  and central processing unit 99
  and heuristics 81, 100
  and memory 87, 99–101
  and mental workload 114
  as open systems 220, 221
  and scripts and narratives 100–1
hypermedia/hypertext 102, 202,
  240
  see also World Wide Web
HyperText Markup Language
  (HTML) 102, 240

IAS machine 94
IBM (International Business
  Machines)
  history 93–5
  IBM 360 series 96
  IBM 370 96
  IBM 650 95
  IBM 701 94, 95
  IBM 702 95
  IBM 1401 95
  IBM token ring 133
  minicomputers 97
  and personal computers 97
  SNA (Systems Network
    Architecture) 186
  and strategic planning 172
  and SYSTEM R 212
**ICIS (International Conference
  on Information Systems)** 9,
  103
IDEF (Integration DEFinition) 72
identifiers
  in data modeling 42–3, 45–6, 48

in ER diagrams 74
and files 83
in object-oriented database
  management systems 156
in object-oriented programs and
  systems 157
IEC *see* International
  Electrotechnical Commission
**IFIP (International Federation
  for Information
  Processing)** 8, **103**
  and system development life-
    cycles 117
  Technical Committee 88, 103
Igbaria, M. et al. 16
image processing 103–6, 191
  applications 104–6
  and compression 104, 152
  digital images 103–4
  functional capabilities and
    benefits 104
  and gradual degradation 154
  in insurance industry 125
  physical components 104, 160
**implementation of information
  systems 106–8**
  and change process 106
  and credibility issues 107
  and management action 107–8
  and problem diagnosis 106–7
  and testing 107
incentives
  and agency theory 3
  rule-based 168
independence, of computer program
  modules 33
index 49, 50
  and multimedia images 153
  tree-structured/hierarchical 48
inference engine 53, 79–80, **108**,
  155
  see also expert systems
INFORM-CIS *see* College of
  Information Systems
  (INFORM-CIS)
information
  access to 77, 189
  acquisition 130
  authenticity 200
  and cognitive fit 87
  concepts 108–13, 139, 732
    decision-making value 111,
      113, 190
    and information quality 111
    and information systems 112–
      13
    and information theory 109–

10, 119
and message reduction
concepts 110–11
non-decision value 112
see also data
and consent 76
extended forms 50
hard/soft 78
integrity 200
load 114
overload 114–15
perfect 111
as resource 140, 173–5
retrieval 115–16
and analysis of information
needs 115–16
and analysis and valuation of
information 116
and data gathering 116
and file transfer protocols 83
and information sources 116
in neural networks 155
software 140, 144
and selected dissemination of
information 116
sharing 10, 15, 36, 57, 91–2, 115,
128
storage *see* storage for information
processing
uncertain 79
underload 114
information architecture 5, 6–7, 72–
3
**information economics 6, 10,
113–14**
information highway 64
see also Internet; World Wide Web
information management (IM) *see*
management information
systems
**information processors,
humans as 87, 99–101, 110,
114**
information services companies 69
information society, and ethics 75–
6, 77
information system function
and business contribution 149,
173
clients 149
growth 118–19
organization 161–5
and coordination of
groups 163–4
and decentralization 164
and design of positions 161–2
and grouping of positions 162–

3
and outsourcing 164–5
outsourcing 167–8
information systems
accounting 1–2
architecture 191
assessment 5–7, 148–9
business contribution
measures 149
growth and learning
measures 149
internal performance
measures 149
user/client measures 149
auditing 9–14
context 5, 6
customer-driven 64–5
design 112, 117
development life-cycle
(SDLC) 3, 117–18, 172,
173, 189
expenditure on 5, 183–4, 238
failure *see* failure of information
system applications
geographic (GIS) 156
implementation 106–8
legacy 51
maintenance 173
methodologies 12, 117–18
planning 7, 12, 117, **171–5**
requirements determination
16, 118, **191–8**, 223, 231
application-level
requirements 192
and critical success factors 39,
196–7
cross-functional
requirements 193–4
database requirements 192
direct 192
and end-user computing 71
improvements in requirement
elicitation 192–5
indirect 192–3, 195–8
organizational-level 191
and prototyping 78, 186, 192,
195, 223
strategies 192
risks 9–10
stage hypothesis 118–19
contagion stage 118
controls stage 118
data administration stage 118
initiation stage 118
integration stage 118
maturity stage 119
success 237

support functions 6, 7
**and system concepts 139, 219–
22**
user evaluation 5, 237
see also management information
systems; security
information technology
acceptance 63, 170
**and education and
training 62–3**
**history of organizational
use 93–7**
in accounting 1–3
investment in 113–14
management 20
standards 213–14
strategic use 140, 216–18
value from 131, 149, 183–4, 190,
217, **238**
information theory 112, 119–20
and coding scheme 109–10, 119
INFORMS *see* Institute for
Operations Research and the
Management Sciences
(INFORMS)
infrastructure
data 141–2
and information systems 6, 71,
73, 113, 138, 144
personnel 142
technology 140–1, 238
telecommunications 231, 232–3,
235
inheritance
in data modeling 43
in object-oriented programs and
systems 157–8, 186
Inmon, W. H. 50–1
**innovation and information
technology 5, 120–1, 144**
barriers to 66–7
and business process re-
engineering 189
general stages 120–1, 139
process 120, 121, 190
research 106
specific stages 121
input devices 30–1, 121–4
in accounting information
systems 1
analog/digital sensors 124
early 95, 121
and image processing 104
joysticks 123
keyboards 74, 121–2
lightpens 122–3
mouse 56, 70, 99, 122

and source data automation 1, 104, 123
and systems analysis 227
touch screens 123–4
trackballs 122
and virtual reality systems 124
voice-based 124
see also bar code; magnetic ink character recognition
Institute for Management Sciences (TIMS) 8–9
Institute for Operations Research and the Management Sciences (INFORMS) 8–9
insurance industry, computer use 124–5, 167
early systems 93
and electronic data interchange 124
and expert systems 125
and imaging technology 105, 123, 125
and privacy issues 177
integrated services digital network (ISDN) 125, 235
intellectual property
and electronic commerce 66
and ethical issues 76–7
intelligence, artificial 4, 191
ethical issues 76–7
interactivity
in processing methods 156
videodisk 190, 191
and World Wide Web 231, 240
interface 6, 7, 125
application programming (API) 52, 156
hypertext 240
multi-user 36
network interface card 234
pen-based 70
process/data-oriented 91
system 219, 221, 226
and systems analysis 226, 227
user 27, 32, 54–5, **86**, 99, 101, 124, 187, 206
internal bus architecture 29–30
International Conference on Information Systems (ICIS) 9, **103**
International Electrotechnical Commission (IEC) 213
International Federation for Information Processing (IFIP) 8, **103**
and systems development life-cycles 117

Technical Committee 88, 103
International Standards Organization (ISO) 19, 53, 213
Internet 73, 125–6, 231, 234
applications 126
and computer viruses 239
as data communication network 234
definition 125
and dispersal of knowledge work 217
and E-mail 68, 69, 105, 125
and electronic commerce 64, 66
and file transfer protocols 83
growth 126, 240
insurance industry use 125
listserves 115
and security 199, 200
software 126
and telecommuting 236
and Usenet 15, 38, 69
as wide area network 126, 235
see also World Wide Web
interorganizational systems (IOS) 67, **126–8**, 140
and electronic data interchange 126–7
and ethical issues 75
and information partnerships 127–8, 190
and privacy issues 176
and process re-engineering 128, 190
and strategic outsourcing 127
and strategic use of information technology 216–17
interviews, group 194, 195
inventory management 95, 148
and bar code use 15, 123
and business accounting cycles 2
and inventory location 148
and sales planning 1, 146
and suppliers 64, 217
and systems requirements determination 193–4, 195, 196
investment
evaluation 96, 238
and information economics 6, 10, 113–14, 138–9, 216
in software 136
stage hypothesis 118–19
in training 17, 165
ISDN (integrated services digital network) 125, 235
ISO
9660 standard 19

and IEC Joint Technical Committee 1 (JTC1) 213–14
standards 19, 53, 213–14

job design, in information systems function 162, 192
job enlargement, in information systems 161–2
job satisfaction, and information systems careers 16, 162, 237
Jobs, Steven 97
joint application design 194, 195
joysticks 123
JPEG (Joint Photographic Experts Group) standard 28
just-in-time (JIT) systems, and electronic data transmission 67
justice 76

kanban 147
kerning 56
keyboard 1
design 74, 121–2
Kilby, Jack 96
King, W. R. 173
kiosks 124
knowledge 129
and computational models 28
domain 78–9, 129
and education and training 62–3
and end-user computing 70
heuristic 4, 81, 100, 151
as primary resource 129
task 98, 101
knowledge base 129
ethical issues 76–7
and expert systems 78–80, 108, 129
personal 129–30
shared 36
see also artificial intelligence; expert systems
knowledge engineers 79
knowledge work 129–31, 217
and acquisition of new information 130
and continuous learning 129, 130
and decision support systems 55
and manipulation of information 130
and personal knowledge base 129–30
and productivity 131
and software packages 209
teams 230–1
Konsynski, B. R. 127–8

Kwon, T. 121

labor
  contract 17, 38
  costs 217
  output 184
LAN *see* local area networks
languages, programming 11, 17,
  33, **184–6**
  algebraic/algorithmic 83–4, 95,
    185, 207–8
  basic assembly 95
  business data programming
    languages 21–6, 51, 53, 95,
    185, 207–8
  data manipulation (DML) 212
  database definition (DDL) 40,
    212
  and database management
    systems 53, 207, 208, 211–
    13
  general purpose 3, 185
  high-level/fourth generation
    (4GL) 53, 70, 185–6, 207
  hypertext markup (HTML) 102,
    240
  and macros 135, 209
  object-oriented 16, 156, 157–8,
    186, 206–7, 208
  procedural 21, 206, 208, 218–19
  query 11, 53, 156, 185, 208, 211–
    13
  and report generators 191
  screen-oriented 186
  simulation 185
  and software 206–8
  specialized 185
  symbolic assembly language 184–
    5, 206
  see also ADA; BASIC; C;
    COBOL; FORTRAN;
    LISP; PASCAL; SQL;
    syntax
laptop computers 149, 167
laser printer 56, 70
lattice, generalization 43
Laudon, K. C. 175, 176
leading, in desktop publishing 56
learning
  continuous 129, 130
  distance 153
  experiential 195
  in neural networks 154–5
  organizational 112
  see also machine learning
Leibnitz, G. W. von 93
Lempel, 28

life-cycle, information system 18,
  172–3
  traditional 117–18, 173, 186
ligatures 56
light pens 122
links, network 59, 102, 240
liquid crystal display (LCD) 166
LISP 80
local area networks (LANs) 78,
  126, **132–4**, 150, 152, 216
  bus network 133
  communications media 133–4,
    234
  CSMA/CD protocol 133
  operating system 134, 206
  ring network 132–3
  star network 132
  and strategic planning 174
  token-passing protocols 133
Locke, John, and property rights 76
logic bombs 76
login procedures 200, 201
logistics information systems 127,
  190
loop, in structured
  programming 33, 218–19

machine language 33, 184, 206
machine learning 4, 81, 85
Macintosh computer 97, 98
MacOS 32
macro program 33, **135**
magnetic ink character recognition
  (MICR) 1, 123, 161
magnetic tape strips 123
mail
  multimedia 153
  voice 160, 216, 231, 236
  see also electronic mail
mainframe computers 31, 57, 96,
  149
  and client-server architectures 21
  and database management
    systems 53
  and operating systems 206
maintenance
  assessment 7
  software 33, 51, **136–7**, 149
    and electronic mail 69
    and expert systems 80, 81
    future prospects 136–7
    and management concerns 136
    and productivity 136
  system 221, 222
make or buy, for software 137–8,
  209
management

decision-making 50, 51–2, 54–5,
  140, 160, 183
  and implementation of
    information systems 107–8
  and information systems
    security 202
  of information technology 20
  strategic 143
  style 5, 38
**management information
  systems (MIS)** 138–44
  assessment 5–7, 139, 228
    analysis of context 6
    and assessment of activities 6, 7
    context of use 5, 6
    metrics 148–9
    and organizational interface 6,
      7
    and system infrastructure 6, 7
  associated knowledge 139–40
  evolution 140
  future prospects 144
  and information concepts 108–9,
    112
  objectives 108
  as organizational function 138–9
  real-time 96
  structure 140–2
  and support for decision-
    making 143–4, 183
  and support for
    management 142–3
  and system concepts 138, 221–2
  see also decision support systems;
    executive information
    systems; information
    systems
manuals 228
manufacturing resource planning
  (MRP)
  and information systems
    use 145–8, 210
  see also manufacturing use of
    information technology
**manufacturing use of
  information
  technology** 145–8, 189
  and artificial intelligence 4
  and business planning 145–6, 148
  and capacity planning 146–7, 148
  and customers 147–8
  early systems 95
  and employees 148
  and inventory locations 148
  and material planning 147
  multiple software packages 210
  and product/process design 147

and production activity
    control 147
and production planning and
    master scheduling 146
and purchasing 147
and sales order processing 146
and sales planning 146, 148
and vendors 148
see also inventory management
mapping, natural, in system
    design 99
March, J. 101
market entry, and electronic
    commerce 67
market grouping, in information
    systems function 163
market share, and information
    technology use 216, 217
marketing
    electronic 64–5, 66
    information systems 127, 216
    and unauthorized use of
        information 176
Mason, R. O. 168
master scheduling, and information
    technology use 147–8, 172–3
matrix structures 164
Mauchley, John W. 94
McCabe, T. J. 136
McCarthy, John 96
McFarlan, F. W. 127–8
McGee, J. V. 127
measurement, and performance
    evaluation 170
meetings *see* electronic meeting
    systems (EMS)
megabytes (MB) 29
memory
    cache 30, 32
    ferrite core 94, 95
    group 36
    human 87, 99–101
    magnetic drum technology 95
    and microcomputers 150
    programmable read-only
        (PROM) 29
    random-access (RAM) 29, 32, 34,
        214
    read-only (ROM) 29, 32, 34
    subsystem management 32
    tube memory technology 94
memory chips 29
messages
    coding 109–10, 119–20, 232
    and communication 231, 233
    electronic 35, 88

in object-oriented programs and
    systems 157–8
and objects 157, 186
reduction 110–11, 112
routing 110, 112
messaging services 68
metadata 40–1, 225
metaphor, in system design 98
**methodology, information
    system 117–18,** 223
**metrics for assessment of
    information systems 148–9**
microcomputer 17, 31, **149–51**
    and client/server
        architecture 21, 150
    and database management
        systems 53
    and disk storage 34, 150
    and end-user computing 70–1
    and expert systems 80
    history 97
    and internal bus architecture 29–
        30
    and macros 33
    and multimedia 152
    and networks 150
    operating systems 16, 150–1, 206
    and peripherals 150, 166
    and security 150, 199, 200
    and speech recognition
        systems 211
    and telecommuting 236
    see also desktop publishing;
        software
microfiche 167
microfilm 167
microprocessor 97
    chips 29
Microsoft 160, 216
Milberg, S. J. 178
Miller, G. A. 99
minicomputers 21, 31, 96–7, 149
Mintzberg, H. 161
**model management
    systems 151**
    and artificial intelligence 151
    see also database management
        systems; decision support
        systems
modeling
    analytical 170
    computational 28
    entity-relationship 18–19, 41–
        2, 73, 159, 191
    object role 159–60
    record-based 159
modems 150

and compression 28
and electronic mail 69
modularity in systems 32, 33, 219,
    220–1, 226–7
monitoring
    electronic 3
    and privacy issues 178
    and security of information
        systems 201
monitors 166
    digital 152
    flat-panel 167
    liquid crystal display (LCD) 166
    in microcomputers 150
    noninterlaced 166
    refresh rate 166, 167
    resolution 166
    size 166–7
monopoly, and information
    control 77
morale, and information systems
    use 10, 70
Mosaic (Web browser) 240
motion video, coding 27, 28, 152
motivation
    and business process re-
        engineering 189
    of IT personnel 136, 162
mouse 56, 70, 99, 122, 150
MPEG-2 (Moving Picture Experts
    Group) standard 28
multimedia 35, 152–3, 191
    applications 153
    browser 105
    and computer-supported
        cooperative work 36
    and databases 50, 53
    and digital images 152
    functional capabilities and
        benefits 152–3
    and hypermedia 102
    and input devices 124
    and object-oriented database
        management systems 156
    output 31
    physical components 152
multitasking 31–2
mutation, and genetic
    algorithms 85–6
MYCIN 80

N–S Charts (Nassi-Schneiderman
    Charts) 226, 227
narratives, in human information
    processing 100–1
NASA-TLX (Task Load
    Index) 114

Nassi-Schneiderman Charts (N-S Charts) 226, 227
Nelson, T. 102
nesting, in data modeling 48, 49
net present value, and information technology use 238
Netscape 216, 240
network interface card (NIC) 234
networks 31, 35, 231
  bus 133
  and client-server architectures 21
  data communication 234
  and database management systems 53
  in distributed systems 57–8, 59
  early 96
  and group decision support systems 89
  isolated 202
  and knowledge workers 130
  local area (LANs) 78, 126, 132–4, 150, 152, 174, 206, 216, 234
  neural 154–5
  operating systems 134
  protocols 233–4
  ring 132–3
  and security 199, 200, 202
  semantic 129
  software 141
  star 132
  value-added (VANs) 67–8
  wide area (WAN) 126, 174, 206, 216, 234–5
  see also integrated services digital network; Internet
Neumann, John von 94
neural networks 144, 154–5
  limitations 154–5
  and nodes 154
Newell, A. 99–100
newspaper, electronic 66
NIAM (Nijssen Information Analysis Method) 159
nodes 59, 60, 102, 234
  activation 154
  and local area networks 132–4
  and neural networks 154
noise, in information theory 109, 110, 112
Nolan, R. L. 118–19
Noyce, Robert 96
Nygren, T. 114

object identifier see identifiers
object linking and embedding (OLE) 160, 161

object-oriented database management systems (OODBMS) 48, 53, 156–7
  and programming languages 156
object-oriented programs and systems (OO) 18, 33, 136, 157–9
  and encapsulation 33, 156, 186, 202, 206, 207
  and programming languages 16, 156, 186, 206–7
object program 33
object-relationship model 41, 43
object role modeling 50, 52, 159–60
objects 41, 157, 159, 186, 207
obsolescence, technological 136, 164
OCR see optical character recognition
OCR-A 161
OCR-B 161
O'Donnell, T. 114
office automation 160, 183
  and computer-supported cooperative work 38
offspring, and genetic algorithms 85–6
OLAP see online analytic processing
OLE see object linking and embedding
Olson, Ken 96
ombudsman, and privacy issues 178
online analytic processing (OLAP) 50, 160–1
online systems 1, 31, 130, 161, 180, 183
  immediate/subsequent processing 181–2
open architecture 97
Open Doc 160, 161
operating system see computer operating system
operational/operations research 203
operations, assessment 7
Operations Research Society of America (ORSA) 8
opportunity cost, and information accuracy 77
optical character recognition (OCR) 104, 123, 152, 160, 161, 179
  see also bar code; digitizer tablets; scanners
optical storage 34, 104, 152, 167, 214, 215

order processing 48–9, 64, 106, 146, 179–80, 193–4, 195–6, 197
organization
  as artificial system 220
  decision-making 101
  effectiveness 230
  as human activity system 204
  and interorganizational systems 126–8
  objectives 20
  as open system 220
  structure
    and information processing 101
    and information technology use 5, 6, 10, 72
  and systems analysis and design 223
  "virtual" 38
  see also enterprise architecture
organization of the information system function see information system function
OSI (Open Systems Interconnect) 186, 202
output devices 1–2, 31, 165–7
  Braillers 167
  computer output microfilm (COM) 167
  early 95
  hard/soft copy 165
  and image processing 104
  multimedia 31
  and output controls 13
  plotters 167
  ports 165
  shared 134
  and systems analysis 227
  and virtual reality 167
  see also monitors; printers; speech recognition and synthesis
outsourcing, strategic 127, 168
outsourcing of information systems 164–5, 167–9
  and agency problems 3
  and careers in information systems 17–18
  co-location 168
  and contract management 168–9
  and cost control 20
  domestic multi-location 168
  global 168
  and payroll systems 2, 167
  rationale 168
  selective 168
  and software development 137
  total 167–8

see also contract work
overflow mechanisms 48

packet switching 9, 68, 96, 126, 202, 234
parallel ports 165
partition, in data modeling 43
partnerships, information 127–8, 190
PASCAL 53
Pascal, Blaise 93
passwords, and access to information systems 83, 150, 181, 201
patches 13
patents, and information systems 217
pattern recognition, and online analytic processing 160–1
payroll systems 32, 124, 167, 221
  and batch processing 1, 2
  early systems 95, 140
  and object-oriented programs 158–9
  outsourcing 2, 167
  and programming language 22–6
peer supervision 163
pel *see* pixel
perception, and information systems failure 82
performance evaluation
  computer systems 170–1, 222
  and information systems use 7, 10, 114, 131, 148–9, 190, 237
  and telecommuting 235
peripherals, computer *see* interface; mouse; printers
person/job fit 162
personal computer *see* microcomputer
personalization, and strategic information technology use 217
personnel management
  and information systems assessment 7, 10
  and information systems auditing 12
  and information systems use 71, 142, 149
pictures, coding 27
pipelining 30
piracy, software 76
pixel 27, 103–4, 166
planning, business systems (BSP) 172
planning

for information systems 7, 12, 117, **171–5**
  current trends 174–5
  evolution 171–4
  strategic 171
  and management information systems function 139
planning, systems integration 173
plotters 167
point-of-sale systems, and suppliers 217
pollution
  and information systems failure 10
  reduction 235
polymorphism, in object-oriented programs 158
portable computers 130, 148, 149, 167
ports, parallel/serial 165
positions, information systems, design 161–2
power, and information systems use 77, 82
power supply systems, uninterrupted 200
Powers, James 93
presentation bias 110–11, 112
price, transfer 20
price-performance ratios 168–9
pricing
  and information systems use 19–20
  nonmarket-based 168–9
principal-agent problem
  in information systems 3
  and productivity 184
printers 150
  impact 165, 166
    daisy wheel 165
    dot-matrix 165, 166
  nonimpact 165–6
    ink-jet 166, 167
    laser 56, 70, 166, 167
    thermal 165, 166
  print quality 166
  print speed 166
  sharing 134, 234
privacy
  and information systems 10, 12, 40, 66, 76, **175–8**
  and combined data 176–7
  corporate approaches 177
  and data collection 175–6, 177
  and errors 176, 177
  and fair practices 177
  and reduced judgment 176

and regulation 177–8
  and unauthorized access 176, 177
  unauthorized secondary use of data 176, 177
  physical 175
  and security in information systems 200
Privacy Act 1974 (US) 76
Privacy Protection Act 1980 (US) 76
problem-solving
  in artificial intelligence 4, 28, 29
  and education 62
  and human information processing 100–1, 194–5
  and soft systems methodologies 203–5
  see also expert systems; group decision support systems
process control, statistical 209
process design, and information technology use 147, 148
processing methods for
  information systems 179–83
  in accounting information systems 1
  batch processing 1, 2, 15, 86, 180–1, 182
  and client/server architecture 21
  and computer programs 33
  concurrent 3, 21, 31, 179, 185
  and controls 13, 182–3
  and data retrieval 182
  decisional 51
  electronic (EDP) 140
  interactive 156
  online systems 1, 31, 130, 161, 179, 180, 181–3
  operational 51
  processing cycle 179–80
  and reference control 183
  vector processing 30
  see also image processing; input devices; transaction processing
processing reference trail 104, 183
processing units, in distributed systems 57–9
product
  for electronic distribution 65
  personalization 217
product data management (PDM), software packages 210
product design, and information technology use 148

production and operations use of information technology *see* manufacturing use of information technology
production rules 79
productivity 70, 113, 138, **183–4**, 203, 238
and information systems use 104, 148, 149, 162, 217
and information technology use 63, 238
and knowledge workers 131
paradox 184
software development 18
in software maintenance 136
and telecommuting 235
professionals
career orientations 16–17
future directions 17–18
information systems 3, 16–18, 116
and quasi-professionals 161–2, 164
and software maintenance 136
see also associations and societies
profitability, and information economics 113, 238
program *see* computer program; macro program; programming
programmable logic controller 31
programming
and construction 117
models 151
outsourcing 137
structured 3, 136, 185, **218–19**
programming languages *see* languages, programming
project management
and information systems implementation 16, 108
software 38, 209
project manufacturing, and information technology use 148
project planning, and information systems use 171–3
project valuation 238
PROM (programmable read-only memory) 29
property *see* intellectual property
PROSPECTOR 80
protection of information resources 181
protocols 131, **186**
CSMA/CD 133
data transmission 12, 133, 186, 233, 234

DSA (digital signature algorithm) 202
file transfer (FTP) 83
four-layer model 233–4
information integrity 200
network 233–5
OSI (Open Systems Interconnect) 186, 202
SHTTP (secure hypertext transport protocol) 202
SNA (Systems Network Architecture) 186
T1 235
TCP/IP 126, 186, 202, **230**
TMN 202
token-passing 133
Token Ring 234
X.25 seven layer model 186
see also ASCII; asynchronous transmission mode; standards
prototyping 55, 107, 151, **186–7**
advantages 187
and requirements determination 78, 186, 192–3, 195, 223
see also systems analysis and design
Prusack, L. 127
Pseudocode 227, 228
publishing
electronic 104
and electronic commerce 65–6
see also desktop publishing
punched cards 93–4, 95, 121, 187
purchasing function, and information systems use 179, 180

quality
of information 111
and information technology use 148
of software 148, 149
quality in information systems *see* management information systems (MIS), assessment
quality tracking, and image processing 104
query languages 11, 53, 156, 185, 208, 211–13
queuing simulations 151, 170, 185
quick-response (QR) systems 67
Quinn, J. B. 127

R1 80
RAM (random access memory) 29,

32, 34, 214
rationality, bounded 101, 160
re-engineering, and information technology 51, 117, **189–91**
and application software 208
and client-server architecture 21
and computer-supported cooperative work 38, 190
definition 189
and information systems planning 174–5
and interorganizational systems 128, 190
reasoning
case-based analogical 100
non-monotonic 79–80
see also inference engine
records 49–50
decomposition 156, 159
recovery *see* backup and recovery processes
redundancy
checks 75, 180
in communication 110, 112, 119–20, 198
data 26, 51, 201
file 59
register, computer 30
regulation
and Internet use 66–7
and privacy of information 177–8
and telecommunications 233, 234
relational database 48, 49, 50, 151, 156, 160, **191**, 208, 212
see also SQL
relationships
binary 41, 74
customer-supplier 63–4
in data modeling 19, 41–6, 48–9, 151, 191, 223
and data structure 50
and degree 74
and fuzzy logic 205
ISA (is a) 43
in object-oriented database management systems 156, 212
in object role modeling 159–60
types 74
see also entities; ER diagrams
reliability
of information 76, 77, 177
of information systems 21, 107, 170
repetitive strain injury, and computer keyboard 122
report generators 191

representation
  analog/digital 26–7, 94, 152,
    233–4
  multidimensional 160–1
  process/data-oriented 91
  of systems 45
  see also image processing
requirements determination *see*
  information systems,
  requirements determination
research
  on information overload 114–15
  and information retrieval 115–16
  and information transfer 115
reservation systems,
  computerized 64, 96, 173–4,
  179, 216
resistance, user 82
resource allocation
  first-in-first-out 193–4
  and management information
    systems 5
resources, information 140, 173–5
reusability, in computer
  programming 33, 81, 136, 158,
  186
reverse engineering 137
reward, and use of information
  systems 10
ring network 132–3
RISC (reduced instruction set
  computer) 30
risk, in information systems use 9–
  10
risk analysis, and group decision
  support systems 88
Roach, S. S. 184
Robert Rules of Order 88
Rogers, E. M. 120–1
ROM (read-only memory) 29, 32,
  34, 214
routers 200–1, 202, 234–5
  see also TCP/IP
RPG (Report Program
  Generator) 185
rules
  business 65–6
  if-then 4, 33, 79, 80, 81, 129, 144

Saaty, 205
SABRE reservation system 96,
  173–4
SAGE computer system 94
sales analysis, and bar code use 15
sales order processing *see* order
  processing
sales planning, and information

technology use 19, 146, 148,
  193
Sarson, T. 224
scanners 1, 56, 103–4, 123, 160, 179
  flatbed 123
  handheld 123
  point-of-sale 15, 64
schemas, and genetic algorithms 86
Schickard, William 93
Scott Morton, M. S. 144
scripts
  in human information
    processing 100–1
  in World Wide Web 240
SDLC *see* systems development,
  life-cycle
search
  and bulletin boards 15
  heuristic 4, 80
  and information needs 116
secondary task method of workload
  measurement 114
secrecy
  and personal data 177
  and security 199
  and strategic applications 217
security of information systems
  7, 10, 13, 21, 36, 40, **199–202**
  and abuse-based losses 199, 201
  and accidents and disasters 200–1
  channel-based 202
  in distributed systems 61
  document-based 202
  and electronic commerce 66
  and electronic mail 69
  firewalls 202
  future problems 202
  intentional violations 199–200
  legislation 76
  and microcomputers 150, 199,
    200
  and networks 134, 199, 200, 202,
    234
  physical 201
  policies 199
  techniques 201
  and telecommuting 235
  see also encryption; privacy;
    viruses
self-employment, and information
  systems professionals 17
self-regulation, and privacy
  issues 178
semantics
  and artificial intelligence 4
  in database management
    systems 53

and debugging computer
  programs 54
and hypertext 102
Semiconductor Chip Protection
  Act 1984 (US) 76
Senn, J. A. 136
sensitivity analysis 144, 151
sentence analysis 45
SEQUEL *see* SQL
serial port 165
service
  differentiated 190
  personalization 217
service sector, and electronic
  commerce 64
Shannon, Claude 109, 119
shell 32
  expert system 80, 209
shipping function, and information
  technology use 147, 148, 195,
  196–7
SHTTP (secure hypertext transport
  protocol) 202
SIGCPR (Special Interest Group on
  Computer Personnel
  Research) 8
SIGMIS (Special Interest Group on
  Management Information
  Systems) 8
signature, digital 157, 200, 202
**SIM (Society for Information
  Management)** 9, **203**
Simon, H. 55, 99–100, 101, 144
simplification, system 221
simulations
  languages 185
  and multimedia 153
  and performance evaluation 151,
    170
  and use of virtual reality 239
skills
  and end-user computing 70
  information systems 17–18, 40,
    127–8
  organization-specific 164
  scarcity 165
  for system analysis and
    design 222, 231
  and training 62
SLDC (systems development life-
  cycle) *see* systems analysis and
  design
SmallTalk programming
  language 156, 157–8, 186
smart card 203
Smith, H. J. 177
Smith, H. J. et al. 175–7

SNA (Systems Network
    Architecture) 186
socialization, in information systems
    function 163
societies, professional, for
    information technology 3, 4,
    7–9, 61, 103, 203
**Society for Information
    Management (SIM)** 9, **203**
sociotechnical design 222, 223
soft copy 165
**soft systems methodologies
    (SSM)** **203–5**, 223
    and analytic hierarchies process
        (AHP) 205
    and fuzzy logic 205
    and multiple criteria evaluation
        methods 205
    and root definitions 205
software **205–9**
    anti-virus 200, 239
    application 205, 206, 208–9, 222
        commercial package 208, 209–
            10
        customized 208, 210, 223
        generator packages 208–9
    application-specific controls 13
    assessment 148–9
    browser 216, 240
    communications 141, 205, 206
    compatibility 126, 150–1
    complexity 136
    design 136
    development professionals 16,
        137, 217
    engineering 139, 149, **209**
    see also CASE
    for executive information
        systems 78
    failures 10
    and file transfer protocols 83
    generalized audit software
        (GAS) 11
    graphics 86, 160
    groupware 37, 91
    Internet 126
    and macros 135
    maintenance 33, 51, 69, 80, 81,
        136–7, 149
    make or buy decisions **137–8**,
        209
    for microcomputers 33, 70, 150
    network 141
    package solutions **209–10**
    approaches to using 210
    and busines system
        solutions 209–10

and knowledge workers 209
performance 222
piracy 76
and programming
    languages 206–8
retrieval 140, 144, 182
security 201, 202, 222
and speech recognition
    systems 211
standardization 151
system 205–6, **222**
user-friendly 36, 78, 97
see also computer-supported
    cooperative work; neural
    networks; viruses
Software Engineering Institute
    (SEI) 149
sound, coding 27
source documents, as input data 1,
    104, 123, 182–3
source program 33
specialization, in information
    systems function 162, 163, 164
**speech recognition and
    synthesis** 99, 107, 152, 167,
    210–11
sponsor
    of executive information
        systems 78
    of information systems 108
spreadsheets
    anomalies 151
    and application generator
        packages 208–9
    and decision support systems 55
    embedding 160
    and knowledge workers 130
    and macros 135
    and manufacturing resource
        planning 145
    and speech recognition
        systems 211
SPS 95
**SQL (Structured Query
    Language)** 53, 185, 208, **211–
        13**
    and data manipulation 212–13
    and database definition 212
SSADM 223
SSL (secure socket layer) 202
**stage model of information
    systems** **118–19**
stakeholders
    and applications failure 82
    and ethics of computer use 75
    and information system
        implementation 106–8

and soft system methodologies
    205
standard business documents 67
standard data format 67
Standard Generalized Markup
    Language (SGML) 102
standardization of work 162
standards
    for CD-ROMs 19
    for electronic data interchange 67
    for information technology
        19, **213–14**
        de facto 213
        de jure 213, 214
    installation standards 213
    for telecommunications 233–4
    see also American National
        Standards Institute;
        International Standards
        Organization; protocols
star network 132
state transition diagrams 19
statistical process control
    packages 209
Stibitz, George 94
**storage for information
    processing** **214–15**, 221, 224
    and CD-ROM 19, 34, 150, 214
    magnetic disk 34–5, 104, 152, 215
    magnetic tape 34–5, 152, 214, 215
    optical 34, 104, 152, 167, 214, 215
    read-and-write 214–15
    read-only 215
    and retrieval time 214
    and ROM (read-only
        memory) 29, 32, 34, 214
    write-once 34, 215
    see also computer storage
Strachey, Christopher 96
STRADIS 223
strategic alliances, and
    interorganizational
    systems 127
strategic outsourcing, and core
    competencies 127, 168
strategic planning, and information
    systems function 138, 140,
    143, 171–5
**strategic use of information
    technology** 67, 138, 140, 171,
    216–18
    and competitive advantage 216,
        217–18
    and information systems
        planning 171, 173
    and power 77, 82
    types 216–17

strategy, organizational, and information systems use 7, 16, 107–8, 139, 171, 173, 216, 238
string, in object-oriented programs 157–8
structure chart 226, 227, 228
structured programming 3, 136, 185, **218–19**
  alternation structure 33, 218
  case structure 218
  recursion structure 219
  repetition structure 33, 218–19
  sequence control structure 33, 218
Structured Query Language (SQL) 53, 185, 208, **211–13**
subjective workload assessment technique (SWAT) 115
subtypes, in data modeling 43, 47
"sugging" 176
summarization, in message reduction 110, 112
supercomputers 21, 30, 31
supertypes, in data modeling 43
supervision, peer 163
supply, and electronic commerce 63–4, 217
Swanson, E. B. 136
Sweden, and privacy regulations 178
Symbolic Assembly Language 95
syntax, in computer programs 22, 53–4, 206
system catalog *see* data, dictionary
system concepts and information systems 139, **219–22**
  abstract/physical 219
  artificial systems 220, 221
  definition and general model 219, 221
  deterministic/probabilistic 219–20
  and management information systems 221–2
  open/closed 219–20, 221
  subsystems 219, 220–1, 226
  and system entropy 221, 222
system engineering *see* CASE
system logs 13
SYSTEM R 212
system representation 45
system software 205–6, **222**
  see also computer operating system; graphical user interface; software
systems analysis and

design 222–8
and data dictionary 40–1, 225–6, 228
and data flow diagrams 40–1, 224–5, 228
and data repository 224–5, 228
and decision-making logic 226
and deliverables 228
design objectives 227
and end-user computing 71
and entity-relationship diagrams 223–4
and human-computer interaction 98–9
and humans as information processors 101
and information system function organization 161
and information systems failure 82
issues 222–3
and management information systems function 139
and modularity and structure charts 226–7
and organizational strategy 107
processes 223
and requirements determination 16, 71, 223
and soft system methodologies 203–5
and software development 137
and systems development life-cycles 106, 117–18, 172, 173, 186, 189, 223
  see also CASE; prototyping
systems development
  and agency problems 3
  and job enlargement 162
  life-cycle (SDLC) 117–18, 172, 173, 186, 189, 223
  methodology 222–3
  outsourcing 167–8
  teams 137, 164, **230–1**
  see also information systems, requirements determination; soft systems methodologies

table 50
  and graphs 87
tabulation, punched-card 93–4, 95, 121, 187
tape storage, magnetic 31, 34–5, 152, 214, 215
target market, and electronic commerce 66
task discretion, in information

systems function 161–2
task/system fit 98, 162, **230**, 237
taxation, and processing reference trail 183
TCP/IP (Transmission Control Protocol/Internet Protocol) 126, 186, 202, **230**
  see also protocols
teams
  cross-functional 161, 190, 231
  knowledge work 230–1
teams, in system development 164, **230–1**
  and make or buy decisions 137
  see also knowledge work
technology
  acquisition 6, 7
  fit 230, 237
  pace of change 17, 31, 62, 164
telecommunication 70, 152, 162, 165, **231–5**
  and data communication 234, 235
  infrastructure 231, 232–3, 235
  and networks 20, 31, 35, 234–5
  protocols and standards 233–4
  and security 234
  services 231, 234
  and strategic planning 174
  switches 200–1
  see also electronic mail; integrated services digital network; Internet; local area networks; networks, wide area; voice mail
telecommuting 64, 76, **235–6**
teleconferencing 160, 231, 236
telemarketing, and privacy issues 176
telephone system 231, 232, 234
television 231, 232
telework *see* telecommuting
Telnet software 126
terminal
  and microcomputer 149–50
  and transaction processing 181, 182
  video display 166
textbooks, and electronic commerce 65–6
Thomas, Charles Xavier 93
threading 36–7
time series forecasting, and neural networks 155
timesharing techniques 96
TIMS *see* Institute for Management Sciences (TIMS)
Token Ring protocol 234

topologies, network 132–3
total quality management, and
    executive information
    systems 78
touch screens 123–4
trackballs 122
training
    and client/server architecture 21
    computer-based 62
    evaluation 62–3
    **in information
        technology** 62–3, 76, 164–
        5
    for information systems use 12,
        17, 71, 87, 107
    methods 62
    and virtual reality 239
transaction processing 1–2, 140,
    142, 179–83, **236**
    controls 182–3
    and data retrieval 182
    methods 180–2
    online 1, 160, 180, 181–3
    processing cycle 179–80
    and productivity 183
    reference control 183
    software 206
    and systems analysis and
        design 222
    see also batch processing;
        processing methods for
        information systems
transfer price, and information
    systems use 20
translation services 68
Transmission Control Protocol/
    Internet Protocol see TCP/IP
transmission of data
    and asynchronous transmission
        mode 9
    and integrated services digital
        network 125
    protocols 12, 133, 186, 234, 235
    see also compression
Transnet system 127
Trojan horses 76
Tufte, E. R. 87
tuples 191, 212
turnover, employee 16, 165, 168,
    169
TV-based home shopping 64
twisted pair cable 133, 233

UK, and privacy regulations 178
uncertainty
    in decision theory 112–13
    in expert systems 79

and information economics 108,
    114
and information theory 119
uniform resource locator
    (URC) 240
UNIVAC computers 95
universal product codes (UPCs) 1,
    15, 123, 161
    see also bar code
UNIX operating systems 16, 32,
    150
USA
    computer societies 8
    and information technology
        expenditure 183
    and privacy regulations 178
    and standard setting 213, 214
Usenet 15, 38, 69
**user evaluation of information
    systems** 5, **237**
user groups, and shared macros 135
user interface 32, 124
    and client-server architectures 21
    and decision support systems 54–
        5
    design 101, 187
    icon-based 99
    software 206
    see also graphical user interface
utilities, computer 32, 41, 206, 222

validation of data 179–80
**value from information
    technology** 131, 149, 183–4,
    190, 217, **238**
Venkatraman, N. 128
video
    coding 27, 28, 152
    and input devices 124
video–conferencing 65, 152–3, 236
videodisk, interactive 190, 191
virtual machine 30
virtual reality 99, 124, 167, **239**
virtue 76
viruses 76, 199, 200, 202, **239**
    anti–virus software 200, 239
visibility, in system design 98–9
Visicalc program 97
vision, strategic 127
VMS 32
voice
    coding 27, 152
    input devices 124
    recognition see speech recognition
        and synthesis
voice mail 160, 216, 231, 236

WANs see networks, wide area
warehousing, data 50, **50–2**, 142
Warnier-Orr diagrams 227, 228
Watson, Thomas J. 93
wave, electromagnetic 26, 232–3
Web see World Wide Web
weight, in neural networks 154
Weiner, Norbert 109, 119
Whirlwind computer project 94
wide area network see networks, wide
    area
Wilkes, Maurice V. 94
Williams, F. C. 94
Williams, Samuel 94
Windows95 32
word processing
    collaborative 36
    and desktop publishing 56
    and knowledge workers 130
    and macros 135
workflow
    and image processing 104, 106,
        125
    management 35, 38
workforce, dispersed 38
working hours, flexible 235
workload
    balancing 104
    human mental 114–15
workplace flexibility, and
    telecommuting 235
workspaces, shared 36, 92
workstations 16, 31, 56, 58, 149
    and client-server architectures 21
    and group decision support
        systems 88–9
    see also microcomputer
World Wide Web 125–6, 217, **240–
    1**
    browsers 216, 240
    and electronic commerce 64–6
    and hypertext language 102, 240
    insurance industry use 125
    and interactivity 231, 240
    and ISO standards 214
    links 240
    and security 199, 202
    and uniform resource locator
        (URC) 240
    see also Internet
WORM (write-once-read-many)
    storage 34, 215
worms 76, 200
Wosniak, Steve 97
write–once–read–many 34, 215
WWW see World Wide Web
WYSIWIS 36

WYSIWYG 36, 86

X.25 seven layer model 186

Young, 199, 200

Zawacki, R. A. 136

Ziv, 28
Zmud, R. W. 121, 173
Zuse, Konrad 94

Compiled by Meg Davies (Registered Indexer)